ONE-PARENT CHILDREN, THE GROWING MINORITY

REFERENCE BOOKS ON FAMILY ISSUES
(VOL. 14)

GARLAND REFERENCE LIBRARY
OF SOCIAL SCIENCE
(VOL. 344)

Reference Books
On Family Issues

ONE-PARENT CHILDREN, THE GROWING MINORITY
A Research Guide

Mary Noel Gouke
Arline McClarty Rollins

GARLAND PUBLISHING, INC. • NEW YORK & LONDON
1990

Library of Congress Cataloging-in-Publication Data

Gouke, Mary Noel
    One-parent children: the growing minority: a research
guide / Mary Noel Gouke, Arline McClarty Rollins.
    p. cm — (Reference books on family issues: vol. 14) (Garland
reference library of social science; vol. 344)
    ISBN 0-8240-8576-0 (alk. paper)
    1. Children of single parents—United States—Bibliography.
2. Single-parent family—United States—Bibliography. 3. Children
of single parents—Education—United States—Bibliography.
I. Rollins, Arline McClarty. II. Title. III. Series: Reference
books on family issues: v. 14. IV. Series: Garland reference
library of social science; v. 344.
Z7164.C5G68   1990
[HQ777.4]
306.85'6—dc20   84-48876
                                                 CIP

Printed on acid-free, 250-year-life paper
Manufactured in the United States of America

CONTENTS

PREFACE

In the United States the traditional family unit has generally been recognized as one consisting of a husband, wife, and their biological children. However, changes in marriage and family patterns over the past two decades have been responsible for tremendous growth in the numbers of children who live in single-parent families. It is difficult to summarize and interpret in a meaningful way the unique experiences of these children. Perhaps the best description is that given by a child from a one-parent family, "you grow up much faster."

Research studies conducted in the 70's, reflecting societal attitudes, suggest that one-parent families were, if not dysfunctional, certainly lacking in many of the characteristics that foster normal psychosocial growth and development in children. Changes in social and behavioral science research methodology in the 80's have resulted in new research that questions many of the findings of these earlier studies. Single-parent families are expected to continue to grow, though at a slower rate. The consequences of the effects of parental absence on children in these families will continue to extend beyond the immediate family to other institutions and agencies in the community.

This bibliography on *One-Parent Children* contains over 1,100 informative abstracts of scholarly books, essays in books, journal articles, and conference papers. Dissertations are also included, but without abstracts. Users are given a citation to *Dissertation Abstracts International* where abstracts may be found. The selection of items is limited to literature published in the English language between 1970 and the first half of 1989. And although the primary focus of the bibliography is on one-parent children in the United States, it includes significant research in many foreign countries published in the English language. Other major factors that influenced the selection of material were the frequency with which the authors were cited in the research literature on the topic and the multi-disciplinary information needs of professionals working with one-parent children.

Abstracts note the purpose of the study, sample size and characteristics, research methods employed, and a brief statement of significant findings. Cross-references are provided in cases where the focus of the material is such that it could appropriately be placed in more than one section of the bibliography. Full bibliographic information has been provided for all entries. The abstracts provided are not intended to replace the documents, but to indicate their usefulness to the researcher. Most items in the bibliography are easily obtainable at large academic or public libraries.

Entries are numbered consecutively throughout the book. The numbers in the indexes refer to entry numbers rather than to page numbers. The subject index reflects terminology from *Psychological Abstracts, ERIC,* and other database thesauri and also includes a special listing of research methods and tests and measurements. Additional indexes, an author index, geographic index, and an index to programs, projects, associations, and institutions, are designed to provide researchers with multiple access to items in the bibliography.

Part I of this bibliography is devoted entirely to works that are general in the scope of their coverage. In most instances each work covers multiple aspects of the subject of one-parent children.

Part II of the bibliography focuses on studies of children in various types of single-parent families. Among the family types represented are: father-absent, mother-absent, single-adoptive, and gay and lesbian families. Also included is a section on reconstituted families, in which the primary research emphasis is on the effects of the transition on children.

Part III of the bibliography includes research on children of unwed mothers, parental loss through divorce, separation, desertion, and death, and parental absence caused by imprisonment, illness, or employment.

Part IV focuses on single-parent children in the schools and the implications for classroom teachers, guidance counselors, school psychologists, school administrators, and for development of school policies and procedures.

The authors hope that this bibliography will prove useful to all those interested in single-parent children, including students, educators, researchers, parents, and finally those professionals involved in mediating the consequences of parental absence.

ACKNOWLEDGMENTS

TO OUR FAMILIES

OHIO STATE UNIVERSITY:
   Libraries' Advisory Committee on Research
   Education/Psychology Library Staff
   Instructional Research Computer Center
   Interlibrary Loan Department
   Marjorie Murfin, Associate Professor, for encouragement
      and proofreading

Other Concerned Colleagues, Associates, and Friends

Garland Publishing for their patience and understanding

AND TO ALL THE SINGLE-PARENT CHILDREN

One-Parent Children,
The Growing Minority

I

GENERAL ASPECTS OF
ONE-PARENT CHILDREN

BIBLIOGRAPHIES AND LITERATURE REVIEW

1. Blechman, Elaine A. "Are Children with One Parent at Psychological Risk?—A Methodological Review." *Journal of Marriage and the Family* 44(1): 179–195 (February 1982).

   The assumption that children from one parent families are at psychological risk is examined. A review of four decades of research studies did not provide conclusive information. If additional controlled studies continue to show no differences attributable to number of parents or cause of parent absence: it is suggested that the risk among one-parent children must be judged without empirical support. Social scientists are cautioned against choosing research designs, statistical analyses and dependent measures that reflect psychological biases. (153 references)

2. Davids, Leo. "The Lone-Parent Family in Canada: the Quantitative Background." In *The One-Parent Family in the 1980's: Perspectives and Annotated Bibliography*

1978–1984, 5th ed., edited by B. Schlesinger, 1–12. Toronto: University of Toronto Press, 1985.

Census information on one-parent families from Statistics Canada is analyzed. The divorce rate between 1971 and 1981 showed an increase of 102 percent. The number of female single parents was roughly five times that of male single parents. The largest single category of one-parent families were widowed people; the smallest category was "single, never-married." The total number of male parents with more than one or two children was small, for females the number was much larger. Males who headed lone parent families had larger incomes; female lone parents had smaller incomes and reported more homes in need of major repairs. (Bibliography)

3. Fassler, Joan. *Helping Children Cope.* New York: Free Press, Collier Macmillan, 1978.

This book attempts to bring to the attention of individuals interested in young children's health a number of books that may be used to help children cope with a variety of stressful life situations. The books that are designed to be used with children in the four-to-eight-year range, deal with the loss of an important person through death, parent/child separation experiences, life-style changes that affect family structure, imprisonment and employment related parental absence. Psychologists, pediatricians, social workers and educators might find the books useful to open channels of communication with children, ease anxieties and encourage growth. (Bibliography)

4. Gongla, Patricia A. "Single Parent Families: A Look at Families of Mothers and Children." *Marriage and Family Review* 5(2): 5–27 (Summer 1982).

The increase in single-parent families has been largely the result of divorce and separation. Research indicates that although single-parent families have characteristics in common, they are not a homogenous group and family conflict may be more important than structure in the dominance of its effect on individual children. Research focusing on the relationship of single-parent families to the broader social environment is suggested as necessary for learning about the functioning of these families. Economic support, vocational assistance for single mothers, and child care services are cited as areas where social policies could benefit family functioning. Recommendations for new directions in research are also offered. (120 references)

5. Horner, Catherine T. *The Single-Parent Family in Children's Books: An Analysis and Annotated Bibliography*, with an Appendix on Audiovisual Material. Metuchen, N.J.: Scarecrow, 1978.

One hundred years of fiction books for children in which one-family parents are portrayed are discussed. Two hundred and fifteen books are analyzed. (Bibliography)

6. Kendall, Earline D., et al. *Effects of Changed Family Structures on Children: A Review of the Literature.* May 1981. 63pp. (ERIC Microfiche ED205281)

This paper examines the effects of changes in the nuclear family on children. Family modifications due to divorce, remarriage, single parenting, father absence, teenage parenting and extended families are discussed. Particular attention is given to the effect of family changes on the child's emotional, social and intellectual behavior. A variety of types of daycare arrangements are described. As families are restructured, supplementary child care is needed. (112 references)

7. Kimmons, Lee, and Judith A. Gaston. "Single Parenting: A Filmography." *Family Relations* 35: 205–211 (January 1986).

Films, filmstrips and videotapes that address in some way a variety of facets of the single parent experience are presented. Entries include annotations, purchase and rental prices and addresses of distributors. *The Educational Film Locator* (Bowker, 1985) is listed as a source of additional information on nonprint media entries included in this article.

8. Lamb, Michael E., and Jamie E. Lamb. "The Nature and Importance of the Father-Child Relationship." *The Family Coordinator* 25(4): 379–386 (October 1976).

The nature and extent of the father-infant relationship is explored through a review of literature on the subject. Observations suggest that infants in stress-free situations show no preference for one parent over the other; however in a stressful situation they show a preference for the mother. In play and physical contact, deemed critical in personality development, it was found that mothers more often engage in conventional play while fathers engage in more physically stimulating games. By the end of the second year of a child's life, the father is more interactive with sons than with daughters. (52 references)

9. Orthner, Dennis K., et al. "Single-Parent Fatherhood: an Emerging Family Life Style." *Family Coordinator* 25(4): 429–437 (October 1976).

Twenty single-parent fathers were interviewed to assess their ability to function as primary parents. Maternal mortality rates, legal custody arrangements, and single parent adoption are factors that have been responsible for the growth in male-headed households. Recommendations are made for support services to ease the stresses caused by the need for day care services, education classes for parenting and big sisters for girls. It is predicted that the number of single-parent fathers will continue to grow and programs are needed in the future. (17 references)

10. Riley, Barb. *Education and the Children of One-Parent Families: A Background Paper.* Manitoba Dept. of

Education, Winnipeg, 1981. 24pp. (ERIC Microfiche ED222838)

Findings in recent research studies on single-parent children can help educators understand the effects of single parenting on children's personality, classroom behavior and academic achievement. Elementary school children may fear abandonment and exhibit aggressive and acting-out behaviors when families separate. Secondary school children may suffer feelings of guilt and anger and display withdrawal symptoms. Not all children react the same way when parents separate. In some cases this experience seems to increase independence and personal strength. Discussion groups and peer counseling programs are often helpful to single-parent children. (47 references)

11. Sadler, Judith DeBoard. *Families in Transition: An Annotated Bibliography*. Hamden, Conn.: Archon Books, 1988.

    This annotated bibliography was prepared as a resource for family professionals from a variety of disciplines who work with nontraditional families. Children from single-parent families, step-families, adoptive and foster care families are represented in separate chapters. Descriptions of films, audiocassettes and video cassettes are provided along with 970 books for children and youth. (Bibliography)

12. Schlesinger, Benjamin. "Children in One-Parent Families: A Review." *Conciliation Courts Review* 19(2): 23–31 (December 1981).

    The author reviews literature studies which have examined various aspects of single-parent families headed by fathers and headed by mothers. Findings in these studies are summarized. It is suggested that more investigations are needed that include larger samples that encompass socio-cultural, racial and economic differences of children growing up in single-parent families. (34 references)

13. ———. *The One-Parent Family: Perspectives and Annotated Bibliography*. 4th ed. Toronto: University of Toronto Press, 1978.

The book consists of three sections: a revised essay section, an updated bibliography section and annotated list of books on children in one-parent families. The essays review and synthesize literature on the various types of single-parent families. The bibliography section is arranged by general topics associated with one-parent families. The Children's book section presents a short description of the books and the school grade level for which it is suitable.

14. ———. *The One-Parent Family in the 1980's: Perspectives and Annotated Bibliography 1978–1984*. Rev. ed. Toronto: University of Toronto Press, 1985.

This book contains four essays reviewing the literature various aspects of the one-parent family in Canada and the United States, and 490 items in the annotated bibliography which updates the literature cited in previous editions by the author. The subject arrangement is outlined in the table of contents. Author index.

15. Sonne, John C. "A Family System Perspective on Custody and Adoption." *International Journal of Family Therapy* 2(3): 176–192 (Fall 1980).

This article considers the psychological state of children who have been uprooted from their families and its likely impact on the construction of a family image as these children become parents, husbands and wives. It is suggested that a child needs a three person family to develop a sense of self even though this psychological family is formed by blood-kin or non-blood-kin. It is further suggested that adults in families, mental health professionals and legal and social agencies that are involved with uprooted children should have a clear gender identity and heterosexual orientation. (Bibliography)

GENERAL WORKS

16. Ambert, Anne-Marie. "Longitudinal Changes in Children's Behavior Toward Custodial Parents." *Journal of Marriage and the Family* 46(2): 463–467 (May 1984).

This exploratory report is a follow-up two and one-half years later of a group of separated single parents and their children. Interviews with 27 families indicated that parental satisfaction for low- and high-income mothers had increased, while custodial fathers' satisfaction remained high. Observed children's behavior had improved in both high- and low- income mother-headed families. The departure of disruptive children in low-income mother-headed families contributed to the mother's parental satisfaction and the level of positive family functioning. Suggestions for future research are offered. (18 references)

17. Angel, Ronald, and Jacqueline Lowe Worobey. "Single Motherhood and Children's Health." *Journal of Health Social Behavior* 29(1): 38–52 (March 1988).

Data from the Hispanic Health and Nutrition Examination Survey and the National Health and Nutrition Examination Survey II are used to explore the effect of a mother's marital status on her report of her child's health for Mexican-American, black and non-Hispanic white children aged six months to eleven years. Results show that single mothers report poorer physical health overall for their children than do mothers from two-parent families. Analysis of a matched sample of Mexican-American children indicated that a mother's report of her child's poorer health was associated with the mother's depression score. General social and cultural factors, such as marital status, acculturation and income, affect the accuracy of mothers' reports. (55 references)

18. Ansteatt, Richard, and Barbara Lewis. "The Single-Parent Family: How an Understanding Physician Can Help." *Postgraduate Medicine* 80(2): 137–140 (August 1986).

Children and adults who have experienced separation
from single-parent or spouse face a great deal of stress
that may result in physical or emotional problems.
Physicians need to inquire about any changes in the
family and make this information part of the patient's
record. The authors discussion could be used to aid single
families. A reading list for adults and children is also
provided. The most effective treatment may be
understanding and reassurance. (No references)

19. Arent, Ruth P. "Understanding the Child from the Single
    Parent Family." *Counseling and Human Development*
    12(8): 1–12 (April 1980).

    Children may vary widely in the way they respond to
    living in a single parent family. Responses are related to
    the degree of personal strength of the child and the
    relative skills of the parent in providing a stable support
    system. Other factors that affect the adjustment of
    children are life-style of the neighborhood, age of the
    child, and circumstances surrounding the single-parent
    arrangement. Differences between children of divorce
    and children whose parents have died are most
    pronounced. Counselors and teachers need to work
    together in helping children adjust. Suggestions for
    counseling single parents and support systems that might
    prove helpful are offered. (43 references)

20. Baden-Marotz, Ramona, et al. "Family Form or Family
    Process? Reconsidering the Deficit Family Model
    Approach." *Family Coordinator* 28(1): 5–14 (January
    1979).

    This article questions whether family form or familial
    process is more likely to contribute to children's positive
    personal and social development. A review of research on
    the effects of alternative family forms on children's
    personality, social behavior and school achievement
    suggests that the interactional dynamics that lead to a
    given outcome may be more important than family form.

It is proposed that future research consider not only the interlinkage of family roles and memberships but also the individual structure and family structure over time. (81 references)

21. Baldwin, Wendy, and Virginia S. Cain. "The Children of Teenage Parents." *Family Planning Perspectives* 12(1): 34–43 (January 1980).

The effect of early childbearing on the children of adolescent parents is the subject of this investigation. Results of studies indicate that children of teenage parents show deficits in cognitive development, are likely to spend a large part of their childhood in a single parent households, and are likely to become teenage parents themselves. This study concludes that most of the negative effects observed in these children are the result of the limited education and poor employment and marriage prospects of the adolescent mother. Implications for the provision of supportive services are discussed. (29 references)

22. Bane, Mary Jo. "Marital Disruption and the Lives of Children." *Journal of Social Issues* 32(1): 103–117 (Winter 1976).

Survey data on marital disruption reveal that nearly 30 percent of all children in the U.S. have been affected by this experience during the past century. It is expected that this percentage will grow larger in the coming decades. Although death rates have remained relatively unchanged, divorce and illegitimacy rates have increased over the past twenty years. Most of the children who experience family disruption live in female-headed families, which have less than half the income of male-headed families. The implications of establishing some type of income support policy to relieve the economic impact on children in single-parent families are discussed. (33 references)

23. Baptiste, D. A. "A Comparative Study of Mothers' Personality Characteristics and Child Rearing Attitudes in Husband-Present and Husband-Absent Families." Ph.D. diss., Purdue University, 1976.

For a summary see: *Dissertation Abstracts International* 37A(10): 6263.

24. Barry, Ann. "A Research Project on Successful Single-Parent Families." *Journal of Family Therapy* 7(3): 65–73 (Fall 1979).

This study reports the variables associated with successful single parenting based on findings in a research sample of twenty-five families. Areas examined included: relations with the absent parent, relations with children and personal outlook and management. Successful single families are identified as those who have completed a series of tasks necessary for positive adjustment to single family life. Implications of the study for counseling single parents and their children are discussed. (1 Reference)

25. Blum, Heather Munroe, et al. "Single-Parent Families: Child Psychiatric Disorder and School Performance." *Journal of the American Academy of Child and Adolescent Psychiatry* 27: 214–219 (March 1980).

The Ontario Child Health Study included 1,869 families with 3,294 children. The incidence of conduct, emotional and somatic disorders, hyperactivity and school performance were investigated. Compared with two-parent children, single-parent children were found to be at a small but statisticially significant risk for a negative outcome. When income welfare status and family dysfunction are controlled, childhood psychiatric disorders and poor school performance as factors in single-parent family status are reduced to significant. The implications of these findings are discussed. (16 references)

26. Bradley, Robert H., et al. "A Comparative Study of the Home Environments of Infants from Single-Parent Black Families." *Acta Paedologica* 1(1): 33–46 (January 1984).

Fifty-eight one-parent and two-parent Black families were studied to compare the home environments of their young children. The HOME observation/interview measure used when the children are six and twenty-four months old suggests that single mothers are less emotionally and verbally responsive to their children than mothers in two-parent homes during the first two years of their children's lives. Mothers did not differ in the amount of punishment given the child or the number of toys available, child-centered organization of their home, or interest in the children's development. The authors suggest the need for additional studies. (19 references)

27. Brenes, Margarita E., et al. "Sex Role Development of Preschoolers from Two-Parent and One-Parent Families." *Merrill-Palmer Quarterly* 31(1): 33–45 (January 1985).

The sex-role development of 41 preschool children from divorced, separated and two-parent families was examined through interviews and observation. Understanding of gender identity, sex-role stereotypes and toy choices were assessed. Children from single-parent families exhibited more knowledge of stereotyped conceptions about sex roles and were less sex-typed in their use of toys than two-parent children. Boys from mother-headed families were not "feminized" in their play behaviors and therefore must not have been deprived of male models. It is concluded that the pattern of sex-role adoption of single-parent children is not indicative of gender confusion. (18 references)

28. Briggs, Beverly A., and Connor M. Walters. "Single-Father Families: Implications for Early Childhood Educators." *Young Children* 40(3): 23–27 (March 1985).

Many research studies indicate that fathers who actively seek child custody are more likely to report that they and their children have adjusted well to the single-parent family lifestyle than those fathers who become single parent custodians without actively seeking that status.

Single-father families were more likely to be better off financially than single-mother families. Early research on father-headed single-parent families suggests that this family structure is healthy and workable. It is recommended that educators become aware of the effects of divorce on children, recognize stress-related behavior changes and be willing to listen to the concerns of both parents and children. (25 references)

29. Bundy, Michael L., and James Gumaer, Eds. "Families in Transition." *Elementary School Guidance and Counseling* 19(1): (October 1984).

   This special issue of the journal is devoted to the transition from traditional two-parent families to single-parent and stepfamily structures. The attendant problems experienced by children and the ways in which their needs can be met by educators, counselors and other family professionals are also discussed. (Bibliographies)

30. Burden, Dianne S. "Single-Parents and the Work Setting: the Impact of Multiple Job and Homelife Responsibilities." *Family Relations* 35(1): 37–43 (January 1986).

   Data from a questionnaire completed by 293 single and married employees of a large corporation showed no significant differences in the number of problems with children between single and married parents. This finding tends to disagree with literature that attributes greater problems to children of female headed families and confirms studies that report that single-parent families with adequate income and support are as viable as the two-parent families. (42 references)

31. Burgess, Jane K. "The Single-Parent Family: A Social and Sociological Problem." *The Family Coordinator* 19(2): 137–144 (April 1970).

   This paper examines the single-parent family primarily on the basis of marital role rather than on parental role. Research that emphasizes sex-role identity problems in children from single-parent families is criticized. It is the author's contention that role learning continues throughout life and that an awareness of the multiple factors related to the socialization process should lessen the anxiety, fear and guilt which single parents sometimes feel about the absence of same-sex role models. (31 references)

32. Butler, Annie L. "Tender Topics: Children and Crises." Paper presented at the Annual Study Conferences of the Association for Childhood Education International, Minneapolis, Minn. April 10–13, 1977. 16pp. (ERIC Microfiche ED147019)

This paper describes children's feelings and reactions to divorce, death, hospitalization and parent imprisonment. It is suggested that adults can help children cope with crisis situations by providing accurate information, encouraging the expression of feelings and by managing their own feelings and attitudes toward the situation. The paper also describes ways in which outside supportive services can help children cope with a crisis situation. (11 references)

33. Canadian Council on Social Development. *The One-Parent Family: Report of an Inquiry on One-Parent Families in Canada*. Ottawa, Canada, 1971.

This study by several Canadian organizations was based on interviews with 113 single parents. Children's reactions to their changed family situation varied as reported by their parents. Danger signals noted in parent-child relationships were: parents using a child for emotional support, scapegoating, over-protectiveness, transfer of feeling about the absent spouse to the child and treating children of different sexes differently. Community services needed to aid single parents and their children are discussed. Statistical data, interview guides and references are included. (30 references)

34. Carter, Larry. "New Boy Scout Programs Target Life
    Skills and Single Parent Kids." *Journal of Physical
    Education Program* 80(3): 22. (February 1983).

    This article discusses the "Prepared for Today" and "Tiger
    Cubs" programs aimed at life skills development and
    single-parent children. These skills include the
    information that children who spend time alone need
    when their parents work. The "Tiger Cubs" program is
    for children under the age of eight years and is family
    oriented. This program is designed to promote search,
    discovery and sharing. Both these programs also
    emphasize helping others, fitness and sports and fun. (No
    references)

35. Cashmore, Ernest E. *Having to: The World of One Parent
    Families*. London; Boston: Allen & Unwin, 1985.

    One-parent families lack many of the constraints of the
    traditional family, and their choices are limited. Children
    in one-parent families may suffer, yet this is not caused
    simply by the absence of one parent. The single male
    parent has usually been deserted, and the emotional
    problems which remain cannot be addressed by legislation.
    Practical solutions must also be social in nature. Means-
    tested benefits such as rent rebate and free schools could
    provide financial relief. The one-parent unit is a functional
    and adequate environment for personal growth and
    general development of both parent and children, but it
    challenges the existing social arrangement. (Bibliography)

36. Cherlin, Andrew, and Frank Furstenberg F., Jr. "The
    American Family in the Year 2000." *Futurist* 17(3): 7–14
    (June 1983).

    At current rates about fifty percent of all marriages will
    end in divorce. Joint custody of children is expected to
    continue to be the exception because of post-divorce
    parental conflict. The most detrimental effect for single-
    parent children is not the lack of a male presence but the
    lack of male income. Remarriage does much to alleviate

economic distress and many couples and their children make a successful adjustment. Unfamiliar family forms are not expected in the year 2000. (No references)

37. "The Children's Experience." *Adolescent Mothers in Later Life,* edited by Frank F. Furstenberg, et al., 77–105. New York: Cambridge University Press, 1987.

This 17–year follow-up of a Baltimore study of adolescent mothers and their children reconstructs the life of the children from birth to adolescence. This study also pinpoints possible negative outcomes for the child during infancy, preschool and high school. Mothers' struggle to avoid poverty may be costly in terms of academic achievement, maladjustment, misbehavior, and early parenting. Little evidence was found that most mothers neglect children. Many rely on families for assistance. (Bibliography)

38. Clark, Homer H., Jr. "The Supreme Court Faces the Family." *Children Today* 11(6): 18–21 (November-December 1982).

Family law defined in recent rulings of the Supreme Court related to marriage, divorce, child custody, children of unwed parents and parent-child relationships is reviewed. Although the Court has eliminated some kinds of discrimination in family law there still exist areas in which court rulings do not seem to support its stated interest in the rights of the child. It is concluded that some of these rulings limit the range of solutions to social problems that states may use. (No references)

39. Clayton, Patricia N. "Meeting the Needs of the Single Parent Family." *The Family Coordinator* 20(4): 327–336 (October 1971).

The needs of the single parent are discussed along with the origin and growth of Parents Without Partners. This organization provides the opportunity for single parents to discuss and share with others mutual concerns and problems. The stated purpose of the organization is to help single parents successfully bring up children alone. Educational programs feature topics that may relate to the special needs of children and/or parents. (2 references)

40. Combrinck-Grahm, Lee, et al. "Hospitalization of Single-Parent Families of Disturbed Children." *Family Process* 21(2): 141–152 (June 1982).

The author describes a hospital apartment treatment program for families in which at least one of the identified patients is a child. The program is designed to provide a transition period that gives the family a chance to practice a different way of parenting, or to involve the family more directly in the treatment process. Six cases involving problems unique to single-parent families are discussed. The family hospitalization plan may provide more support than psychotherapy sessions for a parent who lacks a support network and who may have difficulty dealing with acting-out behavior in a child who is also undergoing stress. (9 references)

41. Cornelius, Georgianna Marie. "An Investigation of Children's Imaginative and Social Play in Relation to Family Structure, Maternal Stress, and Attitudes About Play." Ph.D. diss., Pennsylvania State University, 1986.

For a summary see: *Dissertation Abstracts International* 47A(6): 2013.

42. Daniels, Stacey. "Relationship of Employment Status to Mental Health and Family Variables in Black Men from Single-Parent Families." *Journal of Applied Psychology* 71(3): 386–391 (1986).

A variety of measures were used to assess the effects of employment and underemployment on a group of young black men from female-headed families. The data for this research was taken from a longitudinal ecological study of black men from female-headed one-parent households. Findings indicate that employment status was related to social ratings. The longer the father had been present, the more successful was the subject in employment. A highly educated mother was also a significant factor in success as were high school grades. (25 references)

43. Davidson, Charles W., et al. "The Prediction of Drug Use through Discriminate Analysis from Variables Common to Potential Secondary School Dropouts." *Journal of Educational Research* 72(6): 313–316 (July-August 1979).

Seventy-eight secondary school students from male-present and male-absent families were interviewed in regard to self-image, ability to communicate with parents, sex of student and drug use, and employment status of parents. Findings indicated that the best predictor of drug use was the presence or absence of an adult male who was associated with drug use. Self-image and perceived ability to communicate with parents were the next best predictors. It is recommended that drug education programs focus on enhancement of student self-concept and improvement of communication with parents. (21 references)

44. Doering, William G. *Is Life in a One-Parent Family Damaging to Children? A Look at Both Sides.* 1980. 17pp. (ERIC Microfiche ED193546)

The effect of divorce on children who live in one-parent families is examined. Children of divorced parents have been characterized as having lower I.Q. scores, more behavior problems, and academic handicaps than children from two-parent families. Factors related to living with one parent have been associated with juvenile delinquency and possibly with girls dropping out of high school. Other data support the concept that life in a happy one-parent family is less damaging to children than life in a conflict ridden two-parent family. One- parent children have also been found to be more independent but otherwise similar in all respects to children from intact families. (29 references)

45. Dornbusch, Sanford M., et al. "Single Parents in Extended Household, and the Control of Adolescents." *Child Development* 56(2): 326–341 (February 1985).

Patterns of family decision making and deviant behavior in adolescents were investigated in relation to family structure. A representative national sample of 6,710 subjects 12–17 years old was used as a source of data. Findings indicate that adolescents from female-headed families were more likely to make decisions without parental input and more likely to exhibit deviant behavior. Fewer forms of deviance and less independent decision making among adolescents were found in mother-headed families when another adult was present in the household. (18 references)

46. Edelman, Marian Wright. *Families in Peril: An Agenda for Social Change*. Cambridge, Mass.: Harvard University Press, 1987.

This book is based on the 1986 W.E.B. DuBois Lectures which the author delivered. It focuses on the comparative status of black and white families, the public costs of child and family poverty, and the implications for preventive public policy. Black children are more likely to live in a female-headed household, be born in poverty, be unemployed as teenagers, and not go to college after high school than are children from white families. The birth rate among white unmarried teens has been rising while the birth rate among black teens has been dropping. It is suggested that the key to bolstering black families and reducing child poverty and the growth in female-headed families is to provide improvements in education, training and employment for black males and females supported by public policy agendas that improve the status of families. (Bibliography)

47. Eiduson, Bernice T. "Emergent Families of the 1970's: Values, Practices and Impact on Children." In *The American Family: Dying or Developing*, edited by David

Reiss and Howard A. Hoffman, 151–201. New York: Plenum, 1979.

One hundred and fifty children from social contract families, and single-mother households were compared with 50 children from traditional two-parent families to study the impact on the children's development. Based on interviews, questionnaires and observations, findings suggest risk factors for a child's development include marital discord and disruption; separation of child from the mother after six months of age; depression of the mother; repeated residential changes, and addictive parents. Societal implications of emergent families are discussed. (68 references)

48. Ellwood, David T. "Poverty Among Single-Parent Families." Chap. 5, in *Poor Support: Poverty in the American Family*, 128–188. New York: Basic Books, 1988.

Among the problems female-headed families must deal with are lower wages paid to women, unemployment and the costs of daycare for their children. Since the majority of children in the United States are expected to spend some time in a single-parent home, they are at risk of entering the welfare system. This system antagonizes, stigmatizes, isolates, and humiliates its recipients to the extent that it discourages those who need assistance. Most mothers get almost no help. Child support payments are small and may be used as a weapon by divorced spouses. Changes in social policies and enforcement of job support laws are suggested. (78 references)

49. Evans, Roy, and Patricia G. Evans, trans. (Original text compiled under the direction of Mme le Docteur Viguie, for Documentation Francaise). "Social Measures in France Concerning Children with No Family or, Who Are At-Risk Due to Family Circumstances." *Early Child Development and Care* 15(2–3): 233–263 (June 1984).

This article reviews the various forms of intervention authorized by the Family Welfare Code for children-at-risk in France, and describes the institutions which provide financial aid, home help, temporary care of the child and temporary care of expectant mothers and isolated young mothers. Recent efforts made to improve the lives of children in foster care were aimed at providing clothing, toys and educational programs in a similar way to that of children from intact families. Suggestions are made for improvement in child welfare services. (5 references)

50. "Excerpts from the Ditchley Proceedings: Public Policy Considerations." *National Elementary Principal* 59(1): 59–64 (October 1979).

Excerpts from the Ditchley proceedings regarding public policy related to one-parent famililes feature statements by noted researchers on the effects of parental absence on children and the impact of changes in family structure on the single-parent family. Wallerstein discusses the effect of divorce on learning that is still in evidence after five years. The United States is reported to be the only industrial country without a child allowance system and an adequate public policy. Factors in the U.S. which stand in the way of arriving at a policy for families include competing special interests among professionals, religious differences, racial differences and differences in the constituency being addressed. Although there have been many changes in attitudes on social issues in recent years, they do not extend to income maintenance for families. (No references)

51. Farnworth, Margaret. "Family Structure, Family Attributes, and Delinquency in a Sample of Low-Income Minority Males and Females." *Journal of Youth and Adolescence* 13(4): 349–364 (August 1984).

Data were collected at two points in time to investigate the significance of family structure and its association with self-reported delinquency within a sample of black males and females from low-income families. Results suggest that the importance of family structure for delinquency is greatly exaggerated. When family structure is implicated in delinquency within this sample of youth from low-income families, an integral feature of structure is parental employment. (39 references)

52. Feldman, Wendy S., et al. "A Behavioral Parent Training-Program for Single Mothers of Physically-Handicapped Children." *Child Care Health and Development* 9(3): 157–168 (May-June 1983).

A training program for single mothers of children with physical disorders is outlined. The nine week program is designed to teach behavioral techniques to help mothers provide self-help skills and reduce behavior problems. Subjects in the study were selected from an orthopedic clinic focusing on children with spina bifida. The Miller Social Learning Test, the Behavioral Vignettes Test III and the Performance Inventory were used as measures. Results showed that children were able to acquire the self-help skills their mothers selected for them and were able to maintain them over a period of five months. Results suggest that a single parent faced with multiple stresses benefits from a program which aids the independent functioning of a chronically ill child. (23 references)

53. Ferri, Elsa. *Growing Up in a One Parent Family: A Long-Term Study of Child Development*. Windsor, England: NFER: Atlantic Highland, 1976. (A National Children's Bureau report)

This research is based on data gathered for the National Child Development Study conducted in Great Britain on single parent families. These families were found to be subject to greater financial hardship and earned lower wages which were further reduced by the costs of child care. Children of mothers who worked before they entered school were found to have lower scores in reading and arithmetic, and were judged to be less well adjusted. The crucial factor for the adjustment of single parent children was the social-psychological success of the family not whether the family was legally or physically broken. (Bibliography)

54. Fry, P. S., and Sonja C. Grover. "An Exploration of the Child's Perspective: Children's Perceptions of Parental Treatment, Personal Anxiety and Attributions of Blame in Single-Parent Families." *Journal of Psychiatric Treatment and Evaluation* 5(4): 353–362 (1983).

This study explores children's perceptions of parental conflict and parent-child relationships through individual interviews with sixty children from single-parent families. Findings indicated that the number of problem children in father-headed families was significantly greater than in mother-headed families. The therapeutic implications of the study for single-parent families are discussed. (28 references)

55. Fry, P. S., and R. J. Trifilet. "An Exploration of the Adolescents' Perspective-Perceptions of Major Stress Dimensions in the Single-Parent Family." *Journal of Psychiatric Treatment and Evaluation* 5(2–3): 101–111 (1983).

Adolescents' perceptions of the impact of divorce were probed through interviews with 150 young people from divorced families. Factors found to be stressful were parental conflict, mothers' inability to cope, anxiety about the reoccurence of feared events and reversal in parent-child roles. Family life education programs and further studies are suggested. (31 references)

56. Gardner, R. A. *The Boys and Girls Book About One-Parent Families*. New York: Putnam's Sons, 1978.

This book is written by a child psychiatrist for children who live in single-parent families. Three major sections deal with issues associated with parental absence due to separation or divorce, death or because the mother never married. It is suggested that the book be read and discussed by parent and child together. Not intended as a do-it-yourself manual, it aims to counter the development of psychological problems by encouraging open, honest and direct communication between parents and children. (No references)

57. Garfinkel, Irwin, and Sarah S. McLanahan. *Single Mothers and Their Children: A New American Dilemma.* Washington, D.C.: The Urban Institute Press, 1986.

This book is part of a series on Changing Domestic Priorities. It analyses the effect of changes in government domestic policies on single mothers and their children. Some evidence was found that children who live with single mothers in households with other adults fare better than those who live in homes where their mother is the only adult. Government data indicates that half of all children in female-headed families live in poverty and some black children never escape it. Reagan's domestic policies and proposals are discussed in relation to the plight of one-parent families. Implications for public programs and policy recommendations are presented.

58. Garman, A. R., et al. "Comparative Growth of Primary School Children from One and Two Parent Families." *Archives of Disease in Childhood* 57(6): 453–458 (1982).

Data for this study was taken from the National Study of Health and Growth which included samples from 28 areas in England and Scotland. It was found that one-parent children were shorter than two-parent children. Low birth weights and shorter parents were thought to be responsible for the shorter stature of the children. Further study is suggested to see if obesity will be a health problem for these one-parent children. (21 references)

59. Gasser, Rita D., and Claribel M. Taylor. "Role Adjustment of Single Parent Fathers with Dependent Children." *Family Coordinator* 25(4): 397–401 (October 1976).

Forty single fathers completed a questionnaire to provide
information on their adjustment as heads of one-parent
families. It was found that fathers assumed full
responsibility for all childcare unless the child was old
enough to assume this responsibility for himself/herself.
Most fathers gave up memberships in clubs and social
groups because of demands on their time. Widowed
fathers, unlike divorced fathers, were more reluctant to
give up friendships and club memberships and also
reported better relationships with neighbors. The success
of single fathers in adapting to one-parent families may
encourage more fathers to seek custody of children in
divorce situations. (12 references)

60. George Washington University. *Single Parent Families*,
    Parts 1–4. Institute for Educational Leadership; National
    Public Radio. George Washington University, 1980. 59pp.
    (ERIC Microfiche ED196563)

    Four National Public Radio interviews with single parents,
    their children and concerned others are recounted in
    these transcriptions. The interviews cover a wide range
    of topics, including methods used by single parents to
    resolve family problems. Additionally, the reactions of a
    young girl to her parents' divorce, aspects of the
    relationship between a father and his daughter, and
    resources providing support to single parents and their
    children are described. (No references)

61. Gibbs, Jewelle Taylor. "Identity and Marginality: Issues
    in the Treatment of Biracial Adolescents." *American
    Journal of Orthopsychiatry* 57(2): 265–278 (April 1987).

    The major conflicts and coping strategies of teenagers of
    mixed black and white parentage are examined. Cases
    used to illustrate some of the conflicting feelings included
    children from intact and divorced families as well as
    those born to unmarried mothers. Four areas of special
    concern are: age-appropriate behavior; attitudes of parents
    and family toward biracial identity; self-perceived identity;

and peer relationships. Teens' coping strategies may be adaptive or maladaptive. It is suggested that the major developmental task for biracial adolescents is to merge the dual racial identifications into a single identity that recognizes the positive aspects of each heritage. Therapeutic strategies to use in working with these teenagers are offered. (41 references)

62. Gilbert, Sara. *How to Live with a Single Parent.* New York: Lothrop, Lee & Shepard, 1982.

    This book is written for children who live in single-parent families and for single parents. Children's concerns about the family's economic situation, the addition of more responsibilities at home, dating parents and experiences of peers in the same situation are discussed and suggestions are made for coping with problems. A list of books and organizations that offer support to children and their parents is provided. (Bibliography)

63. Gladow, Nancy, and Margaret P. Wells. "The Low-Income Single Parent." *Journal of Extension* 22: 16–21 (September-October 1984).

    This Washington study examines the problems and support systems of 64 low-income single-parent families. Interviews with parents indicate that the most pervasive problems were associated with finances, health care, transportation, dealing with children's emotional needs and behaviors, and household tasks such as repairs and moving. Parents expressed interest in taking courses which would increase their knowledge and skills in those areas that caused the most problems for them. Single low-income parents are often unable to take advantage of support groups which are often comprised of middle-income and middle-class persons. Implications for the family-living extension agent are discussed. (5 references)

64. Glenwick, David S., and Joel D. Mowrey. "When Parent Becomes Peer: Loss of Intergenerational Boundaries in

Single-Parent Families." *Family Relations* 35(1): 57–62 (January 1986).

This paper discusses the single-parent family in which the intergenerational boundaries between the parent and the child are poorly defined. This situation may occur when a latency child lives with his/her mother and the mother functions more as peer partner than parent in her relations with the child. Two cases are discussed in which the mothers' negative feelings about the absent father affected the mother/child relationships. The therapeutic strategies used to help the mother return to her parental role are described. (13 references)

65. Goldstein, Joseph, et al. *Beyond the Best Interest of the Child*. New York: Free Press, 1973.

In child placement, the state recognizes the need to protect the child's physical well-being but has shown less concern for safeguarding the child's psychological well-being. Each time the parent-child relationship is broken, society risks gaining a person ill suited for becoming an adequate parent for children of the future. Placement decisions should protect the child's need for continuity of relationships. In changing the caretaking person, young children lose the most recently acquired achievements, which are rooted and develop in the intimate interchange with a stable parent figure. A model child placement statute for states is offered. (Bibliography)

66. Gorum, Jacquelyne Wallace. "Stress-Coping Patterns and Functioning of Black Single-Parent Families." Ph.D. diss., Howard University, 1983.

For a summary see: *Dissertation Abstracts International* 45A(7): 2255.

67. Groller, Ingrid. "A Fresh Start for Single Parents." *Parents* 56(1): 66–69 (January 1981).

A unique housing development in Denver aids single-parent families. Sponsored by the Warren United

Methodist Church, Warren Village provides a home for 93 families for an average stay of 12 to 15 months. Daycare facilities, family and career counseling, low-cost rent, and mutual support are among services provided to residents who are primarily women and children. Case histories of several women are used to illustrate the role of Warren Village in helping single mothers with children re-establish themselves without being separated from their children. (No references)

68. Hall, Marilyn C., and Dorellis J. Nelson. "Responsive Parenting: One Approach for Teaching Single Parents Parenting Skills." *School Psychology Review* 10(1): 45–53 (Winter 1981).

Numerous studies have shown that parents can be effective change agents for their children's behavior. The Responsive Parenting (RP) Program was designed to help parents who are concerned about their children's behavior. This program successfully uses parents who have already taken the course in parenting to assist in teaching other parents. After successful implementation with over 3,000 parents in the Shawnee Mission School District, the program has been replicated at a number of places across the country. Variations of the RP Program can be developed to meet the special needs of different areas. (47 references)

69. Hanson, Shirley. "Healthy Single Parent Families." *Family Relations* 35(1): 125–132 (January 1986).

This study explores characteristics of healthy single-parent families such as socio-economic status, social support, religiousness, problem solving and physical and mental health. Eighty-four subjects from forty-two families were interviewed and administered a questionnaire. Results showed that the physical and mental health of single parents and their children were generally good, especially for boys. Single mothers had poorer overall health than fathers. Custody arrangements also affected health as did good communication and social support. Implications for practitioners, educators and researchers are noted. (29 references)

70. ———. "Single Parent Families." *Family Relations* 35(1): 3–8 (January 1986).

This special issue of the journal focuses on the single-parent family. The most common reasons for the incidence of single-parent families are separation, divorce, widowhood, adoption and premarital birth. Although single-parent families constitute a significant family form, not much is known about them. This journal issue brings together articles that report current research, theoretical understandings and clinical observations on single parents and their children which will interest educators, researchers and family practitioners. Areas that need additional study are suggested. (2 references)

71. Harper, Linda E. "Exchange Theory as a Predictor of Parent-Adolescent Conflict in the Single Parent Family." Ph.D. diss., University of California at Los Angeles, 1981.

For a summary see: *Dissertation Abstracts International* 42A(4): 1812.

72. Hawley, Lynn E., et al. "Resident and Parental Perceptions of Adolescent Problems and Family Communications in a Low Socioeconomic Population." *The Journal of Family Practice* 19(5): 651–655 (November 1984).

Seventy-nine parents and 121 adolescents were examined for parentally perceived behavior problems and their correlation with single parenting. Data for the study came from medical records, telephone interviews and questionnaires. Single-parent homes were found to have three times the incidence of behavioral problems, a greater degree of communication and lower use of community resources than two-parent families. Parents reported problems with academic performance, truancy, household chores and siblings. None of the perceived behavioral problems were noted in medical records master problem list. (9 references)

73. Heger, Donna Tubach. "A Supportive Service to Single Mothers and Their Children." *Children Today* 6(5): 2–4, 36 (September-October 1977).

The Single Parent Program of the Child Saving Institute in Omaha, Nebraska is described in this article. The mothers and members of the CSI team make a contract to accomplish certain goals within a time specified frame. The program aims to help the mothers become self-supporting and able to live independently. Several case studies are used to illustrate how the program works. Of 69 young women who participated in the program a success rate of 67 percent was reported. (2 references)

74. "Help for Single Parents: Agencies and Organizations." *Family Relations* 35(1): 213–214 (January 1986).

This is a modified version of a list of agencies, organizations and support groups published in *Single Parent*, March 1985. Addresses, telephone numbers, membership fees, and a description of the kinds of services offered are presented for each agency or organization. Areas represented include pension rights, military benefits, parental rights in schools, advocacy for low income families, child support and custody. (No references)

75. Hetherington, E. Mavis, et al. "The Development of Children in Mother-headed Families." In *The American Family: Dying or Developing*, edited by David Reiss and Howard A. Hoffman, 117–145. New York: Plenum Press, 1979.

The functioning of mothers and children in single-parent families is compared with nuclear families. In the female headed families, mothers suffer from task overload, economic hardship and social isolation. It is suggested that the functioning of the mother who is present may be more critical than simple father absence in the sex-typed behavior of children and that the lower scores on achievement tests may be the result of the quality and quantity of maternal interaction. When the single mother has problems coping in the post-divorce period or has poor parenting skills, her children are more likely to be subject to emotional disturbance and acting-out behavior. Implications for social policy are noted. (74 references)

76. Hofferth, Sandra L. "Updating Children's Life Course." *Journal of Marriage and the Family* 47(1): 93–115 (February 1985).

   Data from the Panel Study of Income Dynamics are utilized for the purpose of analyzing parental marital status and living arrangements as they affect the childhood years of black and white children. In 1980, 11 percent of white children and 55 percent of black children were born to unmarried mothers. Of children born in 1980, 70 percent of the white children and 94 percent of the black children are projected to have spent some time in a single parent family before they reach the age of eighteen. Findings also show that there is considerable movement among family types. Almost all black children will have one-parent family experience. The family type into which a child is born is an important factor in his/her life course. (25 references)

77. Hogan, M. Jannice. "Single Parenting: Transitioning Alone." In *Stress and the Family: Vol.I: Coping with Normative Transitions*, edited by Hamilton I. McCubbin and Charles R. Figley, 116–132. New York: Brunner/ Mazel, 1983.

   Three case studies are used to illustrate the nature of stress in single-parent families. Following divorce or death, family members experience a sense of loss and grief. Problems include redefining family relationships, irregular or inadequate child support payments, and changes in family roles. Families may eat less meat; children may assume more responsibility for helping each other; and single parents may develop more meaningful relationships with their children as major coping strategies. Educators, counselors, friends, relatives, and policy makers can help reduce stress in single-parent families. (No references)

78. Horns, Virginia, and Gypsy Abbott. *A Comparison of Concepts of Self and Parents among Elementary School Children in Intact, Single Parent, and Blended Families.* Paper presented at the Annual Meeting of the Mid-South Education Researcher's Association, Biloxi, Miss. 31pp. November 1985. (ERIC Microfiche ED264481)

Differences in 404 elementary school children's self-concepts and their concepts of the adults they lived with were examined in relation to family structure. Responses to items on the Personal Attribute Inventory for children revealed few differences on self-concepts and concepts of parents. In reporting specific feelings, single-parent children saw themselves as less calm, less complaining, more afraid and nicer than other children. Children from intact families saw themselves as calmer, healthier, stronger and wiser than other children. The relationship between children's self-concept and the level of familial conflict is an area suggested for further study.

79. Hur, K. Kyoon, and Stanley J. Baran. "One-Parent Children's Identification with Television Characters and Parents." *Communication Quarterly* 27(3): 31–36 (Summer 1979).

This study explores the susceptibility of 36 children from single-parent families to the influence of television. Results of individual interviews showed that children with a parent of the opposite sex were more likely to identify with television characters. The presence of a commenting parent in the viewing situation seemed to be important in mediating the impact of the medium and to increase parental identification. Additional research on the nature of parent-child interaction in the one-parent home and the influence of television is suggested. (12 references)

80. Ihinger-Tallman, Marilyn. "Member Adjustment in Single Parent Families: Theory Building." *Family Relations* 35(1): 215–221 (January 1986).

This special issue deals with the unique problems and adjustment processes of those who live in single-parent households. The articles on educational programs, trend data, books, films, newsletter, and organizational information presents educational and information materials that will help educators and clinicians who serve single parents. The broadest and most general findings from the articles are restated in propositional form in this introduction to the issue. Family economic resources, parents and children's psychological characteristics and social support networks and their influence on the functioning of the single-parent family are among other topics covered. (14 references)

81. Johnson, Judy. "Help for the Handicapped Male Child of the Single Parent." *Pointer* 22(1): 71–73 (Fall 1978).

Sometimes the presence of a handicapped child precipitates individual or family breakdown. Should parents divorce, the author suggest that parents share responsibility for the child. The role that the Big Brothers of America program can play in aiding the single female parent in meeting the needs of the handicapped child is discussed. (3 references)

82. Jorgensen, Stephen R., and Elizabeth G. Haley. "Future Families in a Nation at Risk: the Promise and Potential of Home Economics." *Illinois Teacher of Home Economics* 28(3): 94–99 (January-February 1985).

Among the problems which families will continue to face in the future are increasing rates of divorce and teenage pregnancy. The large number of single-parent households associated with divorce and the births of infants to unmarried mothers suggest that one-third to one-half of all children born in the 1970's will spend some part of their lives in a one-parent household. Blacks and other minorities continue to be represented disproportionately in the lower end of the economic, occupational and educational scales. Guidelines are offered for designing home economics programs that will provide information and skills to enable all students to cope with societal problems in the future. (18 references)

83. Kamerman, Shelia B., and Alfred J. Kahn. *Mothers Alone: Strategies for a Time of Change*. Dover, Mass.: Auburn House, 1988.

In departing from traditional lifestyles, single parents face such challenges as temporary or continuing poverty, although there may be some improvement from situations faced in the past. Efforts of the United States and seven other advanced industrialized countries to meet the needs of single parent families include anti- poverty strategies and policies to facilitate participation in the work force. Because it is difficult to limit most public programs to poor mothers, universalism as a policy perspective is suggested. (Bibliography)

84. Kaplan, Barbara J. "Understanding Family Disruption: the Cognitive Development of Children." *Social Service Review* 54(3): 414–422 (September 1980).

An attempt is made to shed light on children's misunderstanding of the reasons for family disruptions by examining their cognitive development. The child's understanding of events is limited to his/her knowledge of the world. The child is likely to assume that his/her actions may cause things that adults view as caused by independent circumstances. It is suggested that the social workers not treat the child's assumptions about the cause of family disruption as meaningless but use their understanding of the child's cognitive development to offer the best explanation of the event they can. (5 references)

85. Kazak, Anne E., and Jean Ann Linney. "Stress, Coping, and Life Change in the Single-Parent Family." *American*

Journal of Community Psychology 11(2): 207–220 (April 1983).

Forty-seven white, employed, divorced women with custody of children were examined for self-perceived competence as parent, social participant, and self-supporter. A battery of self-report instruments were administered to subjects in their homes. The single-parent women felt very competent in their parenting role and rated it highest of the three roles. Single social participant and self-supporter roles may be viewed as more stressful to divorced women because their role as child caretakers is so demanding. (32 references)

86. Kellam, Sheppard G. "The Long-Term Evolution of the Family Structure of Teenage and Older Mothers." *Journal of Marriage and the Family* 44(3): 539–554 (August 1982).

The short-term and long-term effects of teenage motherhood were studied in a population of poor blacks in Chicago. Based on a comparison of fifteen years of family evolution of teenage and older mothers, it was found that teenage mothers frequently begin child rearing as the only adult at home and are at high risk of remaining the only adult at home as long as 15 years after the child's birth. Consequently the teenage mother has less help in rearing her child and participates less in voluntary organizations. Further study of the detrimental outcomes for the teenage mother or her children is advised. (41 references)

87. Kellam, Sheppard G., et al. "Family Structure and the Mental Health of Children." *Archives of General Psychiatry* 34(9): 1012–1022 (September 1977).

This study of family structure and its impact on the mental health of children is based on subjects comprising one-half of the 1,964 first-grade children in a poor black urban community and all 1,966 first-grade children in the same community. Findings suggest that mother-alone families run the highest risk of social maladaptation and of psychological risk. A second adult helps the single-parent family. Mother/grandmother families are almost as effective as mother/father families. Mother/stepfather families were found to be similar to mother-alone families in regard to risk. Implications for social policy and mental health programs are noted. (24 references)

88. Kelly, F. Donald, and Frank O. Main. "Sibling Conflict in a Single-Parent Family: An Empirical Case Study." *American Journal of Family Therapy* 7(1): 39–47 (Spring 1979).

Young children seem to need to differentiate themselves from their siblings, to stand out in contrast with the others. They may compete with each other for their parents' affection and attention. The case discussed in this paper is that of the older boy in a divorced family who did not have access to his father. Bickering, arguing, and fighting characterized his relationship with his younger brother. Results following a ten-week treatment session, the relationship between two brothers improved greatly. Suggestions for further study of sibling relationships are offered. (22 references)

89. Koller, K. "Parental Deprivation, Family Background, and Female Delinquency." *British Journal of Psychiatry* 118: 319–327 (March 1971).

This study probes the relationship between random sample of 121 adolescent girls at a Training School in Great Britain. The group of delinquent girls was matched with 101 girls from the general population. The delinquent girls in this study came from large families with the intermediate female children being more likely to have a history of delinquency. Over half of the delinquent girls had experienced long-term loss of one or both parents. (29 references)

90. Lederer, James B., et al. *Single Parent Families and the Handicapped*. Bergen County Special Services School

District, Paramus, N.J., July 1982 7pp. (ERIC Microfiche ED224216)

This paper reports results of a survey to determine the relationship between severe disabilities in children and single-parent families in Bergen County, New Jersey. Findings indicated that the range of single-parent families extended from 15 percent in the retarded population to 66 percent in the hospitalized emotionally disturbed population. Records of 750 students served by the Special Services School District of Bergen County were reviewed. The relationship between handicapping condition and single parent status could not be determined by the data. Difficulty facing parents in taking part in the child's education is noted. Changes in school policy are suggested. (8 references)

91. *Legal Rights of Children*, edited by Robert M. Horowitz and Howard A. Davidson. Colorado Springs: Shepard's/ McGraw-Hill, 1984. (Family Law Series)

This book is for professionals and others who are involved in providing services related to the rights of children. Among the topics represented that have special significance for single-parent children are child support, custody disputes, parent locator services, illegitimate children's rights, parental kidnapping, maternal and child health grants and public benefit programs. Anticipated changes in the law likely to occur within the next decade are also discussed.

92. Libber, Samuel M., and Donelda J. Stayton. "Childhood Burns Reconsidered: The Child, the Family and the Burn Injury." *The Journal of Trauma* 24(3): 245–252 (March 1984).

The psychological characteristics of 100 burned children and their families were evaluated in this study. Results were then compared with similar studies from Australia, Great Britain and the United States. Findings suggest that the children most at risk for burns are very young, male, economically disadvantaged, and with psychological handicaps and a history of previous burns. The implications for family professionals are noted. (36 references)

93. Lindbald-Goldberg, Marion. *Clinical Issues In Single-Parent Households*. Rockville, Md.: Aspen, 1987.

This volume in the Family Therapy Collections Series focuses on the single-parent family as an alternative family structure with problems unique to one-parent households and other problems shared in common with nuclear families. Among the single-parent issues discussed are: economic problems, social network and kinship systems, impact of divorce on children and teenage single parents. It is suggested that many of the psycho/social problems associated with growing up in a one-parent home are due to economic factors rather than to family structure. (Bibliography)

94. ———. "Successful Minority Single-Parent Families." Chap. 6, in *Children in Family Contexts: Perspectives on Treatment*, edited by Lee Combrinck-Graham. New York: Guilford Press, 1989.

Normative and dysfunctional single-parent family functioning was investigated in 126 low income black families headed by working and nonworking mothers. A model of adaptive single-parent functioning and a model of less adaptive single-parent functioning are used to illustrate the differences between the two types of families. Characteristics of successful one-parent families include: a workable executive hierarchy, clearly defined sibling responsibilies, parental skills to solve problems and attend to personal needs, a sense of control and a positive coping philosophy. (35 references)

95. Lindbald-Goldberg, Marion, and Joyce Lynn Dukes. "Social Support in Black, Low-Income, Single-Parent

Families: Normative and Dysfunctional Patterns."
American Journal of Orthopsychiatry 55(1): 42–58
(January 1985).

This study examines normal and dysfunctional single-parent family functioning in black, low-income, working and non-working, female-headed families with preadolescent and adolescent children. Data were gathered from 126 urban families in two-hour research interviews. It was found that clinic and nonclinic groups were similar demographically and that the black, single-parent family operates as a subsystem of the kinship system, which, in turn, is a subsystem of the community, which is part of the larger society. (34 references)

96. Lindsay, Jeanne Warren, and Deedee Upton Warr. *Do I Have a Daddy?: A Story about a Single-Parent Child with Special Section for Single Mothers and Fathers.* Buena Park, Calif.: Morning Glory, 1982.

This story about a single-parent child describes some of the concerns children may have about father absence and how parents may respond to these concerns. A special section for single mothers and fathers follows the story about the child. The need to stress positive points and to provide honest answers is emphasized. A grandfather, brother or male friends may provide the child with a male role model. Ways to use this book in single-parent situations are discussed. (No bibliography)

97. Lipten, Claire Rose. "The Single-Parent Family as Alternative Lifestyle." Ph.D. diss., Wayne State University, 1979.

For a summary see: Dissertation Abstracts International 40A(4): 2292.

98. Loveland-Cherry, Carol J. "Personal Health Practices in Single Parent and Two Parent Families." *Family Relations* 35(1): 133–139 (January 1986).

A sample of 41 white middle class families with at least one child eight to fourteen years old who lived in one- or two-parent homes was interviewed. A modified version of Pratt's Family Health Interview Schedule was the measuring instrument used to determine differences in health practices. No significant differences for levels of personal health practices were found for children, mothers and total family units. However there was a greater degree of variance in scores for children from single-parent families. Implications for practice are discussed along with suggestions for further research. (21 references)

99. Lowenstein, Joyce S. "A Comparison of Self-Esteem between Boys Living With Single-Parent Mothers and Boys Living With Single-Parent Fathers." Ph.D. diss., University of Maryland, 1977.

    For a summary see: *Dissertation Abstracts International* 39A(2): 1137.

100. Lowenstein, Joyce S., and Elizabeth J. Koopmen. "A Comparison of the Self-Esteem between Boys Living With Single-Parent Mothers and Single-Parent Fathers." *Journal of Divorce* 2(2): 195–208 (Winter 1978).

    The self-esteem of boys in 40 single-parent families were compared. Sons between the ages of nine and fourteen were administered the Index of Adjustment and Values and 20 mothers and 20 fathers were administered the Index of Adjustment and Values. Results show: 1) boys who saw their noncustodial parent once a month had higher self-esteem than those who did not, 2) there is no significant difference in self-esteem between boys living with single-parent mothers and boys living with single-parent fathers, and 3) given comparable economic status, availability and interest, fathers and mothers who want custody can provide equally conducive environments for boys between the ages of nine and fourteen. (16 references)

101. MacKinnon, Carol E., et al. "The Impact of Maternal Employment and Family Form on Children's Sex-Role

Stereotypes and Mothers' Traditional Attitudes." *Journal of Divorce* 8(1): 51–60 (Fall 1984).

Sixty single-parent and 20 intact families were studied to discover the effects of divorce and maternal employment on mothers' and children's sex-role attitudes. Instruments used were Attitudes Toward Women Scale for mothers and the Sex-Role Learning Index for children. It was found that working mothers, single and married, were more liberal in sex-role attitudes, and that children of single-parent families were more liberal in sex-role orientation. It is suggested that children from divorced families, particularly girls, are less aware of sex-role stereotypes of the opposite sex. (3 references)

102. McCarty, Priscilla McAllister. "Parent-Child Relationships in Single Parent Families." Ph.D. diss., Ohio State University, 1981.

For a summary see: *Dissertation Abstracts International* 42A(10): 4608.

103. McCubbin, Hamilton, and Pauline Grossenbacher Boss. "Family Stress and Coping: Targets For Theory, Research, Counseling and Education." *Family Relations* 29(4): 429–444 (October 1980).

This article is written by the guest editors to introduce this special issue of the journal. The issue focuses on family stress and the dynamics of family adjustment in coping with parenthood, retirement and loss of a family member. Reports of investigations include theory and research that offers guidelines for clinical intervention by professionals who work with families during times of extreme hardship. (1 reference)

104. Melli, Marygold S. "The Changing Legal Status of the Single Parent." *Family Relations* 35(1): 31–36 (January 1986).

The legal status of the unmarried mother, who recently was regarded as sole parent, is changing in regard to adoption, custody and visitation. Unmarried fathers who live with the unmarried mother and her children may receive rights approximating those of married fathers. Divorced single parents have less autonomy in the rearing of children. Joint custody is gaining greater acceptance. Increased rights for fathers is the out growth of the equal rights movement and has changed the legal relationship between the custodial and noncustodial parent. The impoverishment of children and increased welfare costs have lead to greater enforcement of support. (26 references)

105. Mendes, Helen A. "Single-Parent Families: A Topology of Life-Styles." *Social Work* 24(3): 193–200 (May 1979).

This article addresses five distinct life-styles adopted by single-parent families and examines the risks and opportunities associated with each. The sole executive, the auxiliary parent, the unrelated substitute, the related substitute and the titular parent are discussed along with related psychosocial factors. Implications for social work practice with each single family type are outlined to help these professionals minimize risks and maximize opportunities for these parents and their children. (30 references)

106. Miller, Jean Baker. "Psychological Recovery in Low-Income Single Parents." *American Journal of Orthopsychiatry* 52(2): 346–352 (April 1982).

This report examines the process by which a group of eight working-class female single parents were able to arrive at a state of healthy psychological functioning and a good self concept after marital separation of three to nine years. Most of the women had some type of job and had established a supportive network with other single parents. They had close emotional interactions with their children and often assumed leadership roles on community issues. Counseling, jobs and responsibility for their children played an important role in their adjustment. (8 references)

    *   Montemayor, Raymond, and Geoffrey K. Leigh. "Parent-Absent Children: A Demographic Analysis of Children and Adolescents Living Apart from Their Parents." *Family Relations* 31(4): 567–573 (October 1982).

    Reported in Reconstituted Families Item No. 319.

107. Morawetz, Anita, and Gillian Walker. *Brief Therapy with Single-Parent Families.* New York: Brunner/Mazel, 1984.

Sociologists, jurists and economists, in particular have had to confront the issues resulting from dramatic increases in the number of single parents and the rise in divorce rates. Case studies are presented to illustrate the factors associated with divorce, desertion, death and custody. Single-parent children are at a disadvantage because educators have assumed for many years that they have more school problems than children from two-parent families. How well a child does is significantly related to the expectation which significant adults have for the child's success or failure. The role of the therapist in resolving school problems is discussed as are public policy implications. (Bibliography)

108. Moreno, Steve. *Parenting Information.* Moreno Educational Company. San Diego, Calif., 1981. 161pp. (ERIC Microfiche ED227928)

Five booklets written in English and Spanish contain information on how parents can help their children learn. One of the booklets designed for single parents provides information on the effect of divorce on children and adolescents. Schools are suggested as a resource for helping children. (Bibliography)

109. Mueller, Daniel P., and Philip W. Cooper. "Children of Single Parent Families: How do They Fare as Young Adults?" *Family Relations* 35(1): 169–176 (January 1986).

A sample of 1,448 persons, 19–34 years of age, from Ramsey County, Minnesota, were surveyed to obtain information on young adults from single-parent families and to compare them with young adults from intact families. Young adults from single-parent families had lower educational, occupational and economic status than those from traditional families. Differences in marital stability and timing of parenthood were also noted. Children from low-income families are at risk of dropping out of school, and educational opportunities for single parent children improve as family income improves. Special programs for at-risk children are suggested. (22 references)

110. Neiman, Jeri Anne. "One-Parent Families: A Study of Short and Long-Term Families Using Family Climate. M.A. Thesis, California State University, 1981.

For a summary see: *Masters Abstracts* 20(3): 0310.

111. Nork, Steven L. "Enduring Effects of Marital Disruption and Subsequent Living Arrangements." *Journal of Family Issues* 3(1): 25–40 (March 1982).

A national sample of 8,224 adults was examined to compare those who had experienced parental loss during adolescence with those who had lived in intact families during this period of their lives. Data from the study are taken from the National Opinion Research Center's General Social Surveys between 1972 and 1977. Few long-term effects associated with family disruption of any kind were observed in results of the study. Where effects were noted, they were positive in nature, indicating the possibility that family disruption may have strengthened some individuals. Suggestions are made for further study of the potentially positive effects of some types of family disruption. (19 references)

112. Norton, Arthur J. "Families and Children in the Year 2000." *Children Today* 16(4): 6–9 (July-August 1987).

Social economic and demographic factors which will have an impact on the lives of children up to the year 2000 are described. More working parents, increased need for daycare and nurseries, some decrease in divorce rates, and continuing concern for children in single-parent families, and in stepfamilies will challenge children, parents, and others upon whom children depend for assistance. (No references)

113. Norton, Arthur J., and Paul C. Glick. "One Parent Families: A Social and Economic Profile." *Family Relations* 35(1): 9–17 (January 1986).

The most recent demographic information is used to determine the extent to which the single- parent family compares unfavorably with two- parent families based on socio-economic characteristics. Sex, race, age, marital status, education, employment, family income and mobility are among factors examined. Single- parent families were found to be in a disadvantaged position relative to other family groups. More research is recommended in the areas of child care and support systems. (14 references)

114. Nunn, Gerald D., and Thomas S. Parish. "Personal and Familial Adjustment as a Function of Family Type." *Phi Delta Kappan* 64(2): 141 (October 1982).

Six hundred and thirty-three white children from lower-middle-income single-parent and intact families were studied to determine the effects of living in single-parent homes. The Personal Attribute Inventory, State-Trait Anxiety Inventory and Behavior Rating Profile measures were used to assess adjustment. Findings indicated that children from intact families had better personal and familial adjustment than children who had suffered parental loss through death. However, the latter were better adjusted in many ways than children from divorced families. (3 references)

115. Olson, Dawn R. "Family Structure and Social Influence." Paper presented at the Annual Meeting of the Midwestern

Psychology Association, May 6–8, Minneapolis, Minn. 1982. (ERIC Microfiche ED226259)

Thirty-eight junior high school students were studied to determine the relative effects of peer and family influence in single-parent and nuclear families. Results of questionnaires showed that children from both family types are more influenced by parents than peers. This finding suggests that regardless of the stress of divorce, parental influence in single-parent and nuclear families is similar. Further research is suggested to discover why there is less parental influence immediately following divorce and what is responsible for the restoration of parental influence later. (9 references)

116. Pardeck, John T., and Jean A. Pardeck. "Helping Children Cope With the Changing Family: Through Bibliotherapy." *Social Work in Education* 9(2): 107–116 (1987).

Children in changing family structures sometimes have difficulty coping with problems related to the transition. They may experience feelings of hostility, guilt, anger and insecurity. Through bibliotherapy children who are experiencing difficulties learn about others with similar problems and ways to cope with them. There are many children's books available that deal with situations related to divorce, living with one parent, and stepfamilies. By identifying those children who would benefit from bibliotherapy, school social workers can help them cope with family transition. A list of children's books that may be used by the professional in bibliotherapy is included.

117. Parish, Joycelyn G., and Thomas S. Parish. "Children's Self-Concepts as Related to Family Structure and Family Concept." *Adolescence* 18(71): 649–658 (Fall 1983).

Four hundred and twenty-six children from divorced, intact and reconstructed families were examined to determine the effect of family structure on the children's self-concepts. The Personal Attribute Inventory for Children (PAIC) was administered to fifth through eighth grade public school students. Findings indicate that children's self-concepts were significantly related to their family structure and their family concept. Implications for parents, educators and family professionals are noted. (22 references)

118. Parish, Thomas S. "Evaluations of Family as a Function of One's Family Structure and Sex." *Perceptual and Motor Skills* 66(1): 25–26 (1988).

Eight hundred and twenty-two college students completed the Personal Attribute Inventory using their family as the target group. Family ratings as a function of their own family structure did not differ significantly for 229 men in the group. However, 33 women from divorced families were significantly more negative in their family ratings than 560 women from intact families or the men from intact or divorced families. Implications for mediating the effects of paternal divorce are noted. (2 references)

119. Parish, Thomas S., and Gerald D. Nunn. "Children's Self-Concepts and Evaluations of Parents as a Function of Family Structure and Process." *Journal of Psychology* 107(1): 105–108 (January 1981).

Self-concepts and perceptions of parents were examined in a sample of 132 children who had lost fathers through death or divorce. The Personal Attribute Inventory for Children and another instrument for rating parents were completed by fifth through eighth grade students. Results showed that children from unhappy and divorced families may experience threats to fulfillment of their basic needs. Children from happy homes or from families where parental loss was due to death responded more positively in regard to their self-concepts and ratings of their parents. Suggestions are made for further research of related factors. (16 references)

120. Parish, Thomas, and Joycelyn C. Parish. "Relationship between Evaluations of One's Self and One's Family by Children from Intact, Reconstituted, and Single-Parent

Families." *Journal of General Psychology* 143(2): 293–294 (December 1983).

Four hundred seventy-one fifth through eighth grade children were administered the Personal Attribute Inventory for children to determine variance in self-perception and perception of family across family structure. Self-concepts were found to be significantly correlated with evaluations of families, except for those subjects from divorced non-remarried families. Findings therefore suggest that two parents, natural or otherwise, provide a home situation in which the child can regain personal stability. (5 references)

121. Parish, Thomas S., and Stanley E. Wigle. "The 16 PF as a Predicator of Familial Background." *Journal of Genetic Psychology* 144(2): 289–290 (June 1984).

Two hundred and ninety-four college students participated in a study to evaluate the Sixteen Personality Factor Questionnaire (16 P F) as predicators of respondents' familial backgrounds. Most of the factors were found not to be significant discriminant predicators of familial background. The Personality Factor (PF 12) showed respondents from divorced, remarried and intact families had more confidence, more self-assurance and less guilt than divorced non-remarried families. (No references)

122. Parish, Thomas S., et al. "Evaluations of Self and Parents as a Function of Intactness of Family and Family Happiness." *Adolescence* 16(61): 203–210 (Spring 1981).

Two hundred and eighty-four children evaluated themselves and their parents as a function of intactness and family happiness. Children in the study who rated their families "happy" also rated themselves and their parents more favorably than those who rated their families "unhappy." Children from intact families rated their parents more favorably than children from divorced families. Males from divorced families rated themselves and their fathers more negatively than females. Findings are discussed in relation to other research studies. (14 references)

123. Pearce, Diana M. "The Feminization of Ghetto Poverty." *Society* 21(1): 70–74 (November-December 1983).

The number of poor female-headed households has increased substantially during the past decade, and the increase has been greatest for black female-headed families. The impact of inequities in the distribution of primary and secondary welfare benefits, as it affects women and minorities, is discussed. The traditional emphasis on jobs rather than careers leaves many women at a disadvantage when it comes to supporting themselves and their children. It is noted that only in a sexist society can the breakup of the family increase the economic status of the father while the mother and children suffer decreases in economic status. (9 references)

124. Phelps, Randy E., and Debra K. Huntley. *Social Networks and Child Adjustment in Single-Parent Families.* Paper presented at the Annual Convention of the American Psychological Association, Los Angeles, Calif., August 23–27, 1985. 16pp. (ERIC Microfiche ED266400)

This paper focuses on the role of the child's social support network on his or her adjustment to parental divorce. Using the Revised Behavior Problem Checklist, mothers were asked to rate the quality and frequency of the child's contact with members of his or her social network. Children used the Child Depression Inventory to rate themselves. Findings indicated that only the network quality measures were significant predictors of the child's adjustment to parental divorce. (12 references)

125. Phillips, Shelley. *Current Issues in Maternal and Paternal Deprivation.* Unit for Child Studies Selected Papers No. 6. New South Wales University, Kesington (Australia) School of Education. October 1980. 20pp. (ERIC Microfiche ED204034)

This paper focuses on the issues of maternal and paternal deprivation. Some areas in which single parents encounter problems in child rearing are not necessarily the effects of single-parenting but may occur in traditional families also. Reversal of parent/child roles, use of the child as a pawn in spousal conflict, sex-role stereotyping, school phobias, delinquency and academic performance are discussed. The social, intellectual and emotional effects of daycare are also noted. (31 references)

126. Porter, Blaine R., and Randy S. Chatelai. "Family-Life Education for Single Parent Families." *Family Relations* 30(4): 517–525 (October 1981).

Problems unique to single parents and their children are discussed and suggestions for ways to deal with the challenges they present are offered. Single parenthood is generally the result of death, divorce, desertion, separation and pregnancy out of wedlock. Each has its own characteristics and responses. However some common challenges can be identified such as, explaining the absence of the other parent, making an honest appraisal of self, exorcising guilt feelings, raising self-esteem and providing a missing sex-role model for children. The family-life educator can help parents understand their children and their needs, help them set goals and aid them in utilizing personal and community resources. (31 references)

127. Quisenberry, James D., ed. *Changing Family Lifestyles: Their Effect on Children.* Washington, D.C., Association for childhood Education International. 1982. 68pp. (ERIC Microfiche ED226854)

Thirteen articles reprinted from the journal CHILDHOOD EDUCATION are organized into three sections: 1) family structure status and stresses, 2) parenting and 3) issues related to the changing family. Areas discussed are divorce and children, support systems for black families, improving the quality of family life, and involving working parents in the schools. (Bibliography)

128. Raschke, Helen J., and Vernon J. Raschke. "Family Conflict and Children's Self-Concepts: A Comparison of Intact and Single-Parent Families." *Journal of Marriage and the Family* 41(2): 367–374 (May 1979).

This study examines the effect of family structure and family conflict on the self- concepts of children. A questionnaire incorporating the Piers-Harris Children's Self-Concept Scale was administered to 289 children from the third, sixth, and eighth grades. There was a significant relationship between self-concept and fighting in the family for both single-parent families and intact families. However, no significant correlation between self-concept scores and family structure was found. The more perceived fighting in the home, the lower the self-concept of children in both single-parent families and in intact families. Suggestions for further longitudinal research are offered. (34 references)

129. Rasmussen, Dennis Duane. "Sex Role Differentiaton in One Parent Families." Ph.D. diss., University of Wisconsin, 1974.

For a summary see: *Dissertation Abstracts International* 35B(11): 5624.

130. Rawlings. Steve W. "Single Parents and Their Children." In *Studies in Marriage and the Family*. U.S. Department of Commerce Bureau of the Cenus. Washington, D.C.: June 1989. (Current Population Reports. Special Studies, Series P-23, No. 162).

Data on single parents and their children are based on estimates reflected in the current population Survey for March 1988 and earlier years. Almost all single parents are mothers who are likely to be younger than single fathers. Teenage mothers require more assistance from parents or from public service agencies. These families are a large and often disadvantaged portion of society.

131. Rhodes, Gregory L., and Mark Real. "Day Care: Investing in Ohio's Children." *Ohio's Children: Ohio's Future, Report*

No. 3 118pp. 1985. (Also ERIC Microfiche ED256469)

This report presents an inventory of Ohio children from single-parent and two-parent families who need daycare services. Daycare policies in the state were compared with those of other states. In addition, families; daycare providers; public officials; and legal specialists were interviewed. Recommendations were made for the improvement of daycare services in Ohio, most of which require no new funding.

132. Risman, Barbara J. "Can Men 'Mother'? Life as a Single Parent." *Family Relations* 35(1): 95–102 (January 1986).

A sample of 141 fathers were examined in regard to their experience as single fathers; the nature of the father/ child relationship; and their satisfaction with their role. Results of a questionnaire showed fathers spend considerable time with their children in household chores and recreational activities. Fathers also felt very close and very affectionate with their youngest child, and are generally satisfied with their role. Children of fathers who earned more income were less likely to exhibit negative emotions. Fathers who fought for custody were more likely to report better relationships with their children. (36 references)

133. Robinson, Mary J. "Sink or Swim: the Single-Parent Family with a Deaf Child." *Volta Review: The Families of Hearing-Impaired Children* 81(5): 370–377 (September 1979).

The single parent of a hearing-impaired child found that her greatest support and source of strength came from other women who had borne a deaf child. The way in which this mother worked through the changes she needed to make in order to help her child cope successfully with the challenge of deafness is discussed. The impact on family life, siblings, relationships with teachers, and school administrators are among the areas covered. The mother felt that her family gained from having to share responsibility for a handicapped member. There are implications for other parents of a physically impaired child. (20 references)

134. Rodgers, Harrell R., Jr. *Poor Women, Poor Families: The Economic Plight of America's Female-Headed Households* Armonk, New York: Sharpe, 1986.

Divorce, separation and out-of-wedlock births have resulted in dramatic increases in female-headed families, and these families are now the major poverty group in the United States. One of the most significant consequences of the high poverty rates for women is the economic deprivation suffered by their dependent children. It is estimated that one in every five children in this country now lives in poverty. Often the most needy female households do not receive public assistance. Female-headed families in Europe are discussed, and recommendations for revision of the American Welfare System are offered. (Bibliography)

135. Roy, Crystal M., and Dale R. Fuqua. "Social Support Systems and Academic Performance of Single-Parent Students." *The School Counselor* 30(3): 183–192 (January 1983).

This study attempts to identify the support systems that enable single-parent children to cope effectively. Results are based on responses to a questionnaire completed by 22 single parents. Results indicate that an adequate support system may mediate the negative effects of single-parent family status on children's academic performance. Implications for intervention are discussed. The questionnaire is included in the appendix. (37 references)

136. Rozendal, Frederick G., and Jo M. Wells. "Use of the Semantic Differential to Evaluate Long-Term Effects of Loss of Parent on Concepts of Family." *Journal of Genetic Psychology* 143(2): 269–278 (December 1983).

The Semantic Differential was used in this investigation

to study its usefulness in assessing differences in concepts of the family between subjects from intact families and those from disrupted families. Forty-eight college students participated in the study. Findings indicated that subjects from disrupted families rated parents, marriage and family less favorably than subjects from intact families. Parent-loss individuals rated divorce more favorably than those from intact families. No long-term effects of parent-loss were found in ratings of self by the two-parent status groups. The Semantics Differential seems to provide more information than a single-dimensional scale. (22 references)

137. Rutter, Michael. "Separation Experience: A New Look at an Old Topic." *Journal of Pediatrics* 95(1): 147–154 (July 1979).

The effects of separation experiences on children as reported in research studies are explored. Various causes of separation and their impact on children are discussed. These include working mothers, mothers or children in hospitals or other institutions, bereavement and broken homes. Research findings indicate that an understanding of the variety of mechanisms operating in the different kinds of separation is necessary if children are to be helped through these experiences. Variables such as length of separation, age of child when the separation occurs, the pre- and post-home separation environment and individual differences in response to stress may be significantly related to the consequences of separation for children. (65 references)

138. Ryan, Patricia. "Single-Parent Families." Administration for Children, Youth and Families. Washington, D. C. (Report No. DHHS-OHDS-79–30247) March 1981, 52pp. (Also ERIC Microfiche ED251236)

This booklet, written for parents, describes children's responses to parental loss and provides information for dealing with these reactions. Children's needs relating to discipline, communication, affection and privacy are also discussed. Suggestions are offered for various types of single-parents: divorced, widowed, adoptive, unmarried and separated. Community agencies and books that may be used as resources for parents and children are listed. (Bibliography)

139. Sack, William H., et al. "The Single-Parent Family and Abusive Child Punishment." *American Journal of Orthopsychiatry* 55(2): 252–259 (April 1985).

Interviews of a random sample of 802 noninstitutionalized adults were reviewed to determine changes in the stress levels of children living in households that experience a change from a two-family to a one-parent family. Abuse was found to be nearly twice as high for single-parent families than for two-parent families and higher in households broken by divorce than by separation or death. Sex of the single parent was not related to reported abuse proportions. Additional insight into patterns of abusive punishment emerges by forming parental compatibility subpopulations of the data. (18 references)

140. Sanik, Margaret Mietus, and Teresa Mauldin. "Single Versus Two Parent Families: a Comparison of Mothers' Time." *Family Relations* 35(1): 53–56 (January 1986).

Data on 210 two-parent/two-child households was compared with data collected on 81 one-parent/two-child households on mothers' use of time. Time spent in child care by employed married mothers was statistically less when compared with nonemployed mothers. Time spent in nonphysical care of children did not differ across the groups and shows that all groups of mothers gave the same amount of time to the needs of their children. Although the time mothers spend with children in all families could be increased, there was not less contact in single-parent families. (9 references)

141. Saucier, Jean-Francois. "Parental Marital Status and

Adolescents' Optimism About Their Future." *Journal of Youth and Adolescence* 11(5): 345–354 (October 1982).

A random sample of 4,539 Montreal adolescents completed a questionnaire designed to measure their optimism about the future. It was found that adolescents from intact families expected, more than those from broken homes, to be successful in the future. Girls who had lost a parent through death were less optimistic than those whose parents were separated. Longitudinal studies are recommended. (67 references)

142. Schlesinger, Benjamin. "Jewish One-Parent Families—A Growing Phenomenon in the 1970's." *Journal of Psychology and Judaism* 7(2): 89–100 (Spring/Summer 1983).

This paper examines the rapid growth of single-parent families in the Jewish population in Canada and the United States. The problems and satisfactions of one-parent families and the services which the Jewish community can provide to aid parents and children are discussed. Two programs for children and adolescents and a program for widows are described. It is suggested that the Noah's Ark syndrome of the two-by-two Jewish family life of yesterday will need to be re-examined in terms of what is today. (16 references)

143. ———. "One Parent Families in Great Britain." *Family Coordinator* 26(2): 139–141 (April 1977).

Great Britain's Finer Report on one-parent families is reviewed. The report, which is reputed to be the most comprehensive in the world, is a two-volume work titled *Report of the Committee on One Parent Families* London: Her Majesty's Stationery Office, which was published in 1974. The majority of one-parent families were headed by females, most of whom were at the poverty level. Findings showed that children of working mothers often carry responsibility beyond what should be expected, may show more negative behavior and may see themselves as different from others because of their single-parent family status. Areas recommended for special attention include: child support collection, financial subsidy, day care services, counseling, male staff in day care centers, and family planning. (5 references)

144. Schnayer, Reuben L. "One-Parent Families: Two Common Assumptions—Re-Examined." Ph.D., diss., University of Windsor (Canada), 1986.

    For a summary see: *Dissertation Abstracts International* 47B(5): 2186.

145. Schorr, Alvin L., and Phyllis Moen. "The Single Parent and Public Policy." *Social Policy* 9(5): 15–21 (April 1979).

    Single-parent families vary considerably and the public is cautioned against stereotyping that has no real basis. Incomes of single fathers are higher than incomes of single mothers, and widowed mothers have higher incomes than divorced mothers. Many problems of single-parent children stem from poverty rather than single parenthood. Recognizing that the public image of single-parent families is related to prevailing public policy, the need to view single-parent families as normal is proposed. Employment, income maintenance, child support and social services are noted as obvious areas of need. (57 references)

146. Scovic, Stephen Patrick, Jr. "An Analytical Study of the Verbal Interaction between the Parent and Child in One-Parent Families." Ed.D. diss., University of Cincinnati, 1974.

    For a summary see: *Dissertation Abstracts International* 35A(5): 2699.

147. Shapiro, Edna K., and Doris B. Wallace. "Siblings and Parents in One-Parent Families." *Journal of Children in Contemporary Society* 19(3–4): 91–114 (1987).

The study reported in this paper describes an investigation of six one-parent families and seven two-parent families. The focus is on sibling and custodial parent in the one-parent home. Interviews with each individual in these families suggest that members of the same family have different perceptions of family experiences and the impact of divorce on their relationships with each other. Single parents and their children seemed to have a closer relationship than children and their married parents. It was also found that the one-parent family with two siblings differed from the four-member two-parents-and-two-siblings family. Suggestions for future research are noted.

148. Shaw, Lois B. "High-School Completion for Young Women: Effects of Low Income and Living with a Single Parent." *Journal of Family Issues* 3(2): 147–163 (June 1982).

This study investigates the effects of living in a single-parent home on the educational chances of young women. The discrepancy between the income of female-headed families and intact families contributes to a higher high school dropout rate for single-parent children. However, in black families, even when incomes were comparable with white families, black daughters were more likely to fail to complete high school if they lived with a single parent. Data from the National Labor Survey indicated that black girls were more likely to drop out of school because they were pregnant while white girls were more likely to drop out because of early marriage. Research suggestions are offered. (Bibliographic notes)

149. Shulman, Samuel, and Moshe Morris Klein. "Resolution of Transference Problems in Structural Therapy of Single-Parent Families by a Male Therapist." *American Journal of Family Therapy* 12(2): 38–44 (Summer 1984).

The male therapist treating the single-parent family may encounter transference problems as the family attempts to induct the therapist into the family system, giving him

the role of husband or father. Structural family therapy
is suggested as a means of overcoming the transference
in order that the single-parent family may function
independently without the need for an outside male
authority figure. Two cases from the authors' clinical
experience in Israel are presented to illustrate and clarify
the therapeutic interventions made to overcome
transference problems. (8 references)

150. Singer, Karla. "A Comparative Study of Self-Concepts:
Children from One-Parent Home Environment, Children
from Two-Parent Home Environment." Ed.D. diss., Florida
Atlantic University, 1978.

For a summary see: *Dissertation Abstracts International*
39A(3): 1409.

151. Skylar, Kathryn Kish. "Some Reforms That Can Help
One-Parent Families." *Education Digest* 48(1): 58–59
(September 1982).

Two thirds of the single-parent families headed by mothers
have children under 18 as compared with one third of the
single-parent families headed by fathers. Suggestions
offered for improving the ability of these families to
maintain a standard of living above the poverty level are:
neighborhood child-care centers, new job opportunities
for women, greater economic and social opportunities for
minority families, welfare policy reforms and improved
child support policies. (No references)

152. Slater, Elisa J., et al. "The Effects of Family Disruption
on Adolescent Males and Females." *Adolescence* 18(72):
931–942 (Winter 1983).

Two hundred and seventeen adolescents from single-
parent and intact families were compared to determine
the effects of divorce and separation on adolescents' self-
concepts and anxiety levels. A variety of questionnaires
were used to provide information on the subjects'
background and perceptions of self and family. Results of

the investigation showed that males from disrupted families had self-concepts and perceptions of their families that were better than males from intact families. This was not found to be true with girls in the study. It is suggested that further research should be done to identify the factors that mediate the adjustment process. (37 references)

153. Smith, Richard M., and Craig W. Smith. "Child Rearing and Single-Parent Fathers." *Family Relations* 30(3): 411–417 (July 1981).

Twenty-seven single-parent fathers rearing a total of 47 dependent children were studied to assess the five variables of goal facilitation transition procedures, normative change, role strain, and ease of role transition during three different phases of their lives. Responses in a semi-structured interview would seem to indicate that the child-rearing problems of single-parent fathers lie in the preparation for fatherhood and the role expectations of that society holds for fathers. Fathers can be successful single parents, and they should receive preparation to rear their children. Resources should be available to provide education and support. (30 references)

154. "Sociologist Looks to Make It Easier for Single-Parent Families." *Black Issues in Higher Education* 5(1): 19 (March 15, 1988).

A Penn State University sociologist is studying a sample of 2,200 black and white single and married mothers and their children to determine how a significant number of black children from single-parent homes overcome unfavorable circumstances to become very successful people. Professor Dennis P. Hogan's research will also assess the contention that black families are often successful because they have strong supportive networks. The findings will have implications for what public policy makers, families and communities can do to make it easier for all single parents to do an effective job of reducing negative consequences on children growing up in single-parent homes. (No references)

155. Stephens, Nancy, and Harold D. Day. "Sex-Role Identity, Parental Identification, and Self-Concept of Adolescent Daughters from Mother-Absent, Father-Absent and Intact Families." *Journal of Psychology* 103: 193–202 (November 1979).

Thirty-nine adolescent girls from intact and one-parent homes were studied for effects of parental absence on self-concepts, sex-role identity and parental identification. The Piers-Harris Children's Self-Concept Scale and the Bem Sex-Role Inventory were administered to participants in the study. It was found that identification with fathers and mothers was greater for children from intact families than identification with the mother was for children from father-absent homes. No negative findings were noted in cases where adolescent daughters were in the custody of fathers. (44 references)

156. Stern, Mark J. "The Welfare of Families." *Educational Leadership* 44(6): 82–87 (March 1987).

This article presents current statistics on the increase of single-parent families in the United States. Increases in the number of children in female-headed families who live in poverty and have school problems are discussed along with implications for school policy. (4 references)

157. Stolberg, Arnold L., and Ann J. Ullman. "Assessing Dimensions of Single Parenting: The Single Parenting Questionnaire." *Journal of Divorce* 8(2): 31–45 (Winter 1984).

This study attempts to develop and validate an instrument for assessing parenting skills. Subjects were 239 divorced parents and their children. A variety of measuring instruments was used in the study. The relationship between the quality of parenting skills and the degree of children's adjustment in the post divorce period was found to be significant. Implications of the study for mental health professionals are suggested. (26 references)

158. Stone, Judith P. "Problems of the Single Parent of the Preschool Child." *Day Care and Early Education* 5(3): 16–17 (Spring 1978).

Single parents may be unwed, divorced, adoptive, widow, widower, foster parent, or older sibling. Money is a critical factor in the lives of the working parent because of the cost of child care. Age of parent, emotional stability, racial and ethnic considerations are significant in their relationship to parent and child support systems. Parents must share what happens at home with the child care staff, and the information should be taken into consideration by the school in its child-care plans. This partnership, which is based on goals that are mutually agreeable, is important for the child's development and adjustment. (No references)

159. Tessman, Lora Heims. *Children of Parting Parents*. New York: Jason Aronson, 1978.

This book is based on the author's clinical experience with children, adolescents and adults who were trying to cope with their reactions to the loss of parents due to separation, divorce and death. Children seemed to be best able to cope with parental death or divorce when other meaningful relationships remained intact. For very young children, this means keeping the same babysitters, nursery school, and contacts with the extended family or neighbors as before. Although a period of stress following parental loss is not unusual for a child, with adequate emotional support to face the situation and work it through, the child may emerge with a greater tolerance for dealing with life stresses in later life. (Bibliography)

160. Thomas, Cheryl Larue. " Perceptions of Intrafamilial Relationships in Single Parent Lower-Class Families and Male Adolescent Anti-Social Behavior." Ph.D. diss., Adelphi University, 1978.

For a summary see: *Dissertation Abstracts International* 39B(4): 1972.

161. Tietjen, Anne-Marie. "Relationships between the Social Networks of Swedish Mothers and Their Children." *International Journal of Behavioral Development* 8(2): 195–216 (June 1985).

In a sample of 72 Swedish mothers and their children, the author found significant relationships between characteristics of the mothers' social networks and those of their children. The greatest dissimilarity was found in the networks between single mothers and their sons. Over all, findings suggest that the nature and extent of the mothers' involvement in their own networks of support and exchange may influence their children's social relations. Swedish single mothers and family policy are discussed. (23 references)

162. Touliatos, John, and Byron W. Lindholm. "Teachers' Perceptions of Behavior Problems in Children from Intact, Single-Parent, and Stepparent Families." *Psychology in the Schools* 17(2): 264–269 (April 1980).

The behavior problems of 3,644 Caucasian children in kindergarten through eighth grade from intact, single-parent, and stepfamilies were the focus of this study. Quay's Behavior Problem Checklist and teacher input was used to provide data on the children. Results indicated that children from broken families evidenced a greater degree of maladjustment than those from intact families. Recommendations for future research are offered. (25 references)

163. Verzaro, Marce, and Charles B. Hennon. "Single-Parent Families: Myth and Reality." *Journal of Home Economics* 72(3): 31–33 (Fall 1980).

This article reports the increasing incidence of divorce in the United States, the updating of divorce laws and implications for the family as an institution. The complexity of assuming double parental roles, changes in lifestyles and the, impact of living in single-parent families on children are discussed. Implications for services by home economists in school and the community are noted. (18 references)

164. Wadsworth, Jane, et al. "The Influence of Family Type on Children's Behavior and Development at Five Years." *Journal of Child Psychology and Psychiatry and Allied Disciplines* 26(2): 245–254 (March 1985).

This study uses data from the third national British cohort to investigating the influence of family type on the behavior and development of five-year-old children. The Child Health and Education Study (CHES) included children of single, widowed, separated, divorced, and married women. Results of several measures showed that children from one-parent families and stepfamilies had "anti-social" scores that were significantly higher than children from two-parent families. Scores on developmental tests were lower for single-parent children than for children from two-parent families. Stepparent children scored between one-parent and two-parent children. (23 references)

165. ———. "Teenage Mothering: Child Development at Five Years." *Journal of Child Psychology and Psychiatry and Allied Disciplines* 25(2): 305–313 (April 1984).

Studies have shown that children of younger mothers suffer more physical, emotional and intellectual handicaps than other children. A subsample of 1031 mothers from the British Child, Health and Education Study included single, widowed, separated, divorced and married women with children. Results suggest that children of teen-age mothers score lower on vocabulary and behavior tests when compared with children of older mothers. Findings also support the assumption that lower maternal age negatively affects children's development through social disadvantage rather than through biological causes. (38 references)

166. Weinraub, Marsha, and Barbara M. Wolf. "Effect of Stress and Social Supports on Mother-Child Interactions in Single and Two-Parent Families." *Child Development* 54(5): 1297–1311 (October 1983).

Social support networks, coping strategies, life changes and mother-child interaction were studied in 28 mother-child pairs from single parent and intact families. Responses to questionnaires indicated single parents have more stressful life changes, fewer social support networks, work longer hours and encounter more social isolation. All of these factors directly affect the child and the amount of time spent with the mother. It was found that single mothers were similar to married mothers in mother-child interactions. Only in regard to household responsibility did single mothers indicate the need for help in coping. Suggestions for helping single parents with social support are offered. (37 references)

167. Weiss, Robert S. "Growing Up a Little Faster: Children in Single-Parent Households." *Children Today* 10(3): 22–25 (May-June 1981).

Changes in children's roles and responsibilities in single-parent families may result in earlier maturity. Some changes for these children may include: 1) reversal of parent-child roles, 2) responsibility for care of younger children and 3) joint decision-making with parents. Possible long-term effects are discussed.

168. ———. "Growing Up a Little Faster: The Experience of Growing Up in a Single-Parent Household." *Journal of Social Issues* 35(4): 97–111 (Fall 1979).

A theory of the structure and workings of single-parent households is proposed on the basis of interviews with over 200 single parents and their adolescent children. In the single-parent home the children share with the parents household tasks and decision-making and thereby become more self-reliant. Whereas the adolescents are pleased with their ability to carry more responsibility, they are

also sorry that this is true. Although the structure of the single-parent family requires that the child
grow up faster, some parental support and nurturance must be available. (8 references)

169. Weltner, John S. "A Structural Approach to the Single-Parent Family." *Family Process* 21(2): 203–210 (June 1982).

Typical problems faced by single female-headed families are discussed. The emotional and physical demands faced by single parents, lack of a partner in a supporting parental role, and the blurring of generational boundaries in assigning family responsibilities are factors which need consideration in setting priorities for therapeutic approaches to single parent problems. It is suggested that the therapist should support the mother's executive management function in the family (with a family cabinet to provide assistance), recognize the extended family and friends as sources of support, and help in establishing generational boundaries prior to taking on more taxing interventions. (3 references)

170. Wilgosh, L., and D. Paitich. "Ratings of Parent Behaviors for Delinquents from Two-Parent and Single-Parent Homes." *International Journal of Social Psychiatry* 28(2): 141–143 (Summer 1982).

The Bronfenbrenner Parent Behavior Questionnaire was administered to 43 male delinquents and their mothers to compare parent behaviors in single-parent and two-parent homes. No significant differences were found for boys and mothers when single-parent and two-parent groups were compared. The assumption of a connection between delinquency and disturbed families was not supported by the findings. (6 references)

171. Wilkinson, Charles B., and William A. O'Connor. "Growing Up Male in a Black Single-Parent Family." *Psychiatric Annals* 7(7): 50–59 (July 1977).

This study focuses on the first two years of a continuing study of 101 males, 16 to 17 years old, who have been living in a mother-headed
household since infancy. Income of nearly all subjects was at or near the poverty level. Data collected through a variety of measures suggest that lifestyles and sons' outcomes are influenced by mothers' employment, location of housing and number of children. Where employment or community support are available for mothers and sons, black single mothers often use child-rearing practices that result in social competence and educational achievement. (29 references)

172. Wilson, Melvin N. "Mothers' and Grandmothers' Perceptions of Parental Behavior in Three-Generational Black Families." *Child Development* 55(4): 1333–1339 (August 1984).

Sixty black families with children between the ages of eight and fourteen participated in a study of perceptions of grandmother/child and mother/child interactions. Bronfenbrenner Parental Behavior Scale (BPBS) was chosen as a measure in this investigation because of its previous use in cross-cultural ethnic and minority group testing. Findings indicated that grandmothers perceived themselves and were perceived by their daughters as being more actively involved in rearing the children when they lived with their single daughters. Further study of the grandmother/grandchild relationship and the quality of the kinship network is suggested. (47 references)

173. *Women As Single Parents: Confronting Institutional Barriers In the Courts, the Workplace, and the Housing Market*, edited by Elizabeth A. Mulroy. Dover, Mass.: Auburn House, 1988.

The myths and realities surrounding single mothers and their families are examined. Sections contributed by scholars and practioners in law, social work, urban planning, housing, economics, and public policy address the issues of alimony, child custody, child support, employment and resources associated with the restructuring of family life. Social reforms recommended for the 1990's include portable benefits to facilitate regional mobility, economic equality, and expanded choices to increase independence. (Bibliography)

174. *Women, Children, and Poverty in America. A Look at the Problems Facing Low-Income Families Headed by Women and at Some Current and Planned Ford Foundation Responses.* A working paper. Ford Foundation, New York, 1985. 53pp. (ERIC Microfiche ED254607)

This paper discusses problems faced by low-income female-headed families and some current and planned responses by the Ford Foundation. Nonpayment of child support, teenage pregnancy and the debate over the federal welfare system are among the issues discussed. Measures supported by Ford Foundation funding aim to improve operation of the welfare system, aid parents and persuade teenagers to postpone childbearing. Future plans of the Ford Foundation in these areas are also discussed. (59 references)

II

CHILDREN IN DIFFERENT TYPES OF ONE-PARENT FAMILIES

FATHERLESS FAMILIES

BIBLIOGRAPHIES AND LITERATURE REVIEW

175. Akins, Faren R., et al. *Parent-Child Separation: Psychosocial Effects on Development (An Abstracted Bibliography)*. New York: IFI Plenum, 1981.

    This bibliography contains 911 titles, 690 of which have abstracts. Major topics represented include maternal or paternal absence due to desertion, military duty, imprisonment, institutionalization and divorce. A subject and author index appears at the end of the book.

176. Coonrod, Debbie. *The Effect of Father-Absence and Inadequate Fathering on Children's Personality*. Bloomington, Ind.: Debcon, 1979. 79pp. (ERIC Microfiche ED187459)

    Research studies were examined to assess the impact of fathers' availability on their children's development. The literature reviewed in this study suggests that a father exerts a strong influence on his son's masculine orientation and also has a strong influence on a girl's heterosexual relationships. The emotional, cognitive, and social development of children would appear to be negatively affected by fathers' absence. Strengthening boys' preparation for fatherhood is recommended. (80 references)

177. Draper, Thomas W. "Sons, Mother, and Externality: Is There a Father Effect?" *Child Study Journal* 12(4): 271–279 (1982).

Data on two samples of women from the National Longitudinal Survey of Labor Market Experience were used to examine mothers' locus of control as it was related to rearing sons alone. The measure of personal locus of control was a 16–point scale made up of four items from the Rotter 1966 Internality-Externality Scale that dealt with perceived control over reinforcement in one's personal life. Two series of Cross Lagged Panel Correlation (CLPC) analyses were conducted on each sample. Over time, single mothers with sons three years of age and under became more externally oriented. This factor was not noted in mothers with spouses or in single mothers with daughters. (10 references)

178. Hanson, Shirley M. "Father/Child Relationships: Beyond *Kramer vs. Kramer*." *Marriage and Family Review* 9(3–4): 135–150 (Winter 1985–86).

The father-child relationship in single- custodial-father families is explored through a review of literature on the subject. Fathers generally have custody of preadolescent and adolescent children, usually boys. Discipline does not appear to be as much an issue in the single-father homes as it is in the single- mother homes. Single fathers and their children are doing well and using fully the resources that the community has to offer. They do have problems and these are noted. Directions for future research are suggested. (140 references)

179. Hirsch, Elisabeth S. *Problems of Early Childhood: An Annotated Bibliography and Guide.* New York: Garland, 1983.

This annotated list of 1,000 books and journal articles covers a wide range of experiences that many children encounter in early childhood and that may have negative effects on their development. Among the topics covered are parental absence due to death, divorce, hospitalization, illness, imprisonment and employment. The impact of parental loss on single-parent families, schools and teachers is also included. Titles of books that can be used with children in the home, classroom, and group intervention programs are listed.

180. Moles, Oliver C. "Trends in Divorce and Effects on Children." Paper presented at the Meeting of the American Academy for the Advancement of Science. January 1982. 21pp. (ERIC Microfiche ED214630)

In this paper an attempt is made to present a comprehensive picture of the effects of separation and divorce on children. Comprehensive reviews of one-parent families are discussed. Because some detrimental effects are associated with father absence, literature focused on family relationships and conditions of family life is reviewed to locate possible explanations for these effects. (30 references)

181. Pedersen, Frank A. "Does Research on Children Reared in Father Absent Homes Yield Information on Father Influence?" *Family Coordinator* 25: 458–464 (October 1976).

Literature on father-absent families is reviewed for effects of paternal influences on child development. Several conclusions that may be drawn from research studies on father absence include the following: 1) differences between groups of children are due to environmental reasons 2) father-absence effects, especially for male children, are more apparent when the absence occurred

in the first five years, and 3) father absence has an
impact on cognitive development and sex role
identification. It is noted that little information on the
psychological factors that produce differences in father-
absent children is present in studies. Directions for future
research are suggested. (25 references)

182. Popplewell, J. Frank, and Anees A. Sheikh. "The Role of
the Father in Child Development: A Review of the
Literature." *International Journal of Social Psychiatry*
25(4): 267–284 (Winter 1979).

Studies on the effect of father absence on sex-role
development, personality and cognitive development in
children are examined. It is concluded that father absence
places boys at a greater disadvantage than girls in regard
to sex-role development. Methodological problems in
research are noted, and suggestions for additional research
are offered. (80 references)

183. Schaengold, Marilyn. "The Relationship between Father-
Absence and Encopresis." *Child Welfare* 56(6): 385–394
(June 1977).

The relationship between father absence and encopresis
in children two to twelve years old is explored in the
literature. Researchers in five studies report that
encopresis has multifactoral etiology, but the father's
absence played a major role. Among variables which
affect a child is the mother's response to the absence of
the father and her treatment of the child. Further study
of this problem is suggested. (21 references)

184. Stevenson, Michael Ray. "The Effects of Single-Parenting
on Sex-Role Development: The State of the Art." Paper
presented at the Biennial Meeting of the Society for
Research in Child Development, Toronto, Canada. April
25–28, 1985. 18pp. (ERIC Microfiche ED257561)

This paper explores the effects of single parenting on
children's sex-role development based on metaanalytic

techniques of literature on this topic. For females, it was found that no clear evidence exists that father absence affects sex-role development. Preschool father-absent boys, in the selection of toys and activities, showed less stereotypical choices than father-present boys. Older father-absent boys showed more stereotypical overt behavior than boys from intact families. Implications of this investigation for future research are discussed. (41 references)

GENERAL WORKS

185. Adams, Paul L., and Jeffrey H. Horovitz. "Psychopathology and Fatherlessness in Boys." *Child Psychiatry and Human Development* 10(3): 135–142 (Spring 1980).

   Two hundred and one Cuban and black boys were studied to examine the relationship between fatherlessness and psychopathlogy. A mini Minnesota Multiphasic Personality Inventory and the Louisville Aggression Survey Schedule-I were used as measures. No association was found between fatherlessness and psychopathology for this group of boys selected from a poverty group. It is suggested that some ideas about black fatherless families need to be rejected. (11 references).

186. Adams, Paul L., et al. *Fatherless Children.* New York: Wiley, 1984. (Wiley Series in Child Mental Health).

   Father absence due to death, divorce, desertion, incarceration, military service, health problems or failure to wed the mother is discussed along with a critical review of studies. The authors suggest that studies showing the negative effects on children's school performance and sex role be examined more closely for flaws in research methodology. The difference between being a father and fathering, policy recommendations, intervention and treatment are also discussed. (Bibliography)

187. Alston, Doris N., and Nannette Williams. "Relationship between Father Absence and Self-Concept of Black Adolescent Boys." *Journal of Negro Education* 51(2): 134–138 (Spring 1982).

An individual's concept of himself is affected by what important persons in the environment think of him. If the father is among those important persons, a child's self image, especially that of boys, is likely to be affected by his absence. A Self-Appraisal Inventory and the Personal Background Data Sheet were used to study the self-concept of 35 randomly selected black adolescent boys from father-present and father-absent homes. A significant relationship was found between father absence and self-concepts of the boys. They placed less value on themselves, had less stable relationships with peers, less interaction with family members and showed a weaker scholastic performance. Recommendations for further study are offered. (16 references)

188. Austin, Roy L. "Race, Father-Absence, and Female Delinquency." *Criminology* 15(4): 487–504 (February 1978).

Data from questionnaires completed by 4,077 youths about to enter junior and senior high schools were examined for the influence of father absence on delinquency. For the four delinquent offenses studied, father absence had detrimental effects only on whites, especially girls. The only other significant effect showed father-absence to be favorable to black girls. It is suggested that reducing the stigma attached to father absence for white girls would be more helpful in reducing delinquency than economic policies to reduce male unemployment. (20 references)

189. Bannon, Jill A., and Mara L. Southern. "Father-Absent Women: Self-Concept and Modes of Relating to Men." *Sex Roles: A Journal of Research* 6(1): 75–84 (February 1980).

The relationship between father absence in childhood

and self-concept and interpersonal relationships with men was studied in 57 female college students. The Tennessee Self-Concept Scale and a self-report questionnaire on modes of relating to men were used as measures. It was found that father absence, or the cause of that absence, was not significantly associated with adult females' interpersonal relationships with men. Father absence was only significantly associated with self-concept in social situations. Future directions for research on the importance of father presence in the childhood of females are suggested. (30 references)

190. Biller, Henry B. "Father Absence and the Personality Development of the Male Child." *Developmental Psychology* 2(2): 181–201 (1970).

The effect of father absence on the personality of the male child is explored through a review of pertinent data in the literature. Developmental stage length of father absence, availability of role models, and individual differences in maternal behavior are among things considered. Possible impact of father absence on behavior, academic functioning, interpersonal relationships and the development of psychopathology as reported in research published between 1943 and 1969, are examined. Further investigation is suggested. (56 references)

191. Boone, Sherle L. "Effects of Fathers' Absence and Birth Order on Aggressive Behavior of Young Male Children." *Psychological Reports* 44(3):Pt.2 1223–1229 (June 1979).

A sample of 50 Hispanic male children, seven to eight years old, was examined to determine the effects of father absence and birth order on aggressive behavior. Several measures of aggression were used in the study and behavior was videotaped. First-born and last-born subjects with fathers absent had higher aggression scores than their counterparts in father-present families. Differences in patterns of interaction, practices and functions are noted as reasons for differences found in father-present and father-absent families. Limitations of the study are noted along with recommendations for further study. (28 references)

192. Brody, Steve. "Daddy's Gone to Colorado: Male Staff Child Care for Father-Absent Boys." *Counseling Psychologist* 7(4): 33–36 (1978).

The Nurtury is a predominately male-staffed child-care center serving mostly single-parent children. Seventy percent of the children are from single-parent homes, and 30 percent are from father-present homes. A pilot study compared the effects of male-staffed in contrast with female staffed schools on the development of gender identity, social sex role and attitude toward men in preschool children. Results indicated that presence of male teachers strengthened gender identity development and aided development of stereotyped social sex roles to some extent although the attitudes of children toward men were not significantly affected. (22 references)

193. Carter, Donald E., and James A. Walsh. "Father Absence and the Black Child: A Multivariate Analysis." *Journal of Negro Education* 49(2): 134–143 (Spring 1980).

The effect of father absence was investigated in 148 black elementary parochial school children from the inner-city. The Comfortable Interpersonal Distance Scale and the Internal-External Locus of Control measure were used as measures. School achievement grades were obtained from teachers. Results suggest that father absence seems to have a greater effect on the interpersonal distancing of the black child than on achievement or locus of control. Further study with additional measures of adjustment, personality, sex-role orientation and moral development is suggested. (25 references)

194. Cashion, Barbara G. "Female-Headed Families: Effects on Children and Clinical Implications." *Journal of Marital and Family Therapy* 8(2): 77–85 (April 1982).

Research published on female-headed families between 1970 and 1980 is reviewed and general findings of effects on children reported. Among findings noted are: same-sex/opposite-sex parents in a family are not necessary for the development of sex-role behavior; children in female-headed households are likely to have good emotional development and good self-esteem unless they are stigmatized. Intellectual development and rates of juvenile delinquency in female-headed families are not different from others of the same socioeconomic status. Suggestions are offered for female heads of families, teachers and other concerned adults. (59 references)

195. Climent, Carlos E., et al. "Parental Loss, Depression and Violence: III. Epidemiological Studies of Female Prisoners." *Acta Psychiatrica Scandinavia* 55(4): 261–268 (April 1977).

In this study of 95 female prisoners, it was found that loss of a father before the age of ten years was more likely to be associated with signs of depression in these women than was loss of a mother. Women with at least one suicide attempt were more depressed on the self-report measure than other women and were more likely to be violent. Those women judged to be most violent had the highest frequency of suicide attempts. Suggestions are offered for future research. (23 references)

196. Collier, Linda, et al. "The Effect of the Father-Absent Home on 'Lower Class' Black Adolescents." *Educational Quest* 17(1): 11–14 (1973).

The impact of father absence on their children's IQ, achievement and self-concept or personality is examined in this investigation. Thirty-one black children from father-present and father absent homes were participants. Results of a variety of measures showed no significant differences between the two groups in IQ, achievement, self-concept and personality. Implications of these findings are discussed. (17 references)

197. Covell, Katherine, and William Turnbull. "The Long-Term Effects of Father Absence in Childhood on Male University Students' Sex-Role Identity and Personal Adjustment." *Journal of Genetic Psychology* 141 (Pt.2): 271–276 (December 1982).

The long-term effects of father absence in childhood were studied in a sample of 173 male college students. Subsections of the California Personality Inventory and Bem's Sex Role Inventory were completed by father-absent and father-present subjects. Males who had experienced father absence prior to age five scored significantly lower on self-esteem, self-confidence and social interaction. No differences were found in performances on sex-role measures. Subjects were no more masculine or feminine than those in two-parent families. Whereas sex role disruptions may be overcome, father absence prior to age five may have lasting effects on the self-esteem and self-confidence of males. (18 references)

198. Decker, Debra Carole. "The Effects of Father Absence During Childhood on Females' Current Marital Satisfaction." Ph.D. diss., California School of Professional Psychology, Los Angeles, 1982.

For a summary see: *Dissertation Abstracts International* 43B(6): 1955.

199. Drake, Charles T., and Daniel McDougall. "Effects of the Absence of a Father and Other Male Models on the Development of Boys' Sex-Roles." *Developmental Psychology* 13(5): 537–538 (September 1977).

The sex role development of 58 father-present and father-absent second-grade white Canadian boys is compared in this study. Measures used in the investigation were the Draw-A-Person and Drawing Completion Tests, the Drake Preference Test and the Vroegh Test. Multivariate test results show that the time of father absence, presence of male siblings and father substitutes do not significantly affect measures of sex role. Boys with fathers present were found to show a more appropriate sex role orientation and sex role preference than father-absent boys. Based on the Vroegh Test, sex role adoption was not significantly affected by the availability of the father. (3 references)

200. Draper, Patricia, and Henry Harpending. "Father Absence and Reproductive Strategy: An Evolutionary Perspective." *Journal of Anthropological Research* 38(3): 255–273 (Fall 1982).

The findings of social scientists on the effects of father absence are reviewed critically and found wanting by the authors. Theory from evolutionary biology is used to explain the factors operational during father absence in early childhood, which influences reproductive strategy in adulthood. (73 references)

201. Duke, Marshall P., and William Lancaster, Jr. "A Note on Locus of Control as a Function of Father Absence." *Journal of Genetic Psychology* 129(2): 335–336 (December 1976).

Fifty-one male children, ages six to twelve, from father-absent and father-present homes were administered the Nowicki-Strickland Locus of Control Scale to measure the effect of father absence. The father-absent boys were significantly more external than the control group. Since externals are more likely to score low on achievement tests than internals, this finding has implications for teachers and counselors. Modification of locus of control orientation toward internality can significantly aid achievement and personal adjustment of father-absent children. (8 references)

202. Earl, Lovelene, and Nancy Lohmann. "Absent Fathers and Black-Male Children." *Social Work* 23(5): 413–415 (September 1978).

This research examines whether latency-age black male children from absent father homes have access to their fathers or other male models. The availability of male role models was explored in a random sample of 53 latency age boys between seven and twelve years old in Knoxville, Tennessee. Findings of interviews with these children indicated that all the boys had access to some black male who could serve as a role model. Interviews with mothers indicated their sons would prefer an uncle as the preferred male adult when seeking advice. However, only 11 percent of the boys agreed with their mother. Most indicated that they would go to a male relative for help. Research to determine the amount and quality of contact with male role models is suggested. (15 references)

203. Earls, Felton. "The Fathers (Not the Mothers): Their Importance and Influence with Infants and Young Children." *Psychiatry* 39(3): 209–226 (August 1976).

The role of fathers on mediating forms of psychopathology in respect to their infants and young children is examined through a review of the literature. Father-child and child-father relationships during pregnancy, infancy and early childhood are surveyed for possible effects of paternal behavior on behavioral deviance in children. Aspects of sex-related inheritance, paternal behavior during pregnancy, paternal attachment, discipline and influences on the adoption of sex-typed behavior by the child are discussed. Further research in these areas is suggested as well as greater coordination between family professionals during the divorce process. (110 references)

204. Eberhardt, Carolyn A., and Thomas Schill. "Differences in Sexual Attitudes and Likeliness of Sexual Behaviors of Black Lower-Socioeconomic Father-Present vs. Father-Absent Female Adolescents." *Adolescence* 19(73): 99–105 (Spring 1984).

This study compares sexual attitudes and likely behaviors of father-absent with father-present black lower-socioeconomic female adolescents. Ninety subjects were administered the Female Premarital Sexual Permissiveness Scale. Results of this investigation indicate that black, father-absent, lower socioeconomic females were not more sexually permissive than black, father-present, lower socioeconomic females. Subjects who experienced father absence before they were five years of age were found to have a significantly higher need for social approval than those whose fathers were absent after they were five years old. The implications of these findings are discussed and the need for further research noted. (15 references)

205. Fields, Ann Brown. *Father Presence/Absence and Its Relationship to Instrumentality in Children.* Paper presented at the Annual Convention of the American Psychological Association, Montreal, Canada. September 1980, 24pp. (ERIC Microfiche ED203238)

Two hundred children, aged five to eleven, participated in a study to determine the effects of father presence/absence on instrumentality in children. Boys scored higher than girls on instrumentality as measured by questionnaires completed by the children and their parents. Children living, with the mother scored significantly lower on instrumentality than children living with the father or with both parents. Girls' scores on instrumentality had a greater relationship to father presence and time spent with father. The author suggests that all children, and girls in particular, would benefit from adult male contact, such as male elementary school teachers and Big Brother programs for girls. (18 references)

206. Fowler, Patrick C., and Herbert C. Richards. "Father Absence, Educational Preparedness and Academic Achievement: A Test of the Confluence Model." *Journal of Educational Psychology* 70(4): 595–601 (August 1978).

The impact of early and continuing father absence on school achievement was the focus of this investigation. One hundred and twenty, lower-class black kindergarten boys and girls were assessed on 12 educational preparedness measures and tested again two years later to measure achievement in math, reading and language arts. Findings indicated no difference in educational preparedness between father- present and father-absent children. Analysis of achievement criteria favored father-present subjects, with the math performance of girls aided more than boys by the presence of fathers. The need for additional research is discussed. (24 references)

207. Frank, Celeste Mary Watts. "Comparison of Family in Single Mother and Two-Parent Family With Sixth Graders." Ph.D. diss., University of Texas at Austin, 1987.

     For a summary see: *Dissertation Abstracts International* 49A(3): 461.

208. Fry, P. S. "The Relationship between Father Absence and Children's Social Problem Solving Competencies." *Journal of Applied Developmental Psychology* 3(2): 105–120 (April/ June 1982).

     Sixty children from father-absent homes were matched with 60 children from father-present homes in Alberta, Canada, to study the effects of father absence on social competence. Half of the children from the father-absent homes were placed in a 15–week problem-solving intervention program. Findings showed that parent-absent children in the treatment program improved their problem-solving skills above those of untreated parent-absent children but did not equal father-present children in social problem-solving skills. Implications for future research are discussed. (31 references)

209. Fry, P. S., and Anat Scher. "The Effects of Father Absence on Children's Achievement Motivation, Ego-Strength, and Locus-of-Control: A Five Year Longitudinal Assessment." *British Journal of Developmental Psychology* 2(2): 167–178 (June 1984).

     Two hundred and forty ten-year old children were studied to assess the effects of father absence on achievement motivation and related interpersonal orientation. A five-year longitudinal follow-up of 170 father-present and father-absent subjects was conducted later. Multivariate analysis of a repeated measures design showed father-absent children, compared with father-present children, declined in areas of achievement motivation. They also showed a corresponding increase in negative ego-strength dimensions of social alienation and self-centeredness. Educational and developmental implications of the longitudinal analysis are discussed. (56 references)

210. Gershansky, Ira S., et al. "Effects of Onset and Type of Fathers' Absence on Children's Levels of Psychological Differentiation." *Perceptual and Motor Skills* 51(3): 1263–1268 (December 1980).

This study examines the psychological differentiation of children growing up in homes where the father is absent. One hundred children between the ages of eight and sixteen years of age from a clinical population were subjects of the investigation. Subjects were tested on the Rod and Frame Test. The effect of father absence on the psychosexual development of the child was found to be significantly related to the age of the child at the time of father loss. Subjects who identified with the mother or other females were found to be more field dependent than those who identified with the father or other males. (9 references)

211. ———. "Maternal Differentiation, Onset and Type of Father's Absence and Psychological Differentiation in Children." *Perceptual and Motor Skills* 46(3): 1147–1152 (June 1978).

The Rod and Frame Test was administered to 209 children and their mothers to measure levels of psychological differentiation and the effects of onset and nature of father absence on this relationship. Subjects were eight and sixteen years of age and included 72 percent black, 12 percent Puerto Rican and 16 percent white children.

Mothers and children with fathers present had higher correlations between their scores than did mothers and children with fathers absent. Mother-child correlations were not significantly different between the group who had a father absent due to death and those who had father absent due to other causes, except, when the age of the child at onset of the father's absence was a consideration. (10 references)

212. Goldstein, Harris S. "Fathers' Absence and Cognitive Development of Children Over a Three to Five Year Period." *Psychological Reports* 52(3): 971–976 (June 1983).

A national sample of 1,774 children was studied at ages six to eleven and again at twelve to seventeen years to discover the effect of father absence on cognitive development. Measures used in the study were the Wechsler Intelligence Scale for Children (WISC) and the Wide Range Achievement Test (WRAT). Although youths whose fathers were absent, in general, did less well than youths whose fathers were present, the difference was not consistently significant. The decrease in academic performance of black youth from father present/absent homes occurred without a significant decrease in their IQ. (8 references)

213. Goldstein, Harris S., and Rosalind Peck. "Maternal Differentiation, Father Absence and Cognitive Differentiation in Children." *Archives of General Psychiatry* 29(3): 370–373 (September 1973).

This study examines the impact of father absence and mother's cognitive style on the cognitive differentiation of their children. The extent of field dependence in 181 black, white and Puerto Rican children, eight to fifteen years of age, and their mothers was assessed by the Rod-and-Frame Test. A high positive correlation was found between the mother's and child's level of field dependence except in father-absent subgroups. Further exploration into the effects of family structure on cognitive differentiation is suggested. (13 references)

214. Graham, John W., and Andrea H. Beller. "A Note on the Number of Children and Living Arrangements of Women with Children Under 21 from an Absent Father." *Journal of Economic and Social Measurement* 13(2): 209–214 (July 1985).

Two problems with the 1979 and 1982 supplements to the Current Population Survey of mothers with children whose fathers were absent are discussed. One is the overestimate of the number of women with children under 21 from an absent father and the consequent underestimate of the proportion of this population awarded, due, and receiving support payments. The other is the large underestimate of the proportion of divorced, separated, and never married-mothers living as subfamilies. Corrected estimates are presented. (7 references)

215. Grossberg, Sidney H., and Louise Crandall. "Father Loss and Father Absence in Preschool Children." *Clinical Social Work Journal* 6(2): 123–134 (Summer 1978).

The reaction of children to the separation, divorce or death of their father is discussed. Critical factors in diagnosis and treatment were: developmental stage of the child at the time of loss, reason for father loss, state of the relationship with the father at the time of loss, mother's reaction to the loss, and the environment provided for the child subsequent to the loss. Three potential counter transference problems in treating fatherless children were pinpointed: identification with the child, with the absent parent or with the remaining parent. A close stable relationship with an adult can be therapeutic. (41 references)

216. Hainline, Louise, and Ellen Feig. "The Correlates of Childhood Father Absence in College-Aged Women." *Child Development* 49(1): 37–42 (March 1978).

This study explored the significance of early father absence in college-age women. Subjects came from intact families and families where father loss resulted from death, divorce or separation. Videotaped interviews, standardized and nonstandardized measures were used to assess the impact of father loss. Results suggest some attitudinal differences about the acceptability of sexual intercourse in love relationships for the father-absent group but no difference in the amount of reported heterosexual behaviors. Differences between the findings in this study as compared with a study by E. M. Heatherington are discussed. (20 references)

217. Hartnagel, Timothy F. "Father Absence and Self Conception among Lower Class White and Negro Boys." *Social Problems* 18(2): 152–163 (Fall 1970).

The effects of father absence and race on the self-concepts of lower-class adolescent high school males were investigated in this study. Responses to questionnaires indicated that black father-absent boys have smaller differences between actual and normative self-potency than white father-absent boys, but Negro and white father-present boys do not differ significantly from one another. Several interpretative approaches to these findings are discussed. (30 references)

218. Herz, Fredda Mae. "The Effects of Maternal Powerlessness and Isolation on the Adjustment of Children in Single Parent Families." Ph.D. diss., Rutgers University, 1978.

For a summary see: *Dissertation Abstracts International* 39B(11): 5647.

219. Herzog, Elizabeth and Cecelia E. Sudia. "Children in Fatherless Families." In *Review of Child Development Research* vol 3, Child Development and Social Policy, 141–231. Chicago: University of Chicago Press, 1973.

This chapter examines the relationship between father absence, juvenile delinquency, school performance and masculine identity. A review of research did not provide findings that were uniformly consistent: The authors suggest caution in the use of a study of children at one point in time as a predictor of long-term development. Negative effects noted may be the result of developmental lag and may not be the forerunners of the problems predicted on the basis of studies in early childhood. Evidence indicates that fatherless children are given a minority status and suffer from unfavorable stereotypes. (212 references)

* Hetherington, E. Mavis. "Effects of Father Absence on Personality Development in Adolescent Daughters." *Developmental Psychology* 7(3): 313–326 (November 1972).

 Reported in Death Item No. 908.

220. Hetherington, E. Mavis, and J. Deur. "Effects of Father Absence on Child Development." *Young Children* 26: 233–248 (March 1971).

 This article focuses on the findings from the best research on the effect of father-absence on the development of children. Studies suggest that father-absence has a negative effect on the sex-role development of boys, especially younger boys, and is most marked when the loss occurs before the age of five. Other effects of father loss reported include delinquency, more impulsive, less self-control, a more externalized standard of moral judgement and more aggressive classroom behavior. Math and language development also seem to be adversely affected by father loss at a young age. Factors modifying the effects of father absence are an emotionally stable mother who reinforces appropriate sex-typed behavior and the presence of male siblings. Suggestions are offered for further research. (39 references)

221. Hirsch, Seth Lewis. "Home Climate in the Black Single-Parent, Mother-Led Family: A Social-Ecological, Interactional Approach." Ph.D. diss., United States International University, 1979.

 For a summary see: *Dissertation Abstracts International* 40B(9): 4485.

222. Hoffman, Martin L. "Father Absence and Conscience Development." *Developmental Psychology* 4: 400–406 (May 1971).

     Moral attributes and overt aggression in a group of father-absent and father-present seventh- grade white children were compared. A variety of morality indexes were used in the study. Results showed that father-absent boys had low scores on all the moral indexes and were rated as more aggressive than father-present boys by their teachers. No consistent pattern was found for girls. Boys without fathers indicated that their mothers expressed less affection than boys with fathers, while girls without fathers indicated that their mother expressed affection more often. Limitations of the study are noted, and areas needing further study are suggested. (23 references)

223. Horne, Arthur M. "Aggressive Behavior in Normal and Deviant Members of Intact Versus Mother-Only Families." *Journal of Abnormal Child Psychology* 9(2): 283–290 (June 1981).

     A clinical sample of 24 female-headed and intact families were compared with 25 families from a non-clinical sample of female-headed and intact families to study the effect of father presence and absence on the aggressive behavior of family members. The Family Interaction Coding System (FICS) was used in this investigation. Findings showed female-headed non-clinical families had the lowest rate of aggressive behavior, followed by intact non-clinical families. Of families from the clinical sample, female-headed families had the highest aggression rate. It is suggested that support systems that include training in parenting would be helpful for single parents. Areas for further research are noted. (7 references)

224. Hunt, Janet G., and Larry L. Hunt. "Race, Daughters and Father Loss: Does Absence Make the Girl Stronger?" *Social Problems* 25(1): 90–102 (October 1977).

This study probes the effects of father loss on sex-role socialization and the relationship of these effects to the race of the subjects. A sample of 462 black and white school students were selected from the original sample used in a study by Rosenberg and Simmons (1972). The pattern of effects of father loss was found to differ by race of subjects. Father-absent white girls had a more negative sex-role identification, a lower sense of control over destiny, higher school grades, and higher self-esteem. In black girls with absent fathers the effects were less dramatic but more uniformly negative. (29 references)

225. Hunt, Larry L., and Janet G. Hunt. "Race and Father-Son Connection: the Conditional Relevance of Father Absence for the Orientations and Identities of Adolescent Boys." *Social Problems* 23(1): 35–52 (October 1975).

A sample of 445 white and black adolescents from father-present/father-absent families were compared for differences in orientation toward success goals and personal identity. Father-absent white boys showed greater withdrawal from conventional paths to success and adult respectability, while no significant effect was found among blacks. Similarly, white boys with absent fathers had less positive self-identification on self-esteem and sex role scales, while black boys showed more positive identities. It is suggested that the nuclear family is probably not perceived to be as necessary to the pursuit of success goals by black boys as it is by whites who have experienced more identity with the male as breadwinner. Areas for further comparative study are noted. (35 references)

226. Huttunen, Matti O., and Pekka Niskanen. "Parental Loss of Father and Psychiatric Disorders." *Archives of General Psychiatry* 35(4): 429–431 (April 1978).

The relationship between maternal stress during pregnancy and subsequent psychiatric and behavior disorders in children is examined in a study conducted in

Finland. One hundred and sixty-seven children whose fathers died before they were born were compared with 168 children whose fathers died during their first year of life. Findings showed that the number of schizophrenics being treated and the number of persons committing crimes were significantly greater for those who suffered prenatal loss than for those who lost their father after they were born. Both groups had a relatively high incidence of alcoholism and personality disorders. (20 references)

227. "Is Life with Father Best for Teenage Boys?" *USA Today* 115(2495):4 (August 1986).

Findings on the effects of father absence on teenage boys by Mary Dolan, Professor of Social Service at the Catholic University of America, are reported in this article. Professor Dolan stresses the need of teenage boys for a male role model to eliminate confusion about sexual identity. Although boys can live successfully with their mothers until adolescence, Professor Dolan feels that both parents need to be aware of behavior and attitudes that indicate a desire to move, but they should also resist manipulation by the child. She advises that a father who has custody of a teenage son must make adjustments in his life to accommodate the needs of the child. (No references)

228. Jones, Hugh Edward. "Father Absence During Childhood, Maternal Attitudes Toward Men, and the Sex-Role Development of Male College Students." Ph.D. diss., Michigan State University, 1975.

For a summary see: *Dissertation Abstracts International* 36B(6): 3047.

229. Kagel, Steven A., et al. "Father-Absent Families of Disturbed and Non-Disturbed Adolescents." *American Journal of Orthopsychiatry* 48(2): 342–352 (April 1978).

Forty-eight white male adolescents and their parents

were subjects of this study of father-present/father-absent families of disturbed and nondisturbed adolescents. A variety of questionnaire measures were administered to sons, mothers, and fathers when present. In father-present and father-absent homes with a nondisturbed adolescent, family members had warm, supportive family relationships that generate positive intra-familial experiences and increase independence of individual members. Male adolescents who were disturbed, in both father-present and father-absent families, had a family environment that was less warm and supportive and with less orientation toward personal growth. Findings did not show that family conditions characteristic of father-absent homes were a factor in adolescent disturbance. (22 references)

230. Kamerman, Sheila B. "Women, Children, and Poverty: Public Policies and Female-Headed Families in Industrialized Countries." *Signs* 10(2): 249–71 (Winter 1984).

Industrialized countries are concerned about the incidence of poverty in female-headed families. Almost half of all poor families in the United States in 1982 were headed by single females. Results of a cross-national study of public income transfer policies in eight advanced industrialized countries are compared. A changing view of women's roles, growth in mother-headed families and concern about the proportion of these families receiving public assistance have led several countries to consider alternative types of income transfer. A new U.S. policy agenda for female-headed families is suggested. (Bibliographic footnotes)

231. Keller, Peter A., and Edward J. Murray. "Imitative Aggression with Adult Male and Female Models in Father Absent and Father Present Negro Boys." *Journal of Genetic Psychology* 122: 217–221 (June 1973).

The imitative behavior of 57 six-year-old Negro boys from father-absent and father-present families was compared.

Two 16mm films of modeled aggression; sex-role preference Picture Choice, play observations, and a five point Aggressive Behavior rating scale were used in the study. Results indicated that father absence or presence did not affect imitative aggression. However, the adult female model used in one of the films had an inhibiting effect on imitative aggression. Aggressive behavior in young Negro boys was viewed as being more directly related to the role of the mother than the presence or absence of fathers. (7 references)

232. Kestenbaum, C. J., and M. H. Stone. "The Effects of Fatherless Homes on Daughters: Clinical Impressions Regarding Paternal Deprivation." *Journal of the American Academy of Psychoanalysis* 4(2): 171–190 (1976).

This paper explores the cases of 13 girls who experienced paternal loss between infancy and adolescence. Case illustrations include psychotic, borderline character disorder, neurotic and normal responses by girls from fatherless homes. Factors which may affect the outcomes for girls include: developmental stage at the time of loss, quality of the relationship with the remaining parent, the socioeconomic environment, and the presence of siblings. (25 references)

233. Ketchum, Gregory Alan. "The Relationship Between Childhood Separation, Availability of Parents and Adult Self-Acceptance and Anxiety Proneness." Ph.D. diss., California School of Professional Psychology, Berkeley, 1980.

For a summary see: *Dissertation Abstracts International* 41B(12): 4638.

234. Kogdsehatz, Joan L., et al. "Family Styles of Fatherless Households." *Journal of the American Academy of Child Psychiatry* 11(2): 365–383 (1972).

One hundred and five children from father-absent homes were compared with fifty-three children from intact families to assess the effects of father absence. Demographic, psychopathological and lifestyle data were extracted from medical records at the Children's Mental Health Unit at the University of Florida. Fatherless families had less income and where the father had been absent for more than two years, the children were most likely to be afflicted by retardation and psychosis, and a greater proportion were out of school and in special education classes. The final personality of the child is the result of many ingredients in addition to the effects of paternal absence. In most cases father absence was no more significant than economic class membership in influencing the nature and severity of a fatherless child's problems. (7 references)

235. Kopf, Kathryn E. "Family Variables and School Adjustment of Eighth-Grade Father-Absent Boys." *Family Coordinator* 19(2): 145–150 (April 1970).

Fifty-two mother-son pairs were studied for possible association of school adjustment with father-absence. A school adjustment measure was developed for the eighth-grade boys, and an interview schedule was constructed for use with mothers. Results showed that the degree of father absence, birth order and sex of siblings, cause of absence and extended family support were not significantly related to adjustment. Participation in household tasks, positive attitudes toward the father and son and some joint mother-son social activities were found to be related to good adjustment in school. The attitudes and behavior of the mothers of father-absent boys can therefore enhance or impede their sons' school adjustment. (10 references)

236. Lancaster, William, W., and Bert O. Richmond. "Perceived Locus of Control as a Function of Father Absence, Age, and Geographic Location." *Journal of Genetic Psychology* 143(1): 51–56 (September 1983).

Three hundred and twelve children from metropolitan and Appalachian areas, four to six and nine to twelve years old, were studied for the effect of father absence on locus of control. Father-present and father-absent families were represented. The Nowicki-Strickland Locus of Control Scale for Preschool and Primary Grade Children was used for the four- to six-year-old group and the Nowicki-Strickland Locus of Control Scale for Children was used with the nine- to twelve-year-old group. Results showed that children from father-absent families tend toward more externality in locus of control and that younger children tended to be less external than older children. Implications for professionals are noted. (20 references)

237. LeCorgne, Lyle L., and Luis M. Laosa. "Father Absence in Low-Income Mexican-American Families: Children's Social Adjustment and Conceptual Differentiation of Sex-Role Attributes." *Developmental Psychology* 12(5): 470–471 (September 1976).

The effect of father absence on 113 Mexican-American fourth-grade students is the focus of this investigation. Several measures were used, including a rating of subjects' personal adjustment by classroom teachers. Father-present children had significantly higher Goodenough-Harris Drawing Test scores, while father-absent children had more Bender Gestalt Test emotional indicators. Father-absent boys also showed more signs of maladjustment in the classroom than father-absent girls. The drawing of the female figure by father-absent children had fewer feminine attributes. It is suggested that the effects of father absence on girls may not be evident until adolescence. (9 references)

238. Lessing, Elise E., et al. "WISC Subtest and IQ Score Correlates of Father Absence." *Journal of Genetic Psychology* 117(2): 181–195 (December 1970).

A clinical sample of 433 children who had completed the Wechsler Intelligence Scale for Children (WISC) were studied for effects of father absence. Father absence for at least two years was found to be significantly related to WISC subtest scores. Working-class children without fathers did score lower on Verbal and Full Scale IQ than father-present children. Father-absent boys had lower arithmetic scores. Children's performances on each WISC subtest are discussed and compared with findings of other studies. (25 references)

239. Levy-Shiff, Rachel. "The Effects of Father Absence on Young Children in Mother-Headed Families." *Child Development* 53(5): 1400–1405 (October 1982).

One hundred and seventy-nine Israeli children below three years of age, 40 from father-absent homes, were studied for effects of father absence in early childhood. Measures were taken of home behavior by mothers, classroom behavior by teachers, and free play behavior by observers. A modified Parental Attitude Research Instrument was also used for assessment of mothers' child-rearing attitudes. Father absence was found to have a negative effect mainly on boys, and to a lesser extent on girls. Mothers in father-absent homes tended to be less controlling than mothers from intact families. Further research on child rearing behavior of mothers in father-absent families and its effect on child behavior is suggested. (14 references)

240. Longabaugh, Richard. "Mother Behavior as a Variable Moderating the Effects of Father Absence." *Ethos* 1(4): 456–465 (Winter 1973).

This study investigates mother-child interaction as a function of father presence or absence in 51 black lower class mother-child dyads. Based on observations and ratings of masculine versus feminine semantic style, father absence was not related to the semantic style of children of either sex. However, father absence was found to be related to the mode of interaction between mother and son. (10 references)

241. Manzitti, Edward Thomas. "Aspects of the Father-Child
      Relationship and Father Availability During Childhood
      and Sex-Role Development Among College Students from
      Intact Families." Ph.D. diss., Michigan State University,
      1979.

      For a summary see: *Dissertation Abstracts International*
      40B(7): 3439.

242. Marsella, Anthony J., et al. "The Effects of Father Presence
      and Absence upon Maternal Attitudes." *Journal of Genetic
      Psychology* 125(2): 257–263 (December 1974).

      The effect of father absence on the personality
      development of the child was examined through a study
      of maternal attitudes during father presence and absence.
      The Parental Attitude Research Instrument (PARI) was
      administered to 34 wives of nuclear submarine personnel
      under conditions of father presence and absence. Results
      of the study indicate that father presence and absence
      affect maternal attitudes. There is more maternal
      domination and marital discord during father presence.
      Increased maternal control during father presence may
      be the result of modeling the husband's behavior and
      changes in children's behavior. Implications for mediation
      of father presence and absence effects on child adjustment
      are reported. (21 references)

243. Martindale, Colin. "Father's Absence, Psychopathology,
      and Poetic Eminence." *Psychological Reports* 31(3):
      843–847 (December 1972).

      The life histories of 42 eminent French and English poets
      were examined for the possibility of cross-sexual
      identification and degree of psychopathology. A
      temporarily stratified sample of poets was selected from
      the *Oxford Anthology of Verse*. Biographical sources were
      searched for mention of childhood behavior or personality
      and ratings assigned for psychopa- thology and cross-
      sexual identification. Fifty percent of the English and 59
      percent of the French poets showed some evidence of

cross- sexual identification in the ratings. Thirty percent received ratings of father absence, and 15 percent were rated as probably psychotic. Forty-four percent who were rated as showing signs of psychopathology had absent fathers at or before the age of eight. (22 references)

244. McCarthy, E. Doyle, et al. "The Behavioral Effects of Father Absence on Children and Their Mothers." *Social Behavior and Personality* 10(1): 11–23 (Midwinter 1982).

The effect of father absence was investigated in a sample of 1,000 welfare families and a subsample of lower-middle income fathers, surrogate fathers and absent fathers. Variables included a measure based on home interviews with mothers. Findings suggest that children residing with natural fathers or children with no father present have fewer behavorial problems than children residing with surrogate fathers. This study does not support the views that father absence is associated with negative characteristics and behavior. Research implications are discussed. (34 references)

245. McLanahan, Sara S. "Family Structure and Stress: A Longitudinal Comparison of Two-Parent and Female-Headed Families." *Journal of Marriage and the Family* 45(2): 347–357 (May 1983).

Two-parent and female-headed families are examined for the effect of chronic life strains, major life events and absence of social and psychological supports. The source of data for the study was the Michigan Panel Study of Income Dynamics. Findings show that female heads are more likely to experience stress from low levels of income and low levels of social support after major life events. Over 20 percent of all families with children live in female-headed households, and these families are part of a growing poverty population. These female heads with children experience more stress than married male heads. (18 references)

246. Meijer, Alexander, and Sabine Himmelfarb. "Fatherless
      Adolescents' Feeling about Their Mothers—A Pilot Study."
      Adolescence 19 (73): 207–212 (Spring 1984).

      This study of 564 Jerusalem high-school students
      examines adolescents' perceptions of their mothers in
      father-absent homes. The Parent-Child Questionnaire
      (PCQ) was used as a measure of children's feelings about
      their parents. Results of the investigation, based on
      responses of the eighteen father-absent children in the
      sample, showed that fatherless girls perceived their
      mothers as less benevolent than girls from intact families.
      No differences were found for boys. Further investigations
      of the feelings of father-absent adolescents about their
      mothers are suggested. (15 references)

*   Moffitt, Terrie E. "Vocabulary and Arithmetic Perform-
      ance of Father-Absent Boys." *Child-Study Journal* 10(4):
      233– 241 (1981).

      Reported in School Item No. 1075.

247. Montare, Alberto, and Sherle L. Boone. "Aggression and
      Paternal Absence: Racial-Ethnic Differences among Inner-
      City Boys." *Journal of Genetic Psychology* 137(2): 223–232
      (December 1980).

      One hundred and thirty-two preadolescent inner-city boys
      were examined for effect of father absence on aggressive
      behavior. Three dimensional games, questionnaires, and
      videotapes were used to measure aggressive responses of
      Puerto Rican, black and white youths from father-present
      and father-absent families. Findings showed father
      absence had no effect on Puerto Rican boys; white boys
      from father-absent homes showed more aggression than
      white-boys from father-present homes. Black boys from
      father-absent homes showed less aggression than black
      boys from father-present homes. No overall main effect of
      father absence upon aggression was observed when racial
      differences were not considered. Suggestions for further
      study are offered. (22 references)

248. Oberfield, Richard, and Claire Ciliotta. "School-Age Boys/ Single Mothers Group." *Journal of American Academic Child Psychiatry* 22(4): 375–381 (July 1983).

The group therapy model described here was developed to treat school-age boys with moderately severe behavior problems and their mothers. Themes surfacing in the mother/son therapeutic sessions related to communication, separation/individuation, discipline, alienation and the mother's depression and rage. Four of five boys completed the group sessions with their mothers and reported positive outcomes at a six-month follow-up. Group therapy is suggested as a cost-effective means of helping single-parent children who are having problems. (22 references)

249. Parish, Thomas S. "The Relationship between Factors Associated with Father Loss and Individuals' Level of Moral Judgment." *Adolescence* 15(59): 535–541 (Fall 1980).

Twenty-four undergraduate students who had lost their fathers through death or divorce were asked to complete the Rest Defining Issues Test (DIT) to assess moral judgment. Results suggest that the longer one is raised without a father or father figure, the more likely he or she will experience depressed levels of moral judgment if father loss was due to divorce rather than death and especially for females. Replication of the study with a larger more diverse sample from the general population is suggested. (20 references)

250. ——. "Replications and Refinements: Relationship between Years of Father Absence and Locus of Control." *Journal of Genetic Psychology* 138: 301–302 (June 1981).

Studies related to the relationship between father absence and locus of control are summarized briefly. Forty undergraduate students who had experienced father loss through death or divorce were administered the Rotter Internality/Externality Scale. No significant relationship was found between the number of years of father loss and the subject's level of externality across sexes. Significant relationship was found in the inverse relationship between the number of years of father loss and the level of subjects' externality when father loss resulted from death. (5 references)

251. Parish, Thomas S., and Terry F. Copeland. "The Impact of Father Absence on Moral Development in Females." *Sex Roles: A Journal of Research* 7(6): 635–636 (June 1981).

Fifty female undergraduate students participated in a study to determine the effect of father absence on moral development. Each woman was asked to describe the conditions of growing up with or without a father. In addition they were administered the Rest Defining Issues Test. For women from broken homes, the age at loss of the father was strongly correlated with the level of the subject's moral development. However, there was no significant difference between groups of women that could be attributed to the fact that they were from homes broken by death or divorce or from father-present homes. Findings seem to indicate that the younger the child at the time of father absence, the less likely the female child will advance in level of moral development. (4 references)

252. ———. "Locus of Control and Father Loss." *Journal of Genetic Psychology* 136: 147–148, (March 1980).

Two hundred and twenty-seven undergraduate students from father-absent and intact families completed Rotter's Internality-Externality Scale to determine whether male and female college students reared in father-absent or intact homes differed in locus of control. No significant difference was found between groups from intact or father-absent homes. No significant difference was found between sex groups either. However, a Least Significant analysis showed that father loss through death resulted in males being more externally oriented. (3 references)

253. Parish, Thomas S., and Gerald D. Nunn. "Locus of Control

as a Function of Family Type and Age at Onset of Father Absence." *Journal of Psychology* 113: 187–190 (March 1983).

Six hundred and forty-four undergraduate students were examined to determine whether differences in locus of control are influenced by family type and age at onset of father loss. Students completed the Rotter Internality-Externality Scale and answered questions about family type, cause of father loss and age when father absence occurred. Findings indicated that children who experienced father loss from divorce between zero to six and seven to thirteen years were more externally oriented than those from intact families, with higher externality scores for the younger group of subjects. For those students who suffered father loss through death, externality scores were higher for the seven- to thirteen-year-old group. (10 references)

254. Parish, Thomas S., and James C. Taylor. "The Impact of Divorce and Subsequent Father-Absence on Children's and Adolescents' Self-Concepts." *Journal of Youth and Adolescence* 8(4): 427–432 (December 1979).

The self-concepts of 406 grade school and junior high school students were assessed by the Personal Attribute Inventory for Children (Parish and Taylor, 1978). It was found that children and adolescents who had experienced father loss through divorce and whose mothers had not remarried had lower self-concepts than those from intact families. Children of mothers who had remarried had lower self-concepts than intact families, but the difference was not statistically significant. The findings are discussed in relation to current trends toward an increasing divorce rate and the increasing number of stepfathers in American families. (4 references)

255. Parish, Thomas, S., et al. "Father Loss and Individual's Subsequent Values Prioritization." *Education* 100(4): 377–381 (Summer 1980).

Human value priorities of 227 undergraduate students

were examined in relation to the effects of father loss. The Rokeach (1967) Value Survey was the measure used in the study. Findings indicate that males who had lost fathers through death placed a lower priority on the value "Mature Love." Females placed greater priority on the values of "Happiness" and "Family Security." Suggestions are made for further research. (10 references)

256. *Paternal Absence and Fathers' Roles.* Hearing before the Select Committee on Children, Youth, and Families. House of Representatives, Ninety-Eighth Congress, First Session. November 10, 1983. 177pp. (ERIC Microfiche ED254334)

The effects of paternal absence and the role of fathers were the focus of statements presented before the Select Committee on Children, Youth, and Families of the House of Representatives. Among the topics discussed were: father absence in military families and the army's efforts to address the subsequent stresses experienced by these families, effects of father absence on children, economic security as it relates to Black fathers and fathering, the role of the private sector and voluntary agencies in mediating the impact of father absence, and the problems of families of men in prison. (No references)

257. Peck, Bruce B., and Dianne Schroeder. "Psychotherapy with the Father-Absent Military Family." *Journal of Marriage and Family Counseling* 2(1): 23–30 (January 1976).

World conditions have made military assignments more dangerous in some areas, and more servicemen must accept these tours of duty without their families. Dynamics of the father-absent military family are discussed. Father absence may seem "as if" it is divorce or pretend separation. This may cause feelings of terror or uncertainty about family continuity when the usual family boundaries are ruptured. A psychotherapy strategy is suggested that has demonstrated value in aiding in the growth of the father-absent military family. (8 references)

258. Pedersen, Frank A., et al. "Infant Development in Father-Absent Families." *Journal of Genetic Psychology* 135(1): 51–61 (September 1979).

The effects of father absence on a sample of 55 black lower-middle-class infants five to six months old are reported. The amount of father interaction with the infant, the Bayley Tests of Infant Development and home observations of the infant with the primary caregivers were used to assess the infants' development. No significant relationships on any measures were found for female infants. However, findings did show that fathers play a significant role in the development of male infants as early as the first six months of their lives. The frequency of father interaction was also found to be significantly related to the level of infant functioning. (9 references)

259. Phelps, Randy Eugene. "Mother-Son Interaction in Single-Parent Families." Ph.D. diss., University of Utah, 1981.

For a summary see: *Dissertation Abstracts International* 42B(8): 3436.

260. Pipher, Mary Bray. "The Effects of Father Absence on the Sexual Development and Adjustment of Adolescent Daughters and their Mothers." Ph.D. diss., University of Nebraska at Lincoln, 1977.

For a summary see: *Dissertation Abstracts International* 38B(2): 913.

261. Polansky, Norman A., et al. "The Absent Father in Child Neglect." *Social Service Review* 53(2): 163–174 (June 1979).

The impact of father absence as a possible factor in child neglect was explored in a group of father-absent and intact families. Father-present families were found to have markedly more income. A decrement in the physical care of fatherless families was evident. However no effect of fatherlessness was found for psychological care or on level of intelligence. Family practice implications are discussed. (19 references)

262. Reyes, T. F. "Father Absence and the Social Behavior of Pre-School Children." Ph.D. diss., Michigan State University, 1977.

   For a summary see: *Dissertation Abstracts International* 39(1–A): 185–186.

263. Rodgers, Joann Ellison, and Michael F. Cataldo. *Raising Sons: Practical Strategies for Single Mothers.* New York: New American Library, 1984.

   Boys are being reared under different guidelines than those under which their fathers were reared. Because so many boys now live in households without fathers, they will influence future generations. However, even well-intentioned relatives, teachers and family friends often have negative expectations for the outcomes of boys reared by single mothers. Although no one theory of homosexuality has stood the test of time or experience, confusion still reigns over the role mothers play in determining the sexuality or homosexuality of sons. Boys reared by single women generally live in a household with greatly reduced income, grow up faster as a result of increased responsibility and must often make room in their emotional lives for their parents' lovers or stepparents. Interviews with single mothers of sons suggests that mothers can be good, loving, effective parents and model persons for their sons. (Bibliography)

264. Rosenthal, David, et al. "Home Environment of Three- to Six-Year-Old Children from Father-Absent and Two-Parent Families." *Journal of Divorce* 9(2): 41–48 (Winter 1985–1986).

   The differences in the home environments of children in single-parent and intact homes are compared in this study. Results of the Home Observation for Measurement of the Environment Scale administered to 60 families showed similarities on all subscales between the groups studied. The quality of the mother-child relationship in homes with different family structure was found to be similar one year following divorce. Implications for researchers are noted. (15 references)

265. Rowland, Virginia T., and Sharon Y. Nickols. "How Is the Time Spent?" *Journal of Extension* 23:13–16 (Spring 1985).

Fifty-nine mothers, nearly half of whom were divorced, were interviewed regarding their perceptions of the adequacy of resources, including time, for personal and family roles. Findings show that divorced mothers spent over twice as much time working as married mothers but spent only about half as much time doing housework and two-thirds as much time on leisure activities. However, married and divorced mothers spent about the same amount of time in direct child care. Divorced mothers felt they had insufficient time to help their children participate in organized youth activities. It is suggested that extension personnel should find ways to help single-parent families so that their children can participate in extension programs. (4 references)

266. Rubin, Roger Harvey. "Adult Male Absence and Self-Attitudes of Black Children." *Child Study Journal* 4(1): 33–46 (1974).

A sample of 280 fifth- and sixth-grade public school children participated in a study to measure the effects of adult male absence on the self-attitudes of black children. Results of self-attitude measures revealed no significant differences between the self-attitudes of boys from homes lacking adult males and those from homes with adult males. There was also no difference between boys without adult males at home and girls from homes with and without male adults. (31 references)

267. ———. *Family Structure and the Self-Attitudes of Negro Children.* San Francisco: R. and E. Research Associates, 1976. 75pp. (Also in ERIC Microfiche ED137428)

A questionnaire designed to measure self-attitudes was administered to four groups of fifth- and sixth-grade students: boys living with an adult male in the home, boys living in a home without an adult male, girls having adult males living at home and girls living in homes without an adult male. No significant differences in self-attitudes of boys without adult males in the home and boys and girls from homes with adult males. Girls had slightly more positive self-attitudes than boys, and children in bright classes also had slightly more positive self-attitudes. The author makes suggestions for further research. (Bibliography)

268. Samuels, Morris Robert. "A Study of Maternal Role Performance in One-Parent Negro Families." Ed.D. diss., Columbia University, 1970.

For a summary see: *Dissertation Abstracts International* 31A(4): 1917.

269. Santrock, John W. "Effects of Father Absence on Sex-Typed Behaviors in Male Children: Reason for the Absence and Age of Onset of the Absence." *Journal of Genetic Psychology* 130(1): 3–10 (March 1977).

The effects of father absence on sex-typed behaviors were studied in 45 fifth-grade boys from intact and father-absent families. A variety of measures were used in the study, including teachers' ratings. It was found that father presence was not necessary for the development of masculine behaviors. Preadolescent father-absent boys in the study had more masculine behaviors than father-present boys. Boys from divorced families were more aggressive than boys who had experienced father loss through death. It was also found that the later father absence occurs, the greater the likelihood that boys will show more aggressive behavior toward peers and family members. The suggestion is made that male adult attention may be needed to supplement mothers' efforts to modify aggressive behavior. (10 references)

270. ———. "Relation of Type and Onset of Father Absence to Cognitive Development." *Child Development* 43(2): 455–469 (June 1972).

Comparisons are made of third- and sixth-grade IQ and achievement scores with 286 father-absent and 57 father-present, white, predominantly lower-class boys and girls. Father absence was analyzed by onset, age, type of absence, or presence of stepfather. Father absence due to divorce, desertion or separation had the most negative impact in the first two years of the child's life. Death of the father had the most negative effects during ages six to nine for boys. Father-absent boys performed more poorly than father-absent girls or father-present boys. Remarriage of boys' mother in the first five years of the son's life had a positive influence. (15 references)

271. Schenenga, Keith. "Father Absence, the Ego Ideal and Moral Development." *Smith College Studies in Social Work* 53(2): 103–114 (March 1983).

This investigation probes some differences in the moral development of 25 white young adolescent males related to the presence or absence of a father. Results of several measures used for assessment suggest that father-absent boys used principled moral reasoning to a lesser degree and had a lower level of ego ideal development than father present boys. Further study of how a father's participation in the psychological development of his son relates to the son's moral judgement is recommended. (29 references)

272. Schilling, Robert F., et al. "Single Mothers with Handicapped Children: Different from Their Married Counterparts?" *Family Relations* 35(1): 69–77 (January 1986).

Questionnaires were administered to 33 single and 48 married custodial mothers with handicapped children. A modified version of a measure on Resources and Stress was used in the study. Differences between single and married mothers were noted on 24 of 135 items. Most of the significant differences were related to quality of family life rather than rearing of a handicapped child. It is noted that coping and social-support interventions for parents cannot take the place of adequate economic and institutional supports. Parents experience stress related to the special needs of the handicapped child and in proportion to the degree and nature of the handicap. Implications for professional intervention are presented. (73 references)

* Sciara, Frank J. "Effects of Father Absence on the Educational Achievement of Urban Black Children." *Child Study Journal* 5(1): 45–55 (1975).

Reported in School Item No. 1105.

273. Shill, Merton A. "TAT Measures of Core Gender Identity, (Castration Anxiety) Parental Introjects, and Assertiveness in Father Absent Males." Ph.D. diss., University of Michigan, 1978.

For a summary see: *Dissertation Abstracts International* 39B(10): 5087.

274. Shinn, Marybeth. "Father Absence and Children's Cognitive Development." *The Psychological Bulletin* 85(2): 295–324 (March 1978).

The negative effects of father absence on children's cognitive development as measured by IQ and achievement tests is examined in the findings of research literature. Results of these studies show that anxiety, financial hardship, and reduced levels of parent interaction contribute to poor performance on cognitive tests by children from single-parent families. The mother's interaction with her children as a compensatory factor in father absence is discussed. Suggestions for future studies are offered. (77 references)

275. Stanley, Barbara K., et al. "The Effects of Father Absence on Interpersonal Problem-Solving Skills of Nursery School

Children." *Journal of Counseling and Development* 64(6): 338–385 (February 1986).

Fifty nursery school children from father-absent families and intact families were studied to determine the effects of father absence on problem solving. The Preschool Interpersonal Problem Solving Test was used to measure the child's ability to recognize alternative solutions to problem solving. Father-present children were found to have higher scores on the PIPS test. Results suggest that father-absent children may be deficient in social adjustment skills which may be essential in a child's adjustment to other persons. Additional study is suggested. (14 references)

276. Stern, Edgar E. "Single Mother's Perceptions of the Father Role and of the Effects of Father Absence on Boys." *Journal of Divorce* 4(2): 77–84 (Winter 1980).

A questionnaire was administered to a sample of 96 single and nonsingle mothers with male children to assess mothers' perceptions of a father's role and the effect of his absence on the development of boys. Single-mother respondents rated a father more important than nonsingles and also rated a mother more important. Concern about the effects of father absence on a boy's sex-identity development was expressed by all mothers. The need for a male adult in certain types of play and recreational activities was noted. Implications of these findings for family health professionals are discussed and further research is suggested. (15 references)

277. Stern, Marilyn, et al. "Father Absence and Adolescent "Problem Behaviors": Alcohol Consumption, Drug Use and Sexual Activity." *Adolescence* 19(74): 301–312 (Summer 1984).

A sample of 813 adolescents between the ages of 12 and 18 were asked to complete a questionnaire related to attitudes and behavior regarding the use of alcohol, drugs and sex. Results showed that father-absent youths, especially males, were at greater risk due to higher rates of behaviors involving alcohol and marijuana use and sexual activity. However, adolescents were more likely to seek help with their problems from peers rather than their fathers. Implications for family service professionals are noted. (16 references)

278. Stevenson, Michael Ray. "The Effects of Paternal Absence on Sex-Role Development: A Meta-Analysis." Ph.D. diss., Purdue University, 1984.

For a summary see: *Dissertation Abstracts International* 45B(10): 3356.

279. Stevenson, Michael Ray, and Kathryn N. Black. "Sex-Role Development and Father-Absence: Comparing Meta-Analyses." Paper presented at the Annual Meeting of the Midwestern Psychological Association. Chicago, Il., May 5–7, 1983. 14pp. (ERIC Microfiche ED229125)

Effects of father absence on the sex role development of male and female children through meta-analysis of pertinent published and unpublished literature are reported. Findings show that the effects of father absence on boys under the age of six were significant, although no significant difference was found to be associated with the age of female subjects. When sex role preference was assessed, father-absent males were less masculine and father-absent females were more feminine when compared with father-present children. However, measures of sex-role adoption showed that father-absent boys were more masculine, while father-absent girls were less feminine. (39 references)

280. Sugar, Max, ed. "Group Therapy for Pubescent Boys with Absent Fathers." Chap. 4, in *The Adolescent in Group and Family Therapy* 49–67, Chicago: University of Chicago Press, 1986.

This chapter describes therapeutic sessions with a group of pubescent boys who had experienced some degree of paternal loss. The boys were brought to the clinic by their mothers on the advice of school officials or friends or because of school performance and behavior. It is suggested that having a male therapist, especially for early adolescent boys, meets their special needs at this time in their lives. It removes them from their mother and mother-substitutes and gives them a male figure with whom they can identify. The mothers of the boys were also brought into therapy and later into a group with their sons' therapist. The intervention strategies provided the means of dealing with conflicts before pathological defenses became fixed. (29 references)

281. Svanum, Soren, et al. "Father Absence and Cognitive Performance in a Large Sample of Six- to Eleven-Year-Old Children." *Child Development* 53(1): 136–143 (February 1982).

This study investigates the educational performance and intellectual development of six-to eleven-year-old father-absent boys in a national sample of 6,109 children from single-parent and intact families. Subtests of the Wechsler Intelligence Scale for Children (WISC) and Wide Range Achievement Test (WRAT) were used as a control variable. It was found that differences attributed to father absence can often be accounted for by socioeconomic status. Black children with absent fathers showed a decrease only on tests which measured achievement. When control for socioeconomic status was introduced, no decreases were found for children from father-present or father-absent homes. Without control for SES, WISC and WRAT scores for father absent white children were reduced. (17 references)

282. Trachtman, Richard. "Post-Oedipal Development and Adaptation in Father-Absent and Father-Present Boys." *Smith College Studies in Social Work* 51(2): 126–137 (1981).

The experiences of 16 early latency-aged boys who had undergone father absence during at least part of the

Oedipal phase of development were compared with ten father-present boys of similar age. Two semi-structured interviews were used, one for mothers and one for the boys. Little evidence was found that father-absent boys had, as a group, experienced unusual adaptational reactions which differed from father-present boys. The weak connection found between Oedipal resolution and father presence is discussed. It is suggested that given good enough care by the remaining parent, a child may be able to find adaptive routes to normal development. (12 references)

283. Wakerman, Elyce. *Father Loss: Daughters Discuss the Man that Got Away*. Garden City, New York: Doubleday, 1984.

Currently there are five and a half million girls in the United States without fathers. Six hundred and eight women volunteered to complete questionnaires for a father-loss study. Subjects included women who had lost fathers through death or divorce and whose mothers did not remarry, women who had lost fathers through death or divorce and whose mothers remarried, and women who grew up with fathers. It was noted that fathers are important to sex-role development and foster a positive feminine identity and achievement orientation that enables daughters to acknowledge and develop the many aspects of themselves. An unrealistic picture of the father may negatively affect childhood, adolescence, attitude toward self, relationships, careers and family. (83 references)

284. Woodard, Queen E. "Effect of Father-Presence and Father-Absence on the Self-Concept of Black Males in Special Education and Regular Education Classes." ED.D. diss., Western Michigan University, 1984.

For a summary see: *Dissertation Abstracts International* 46A(4): 951.

MOTHERLESS FAMILIES

BIBLIOGRAPHIES AND LITERATURE REVIEW

285. Bradley, Susan J. "The Relationship of Early Maternal Separation to Borderline Personality in Children and Adolescents: A Pilot Study." *American Journal of Psychiatry* 136(4A): 424–426 (April 1979).

A clinical population of 14 borderline patients were compared with a control group of 68 to assess the relationship of maternal separation before the age of ten with borderline personality. The six criteria used by Gunderson and Singer (1975) were employed to identify the borderline patients. Results of data gathered on these patients indicated that the history of early separation in the borderline patients was greater than that of the control subjects. Borderline adolescents, compared with psychi- atrically referred delinquents, also had a history of early separations. Replication of the study with a larger sample size is suggested. (11 references)

286. Hanson, Shirley M. H. "Single Fathers with Custody: A Synthesis of the Literature." *The One-Parent Family in the 1980's: Perspectives and Annotated Bibliography 1978–1984,* edited by B. Schlesinger, 57–98. Toronto: University of Toronto Press.

The history of fathers as custodians of their children is reviewed and a synopsis of the findings in studies published during the past eight years is given. Single fathers with custody do well as primary care givers. Those who are doing best have involved themselves in child care and household tasks before divorce, have actively sought additional counseling and education, and have worked toward a more meaningful interaction between themselves and their children. Most custodial fathers are happy with custody and feel they were the best choice as parent. Children report happiness with the arrangement and do not seem to yearn to live with the noncustodial parent. (Bibliography)

287. Honig, Alice Sterling. *Fathering: A Bibliography.* National Institute of Education, Washington, D.C., August 1977. 78pp. (ERIC Microfiche ED142293)

This bibliography on the father's role in the child's development contains over 1,000 citations of material published between 1941 and 1977. Areas represented include socialization, sex-role identity, cognitive ability and child behaviors. Children's ideas about fathering and nontraditional fathering are also covered. Some of the items in the bibliography are annotated. (Bibliography)

288. Klinman, Debra G., and Rhiana Kohl. *Fatherhood USA: The First National Guide to Programs, Services, and Resources for and About Fathers.* New York: Garland, 1984.

Changes in the American family have been accompanied by changes in social expectations of fatherhood. This compilation of resources available nationwide includes the programs, services and resources which have been developed to meet the needs of single fathers, stepfathers, teenage fathers, gay fathers incarcerated fathers and fathers in general. Also included are books, films and videocassettes, newsletters and organizations.

GENERAL WORKS

289. Ferri, Elsa "Characteristics of Motherless Families." *British Journal of Social Work* 3(1): 91–100 (Spring 1973).

Data for this investigation of characteristics of motherless families came from the follow-up study for the National Child Development Study in Britain. Two hundred and thirty-seven cases of motherlessness among 11–year old children were examined for cause of loss and the relationship of background factors and changes in child care which result. One-half of the cases of mother absence were due to marital dissolution and the other half were due to death. Findings showed that mothers were more likely than fathers to be caring for their children in single-parent homes. Availability of a mother substitute in father-headed households was related to the father's age and the number of children he had. Mother-absent families had a higher proportion of fathers from lower-class backgrounds, and a higher rate of unemployment was reported by fathers who were coping alone. (11 references)

290. Fischer, Judith L. "Mothers Living Apart from Their Children." *Family Relations* 32(3): 351–357 (July 1983).

The various processes by which mothers come to live apart from their children are discussed. Negative societal attitudes are contrasted with the findings of empirical research. No particular traits, dispositions or life styles appear to characterize women who live apart from their children. Most mothers did not run away, nor were they found to be unfit by the courts. Personal conflicts facing the non-custodial mother may be: 1) the best interests of the child, 2) the wishes of society, 3) a situation which may have been imposed and 4) unsettled and fluctuating aspects of custody. Family life educators, counselors and therapists can help mothers who live apart from their children by negation of the unflattering stereotype of the non-custody mother. (11 references)

291. Greif, Geoffrey L. "Children and Housework in the Single Father Family." *Family Relations* 34(3): 353–357 (July 1985).

A survey of 1,136 single fathers responding to a questionnaire in *Parents Without Partners* magazine indicated that children participated more in housework as they got older. Fathers raising teen-age girls received more help from them than fathers raising teen-age boys. However, single fathers may expect less from children in the way of participation in housework than was found in a study of two-parent families. It is suggested that males of all ages need to be more involved in housework if a future generation will be better prepared for roles in single parent families. (18 references)

292. Jenkins, Sue. "Love, Loss, and Seeking: Maternal Deprivation and the Quest." *Children's Literature in Education* 15(2): 73–83 (Summer 1984).

This article explores some results of the common experience of mother loss in childhood or adolescence upon the imaginative writings of a number of authors such as George MacDonald, C. S. Lewis, and J. R. Tolkien. It is suggested that adults, older children, toddlers and displaced babies all need help in coping with grief and maternal loss. This loss results in many deep and long-term effects on an individual's growth and development. (14 references)

293. Jones, Elsa. "Leaving Whom? Motherless Families: Problems of Termination for the Female Family Therapist." *Journal of Family Therapy* 5(1): 11–22 (February 1983).

In the single-parent male-headed family, the family may view itself as incomplete and attempt to draw the female therapist into the family to replace the mother. The therapist may also feel that the family cannot cope without her. The author discusses some strategies for dealing with termination of therapy. Two case studies are used to show how the therapist and family may be disentangled from each other. (24 references)

294. Keshet, Harry Finkelstein. "Single Parent Fathers: A New Study." *Children Today* 7(3): 12–19 (May/June 1978).

This article reports the results of interviews with 49 separated or divorced fathers who are rearing their children. The guidance and nurturing activities reported most often by fathers were discipline, serving meals, bathing children and helping them with feelings and emotional upsets. Meeting the needs of their children required single fathers to make changes in lifestyles and priorities. (9 references)

295. MacKinnon, Carol E., et al. "The Impact of Maternal Employment and Family Form on Children's Sex-Role Stereotypes and Mothers Traditional Attitudes." *Journal of Divorce* 3(1): 51–60 (Fall 1984).

Sixty single-parent and 20 intact families were studied to discover the effects of divorce and maternal employment on mothers' and children's sex-role attitudes. Instruments used in the study were the Attitudes Toward Women Scale for mothers, and the Sex Role Discrimination Subscale of the Sex Role Learning Index for children. It was found that working mothers, single and married, were more liberal in sex-role attitudes, and that children of single-parent families were more liberal in sex-role orientations. It is suggested that children from divorced families, particularly girls, are less aware of sex role stereotypes of the opposite sex. (3 references)

296. Mendes, Helen A. "Single Fathers." *Family Coordinator* 25(4): 439–444 (October 1976).

Thirty-two single fathers were interviewed to access their experiences in one-parent homes. It was found that once children entered school many fathers did not hire others to supervise their children after school, although they expressed apprehension about the lack of supervision. Single fathers also reported that they were less affectionate with their adolescent children. It is suggested that male students should be taught something about homemaking, budgeting and marketing. The quality of the parent-child emotional relationship suggested a need for family life education and a second look at the socialization of males in our society. (4 references)

297. Norris, Christopher Saurin. "The Effect of Early Childhood Maternal Deprivation of Adolescent Females' Ability to

Delay Gratification as Measured by Their Response to Varying Reward Schedules." Ph.D. diss., United States International University, 1980.

For a summary see: *Dissertation Abstracts International* 41B(2): 696.

298. Parish, Thomas S., and John A. Hortin. "Locus of Control and Mother Loss." *Journal of Genetic Psychology* 142(2): 317–318 (December 1983).

Seven hundred and eighty-two undergraduate students completed the Rotter Internality Scale to measure the impact of mother absence on locus of control. Findings suggest that mother loss fosters an external locus of control in males whose mothers had died and whose fathers had not remarried. Mother loss did not affect locus of control for females. (3 references)

299. Rutter, Michael. "Maternal Deprivation, 1972–1978: New Findings, New Concepts, New Approaches." *Child Development* 50(2): 283–305 (June 1979).

Research since 1972 on the effects of mother absence on the development of children is reviewed. New concepts and ideas related to social relationships, the process of bonding, critical periods in a child's development and the connection between childhood experiences and parenting receive special attention. Possible reasons why many children show little or no effects of mother absence and those factors which mediate mother loss are areas suggested for more scrutiny because of implications for policy and intervention strategy. (222 references)

300. Schlesinger, Benjamin, and Rubin Zodres. "Motherless Families: An Increasing Societal Pattern." *Child Welfare* 55(8): 553–48 (October 1976).

Seventy-two father-headed single-parent families, including divorced fathers, separated fathers, widowers and unmarried persons, were studied to determine the problems these motherless families face. Most fathers described the family breakup as upsetting to their children. Fathers seemed to be more affected than their children, in terms of changes in sleeping, eating, peer relationships, work, leisure and appearance. Implications of the findings for financial support services, family law and research are noted. (5 references)

301. Smith, Richard M., and Craig W. Smith. "Child Rearing and Single-Parent Fathers." *Family Relations* 30(3): 411–417 (July 1981).

This study consisted of a sample of 27 predominantly middle class Caucasian fathers who had sole custody of at least one dependent child and no live-in female companion. The interview was designed to access the five variables of goal facilitation, transition procedures, normative change, role strain and ease of role transition during three phases of their lives. Also included were questions on discipline, interpersonal interaction, and emotional needs of children. It was concluded that single fathers are able to adjust successfully. Types of experiences and activities which would be helpful to single fathers are identified. (29 references)

302. Wilding, Paul, and Victor George. *Motherless Families*. London; Boston: Routledge & K. Paul, 1972.

This study of nearly 600 families covers five types of motherless families: widowed, divorced, separated families where the mother was hospitalized for at least six months and families where the mother was in prison for at least nine months. Although Society expresses concern for family life and the well-being of children, the majority of respondents in the study felt that a man should go out and work. They made little mention of combining work and child care. It is suggested that motherless families need child day-care centers, domestic assistance, supplementary income to cover the cost of combining two roles, and funded research on mother absence in families. (Bibliography)

RECONSTITUTED ONE-PARENT FAMILIES

BIBLIOGRAPHIES AND LITERATURE REVIEW

303. Brody, Gene H., et al. "Serial Marriage: A Heuristic Analysis of an Emerging Family Form." *Psychological Bulletin* 103(2): 211–222 (March 1988).

This article analyzes existing empirical, clinical, and theoretical information on three or more marriages severed by divorce and views of the consequences of this lifestyle for family members. Negative marital behavior may be repeated in subsequent marriages; experience with marriage dissolution may condition divorced persons toward greater acceptance of divorce as a solution to marriage problems. Family turmoil associated with parental divorce affects children's social, emotional and intellectual adjustment and one to two years may be required to overcome the disruption in their functioning. In serial marriages, the amount of parental conflict a child experiences can increase proportionally to the number of marriages and divorces. Future directions for research are discussed. (92 references)

304. Jolliff, David. "The Effects of Parental Remarriage on the Development of the Young Child." *Early Child Development and Care* 13(3–4): 321–334 (1984).

This study undertakes a review of literature of parental remarriage in order to examine the effects on task development of children. Findings suggest that children of remarried families may experience considerable difficulty initially but suffer no significant long-range developmental effects. The quality of family life, rather than family structure seems to be the most important factor in child development. Additional research on this topic is suggested. (28 references)

305. Rosenberg, Elinor B. "Therapy with Siblings in Reorganizing Families." *International Journal of Family Therapy* 2(3): 139–150 (Fall 1980).

Loss of a parent through death, divorce, or other types of separation leaves children without traditional family support and may foster fears of abandonment. On the other hand, the relationship of siblings lasts a lifetime and therefore offers an important support system that continues through developmental stages of the life cycle. However, siblings are not always supportive and helpful to each other even in times of stress. Results of case work with sibling groups from reorganizing families are discussed on a case-by-case basis. It is suggested that negative forces with a sibling group can be reworked into a positive mutually supportive system. Extension of the study of siblings and sibling subgroups as they move through life cycles and strengthen their natural bonds is proposed. (6 references)

GENERAL WORKS

306. Amato, Paul R. "Family Processes in One-Parent, Stepparent, and Intact Families: The Child's Point of View." *Journal of Marriage and the Family* 49(2): 327–337 (May 1987).

This study examines the effects of divorce and remarriage on the adjustment and development of children. Data on a sample of 402 children and their families were obtained from a study conducted by the Australian Institute of Families Studies in 1982–1983 and were limited to the state of Victoria. Similar levels of support and punishment from mothers were reported by children regardless of family type. However, less father support, control and punishment were reported by children with one parent. Stepfathers were paid to provide less support, control and punishment than biological fathers. (31 references)

307. Bryan, Linda R., et al. "Person Perception: Family Structure as a Cue for Stereotyping." *Journal of Marriage and the Family* 48(1): 169–174 (February 1986).

Perceptions of stepparents and stepchildren were compared to perceptions of adults in other family structures, including married, widowed, divorced, or never-married parents. Perceptions of 696 subjects were measured with the First Impressions Questionnaire. It was found that family structure is a cue by which stereotypes are formed. Children in stepfamilies are viewed more negatively than children in other family types. (28 references)

308. Clingempeel, W. Glenn, and Sion Segal. "Stepparent-Stepchild Relationships and the Psychological Adjustment of Children in Stepmother and Stepfather Families." *Child Development* 57(2): 474–484 (1986).

This investigation examines the quality of stepparent-stepchild relationships. Sixty randomly selected Caucasian stepfamilies were assessed with a variety of measures by doctoral students in clinical psychology. Results indicated more positive relationships between stepmother and stepchild were associated with better psychological adjustment of stepchildren of both sexes. For girls living with biological fathers, more frequent visits by the biological mother were associated with less positive relationships with stepmothers. For boys, lower aggression and inhibition ratings and positive communication behaviors were significant in relationships with stepmothers. Limitations of the study are discussed and recommendations for future research are offered. (39 references)

309. Coleman, Marilyn, and Lawrence Ganong. "An Evaluation of the Stepfamily Self-help Literature for Children and Adolescents." *Family Relations* 36(1): 61–65 (January 1987).

Eleven stepfamily self-help books for children and

adolescents were reviewed and evaluated for possible usefulness in bibliotherapy. Factors considered in the evaluation were: audience, author's background, issues identified, advice given and strengths of parental remarriage. Use of the books in facilitating therapy is discussed. (17 references)

310. Collins, Stephen. *Step-Parents and Their Children.* London: Souvenir Press, 1988.

This book focuses on a positive approach to stepparenting based on the author's own experience as a stepparent and counseling work with stepparents. The first hurdle stepfamilies face is adjusting attitudes. While stepchildren may have particular problems arising from upheavals in their lives, these are not insurmountable. However, the interrelationships of children and adults require special understanding. Guidelines for easing adjustment of these new relationships are offered. Relevant points of law, sources of help for stepfamilies and suggestions for further reading that may be useful are also presented. (bibliography)

311. Furstenberg, Frank F., Jr., and Christine Winquist Nord. "Parenting Apart: Patterns of Childrearing After Marital Disruption." *Journal of Marriage and the Family* 47(4): 893–904 (November 1985).

Today many parents remarry following divorce and their children grow up with more than one set of parents. Data from interviews with 2,279 preadolescent children in 1,747 homes were used to learn about relations among children, parents, stepparents and children following separation and divorce. Findings showed that most children had little contact with nonresident parents, and any contact tended not to be influential in decision-making. Where the former spouse was active in the child's life, there was little evidence of difficulty in stepfamilies consisting of the child's mother and stepfather. (21 references)

312. Goetting, Ann. "The Six Stations of Remarriage: Developmental Tasks of Remarriage After Divorce." *Family Relations* 31(2): 213–222 (April 1982).

This article focuses on six developmental tasks which are encountered in the passage from divorced to remarried. The task of parenting is associated with a great number of the problems experienced in remarriage. There may be the new husband and wife, former spouses, two sets of children, four sets of grandparents, and relatives and friends associated with the previous marriage that have the potential to affect the adjustment of children and add complexity to the task of parenting. (29 references)

313. Harper, Patricia. *Children in Stepfamilies: Their Legal and Family Status.* Institute of Family Studies Policy Background Paper No. 4. Institute of Family Studies, Melbourne Australia. (ERIC Microfiche ED245827)

The changing nature of the family in Australia is discussed. Changes have occurred in family formation and breakdown, composition and structures, family relationships, and in status, rights, and obligations of family members. Some families use adoption to clarify and establish legal status and family relationships of children and stepparents. Changes in legislation are suggested in order to clarify relationships in stepfamilies. It is suggested that stepparents should be able to seek guardianship or custody rights but that adoption of stepchildren should be abolished. (32 references)

314. Hayes, Richard L., and Bree A. Hayes. "Remarriage Families: Counseling Parents and Their Children." *Counseling and Human Development* 18(7): 1–8 (March 1986).

Although the nuclear family is still accepted as the standard, with one in three children under the age of eighteen expected to spend a portion of his/her life with a single parent by the year 1990, it is not the norm. Single parent and remarriage families will comprise about 45%

of all families. Support for the child in restructured families must come from the school and from interaction with peers. Counselors need to understand the changes taking place in the life of the child and be mindful that the outcomes for the child are not predetermined and that remarriage families are part of normal responses to changing social conditions. (44 references)

315. Hyde, Margaret O. *My Friend Has Four Parents*. New York: McGraw-Hill, 1981.

This book for young readers explores the feelings children experience when their families fall apart. Other problems which these children may face such as the changes that come from living with one parent, custody and parental kidnapping and living in stepfamilies are also discussed. A list of titles suggested for further reading includes fiction and nonfiction titles. There is also a list of suggested readings for parents.

316. Isaacs, Marla Beth, and George H. Leon. "Remarriage and Its Alternatives Following Divorce: Mother and Child Adjustment." *Journal of Marital and Family Therapy* 14(2): 163–173 (April 1988).

This five-year longitudinal study explores the effects on mothers and children of new parental relationships following divorce in 87 female families. Remarriage, unmarried living together, seriously involved but not remarried, and not seriously involved are the categories of blending represented. Only one arrangement was found to have a significant effect on the adjustment of children, and that was the situation where the mother had a live-in partner but was not married. None of the other arrangements nor the child's sex significantly affected the child's adjustment. Suggestions are made for future studies. (13 references)

317. Marotz-Baden, Ramona, et al. "Family Form or Family Process? Reconsidering the Deficit Family Model

Approach." *Family Coordinator* 28(1): 5–14 (January 1979).

This article questions whether family form or familial process is more likely to contribute to children's positive personal and social development. A literature review of research on the effects of alternative family forms on children's personality, social behavior and school achievement suggests that the interactional dynamics that lead to a given outcome may be more important than family form. It is proposed that future research consider not only the interlinkage of family roles and memberships but consider also the individual and family structure over time. (81 references)

318. Michael, Brad Eugene. "Family Structure, and Behavioral Outcome for Children in Stepfather and Non-Divorced Family." Ph.D. diss., University of Houston, 1987.

For a summary see: *Dissertation Abstracts International* 49B(6): 2382.

319. Montemayor, Raymond, and Geoffrey K. Leigh. "Parent-Absent Children: a Demographic Analysis of Children and Adolescents Living Apart from Their Parents." *Family Relations* 31(4): 567–573 (October 1982).

U.S. Census Population figures were utilized in compiling a statistical profile of children who do not live with their parents. In 1980, nearly three million unmarried noninstitutionalized children under the age of eighteen were reported in this group. Most of these children live in families with a relative, usually the grandparents. The percentage of white children living in institutions or with non-relatives was far greater than that of black children. The reasons children live apart from parents, such as divorce, illegitimacy, unemployment and inflation, are discussed. Suggestions are made for further research on parent-absent children. (24 references)

320. Nunn, Gerald D., et al. "Perceptions of Personal and

Familial Adjustment by Children from Intact, Single-Parent, and Reconstituted Families." *Psychology in the Schools* 20(2): 166–174 (April 1983).

Children's personal and familial adjustment variables were studied to see if they vary as a function of their present familial configuration and/or gender. Adjustment factors surveyed included self-concept, perception of school adjustment, home adjustment, peer relationships state and trait anxiety as well as their evaluations of mother, father and family. The results showed a) less positive adjustment among children from divorced families, whether the remaining parent remarried or not; b) mixed findings regarding comparisons of psychosocial adjustment between single-parent and remarried groups; and c) a pattern of effects related to significant interactions of family type and gender in which males appeared to be favorably affected within the single-parent configuration, while females were more favorably adjusted within the reconstituted family. (31 references)

321. Parish, Thomas S., and Judy W. Dostal. "Evaluations of Self and Parent Figures by Children from Intact, Divorced, and Reconstituted Families." *Journal of Youth and Adolescence* 9(4): 347–351 (August 1980).

Seven hundred and thirty-eight school-age children from 14 school districts in Kansas completed the Personal Attribute Inventory, which was used for the purpose of evaluating themselves, their mothers and fathers. Responses showed that children from intact families generally evaluated themselves and their parents more favorably than children from divorced families. Children from reconstituted families, in contrast with nonremarried children, rated themselves somewhat more favorably, their absent fathers significantly more favorably and their mothers less favorably. Results of these findings are discussed. (14 references)

322. Quinton, David, et al. "Institutional Rearing, Parenting Difficulties and Marital Support." *Psychological Medicine*

14(1): 107–124 (February 1984).

In a follow-up study, 94 girls reared in institutions subsequent to failure in parenting were compared with 51 girls in a general population sample. Subjects and their spouses were interviewed, and parenting skills in handling control, peer relationships and distress were evaluated. Findings indicated that institution-reared women had a significantly increased rate of psychosocial functioning and parenting problems in adulthood. However, there was evidence that a good marriage relationship with a non-deviant partner and good living conditions mediated effects of institutionalization. (33 references)

323. Shafer, L. Loyet. "Presenting Concerns and Treatment Issues of Children from Intact, Single-Parent and Stepfamilies." Ph.D. diss., Oklahoma State University, 1988.

For a summary see: *Dissertation Abstracts International* 49B(10): 4560.

324. Steinberg, Laurence. "Single Parents, Stepparents, and the Susceptibility of Adolescents to Antisocial Peer Pressure." *Child Development* 58 (1): 269–275 (February 1987)

This study compares 865 fifth-, sixth-, and ninth-grade students who lived with mother alone, two natural parents and one natural parent/one-stepparent. Findings showed that children from two-parent homes were less likely to participate with peers in deviant behavior than children in other family types. Children in stepfamilies were as much at risk for involvement in deviant behavior as were their peers in single-parent homes. Research on the relationship between physical maturation, family structure and susceptibility to antisocial activity is suggested. (15 references)

325. Tropf, Walter D. "An Exploratory Examination of the

Effect of Remarriage on Child Support and Personal Contacts." *Journal of Divorce* 7(3): 57–73 (Spring 1984).

This study examines the effect of remarriage on voluntary support and personal contacts between father and child following divorce. Results of interviews from a convenience sample of 101 divorced men in the Orlando Florida area are reported. All the men had children by a previous marriage. Evidence suggests that visiting frequencies decrease, but voluntary support increases after the father's remarriage. However, voluntary support decreases after the remarriage of the wife. Further study of the complexity of role configurations created by remarriage is suggested. (15 references)

326. Visher, Emily, et al. *Old Loyalties, New Ties: Therapeutic Strategies with Stepfamilies.* New York: Brunner/Mazel, 1988.

An overview of stepfamilies in the 1980's is presented. Also described are intervention strategies designed to build and strengthen self-esteem and supportiveness, teach negotiation and encourage dyadic relationships. Family members are helped to deal with change and loss, resolve loyalty conflicts and develop boundaries that encourage integration and stability. The appendix includes separate reading lists for adults and children. Therapists and counselors will find guidelines for working with stepfamilies.

327. Vosler, Nancy R. "Children in Intact, One-Parent, and Blended Families: Psychosocial Consequences of Family Structure." Ph.D. diss., Virginia Commonwealth University, 1985.

For a summary see: *Dissertation Abstracts International* 46A(7): 2077.

SINGLE-PARENT ADOPTIVE FAMILIES

BIBLIOGRAPHIES AND LITERATURE REVIEW

328. Kadushin, Alfred. "Single-Parent Adoptions Overview and Some Relevant Research." *Social Service Review* 44(3): 263–274 (September 1970).

The idea of single-parent adoption as a source for meeting the need for a larger number of adoptive applicants is explored through a review of research literature on the subject. Standards which adoption agencies apply to single applicants relate to the availability of male role models, ability to support the child financially, sexual identification of the applicant, health status and motivation. Adopted children of single parents are subject to many of the risks of biological children in father-absent homes, which, in turn, affects the social worker's attitude about single-parent adoption. However, the two-parent family is not necessarily free of pathogenic findings, and neither is the single-parent family necessarily a pathogenic family. An overview of the literature leads to the conclusion that children can be reared without damage in family situations that embrace a variety of contexts. (56 references)

329. Kim, S. Peter. *Special Adoptions: An Annotated Bibliography on Transracial, Transcultural, and Nonconventional Adoption, and Minority Children. For Mental Health, Health, and Human Services Professionals.* American Academy of Child Psychiatry. Washington, D.C., National Institute of Mental Health, Bethesda, Md., 1981. 149pp. (ERIC Microfiche ED216294)

This bibliography on special adoptions mirrors changing trends and legislation. Black, Indian, American Indian, Eskimo, Oriental, Puerto Rican, Mexican and hard to place children are among the groups represented. Social attitudes, parent-child relationships, adjustment, health and development are also considered, along with cultural identity. A detailed subject index provides easy access to the 271 annotations in the bibliography.

330. Murray, L. "A Review of Selected Foster Care - Adoption Research from 1978 to Mid-1982." *Child Welfare* 63(2) 113–124 (March-April 1984).

This article summarizes the research on permanent planning, adoption outcomes, foster parents, and recidivism in foster care. This research indicates that: 1) children adopted at older ages encounter more difficulties and, when the effects of age are controlled for, 2) children adopted transracially or by single parents do as well as children adopted in-racially or by two-parent families. Suggestions are offered for additional research. (27 references)

331. Schlesinger, Benjamin. "Single Parent Adoptions: A Review." *Australian Journal of Social Issues* 14(2): 112–117 (1979).

This paper reviews findings of research studies on single-parent adoptions reported in the United States early as 1970. The availability of male role models in the extended family may be one of the agency's considerations in adoption placement. The special needs of some children may best be served by single adults who are qualified to meet those needs. Results of single-parent adoptions in Chicago and Los Angeles are mentioned. Single-parent mothers and fathers report parenting experiences similar to those reported by other adoptive couples. Research findings support the growing practice of single-parent adoption. (10 references)

332. VanWhy, Elizabeth Wharton. *Adoption Bibliography and Multi-Ethnic Sourcebook*. Hartford, Connecticut: Open Door Society of Connecticut, 1977.

This bibliography includes articles, dissertations, books

and audiovisuals on multiethnic adoptions for adults and children. Many of the items listed in the bibliography are annotated. A multiethnic sourcebook section provides information on places from which ethnic dolls, calendars, musical instruments periodicals, workshops, toys, games and bilingual educational materials may be obtained.

GENERAL WORKS

333. "Adopting Illegitimate Children: When Does a Putative Father's Claim Have Merit." *Children's Legal Rights Journal* 4(4): 1–5 (January-February 1983).

    Although the U.S. Supreme Court has issued several key decisions regarding the rights of fathers of illegitimate children in cases where the child was freed for adoption by the natural mother, both the Supreme Court and lower courts are still having to contend with variations of the problem. Issues in several cases decided by the Court involving the rights of fathers of illegitimate children are discussed in relation to a case pending before the Court that asks that an adoption be voided through retrospective application of the law. (5 references)

334. Amos, Iris E. "Child Advocacy and the Adversary System: Round Peg in a Square Hole." *Journal of Clinical Child Psychology* 10(4): 56–58 (Winter 1981).

    This article describes a recent adoption decision that focuses on the participation of six psychologists who appeared as expert witnesses in a case involving the child of divorcing parents. An argument is made for the use of the consultation model, implemented by identifiable child specialists, as an alternative to the multiple expert witness approach. Guidelines for an alternative model are presented. (13 references)

335. Beckman, Gail McKnight. "Changes Highlight Need for Making Special Provisions for Adopted or Illegitimate

Children." *Estate Planning* 12(6): 352–355 (November 1985).

Recent changes regarding the inheritance rights of adopted and illegitimate children and how they may affect client expectations and malpractice claims against estate planners are discussed. Language that needs to be included in the wills to meet a variety of situations and the need for certain pre-death documents to protect the rights of children post-death are mentioned. There is also a need for a third-party beneficiary to enforce the father's obligation. (15 references)

336. Branham, Ethel. "One-Parent Adoptions." *Children* 17(3): 103–107 (May-June 1970).

Single persons are being considered as adoptive parents for children with special needs along with long-term foster care, subsidized adoptions and adoption across racial lines. This article reports on the first 36 placements of children in single-parent families by the Los Angeles Department of Adoptions. The factors considered by the agency in making placements are discussed along with case presentations that address the concerns of many adoptive agencies when considering single-parent adoptions. The Los Angeles agency plans a longitudinal study which is expected to shed more light on single-parent children of all types. (6 references)

337. David, Winston R. "The Unwed Father: Conflict of Rights in Adoption Proceedings." *Florida State University Law Review* 7(3): 559–570 (Summer 1979).

The assumption that natural fathers have a constitutionally protected relationship with their illegitimate children is a recent concept. Rulings in cases discussed indicate that the court recognizes that persons with no biological relationship with the child may develop a constitutionally protected interest that may support a claim that the best interest of the child is served through adoption by a psychological parent. The adoption of illegitimate children is thereby encouraged by these rulings. However, it is noted that adoption should not be promoted at the cost of protected interests of either natural parent. (72 references)

338. Dougherty, Sharon A. "Single Adoptive Mothers and Their Children." *Social Work* 23(4): 311–314 (July 1978).

This study is an attempt to identify the characteristics of single adoptive mothers and their children and their sources of support. The study sample of eighty-two adoptive mothers, ranging in age from 21 to 64 completed a questionnaire. Most mothers had never married, were well educated, employed, older than biological mothers, had above-average incomes, and wanted a child to satisfy their own needs. The 121 children ranged in age from one day to 12.5 years at adoption, came from a variety of racial backgrounds and two thirds were in the hard-to-place category. Adoption fees ranged from none to $8,000. Adoptive mothers viewed the adoption itself as satisfying their own needs and meeting the needs of the children. Other single parents, friends and relatives were the preferred sources of support. Few of the mothers indicated a need for the type of support a social service agency provides. Suggestions for further inquiry into the adjustment needs of adoptive mothers and the type of social services needed by the few who desire this support. (4 references)

339. Feigelman, William, and Arnold R. Silverman. "Single Parent Adoptions." *Social Casework* 58(7): 418–425 (July 1977).

This study compares responses to questionnaires by single adoptive parents with those of adoptive couples. The nationwide study sample of 713 respondents included 58 single parents. The latter tended to be more highly educated, had higher-status occupations, less income, and were employed in human service fields. More emotional adjustment problems for children were reported by single parents. However, this difference disappeared when age was controlled. Data did not show a significant correlation between frequency of contact with the extended family and the emotional development of the adopted children. Single adoptive parents, especially males, encountered more resistance from the courts, friends and social agencies. Additional studies of single parent adoptions are recommended. (12 references)

340. Fox, Lorraine M. "Parental Rights and One-Parent Families." *Adoption and Fostering* 7(3): 29–33 (1983).

This article focuses on the legal practices related to the assumption of parental rights over children in local authority care. The National Council for One-Parent Families is especially concerned about single parents who need short-term help in caring for their children and who consequently find themselves deprived of their children permanently. Preliminary analysis of data from a study suggests that single parents are disproportionately at risk for loss of parental rights. (No references)

341. Hill, Robert B. *Informal Adoption Among Black Families.* Washington, D.C.: National Urban League, 1977.

Approximately 67 percent of white children born to unmarried mothers are given away for formal adoption, while nine out of ten black children born out of wedlock are kept by the extended family in informal adoption. During various periods in their lives, these black children are being cared for by grandmothers, aunts, uncles or other relatives. Social agencies have not generally been concerned with the quality of care provided children in informal adoption, and little attention has been paid to their needs. Implications for social policies are discussed. (Bibliography)

342. Lambert, Lydia. *Children in Changing Families: A Study of Adoption and Illegitimacy.* London; New York: Macmillan, 1980.

This is a follow-up study of illegitimate and adopted

children that was first undertaken by the National
Children's Bureau in Great Britain in 1958. The sample
for this investigation included 294 illegitimate children,
115 adopted children and 12,076 legitimate children at
age 11. Many of the illegitimately born children were
living in families that, in outward appearances resembled
the norm. Findings indicate a lack of association between
children's physical development or school achievement
and their birth status. The study highlights less the
differences between legitimate and illegitimate children
than it underlines the needs shared by all children in
changing families. (Bibliography)

343. Pannor, Ruben, and Byron W. Evans. "The Unmarried
Father Revisited." *Journal of School Health* 45(5): 286–291
(May 1975).

Supreme Court decisions have indicated that the
unmarried father has rights that cannot be ignored.
Adoption agencies must involve the single father in
adoption to the extent required by state laws. Suggestions
for counselors and social workers who are working with
unmarried mothers and fathers are outlined. The welfare
of the child should be the primary consideration when
options for the child's care are being considered and the
rights of the father who wants and is competent to care
for the child should be protected. Interagency cooperation
is suggested in cases where the single father resides in a
different community. (7 references)

344. Radford, Mary F. "Constitutional Law—Equal Protection."
Emory Law Journal 29(3): 833–858 (Summer 1980) New
York Statute Requiring Consent of Mother, but not of
Father, as Prerequisite to Adoption of Illegitimate Child
Violates the Fourteenth Amendment Because it Draws
Gender-based Distinction Which Bears No Substantial
Relation to State Interest in Encouraging Adoption of
Illegitimate Children (case note).

This article traces the legal path of the case of *Caban v.*
Mohammed that challenged the part of a New York

Domestic Relations Law that held that only the mother's consent for adoption was required in the case of children born out of wedlock. (148 references)

345. Rosenthal, Perihan Aral. "Triple Jeopardy: Family Stresses and Subsequent Divorce Following the Adoption of Racially and Ethnically Mixed Children." *Journal of Divorce* 4(4): 43–55 (Summer 1981).

The adoption of racially and ethnically or culturally different older children causes stress for both parents and children. This study concentrates on problems in regard to 15 black, black-Vietnamese and American Indian children who were adopted by five white middle-class families who had two or three biological children. The problems of the children with ethnicity, identity and rejection were further magnified when their parents later divorced. Therefore the need for families considering transracial adoption to be more carefully screened during the preadoption period is stressed. Findings in the cases examined in the study were all negative for the adopted children, the biological children and the divorced mothers with whom the children lived. (14 references)

346. Shireman, Joan F., and Penny R. Johnson. *Adoption: Three Alternatives. A Comparative Study of Three Alternative Forms of Adoptive Placement.* Chicago Child Care Society. Chicago, 1980. 74pp. (ERIC Microfiche ED197811)

This is the second report in a longitudinal study of the experiences of black children adopted by white couples, black couples and single parents. Data from interviews with 96 families showed that children raised by white families did not have problems forming racial identity, and black children raised by single parents did not have problems forming sexual identity. Descriptive components of the study focus on family interaction, roles, and ways of managing family life and crises. Particular emphasis was placed on the single adopting parent as well as parental handling of adoption and perceived need for support groups or services. (45 references)

347. ——. "Single Persons as Adoptive Parents." *The Social Service Review* 50(1): 103–116 (March 1976).

This study focuses on the child's handling of his identity as assessed four years after adoption. Children in the study were black infants who were adopted under the age of three by black couples, white couples and 31 single persons. Parents interviewed were judged to be well educated, emotionally stable, employed and competent. Children placed in the single-parent homes were considered low risk and generally were of the same sex as the adoptive parent and possessed the characteristics initially requested by the applicants. In the period immediately following placement, some symptoms of disturbance or readjustment were reported. At the end of four years only two children exhibited behavior that indicated emotional adjustment problems. Further study of adoptive single-parent families is suggested. (3 references)

348. ——. "A Longitudinal Study of Black Adoptions: Single Parent, Transracial, and Traditional." *Social Work* 31(3): 172–176 (May-June 1986).

This study on nontraditional adoptive placement of black children by Chicago child care agencies discusses single-parent, transracial and black couple adoptions. Most children in each type of family were found to be handling developmental tasks well with few differences between adoptive groups. Children in traditional homes experienced the development of a sense of racial identity much later than those in transracial families. A follow-up study is expected to take place in four years. (21 references)

349. ——. "Single-Parent Adoptions: A Longitudinal Study." *Children and Youth Services Review* 7(4): 321–334 (1985).

An eight-year study of 22 single adopting families compares their experiences with those of two-parent adopting families. Interviews with single parents indicated that they were successfully employed, had no problems with child care and made use of extended family supports. Although a higher proportion of single-parent children were found to be disturbed compared with those of adopting couples, the problems seemed to be, for the most part, those which could be remedied with time. In general many problems anticipated in single-parent adoptions were not evident in the study. (10 references)

350. ———. *Single Parent Adoption*. Administration for Children, Youth, and Families. Washington, D.C. April 1981. 29pp. (ERIC Microfiche ED252306)

Two views of the single-parent family present in this document includes articles by William Feigleman and Arnold R. Silverman and a brief statement by an adoptive parent, Amanda Richards. The first paper summarizes research findings on single-parent adoptions and presents results of a nationwide survey of 713 adoptive parents. Adoptive single parents reported more difficulty than adoptive couples in adopting children and were more likely to adopt hard-to-place children. Although adoptive single parents reported more adjustment problems on the part of their children, this was thought to be due to the fact that they tended to adopt older children more often than couples. In the second paper, a single-parent describes her experience in becoming an adoptive parent. (12 references)

ONE-PARENT FAMILIES WITH
ALTERNATIVE LIFE STYLES

BIBLIOGRAPHIES AND LITERATURE REVIEW

351. Cramer, David. "Gay Parents and Their Children: A
     Review of Research and Practical Implications." *Journal
     of Counseling and Development* 64(8): 504–507 (April
     1986).

     Research on the legal and developmental questions that
     often surface regarding the effect of a parent's
     homosexuality on his or her children is discussed. A gay
     parent seeking custody or visitation is often at a legal
     disadvantage in the courts, especially if sexual orientation
     is an issue in custody hearings. Legal concerns center
     around three issues: effect on the child's sexual orientation
     risk that the child of the same sex as the parent will be
     abused or that the child of the opposite sex will be rejected
     and stigmatizing of the child by peers. Research findings
     suggest that children raised by gay parents are
     emotionally and sexually similar to those raised by non-
     gay parents. Organizations are available to provide
     emotional and practical support for gay parents in
     metropolitan areas. Less help is available for children,
     but a supportive teacher, counselor or therapist can be an
     important resource. (21 references)

352. Riddle, Dorothy I. *Gay Parents and Child Custody Issues.*
     1977 22pp. (ERIC Microfiche ED147746)

     Homophobia is so widespread that gay parents have about
     a 50–50 chance of getting custody of their children when
     a divorce occurs. Not much research has been done on
     children in gay families but these studies have indicated
     that children suffer no negative effects from living with a
     gay custodial parent. Any difficulties they experienced
     were similar to those of children of heterosexual divorced
     parents. The parent's sexual orientation has no effect on

a child's sexual identity or whether the child will become heterosexual. Psychologists may be called as expert witnesses in custody cases to counter inaccurate opinions that others may have of homosexuals. (24 references)

GENERAL WORKS

353. Bozett, Frederick W. "Gay Fathers: Evolution of the Gay-Father Identity." *American Journal of Orthopsychiatry* 51(3): 552–559 (July 1981).

This is an exploratory study of the development of the gay-father identity based on in-depth interviews of 18 gay fathers with children ranging in age from two to twenty-five years. Findings indicate that fathers who were homosexually active before marriage could more easily achieve the gay-father identity. Those fathers who became homosexually active after marriage had more difficulty resolving what initially seemed to them to be an unsolvable conflict. In the latter case, serious role conflict and inner turmoil resulted when the fathers had to hide their gay identity from wives and children. (19 references)

354. ———. "Gay Fathers: How and Why They Disclose their Homosexuality to Their Children." *Family Relations* 29: 173–179 (April 1980).

Interviews with eighteen gay Caucasian fathers indicate that many disclose their homosexuality to their children, and this disclosure tended to improve their relationship. However, gay fathers avoided overt expressing of their homosexuality in order to protect their children from the hostility of other persons. Nondisclosure by gay fathers may cause severe psychological distress to the father who wants his children to know about his sexual orientation but fears the consequences of disclosure. (14 references)

355. Fishel, Anne Hopkins. "Gay Parents." *Issues in Health Care of Women* 4(2–3): 139–164 (1983).

This paper reviews research studies and personal accounts about gay parents. More lesbian parents have been given custody of their children than gay male parents. Of primary concern in custody considerations is: exposing the child to stigma, conflict regarding sex-role identity, and suitability of the home environment. Research conclusions do not show that these concerns are justified. Although parent-child relationships are better when parents are honest with their children about their sexual orientation, prevailing social attitudes mandate the need to exercise discretion in employment, housing and with their children's peers. (54 references)

356. Gantz, Joe. *Whose Child Cries: Children of Gay Parents Talk about Their Lives.* Rolling Hills Estate, Calif.: Jalmar, 1983.

The experiences of five homosexual families who are raising children are described. The book is written from the point of view of the children. One common thread in all the homes is the children's isolation from their peers, although most of them had never mentioned to a friend that their parents were gay. Societal attitudes are hurtful. Although role models, to some likely extent, play a part in sexual preference, most homosexuals are from heterosexual homes. (Bibliography)

357. Golombok, S. "Children in Lesbian and Single-Parent Households: Psychosexual and Psychiatric Appraisal." *Journal of Child Psychology and Psychiatry* 24(4): 551–572 (October 1983).

Fifty-four female-headed single parent families, one-half lesbian in sexual orientation, the other half heterosexual, were studied to identify the effects of the mother's sexual orientation on children living with them. Children and mothers were interviewed, and parents and teachers completed questionnaires. Findings show no difference between children reared in a lesbian home and children reared in a heterosexual single-parent home in regard to gender identity, sex role behavior and sexual orientation. Most of the children had been born into a heterosexual household and had spent a minimum of two years there, and most of the children in lesbian families had regular contact with their fathers. In psychological development, and in their emotions, behavior and relationships, children from lesbian and heterosexual homes did not differ. (38 references)

358. Goodman, Bernice. "The Lesbian Mother." *American Journal of Orthopsychiatry* 43(2): 283–284 (March 1973).

This paper focuses on the development of the child and the mother-child relationship with the lesbian mother. Data were drawn from the author's experiences with lesbian mothers in individual and group therapy. Similarities and differences in relationships with male or female children, helping the child understand the mother's lifestyle, children's peer group experiences and the roles of the child's father, grandparents and the mother's lover are addressed. Due to limited data in this area, no definite findings or conclusions are presented. (No references)

359. Green, Richard. "The Best Interests of the Child with a Lesbian Mother." *Bulletin of the American Academy of Psychiatry and the Law* 10(1): 7–15 (1982).

This discussion addresses the issue of whether having one homosexual parent or two homosexual adults in parenting roles increases the probability of a homosexual orientation by the child. The etiology of a homosexual orientation is discussed. The author then describes the factors he considers when asked to evaluate adults and children in custody cases. Results of research conducted on children being raised by lesbian mothers, who were compared with children being raised by divorced heterosexual mothers showed no significant differences for the boys and girls in either group of families. (15 references)

360. ——. "Sexual Identity of 37 Children Raised by Homosexual or Transsexual Parents." *American Journal of Psychiatry* 135(6):692–697 (June 1978).

This article discusses 37 children from a clinical population who are being raised by homosexual or transsexual parents. The subjects, ranging in age from three to twenty years have lived in sexually atypical families for one to sixteen years. Findings suggest that children who are being raised by homosexual or transsexual parents do not differ significantly from children raised in more conventional families. (6 references)

361. Hall, Marny. "Lesbian Families: Cultural and Clinical Issues." *Social Work* 23(5): 380–385 (September 1978).

This article focuses on the issues that confront social workers in their work with lesbian families. A multi-faceted approach, including practioner's own attitude toward lesbians, clinical familiarity with lesbian lifestyles, and a willingness to assume an advocacy role with lesbian clients. Finally, social workers may serve as expert witnesses in custody cases, adoption and foster care placement and as family counselors. (11 references)

362. Harris, Mary B., and Pauline H. Turner. "Gay and Lesbian Parents." *Journal of Homosexuality* 12(2): 101–113 (Winter 1985–1986).

The impact of parents' sexual orientation on their children was studied in 23 male and female homosexuals and 16 heterosexual single parents. Questionnaires used in the investigation were designed to protect the anonymity of participants. Identified as problems by the gay/lesbian parents were finances and disagreement with partners about disciplining children. Relationships with their children were rated good, and most did not encourage sex-typed toys and activities for their own children. Few differences were found between the gay, lesbian and heterosexual parents. Results suggest that being gay is not incompatible with effective parenting. (16 references)

363. Hill, Marjorie Jean. "Effects of Conscious and Unconscious Factors on Child Rearing Attitudes of Lesbian Mothers. Ph.D. diss., Adelphi University, 1981.

For summary see: *Dissertation Abstracts International* 42B(4): 1608.

364. Hoeffer, Beverly. "Children's Acquisition of Sex-Role Behavior in Lesbian-Mother Families." *American Journal of Orthopsychiatry* 51(3): 536–544 (July 1981).

Sex-role traits and behavior of children from lesbian and heterosexual single-mother homes are compared. Twenty lesbian and twenty heterosexual single mothers and their oldest child, ages six to nine, were subjects of the study. Block's Toy Preference Test was administered to children and a modified Fling and Manosevitz's Parental Interview was used to measure mothers' encouragement in toy selection and play activities. There was found to be no significant difference between the two groups of children that could be related to mother's sexual orientation. Boys of both lesbian and heterosexual mothers selected more sex-typed masculine toys, and girls of both groups of mothers selected more sex-typed feminine toys. Findings on sex-role behavior indicated no significant differences between children from the two groups of single-mother families. (8 references)

365. Hotvedt, Mary E., and Jane Barclay Mandel. "Children of Lesbian Mothers." In *Homosexuality: Social, Psychological, and Biological Issues*, Chap 23, edited by William Paul, et al., 275–295. Beverly Hills, Calif.: Sage, 1982.

This chapter focuses on issues related to child custody and research studies on lesbian mothers and their prepubescent children. Findings do not support assumptions that lesbian mothers' children suffer from neglect, unpopularity, confused gender identification, or homosexuality. Implications for court policy in regard to lesbian mothers are discussed. Research on the child's development in a gay father's household is suggested. (Bibliographic citations in text)

366. Hunter, Nan D., and Nancy D. Polikoff. "Custody Rights of Lesbian Mothers: Legal Theory and Litigation Strategy." *Buffalo Law Review* 25(3): 691–733 (Spring 1976).

It is estimated that one out of every ten women in America is a lesbian and 1.5 million are lesbian mothers. The legal standards in custody disputes based on the "best interests of the child" is said to be purposefully vague allowing the trial court great latitude. Since custody decisions are never final, the person who lost custody can later ask the court to reconsider. The lesbian mother who wins custody may later be subject to ligation under the "material change in circumstances." Both lesbian mothers and homosexual fathers may face problems in trying to keep their children. Strategies and tactics for use by attorneys representing lesbian mothers are suggested. (18 references)

367. Kirkpatrick, Martha, et al. "Lesbian Mothers and Their Children: A Comparative Survey." *American Journal of Orthopsychiatry* 51(3): 545–551 (July 1981).

Forty preadolescent children of self-identified lesbian and heterosexual mothers were subjects of a comparative survey reported in this article. Results of a variety of psychological measures indicate that gender development of boys and girls in the study were not identifiably different in the two groups, and the prevalence of disturbance among the children was not found to be related to the mothers' sexual orientation. Similarities between the two groups were quite evident and consistent with findings of previous studies of children from two-parent families. (7 references)

368. Kuba, Sue Anne. "Being-In-A-Lesbian Family: The Preadolescent Child's Experience." Ph.D. diss., California School of Professional Psychology at Fresno, 1981.

For a summary see: *Dissertation Abstracts International* 42B(10): 4196.

369. Lewin, Ellen. "Lesbians and Motherhood: Implications for Child Custody." *Human Organization* 40(1): 6–14 (Spring 1981).

The attitude of the courts in child custody rulings involving lesbian mothers is examined in light of data gathered on 80 lesbian and nonlesbian mothers and their families in the San Francisco Bay area. The courts' reluctance to grant custody to lesbian mothers is generally based on the assumption that it would not be in the best interests of the child. Findings from interviews with subjects in this study indicate that both lesbian and nonlesbian mothers face similar problems and have similar parenting behavior patterns but that lesbian mothers' adaptations as single parents reflect the greater vulnerability of their position. (57 references)

370. Lewis, Karen G. "Children of Lesbians: Their Point of View." *Social Work* 25(3): 198–203 (May 1980).

Twenty-one children, nine to 21 years of age, eight lesbian families, were interviewed for this study. The children learned of their mother's homosexuality when their parents separated. The children were in agreement that their parents' divorce was more traumatic than their mother's disclosure of lesbianism. Young and older children were concerned about reactions of their peers. Family discord prior to divorce made the children less able to deal with new problems. Most them had been in therapy at the time of parental separation or their mothers' disclosure of lesbianism. Implications for mental health professionals are noted. (7 references)

371. Louis, Arlene Joyce. "Homosexual Parent Families: Gay Parents. Partners, and Their Children." Ed.D. diss., Columbia University Teachers College, 1985.

For a summary see: *Dissertation Abstracts International* 46A(9): 2729.

372. Miller, Brian. "Gay Fathers and Their Children." *Family Coordinator* 28(4): 544–552 (October 1979).

This research is based on interviews with 40 gay fathers and 14 of their children. All children in the study had been told about their fathers' homosexuality prior to the interview. Findings indicate that most gay fathers do not have children to compensate for homosexual feelings, they do not sexually abuse their homophobic children, they do not expose their children to harassment, and they do not have a disproportionate number of gay children. (43 references)

373. Norton, Joseph L. "Integrating Gay Issues into Counselor Education." *Counselor Education and Supervision* 21(3): 208–212 (March 1982).

This article discusses ways to reeducate counselors-in-training about gays in order that they will be better prepared to work with their counselees. Among topics discussed are community resources; heterosexual bias in tests; counseling the disabled; and counseling gay couples about child custody problems, and harassment of children. It is suggested that gay issues are appropriate for discussion in any counselor education course. (20 references)

374. Nungesser, Lonnie G. "Theoretical Bases for Research on the Acquisition of Social Sex-Roles by Children of Lesbian Mothers." *Journal of Homosexuality* 5(3): 177–188 (Spring 1980).

This study probes the socialization effects of lesbian mothers on their children. The classification and measurement of sex-typed behaviors are discussed and lesbian lifestyles and values as reported in the literature are reviewed. Theoretical modeling is presented to determine the socialization effects on the children. Suggestions for research are offered. (20 references)

375. Pagelow, Mildred D. "Heterosexual and Lesbian Single Mothers: A Comparison of Problems, Coping and Solutions." *Journal of Homosexuality* 5(3): 189–204 (Spring 1980).

Twenty-three heterosexual single mothers and twenty lesbian mothers were subjects of a study to compare their adaptations to problems of child custody, housing and employment. Participant observation in a variety of discussion groups and group activities, interviews and questionnaires were used to gather data. Although both groups reported problems in the areas of housing, child custody and employment, the lesbian mothers felt their problems were greater. Most lesbian subjects "passed" and were more independent in order to meet their needs. (27 references)

376. Rand, Catherine, et al. "Psychological Health and Factors the Court Seeks to Control in Lesbian Mother Custody Trials." *Journal of Homosexuality* 8(1): 27–39 (Fall 1982).

This study examines the psychological health of 25 self-identified lesbian mothers and the behaviors which the court wishes to control in lesbian-mother custody trials. Three scales from the California Psychological Inventory administered to subjects indicated some support for a positive association between psychological health and disclosure of lesbianism to employer, ex-husband, children and a lesbian community. However no correlation between disclosure to parents and psychological health was found. If the psychological health of parents is a mediating factor in the adjustment of children then results of the study would indicate that the courts are wrong in assuming that the disclosure of her lesbianism by a mother is not in the best interests of her children. (42 references)

377. Rees, Richard Louis. "A Comparison of Children of Lesbian and Single Heterosexual Mothers on Three Measures of Socialization." Ph.D. diss., California School of Professional Psychology at Berkeley, 1979.

For a summary see: *Dissertation Abstracts International* 40B(7): 3418.

378. Rice, Katherine Virginia. "Children Raised by Lesbian

Mothers." Ph.D. diss., University of California, Los
Angeles, 1981.

For a summary see: *Dissertation Abstracts International*
42B(8): 3444.

379. Steinhorn, Audrey. "Lesbian Mothers—The Invisible
      Minority: Role of the Mental Health Worker." *Women
      and Therapy* 1(4): 35–48 (Winter 1982).

      The problems facing lesbian mothers and their children
      from social workers' point of view. Among the problems
      the mother faces are social attitudes toward her lifestyle,
      establishing her suitability as a custodial parent, fear of
      losing custody of her children if she participated in
      enforcing child support and the need for children and
      mother to keep her lifestyle secret from those who may be
      disapproving. The author concludes that institutionalized
      support systems can be developed to help lesbian mothers
      involved in custody litigation. (14 references)

380. Voeller, Bruce, and James Walters. "Gay Fathers." *The
      Family Coordinator* 27(2): 149–157 (April 1978).

      An Executive Director of the National Gay Task Force, a
      gay father of three children, answers questions about gay
      fathers posed by the editor of this journal. Responses
      suggest that: many gay fathers are still married and
      their spouses do not know they are gay; homosexuals are
      screened out when foster care, adoption, or custody and
      visitation in divorce cases are considered; homosexuals
      have a smaller incidence of child molestation than
      heterosexuals; and children of homosexuals are no
      different in their sexual orientation than those in the
      general population. (No references)

III

CHILDREN WHO LACK OR HAVE LOST A PARENT

LACK OF A PARENT THROUGH ILLEGITIMACY OR SINGLE PARENTHOOD

GENERAL WORKS

381. Babb, Susan E. "Analysis of an Analogy: Undocumented Children and Illegitimate Children. (case note)." *University of Illinois Law Review* 3: 697–729 (Summer 1983).

This article reviews the analogy between illegitimate children and undocumented alien children in light of the Supreme Court ruling in the *Pyler v. Doe Decision.* Legislation placing disabilities on groups because of circumstances beyond their control was found to be contrary to the 14th amendment. Consequently state benefits granted to children generally and excluding illegitimate children discriminated against illegitimates. (155 references)

382. Banks, Mildred Linda. "Family Structure and Child
      Development in Anguilla, West Indies." Ph.D. diss.,
      Pennsylvania State University, 1986.

      For a summary see: *Dissertation Abstracts International*
      47B(11): 4671.

383. Barret, Robert L., and Bryan E. Robinson. "A Descriptive
      Study of Teenage Expectant Fathers." *Family Relations*
      31(3): 349–352 (July 1982).

      This study reports results of responses to a questionnaire
      administered to 26 teenage expectant fathers who were
      largely black, about their relationship with the expectant
      mothers and their families. Findings indicated that the
      teenage fathers maintained positive relationships with
      the expectant mothers' families and continued contact
      with expectant mothers. Most of the respondents indicated
      a willingness to participate in counseling and in some
      aspects of the fathering experience including the
      assumption of some financial responsibility for their child.
      Policy implications are noted. (14 references)

384. Bolton, F. G., Jr., and Roy H. Laner. "Children Rearing
      Children: A Study of Reportedly Maltreating Younger
      Adolescents." *Journal of Family Violence* 1(2): 181–196
      (June 1986).

      This study examines the differences in maltreatment of
      children by younger and older adolescent mothers as
      found in a study by the Children Protective Services in
      Maricopa County, Arizona. The mothers under sixteen
      years of age were under greater financial stress, were
      often minorities, and were less likely to be receiving
      economic assistance as compared with mothers aged 16
      to 19 years. Psychotherapy alone was not seen as a tenable
      solution to the problems of the younger group of
      adolescents.

385. Clark, Tobin K. "An Equal Protection Challenge to
      Alabama's Intestacy Scheme as it Affects Illegitimate

Children: Everage v. Gibson." *Alabama Law Review* 31(2): 493–507 (Winter 1980).

The case discussed in the article involves an illegitimate adult child who is considered to be the heir of her mother but not of her father. The Everage Court declared that a judicial determination of paternity legitimizes the child in order that it may inherit from the intestate father's estate in the same way that a legitimate child inherits. However, the paternity action had to be commenced not later than two years after the child's birth. The appellant in Everage did not meet this requirement. (84 references)

386. Crellin, Eileen, et al. *Born Illegitimate: Social and Educational Implications.* England: Windsor, Berks, 1971.

In this longitudinal study of children born out of wedlock in Great Britain over 600 illegitimate children were compared with some 16,000 children all born in the same week in 1965 and 1969. Children born of illegitimate birth had very young mothers, lower birth weight, more unfavorable home environments, and a higher incidence of behavioral and academic problems than legitimate children. Changes are suggested for reducing the disadvantages of children of illegitimate birth. Additional follow-up studies are planned by the National Children's Bureau. (Bibliography)

387. Curry, Randy. "Illegitimate Children-Protecting Their Rights in the Courtroom." *Journal of Juvenile Law* 8(1): 234–236 (Annual 1984).

This article is concerned with recent court decisions relating to burden of proof in paternity actions; who can sue to protect the rights of the illegitimate child, and the effect of criminal prosecution on subsequent civil action relative to the rights of illegitimate children. Following examination of court findings related to these issues, it is suggested that conflicts between protecting illegitimate children and protecting those sued for paternity bears watching by attorneys. (13 references)

388. Cutright, Phillips. "AFDC, Family Allowances and
     Illegitimacy." *Family Planning Perspectives* 2(4): 4–9
     (October 1970).

     Critics often see AFDC programs as providing benefits
     that encourage illegitimate births. Preliminary
     investigation of the relationship between AFDC coverage,
     benefits and illegitimacy rates found no association
     between AFDC benefits and illegitimacy rates. Data
     suggests that illegitimate white children are more likely
     than illegitimate nonwhite children to be on AFDC. No
     connection between AFDC benefit levels and illegitimacy
     rates were found in programs in Canada and other
     developed countries. (3 references)

389. Danvers, G. H. *Duquesne Law Review* 21(2): 529–545
     (Winter 1983) "Constitutional Law—Fourteenth
     Amendment—Equal Protection—illegitimate Children—
     Paternity Suits—the United States Supreme Court has
     Held That a Texas Statute Which Precludes Paternity
     Suits From Being Brought on Behalf of Illegitimate
     Children more Than One Year After Birth Violates the
     Equal Protection Clause of the United States Constitution"
     (case note).

     This article discusses the *Mills v. Habluetzel* case in
     which the Texas Department of Human Resources and
     the mother of a nineteen month old illegitimate child
     sought a declaration of paternity in order to obtain child
     support from the father. The U.S. Supreme Court reversed
     the findings of the Texas courts which held that the
     paternity action was not timely under Texas law. (115
     references)

390. Derrick, Sara M. *Cognitive Performance Among Head
     Start Children from Three Family Types.* Department of
     Home Economics, Bowling Green State University. Bowl-
     ing Green, Ohio. May 1984, 28pp. (ERIC Microfiche
     ED238586)

One hundred and seventeen head start children from unwed mother families, father absent families, and father present families were administered a variety of measures to determine cognitive performance among children from the three family types. Results indicated that children from unwed mother families demonstrated a trend toward lower scores on four measures than did children from the other two family types. Multivariate Analysis of Variance showed no significant difference in cognitive performance on the basis of family structure or sex of children. Scores on all measures were accelerated with chronological age. The need for longitudinal data is noted. (17 references)

391. Durdines, David. "Lois Mae Mills, Appellant v. Dan Habluetzel, U.S. 102 S Ct. 1549 (1982). (Equal Protection to Illegitimate Children) (case note)." *Journal of Juvenile Law* 7(1): 183–185 (Annual 1983).

In this case, the U.S. Supreme Court declared that the Texas Family Code denied equal protection to illegitimate children, and therefore the one-year limitation to establish paternity was not realistic and could only increase the state welfare system load.

392. Dwyer, John M. "Equal Protection for Illegitimate Children Conceived by Artificial Insemination. *San Diego Law Review* 21: 1061–1075 (September-October 1984).

Section five of the Uniform Parentage Act grants to children whose mother was artificially inseminated by a donor the right to a legal father. The donor has no legal-paternal responsibility only if the mother is married and her husband has consented to the insemination. In California, the donor has no legal-paternal responsibility regardless of the mother's marital status. It is suggested that the California Version of the Uniform Parentage Act should be revised. (Bibliographic footnotes)

393. Filinson, R. "Illegitimate Birth and Deprivation: Recent Findings From an Exploratory Study." *Social Science and Medicine* 20(4): 307–314 (1985).

The association between illegitimate birth and deprivation documented in studies from the 1950s is re-examined using data from an exploratory investigation of three cohorts of illegitimate children born in the 1970s. Because the link between illegitimate birth and disadvantage has been complicated by the complex set of birth and interrelationships between birth and illegitimacy, specific demographic characteristics of the illegitimate childbearing population, familial organization preceding and succeeding illegitimate birth and consequences for the illegitimate child and his mother, recent changes in the incidence, demographic patterning and familial configurations of illegitimacy are outlined before living conditions are described. (34 references)

394. Force, Jill L. "Constitutional Law—Tennessee Statute Imposing Two-Year Limitation Period on Paternity and Child Support Actions Brought on Behalf of Illegitimate Children Violates Equal Protection." (case note). *Journal of Family Law* 2: 371–375 (January 1984).

The alleged father sought dismissal of an action by a mother seeking to establish paternity and right to support for her nine-year-old son, on the basis that such action, was barred by the two-year statue of limitations in the state of Tennessee. The mother in turn challenged the constitutionality of the two-year limitation statute on due process and equal protection grounds. This article traces the mother's challenge through the courts. (20 references)

395. Hailey, C. David. "The Inheritance Rights of Illegitimate Children in Georgia: the Role of a Judicial Determination of Paternity." *Georgia Law Review* 16(1): 170–196 (Fall 1981).

The inheritance rights of illegitimate children are reviewed in historical perspective under English common law and in the state of Georgia. In 1980, the *Georgia Code Annotated* section 113–904 was amended to allow inheritance if there has been judicial determination of paternity. Inconsistences between sections of the *Georgia Code Annotated* in regard to inheritance rights of illegitimate children and the implications for custody, adoption, support and paternity are discussed. (151 references)

396. Hamner, Barbara Ann. "Illegitimate Children." *American Journal of Trial Advocacy* 4(2): 478–480 (Fall 1980).

Recent rulings by the U.S. Supreme Court related to the rights of illegitimate children are discussed. The case of *United States v. Clark* involving survivors' benefits under the Civil Service Retirement Act is traced. Court rulings in this and other cases in recent years lean toward equalization of the rights of all natural children. (Bibliographic footnotes)

397. Harris, D. J. "Right to Family Life." Right to the Peaceful Possession of One's Property (Article 1, First Protocol)—Discrimination in the Protection of Each of the Above (Article 14) —Their Application to the Status of Illegitimate Children and Their Parents." (Article 8) *British Yearbook of International Law* 260–264 (Annual 1979).

This article reports the decision of the European Convention on Human Rights in the Marckx case which involved rules of Belgian law discriminating against illegitimate children. It was noted that at the time the Convention was drafted, it was acceptable to distinguish between legitimate and illegitimate families but that the Convention must be interpreted in light of present-day conditions. A bill to bring Belgian law into line with the plenary court decision on the rights of illegitimate children was submitted to the Belgian Senate in 1979. (4 references)

398. Hedden, Ellen M. "Family Law—Support for Illegitimate Children." *Canadian Bar Review* 60(1): 171–179 (March 1982).

Ontario's Children's law reform Act, 1977 recognized all

children, whether born in or out of wedlock, equal in the eyes of the law of the province. The Family Law Reform Act, 1978 removed any statutory limitation periods affecting a child's rights. However, in Re: Bagaric and Juric the declaration of parentage was allowed to proceed, but the application for child support was struck out. This case, which is the focus of the article, is analyzed in relation to interpretation of applicable laws. (31 references)

* Heger, Donna Tubach. "Supportive Services to Single Mothers and Their Children." *Children Today* 6(5): 2–4, 36 (September 1977).

Reported in General Aspect Item No. 73.

399. Isaacson, Scott E. "Equal Protection for Illegitimate Children: A Consistent Rule Emerges." *Brigham Young University Law Review* 142–164 (Fall 1980).

Inconsistency has characterized the approach of the Supreme Court in its decisions related to equal protection of illegitimate children. A review of the cases suggests that the Court weighs competing interests and applies differing degrees of judicial scrutiny in different illegitimacy cases. Where a state statute's primary purpose is to condemn illicit behavior, the statute is strictly scrutinized and is likely to be declared unconstitutional. However, if the statute serves primarily an administrative purpose not associated with moral condemnation of illegitimacy, it is likely to be held constitutional. (124 references)

400. Keller, J. Clarke. "Inheritance Rights of Illegitimate Children in Kentucky: A Need for Reform." *Kentucky Law Journal* 71(3): 665–683 (Summer 1983).

Recent decisions regarding the inheritance rights of illegitimate children and the implications of these decisions are discussed and analyzed. Other states' handling of this issue through statutory provision and case law is examined. Recommendations are made for specific legislation to update Kentucky's law's on inheritance rights of illegitimate children. (111 references)

401. Krause, Harry D. *Illegitimacy: Law and Social Policy.* New York: Bobbs-Merrill, 1971.

The author investigates the current law of illegitimacy, the constitutional right to equality, determination of paternity, attitudes on law and illegitimacy, approaches to illegitimacy in foreign countries and a Uniform Legitimacy Act. It is suggested that the groups hit hardest are the same groups that have traditionally been disadvantaged by the law. Illegitimacy and poverty are said not to necessarily equate with child neglect and dependency. (Bibliographic footnotes)

402. Kreech, Florence. "The Current Role and Services of Agencies for Unwed Parents and Their Children." *Child Welfare* 53(5): 323–328 (May 1974).

Changing times and morales have increased rather than diminished the need for agency services for unmarried pregnant women and unmarried mothers. In the past these agencies were not so much concerned with the mothers as with the placement of their children for adoption. It is suggested that agencies need to assist these mothers in the areas of housing, education, and child care in order to help them become self-supporting, as most mothers keep their children today. Flexibility in meeting the changing needs of unwed mothers and inter-agency cooperation is recommended.

403. Kurz, Brenda Jo. "The Impact of Adolescent Illegitimacy on Academic Achievement: An Analysis Within Racial and Socio-Economic Status Groups." Ph.D. diss., University of North Carolina at Chapel Hill, 1986.

For a summary see: *Dissertation Abstracts International* 47B(5): 1950.

404. "The Legitimate Claims of Illegitimate Children." *Children's Legal Rights Journal* 7(1): 18–19 (August 1982).

The U.S. Supreme Court has increasingly overturned state laws which make distinctions between the rights of legitimate and illegitimate children. Two cases heard by the Court relating to rulings involving Texas one year statute in paternity claims are discussed. When the U.S. Court found the statute to be unconstitutional, the Texas legislature amended the law to increase to four years the time in which paternity claims could be filed. (13 references)

405. Levitan, Barbara. "Unequal Protection for Illegitimate Children and Their Mothers." *New York University Review of Law and Social Change* 9(2): 241–269 (Winter 1980).

The ambiguous findings by the Supreme Court on the constitutional status of illegitimates is discussed in relation to *Califano v. Boles*. Cases that illustrate the Court's inconsistencies in applying the equal protection claims of illegitimates are analyzed. In *Califano v. Boles*, the Court held the unwed mother had not married the deceased wage earner and was not entitled to mothers' insurance benefits under the Social Security Act, thereby denying illegitimate children the right to treatment equal to legitimate children. (238 references)

406. Macqueen, Julie-Ann, ed., *Unmarried Parents and Their Children; Innovative Community Approaches*. 3rd.ed. Edinburgh: Scottish Council for the Unmarried Mother and her Child, 1972.

The book is a reference guide to services for the unmarried mother and her family. It lists places of accommodation for mothers and babies, types of day care available, sources of financial aid, legal aid information, medical services and social service agencies for places in England, Scotland and Wales. (Bibliography)

407. Martin, Robert W. "Legal Rights of the Illegitimate Child." *Military Law Review* 102: 67–76 (Fall 1983).

The illegitimate child's right to support, inheritance and military benefits are among the issues discussed in this article. Historical and constitutional treatment of the child born out of wedlock is briefly outlined. The U.S. Supreme Court has held that a statute that grants enforceable support to legitimate children from their biological fathers violates the constitution if illegitimate children are denied the same right. However, until recently most states did not provide the illegitimate child the right to inherit from its intestate father, even where paternity had been adjudicated by a court. As a result of recent Court decisions, the Army provides a basic allowance for quarters for an illegitimate child, if a court has judicially ordered the father to pay support, or if the father has admitted paternity in writing. (Bibliographic footnotes)

408. ———. "Legal Rights of the Unwed Father." *Military Law Review* 102: 77–84 (Fall 1983).

This article provides an overview of the legal role of unwed fathers in the military in regard to parental rights and obligations. The unwed father generally has no legal obligation to support an illegitimate child until paternity has been established in a judicial proceeding. Generally, to have any chance in adoption proceedings, the father first must have asserted or established his parental role. If a father has been judicially decreed to be the father of a child and judicially ordered to pay child support, or acknowledged paternity in writing, basic allowance for quarters may be granted for the illegitimate child. (Bibliographic footnotes)

409. May, David. "Illegitimacy and Juvenile Court Involvement." *International Journal of Criminology and Penology* 1(3): 227–252 (August 1973).

This paper explores the relationship between illegitimacy and delinquent behavior. Data related to a population of Aberdeen (Scotland) school boys indicates illegitimate boys are more likely than legitimate boys to make a court appearance and to make additional court appearances, and the same thing is true for illegitimate sons born into single-parent families and sons of stable cohabitees. The author notes that the data from the Aberdeen study do not necessarily tell anything about delinquent behavior, only about court appearances. (44 references)

410. Mendel, Elizabeth Ullmer. "Illegitimate Children—Trial Court did not Abuse Discretion by Ordering Illegitimate Child's Name Changed to That of the Father, Despite Mother's Opposition." *Journal of Family Law* 19(4): 773–778 (August 1981).

Indiana Appeals Court orders illegitimate child's name changed to that of the father's in case where the father acknowledges paternity and helps support the child. (23 references)

411. Morrisroe, Patricia. "Mummy Only: the Rise of the Middle-Class Unwed Mother." *New York* 16(8): 22 (June 1983).

The number of planned unwed mothers are increasing, especially in the middle-class and over 30's area. Fertility clinics allow women to avail themselves of artificial insemination. Planned unwed mothers and doctors are interviewed. Dr. John Munder Ross believes that unwed mothers are egocentric and bad for children. Ruth Hamilton is a working unwed mother, with no marital intentions. On the other hand Dr. Martin V. Cohen believes that society will accept the present bad marriage syndrome. When Ann M. had her child through artificial insemination her parents' initial dismay turned to delight. Dr. Cohen believes that a woman's failure to sustain a relationship does not mean that she will be a bad mother. Ellen Robbins believes that her child will not suffer any social disgrace because of her illegitimacy.

412. National Council on Illegitimacy. *Illegitimacy: Changing Services for Changing Times.* New York: National Council on Illegitimacy, 1970.

Seven papers on the unwed mother and her child

presented at the 1969 National Conference on Social Welfare examine and refute some of the stereotypes which have been assumed in popular attitudes toward illegitimacy. More unmarried mothers are keeping their babies and while adoption is a solution for the majority of white mothers, it has been available for only a small number of nonwhite children. It is suggested that the social stigma and legal, social and economic discrimination that society imposes on the unwed mother and her child is a greater determinant of what the outcome will be for them, than the birth status of the child. (Bibliographies)

413. O'Neil, Agnes E. "Illegitimacy in Canada: Bridging the Communication Gap." *Canadian Journal of Public Health* 62(2): 156–158 (March-April 1971).

Between 1961 and 1966, the number of illegitimate births in Canada was highest for teenage mothers. Some programs have been established to enable pregnant young women to continue their education and to make it easier for them to cope in the future. Implications of this high rate of illegitimacy for social policy are discussed. (2 references)

414. Pannor, Reuben, and Byron W. Evans. "The Unmarried Father Revisited." *Journal of School Health* 45(5): 286–291 (May 1975).

Supreme Court decisions have indicated that the unmarried father has rights that cannot be ignored. Adoption agencies must involve the single father in adoption to the extent required by state laws. Suggestions for counselors and social workers who are working with unmarried mothers and fathers are outlined. The welfare of the child should be the primary consideration when options for the child's care are being considered. The rights of the father who wants, and is competent to care for the child should be protected. Interagency cooperation is suggested in cases where the single father resides in a different community. (7 references)

415. Peach, Lucinda J. "Ending Discrimination Against Unwed Fathers and Their Illegitimate Children under the Immigration Laws." *New York University Law Review* 58(1): 146–182 (April 1981).

This article discusses the denial of preferred status for the illegitimate child of an immigrant father in a case where the mother's death occurred. Had the petitioner been the child's mother, preferential status could have been granted. Inadequacies of current interpretations of legitimation requirements under the Immigration and Naturalization Act are explored and suggestions are made for remedies. (144 references)

416. Ramberan, Edith McMillan. "Constitutional Law— New York Statute Requiring Illegitimate Children Who Would Inherit from Their Fathers by Intestate Succession to Provide a Particular Form of Proof of Paternity is not Violative of the Fourteenth Amendment. (case note)." *Howard Law Journal* 21(3): 577–598 (Summer 1980).

This article reports court findings in the case of *Lalli v. Lalli* as it relates to New York estate law that says that an illegitimate child can inherit from his intestate father only if a court has declared paternity during the father's lifetime. The U.S. Supreme Court's ruling in Lalli and related cases are reported. (439 references)

417. Rix, Nancy E. "A Survey of Recent Changes in Intestate Succession Law Affecting Illegitimate Children—the Informally Acknowledged Child is the Ultimate Loser." *Loyola Law Review* 29(2): 323–351 (Spring 1983).

Changes in Louisiana succession law affecting illegitimate children are discussed in relation to findings in significant cases. The new succession statutes and inter-related articles expand the rights of formally acknowledged illegitimates, but deprives informally acknowledged illegitimates of their inheritances. Suggestions are made for ways to remedy discrimination against illegitimates resulting from changes in the statutes. (226 references)

418. Roboz, Paul, and David Pitt. "Illegitimacy and Mental Retardation." *The Australian Journal of Mental Retardation* 2(7): 197–199 (September 1973).

The incidence of illegitimacy varies according to social environment and seems to be greatest where populations live in depressed social conditions. In a institutional group of 1,400 retarded individuals, the rate of illegitimacy was found to be similar to that in the general population. The illegitimate individuals tended to have lower birth rates and a higher incidence of congenital malformations, but a lower incidence of Down's syndrome. The rate was also high in cases of cultural-familial mental retardation. (6 references)

419. Sauber, Mignon, and Eileen M. Corrigan. *The Six-Year Experience of Unwed Mothers as Parents: a Continuing Study of These Mothers and Their Children*. New York: Council of Greater New York, 1970.

In this study of unwed mothers and their children three hundred and twenty-one mothers were interviewed in 1962. Follow-up studies were done 18 months following confinement and again six years later. As the children reached school age 40 percent who had lived with a member of their family now lived alone. Thirty-one percent lived with their husbands and children, and 21 percent continued to live with relatives. Findings indicate that not all unmarried mothers are alike and their children are not all alike. The majority of mothers have very low incomes. The study suggests the need for sex education in the schools, preschool programs that go beyond custodial care, and help with housing. The majority of the mothers and children were found not to be clearly distinguishable from other large groups of mothers and children. (Bibliographic footnotes)

420. Schlesinger, Benjamin. "Australia's Council for the Single Mother and Her Child." *Children Today* 2(4): 26–27, 36 (July-August 1973).

The program of the Australian Council for the Single Mother and Her Child is described. The council aims to provide emotional support for the single mother and encourage continuing education to facilitate self-reliance. It also seeks to influence public policy to the extent that single mothers and their children are treated the same as widows and deserted wives and their children. (No references)

421. Smith, Leo Gerard. "Illegitimate Children—the Illegitimate Children of a Deceased Federal Civil Service Employee are Entitled to Survivors Benefits under the Civil Service Retirement Act." *Journal of Family Law* 19(1): 166–171 (November 1980).

The right of illegitimate children to survivor's benefits under the Civil Services Retirement Act where the employee lived with the children as a family though not at the time of death is discussed in regard to *United States v. Clark.* The Court concluded that the children did not necessarily have to have lived with the deceased at his death in order to receive an annuity. (16 references)

422. Stenger, Robert L. "Expanding Constitutional Rights of Illegitimate Children." *Journal of Family Law* 19(3): 407–444 (May 1981).

Supreme Court action involving statutory classifications related to illegitimacy between 1968 and 1980 are discussed. The author summarizes the results of Court rulings and analyzes the reasoning employed in reaching them. (131 references)

423. Stewart, Timothy L. "Illegitimate Children and Social Security Benefits." *Indiana Law Review* 16(4): 887–910 (Fall 1983).

Illegitimate children still face problems in many areas in which legitimate children do not, including the area of participation in government benefits. The supreme court decisions in Labine, Trimble, and Lalli challenged state intestacy laws that discriminate against illegitimate children where the laws are not carefully tailored to achieve important state interests. The case of *Jones v. Schweiker*, which is the focus of this article, is discussed in detail. This case, which involves denial of surviving children's benefits under the Social Security Act, had not been completely resolved at the time this article was written. (139 references)

424. Tabler, Norman G. "Paternal Rights in the Illegitimate Child: Some Legitimate Complaints on Behalf of the Unwed Father." *Journal of Family Law* 11(2): 231–254 (1971).

The unwed father's legal position as regards his right to visit his child is analyzed. At the time the article was written, only six states had allowed visitation over the objections of the custodial mother. Fathers who refused to pay child support were never granted visitation. The method by which a father may legitimatize his child is not clear in many states. Different rulings in custody disputes emerge based on the legitimacy or illegitimacy of the child. Reasons for strengthening the rights of unwed fathers are presented. (104 references)

425. Teele, James E., and William M. Schmidt. "Illegitimacy and Race." *Milbank Memorial Fund Quarterly* 48(2): 127–144 (April 1970).

Published data show that in the U.S. illegitimate birth for blacks began to taper off in the 1960's, while rates and ratios for whites appear to be increasing. Lack of uniformity in reporting among states, lack of data from nonreporting states, the inclusion of children from consensual marriages, and the exclusion of illegitimate births to married women are cited as factors that present an inaccurate picture of illegitimacy. It is suggested that more accurate data might tell more about the causes of illegitimacy and the amount and type of services needed than do present methods, and might also correct the assumption that illegitimate children are born only to the unmarried and the black. (14 references)

426. Tomic-Trumper, Patricia Del Carmen. "The Care of Unwed Mothers and Illegitimate Children in Toronto, 1867–1920: A Study in Social Administration." Ph.D. diss., University of Toronto (Canada).

For a summary see: *Dissertation Abstracts International* 47A(10): 3891.

427. Urwin, Charlene Ann. "Single Mothers by Choice: Elements in Decision Making." Ph.D. diss., University of Texas at Austin, 1986.

For a summary see: *Dissertation Abstracts International* 47A(5): 1884.

428. Vinovskis, Maris A. *An "Epidemic" of Adolescent Pregnancy?: Some Historical and Policy Considerations.* New York: Oxford University Press, 1987.

An overview of teenage pregnancy from colonial times to the present is provided. The importance attributed to the father's role in child rearing, and his responsibility for the care and support of his children is traced. A series of recommendations for policies address teenage sexuality, care programs for pregnant and adolescent mothers and access to medical and economic assistance to eliminate negative consequences for mothers and children. (Bibliography)

429. Wadsworth, Jane, et al. "Teenage Mothering: Child Development at Five Years." *Journal of Child Psychology and Psychiatry and Allied Disciplines* 25(2): 305–313 (April 1984).

Studies have shown that children of younger mothers suffer more physical, emotional, and intellectual handicaps than other children. A subsample of 1,031 mothers from the British CHES survey, under 20 years of age when their children were born, and their five year old children were subjects of a study of the effects of maternal age on children's development. A variety of measures were used in the investigation. Results suggest that children of teen-age mothers score lower on vocabulary and behavior tests when compared with children of older mothers. Findings also support the assumption that lower maternal age negatively affects children's development through social disadvantage rather than through biological causes. (38 references)

430. Webb, David D. "The Prodigal Father: Intestate Succession of Illegitimate Children in North Carolina under Section 29–19." *North Carolina Law Review* 63(6): 1274–1285 (August 1985).

This article reports the case of In re Estate of *Stern v. Stern* which involved the right of lineal and collateral kin of an illegitimate child's father to inherit from the child's intestate estate when the father failed to acknowledge paternity by statutorily prescribed method in North Carolina. This case is discussed in relation to regard to statutes affecting intestate succession. (74 references)

431. Winter, Robert A., Jr. "Constitutional Law-State Statute Providing Illegitimate Children One-Year Period Commencing at Birth to Establish Paternity and Obtain Support When Legitimate Children are not Similarly Burdened is Deprivation of Equal Protection" (case note). *Journal of Family Law* 21(1): 150–154 (November 1982).

Texas court rulings in the *Mills v. Habluetzel* case are discussed. The U.S. Supreme Court overturned decisions of the state courts by finding that Texas law discriminated against illegitimate children by denying them support which was generally available to legitimate children. (No references)

432. Wolff, Morris H., and Stephen Cirillo. "The Bastard's Cause of Action: A Statutory Cause of Action for

Illegitimate Children." *Journal of Family Law* 19(3): 463–473 (May 1981).

A series of actions by the United States Supreme Court in recent years have resulted in gains for illegitimate children that approximate those of legitimate children in a number of areas such as wrongful death, child support, workman's compensation and some types of inheritance. Cases are cited of the failure of state courts to compensate the illegitimate child for injuries suffered because of the child's status. It is suggested that civil damages suits for illegitimate children have become more important as their numbers of cases have increased and society shares the cost. (40 references)

433. Zingo, Martha T. "Equal Protection for Illegitimate Children: the Supreme Court's Standard for Discrimination." *Antioch Law Journal* 3(13): 59–97 (Spring 1985).

This article examines inconsistencies in the Supreme Court's decisions regarding its equal protection analysis of laws affecting illegitimate children. Through opinions justice presented, legislators can predict with some degree of accuracy whether a law affecting illegitimate children can survive a constitutional challenge. It is suggested that strict scrutiny applied by the Court would provide full predictability to legislators, and more consistently protect the rights of illegitimate children against discrimination. (132 references)

TEMPORARY LOSS OF A PARENT

GENERAL WORKS

434. "Children of Exceptional Parents." edited by Mary Frank. *Journal of Children in Contemporary Society* 15(1): Whole Issue. New York: Hawthorn 1983.

Ten papers by recognized professionals in the fields of child development, social work, social science, medicine, psychology and psychiatry focus on the alcoholic parent, the mentally ill parent, and the incarcerated parent. The impact of parents' problems on family relationships and child rearing patterns are addressed. Intervention to prevent a second generation from having to deal with similar problems is a major concern of professionals who work with exceptional parents. (Bibliographies)

Illness

435. American Psychiatric Associiation. *Crises of Family Disorganization: Programs to Soften Their Impact on Children*, edited by Eleanor Pavenstedt and Viola W. Bernard. New York: Behavioral Publications, 1971.

The papers included in this work are selected works previously presented at a Meeting of the American Psychiatric Association. Three papers address the problems of children of mentally ill parents, three focus on dysfunctional parenting due to unmanageable stress and two papers discuss programs to assist parents. The need for crisis-oriented services and resources for the children and families of the mentally ill is noted. (Bibliographies)

436. Cain, Lillian Pike, and Nancy Staver. "Helping Children Adapt to Parental Illness." *Social Casework* 57(9): 575–580 (November 1976).

This article examines the effect of long-term serious illness of a parent on their children. Data for the study was based on interviews with parents in 25 families and professionals who had been associated with the family members of kidney transplant patients. Parents may help children cope with frequent hospitalization of the ill parent by being able to handle and communicate information about the etiology of the disease and the prognosis following the transplant. Further study is suggested regarding the effect of prior stresses in the family, parental role changes dictated by the illness, and alterations in the relationship with the extended family. (No references)

437. Cohler, Bertram J., et al. "Child-Care Attitudes and Development of Young Children of Mentally Ill and Well Mothers." *Psychological Reports* 46(1): 31–46 (February 1980).

The child-care attitudes of mentally ill mothers and the development of their children is the focus of this study. Data is derived from a long-term study of parent-child relations among mentally ill and well mothers of young children. Mothers were administered several measures and were observed with their child in a test situation. It was found that child-care attitudes are related to the child's cognitive development and to the mother's behavior as observed in the laboratory. Mentally ill mothers seem less involved in their child's performance than well mothers. Intensive home nursing aftercare was provided for the mentally ill mothers of young children. (63 references)

438. Grunebaum, Henry, et al. *Mentally Ill Mothers and Their Children.* Chicago: University of Chicago Press, 1975.

A joint mother-child admission program developed at the Massachusetts Mental Health Center is described. The program provides the mother with the opportunity to resume the care of her child in a protected and therapeutic environment. Case studies illustrate the development of joint admission children. Children of hospitalized mothers in contrast with nonhospitalized mothers, tended to have poorer interpersonal relations but did not experience cognitive impairment. Some non-joint admisson children did more poorly on some aspects of cognitive development, and joint admission children consistently did better, than children of normal nonhospitalized mothers. (Bibliographies)

439. "Impact of Parental Illness on Children." In *Children of Mentally Ill Parents: Problems in Child Care,* edited by Elizabeth P. Rice et al., 70–103. New York: Behavioral Publications, 1971.

Results of three studies on families and the ill parents show that children are involved in the disturbances and disruptions caused in families by the mental illness of a parent more than they are by those associated with tuberculous parents. Children's problems included behavioral difficulties and neurotic traits, some of which were minor and transient and others that were of major or critical proportions. Children with above grade placement in school were those from single parent families. Fewer children from one-parent families had repeated grades than children from two-parent families. Teachers also reported that fewer one-parent children had problems in their home situations, including child-care problems than children in two-parent families. Implications for schools and social workers are noted.

440. Quinton, David, et al. "Institutional Rearing, Parenting Difficulties and Marital Support." *Psychological Medicine* 14(1): 107–124 (February 1984).

In a follow-up study, 94 girls reared in institutions subsequent to failure in parenting were compared with 51 girls in a general population sample. Subjects and their spouses were interviewed and parenting skills in handling control, peer relationships and distress were evaluated. Findings indicated that institution-reared women had a significantly increased rate of psychosocial functioning and parenting problems in adulthood. However, there was evidence that a good marriage relationship with a non-deviant partner and good living conditions mediated effects of institutionalization. (33 references)

441. Rice, Elizabeth P., and Leo Miller. *Children of Mentally Ill Parents: Problems in Child Care.* New York: Behavioral Publications, 1971.

Hospitalization of ill parents causes disruptions in the normal routines of families. Three studies are described. Study I, showed that there are problems for children when a parent is hospitalized for physical or mental illness and that families made little use of health and social agencies. In study II, families of hospitalized patients were referred to community health and social agencies. Study III, was designed to help families prior to hospitalization of the parent. It is suggested that attention should be focused on the whole family situation rather than just on the patient. (Bibliography)

Employment

442. Cohen, Gaynor. "Absentee Husbands in Spiralist Families." *Journal of Marriage and the Family* 39(3): 595–604 (August 1977).

This paper explores the way in which wives cope with the lack of support in rearing children when their husbands are absent due to career pressures. Data is derived from observation, interviews, and records of 42 British families living on a suburban housing estate. The majority of fathers worked in managerial or professional positions in large organizations that required a great deal of mobility. The educational levels of most of the mothers were lower than that of their husbands, and employment opportunities were limited due to the demands of child rearing. Only in relation to formal schooling did the fathers participate in decision-making. The mothers responded to the absence of fathers on a collective rather than an individual basis. This estate subculture offered support to newcomers if they adopted its symbols and unwritten rules. When husbands were forced to move again, the women chose a similar type of housing estate. (36 references)

Military Service

LITERATURE REVIEW

443. "Children." In *Review of Military Family Research and Literature*, 31–36, Arlington, Va.: Military Family Resources Center, 1985.

This section provides an overview of Library holdings in the Military Family Resource Center that relates to children and the impact of military life upon them with full bibliographic information for books, articles and research studies cited in the text is given in the second half of the book.

444. Jensen, Peter S., et al. "The Military Family in Review: Context, Risk, and Prevention." *Journal of the American Academy of Child Psychiatry* 25: 232–234 (March 1986).

Psychosocial dysfunction in military families is explored through a review of the literature. Father absence and geographic mobility are among the specific risk factors discussed. Relatively few families seem to be overtly dysfunctional despite exposure to one or more risk factors. It is suggested that a supportive military network may mediate some of the negative effects of military life. Suggestions for further research are offered. (102 references)

GENERAL WORKS

445. Allen, Harold E. "Schilling Manor: A Survey of a Military Community of Father-Absent Families." Ph.D. diss., University of Michigan, 1972.

For a summary see: *Dissertation Abstracts International* 33A(3): 1229.

446. Bowen, Gary L., and Dennis K. Orthner. "Single Parents

in the U.S. Air Force." *Family Relations* 35(1): 45–52
(January 1986).

This study examines the work, personal, and family
responsibilities of 157 single U.S. Air Force parents. Those
who guestioned the effects of Air Force life on children
frequently cited the family separations and long hours of
work. Single parents also cited changes in relationship
with their children. Children sought more autonomy and
participated more in making decisions. Child care did not
present major problems for most parents. Although most
parents were aware that parent education programs were
available, most parents did not participate and had not
made use of parent support groups. (13 references)

447. Crumley, Frank E., and Ronald Blumenthal. "Children's
     Reactions to the Temporary Loss of the Father." *American
     Journal of Psychiatry* 130(7): 778–782 (July 1973).

     Psychiatric evaluations of 200 children and parents in an
     Army child psychiatric clinic provided data on the effects
     of father loss on the development of children. Subjects in
     the study were between the ages of three and eighteen
     and nearly all had a history of regular separation from
     their fathers. Findings indicated that father absence
     magnified existing deficiencies in father-child
     relationships, aggravated personality problems, and
     affected relationships with the remaining parent and
     others. Military separation was found to result in clinically
     observable reactions in children. Limitations of the study
     are noted. (32 references)

448. Dahl, Barbara B., et al. "Second Generational Effects of
     War-Induced Separations: Comparing the Adjustment of
     Children in Reunited and Non-Reunited Families."
     Military Medicine 14(2): 146–147, 150–151 (1977). (Also
     ERIC Microfiche ED 117629)

     This investigation probes the long-term effects of father
     absence on 105 children whose fathers were reported
     missing in action and 99 children whose fathers were

prisoners during the Vietnam war but returned to their families. Responses to the California Test of Personality indicate that the children whose fathers did not return had poorer personal and social adjustment than those children whose fathers returned. Recommendations are made for future research. (25 references)

449. Frances, Allen, and Leonard Gale. "Family Structure and Treatment in the Military." *Family Process* 12(2): 171–178 (June 1973).

The impact of periodic separations and frequent moves on military families are discussed. Young children may have been seen clinically due to school phobias, inappropriate sphincter control, behavioral disorders and overt depressions. Teenagers may present the usual teenage problems but may be labeled the patient because of parents' intolerance of age-appropriate rebellion. Therapy directed toward a family approach is recommended. (3 references)

450. Grant, Thomas Moore. "Impact of Father Absence on Psychopathology of Military Dependent Children." Ph.D. diss., U.S. International University, 1988.

For a summary see: *Dissertation Abstracts International* 49B(7): 2884.

451. Hillenbrand, Elizabeth D. "Father Absence in Military Families." *Family Coordinator* 25(4): 451–458 (October 1976).

One hundred and twenty-six sixth-grade boys and girls at a school for military dependents were assessed on school achievement, classroom behavior, parental identification and parental dominance. A variety of measures involving parents, teachers and students were used. Results of paternal absence indicate that first born males show increased mathematical ability, while younger brothers exhibit more aggressiveness and dependence, and more verbal ability than quantitative ability. Paternal absence seemed to have less import on girls. Parents believed that father absence was stressful to their children, and lowered their achievement in school, but also noted that the children showed growth in responsibility. Suggestions are made for intervention to modify the effect parental absence and to help them take advantage of this experience as a means of growth. (43 references)

452. Howe, Harriet M. "Children of the Military. New Support to Families Improves Their Lives." *Children Today* 12(3): 12–14, 37 (May-June 1983).

This article focuses on efforts by the military to strengthen the network if family service/support centers being established in each branch of the armed services. Areas of stress on military families include frequent moves and lengthy separations from the service member. Children in these families must adjust to unpredictable changes, including parental absence and frequent shifting of schools. The military is committed to upgrading child care facilities and is also exploring family day care as a supplement to child care centers.

453. Hunter, Edna J., and Stephen D. Nice. "Children of Military Families: A Part and Yet Apart." Chapters of this volume are based upon Papers Presented at the Military Family Research Conference, San Diego, September 1–3, 1977. 175pp. (ERIC Microfiche ED175565)

This volume is a collection of 11 articles that focus on the problems of family life among military personnel with dependent children. Chapter IV explains the effects of the absent parent on Rorschach "T" responses by Gael E. Pierce. John Exner, Jr. (1974) states that his research seemed to indicate that the Rorschach texture "T" response differed from the norm for rejected children or children with an absent parent during the ages from birth to five. The population of the study reported in this Chapter consisted of 52 children (40 males, 12 females) who had been referred to the Guidance Center either by the school or by parents. The children ranged in age from six to seventeen with a mean age of 12.2 years. (135 references)

454. Knowles, Richard K. "A Manual for Ministry with Single-Parent Families in the Air Force." Diss., Western Theological Seminary Theology, 1984.

   Not available through UMI.

455. Lee, Bernard J. "Multidisciplinary Evaluation of Preschool Children and its Demography in a Military Psychiatric Clinic." *Journal of the American Academy of Child Adolescent Psychiatry* 26(3): 313–316 (May 1987).

   This article focuses on methods and results of psychiatric evaluation of preschool children in a military clinic by a multidisciplinary team. Parents usually reported a cluster of symptoms related to problematic behavior. Of 129 children referred by medical services, school, or parents, about 40 percent had developmental disorders and most children needed only brief intervention. The advantages of seeing children in a group setting are described. (3 references)

456. McCubbin, Hamilton I., et al. "Residuals of War: Families of Prisoners of War and Servicemen Missing in Action." *Journal of Social Issues* 31(4): 95–109 (1975).

   This article focuses on the adjustment problems experienced by 215 families of servicemen who were prisoners of war or who were missing in action. Data was gathered through personal, indepth interviews. Results indicated that normal patterns of coping with father-husband absence were disturbed by the indeterminate length of absence when fathers were missing in action or prisoners of war. 69 of 405 children were reported by their mothers as having significant emotional problems due to father absence. (25 references)

457. McCubbin, Hamilton I., et al. "The Prisoner of War and His Children: Evidence for the Origin of Second

Generational Effects of Captivity." *International Journal of Sociology of the Family* 7(1): 25–36 (January-June 1977).

The effect of father absence on the father-child relationship was studied in 42 families of returned prisoners of the Vietnam War. Instruments used in the study included interviews, questionnaires and other military records. The severity of physical abuse suffered by the father as a POW was negatively correlated with his perception of his relationship with his children one year following his release. This finding is discussed in comparison with findings of the Canadian study of concentration camp survivors. Adequate preparation for war induced separation was found to facilitate the father's reintegration. (16 references)

458. Morrison, James. "Rethinking the Military Family Syndrome." *American Journal of Psychiatry* 138(3): 354–357 (March 1981).

Clinical data on 140 military dependents and 374 non-military dependents, one to nineteen years of age, gathered during a six-year period in private practice was examined for military family syndrome and susceptibility to psychiatric disorders in children of servicemen. Personality disorder was equally represented in the two groups, however military dependents were found much less likely to have psychosis. The results of the study indicates that if a military family syndrome exists at all, its effects and causes are less obvious than has been previously stated. (9 references)

459. Peck, Bruce B., and Dianne Schroeder. "Psychotherapy With the Father-Absent Military Family." *Journal of Marriage and Family Counseling* 2(1): 23–30 (January 1976).

Military service tour assignments that exclude dependents mean that mothers must assume full responsibility for the children and household for 18 months or more while the father is absent. Mothers experience difficulty controlling children and children exhibit behavior problems at school. Techniques used by a male-female therapy team in working with mothers and children are described. Strategies discussed were found to be of value in promoting continued growth in the father-absent military family. (8 references)

460. Rienerth, Janice G. "The Impact of Male Absenteeism on the Structure and Organization of the Military Family." Ph.D. diss., Southern Illinois University, 1977.

For a summary see: *Dissertation Abstracts International* 38A(5): 3086.

461. Rosenfield, Jona M., et al. "Sailor Families: the Nature and Effects of One Kind of Father Absence." *Child Welfare* 52(1): 33–44 (January 1973).

The wives and children of ten Israeli seamen's families were interviewed to determine the effect of father absence. The seamen were away from their families from ten days to one year. Among problems that surfaced were behavior problems, academic difficulties, nervousness, fears and depression in children. Comparison of these findings with those of the Norwegian study of sailors' families indicate some similar concerns about children. Questions are raised which have further implications for future research. (23 references)

462. Watanabe, Henry K. "A Survey of Adolescent Military Family Members' Self-Image." *Journal of Youth and Adolescence* 14(2): 99–108 (April 1985).

One hundred and thirty-five adolescents from military families were studied to determine the effect of various stresses on the children's self-image. Results of data based on responses to the Offer Self-Image Questionnaire suggests that the usual demands placed on children in military families do not prevent these children from developing a healthy self-image. The frequency of moves, parental absence and other military experiences, left military children with a psychological profile not unlike that of their nonmilitary counterparts. (10 references)

463. Yeatman, Gentry W. "Paternal Separation and the Military Dependent Child." *Military Medicine* 146:320–322 (May 1981).

Parents of 258 patients being treated at the Pediatric clinic at an army hospital completed a questionnaire assessing the effects of father absence. Responses indicated problems with discipline, phobias, school performance, and self-esteem. Suggestions for future studies are offered. (8 references)

Imprisonment

464. Ash, Peter, and Melvin Guyer. "Involuntary Abandonment: Infants of Imprisoned Parents." *Bulletin of the American Academy of Psychiatry and the Law* 10(2): 103–113 (June 1982).

This article focuses on the plight of children when their parents are imprisoned and the courts exercise their power to terminate parental rights in some situations. A case is used to illustrate the adversarial role a state may assume in disregarding a mother's recommendation for care of her child and terminating parental rights. Research has shown that infants raised in prison nurseries by delinquent minor mothers soon approached family reared infants and surpassed those orphans in a foundling home. The child's need for continuity would suggest that the child remain with the mother in prison for the first two years. Various aspects of the situation involving the imprisoned mother and her child are discussed. (35 references)

465. Balthazar, Mary L., and Ruall J. Cook. "An Analysis of the Factors Related to the Rate of Violent Crimes Committed by Incarcerated Female Delinquents." *Journal*

of Offender Counseling, Services, & Rehabilitation 9(1–2): 103–118 (Fall-Winter 1984).

This study explores the connection between age, educational level, I.Q., family structure, and geographical location with the rate of violent crimes among female juveniles. Sixty-three female students confined at a juvenile institution were subjects of this investigation. No significant relationship between age, educational level, I.Q., family structure, and geographical location and the rate of violent crime committed by juveniles in this institution were found. It is therefore suggested that other factors not considered in this research may have been responsible for the rate of violent crimes. Additional research is recommended. (47 references)

466. Beckerman, Adela. "Incarcerated Mothers and Their Children: The Dilemma of Visitation." *Children and Youth Services Review* 11: 175–183 (1989).

The Adoption Assistance and Child Welfare Act of 1980 (P.L. 96–272) aims to reduce the number of children in foster-care and encourage permanency planning. A mother's incarceration and inability to visit regularly with her children affects permanency planning. Courts and correction institutions are recognizing that incarceration of parents is not necessarily associated with child neglect and abandonment. There are still no clear criteria for determining how long a child of an imprisoned mother should remain in foster-care. Additional policy-directed research is suggested. (37 References)

467. Brislin, Virginia High. "The Effect of Immediate Versus Delayed Separation from Infants on Several Dimensions of Inmate-Mothers' Perception and Enactment of the Maternal Role." Ph.D. diss., University of Kentucky, 1984.

For a summary see: *Dissertation Abstract International* 45B(4): 1317.

468. Cottle, Thomas J. "Angela: A Child Woman." *Social Problems* 23(4): 516–523 (April 1976).

This study reports the reactions of a 12–year old girl during the two years her mother was imprisoned. The child's own words are used to illustrate her feelings of abandonment, loss, anger, love, and threatened self-esteem.

469. DeChillo, Neal, et al. "Children of Psychiatric Patients: Rarely Seen or Heard." *Health and Social Work* 12: 296–302 (Fall 1987).

This study probes the effect of parental mental illness on children as reported in the literature and then looks at the way inpatient psychiatric social workers deal with patients' children. Interviews with inpatient staff and a review of 121 patient charts were used to collect data for the study. Although research reports address the impact of parental psychiatric illness on children, findings indicate that despite the social workers' familiarity with the literature, attention to the needs of patients' children was limited. Clinical and policy implications are discussed.

470. Fritsch, Travis A., and John D. Burkhead. "Behavioral Reactions to Parental Absence Due to Imprisonment." *Family Relations* 30(1): 83–86 (January 1981).

This study examines behavioral reactions in 194 children of 91 inmates based on their responses to a questionnaire. Sex of the absent parent was found to correlate with the type of behavior manifested, absence of the father with "acting-out" behavior and absence of the mother with "acting-in" behavior. The relationship existed regardless of whether parental absence precipitated the problematic behavior or caused an already existing problem to worsen. Parental absence takes on additional meaning depending on whether the child is told the parent is incarcerated or whether more socially acceptable reasons are given to explain the parent's absence. (22 references)

471. Gibbs, Carole. "The Effect of the Imprisonment of Women upon Their Children." *British Journal of Criminology* 11(2): 113–130 (October 1971).

The effect of imprisonment on a woman's family was investigated in 638 women, 223 of whom had dependent children. Interviews completed soon after prison reception were later recorded on the questionnaire, along with data from the prison welfare officer and from other records were used to assess the effect of imprisonment on women's children. Of the women with dependent children, 60 were single, 71 divorced or separated, and four were widowed. Of all children in the sample, only 57 percent were reported as normally living with the mother, 37 percent not normally living with the mother resided with the father, relatives or friends, or were in the care of the local authority. The immediate effect on the children of women going to prison was less than had been suggested in prior studies of the Home Office Census. (5 references)

472. Hairston, Creasie Finney, and Patricia W. Lockett. "Parents in Prison: New Directions for Social Services." *Social Work* 32: 162–164 (March-April 1987).

Parent-child relationships are weakened when one-parent is imprisoned. This article describes a program designed to help inmates strengthen family relationships. It was developed with the approval of the Tennessee Department of Correction and is operating successfully. Home study courses, structured classroom courses, special event rap sessions, and special projects comprise the major components of the program. Parents in Prison has received local, state and national recognition. (12 references)

473. Hannon, Ginger, et al. "Incarceration in the Family: Adjustment to Change." *Family Therapy: The Journal of California Graduate School of Marital and Family Therapy.* 11(3):253–260(1984).

The effects of incarceration on spouses, children and siblings are discussed. Families of prisoners are faced with major adjustments. Among the things they must cope with are finances, embarrassment, separation and geographical problems with visitation. Many children are

often left in ignorance about the the real reason for the
parent's absence. Imprisoned mothers have the additional
problem of child care during their absence. Often children
are not told the truth about the parent's absence and
many may exhibit acting-out behaviors. It is suggested
that family therapy would be helpful to the family. (19
references)

474.　Henriques, Zelma Weston. *Imprisoned Mothers and Their
Children: A Descriptive and Analytical Study.* Washington,
D.C.: University Press of America, 1982.

As more women are being imprisoned for the commission
of serious crimes, a substantial number of children are
being deprived of parental care and may be subject to
neglect and abuse. Data for this study were obtained
through interviews with mothers, children, guardians,
foster care workers, institutional and agency personnel.
Children of incarcerated mothers were young, had little
contact with their fathers. Many were supported by public
assistance. Imprisoned mothers preferred child care by
relatives and viewed foster care negatively. Implications
for social policies are discussed. (Bibliography)

475.　Koban, Linda Abram. "Parents in Prison: A Comparative
Analysis of the Effects of Incarceration on the Families of
Men and Women." *Research in Law, Deviance and Social
Control* 5: 171–183 (1983).

Structured interviews were conducted with 70 female
and 62 male prisoners in Kentucky institutions to compare
the effects of family disruption on these prisoners and
their children Findings showed that: Women prisoners
were more likely to have children, these children lived
equally with extended family, fathers or foster homes,
and women were more concerned about their children
and had greater expectations of eventual reunion with
them. In general, women prisoners and their children
suffer more negative effects than male prisoners. (11
references)

476. Lowenstein, Ariela. "Temporary Single Parenthood—the Case of Prisoners' Families." *Family Relations* 35(1): 79–85 (January 1986).

This study examines the adjustment problems of children whose fathers were in prison. The sample consisted of 118 married mothers whose Jewish husbands were imprisoned for the first time and were sentenced from 13 months to life. Inmates and wives were interviewed and family systems functioning measured by the Family Resource Inventory and Coping with Separation Inventory. The criterion variable was the children's adjustment as perceived by the mother and measured by Children's Adjustment Inventory. In about 40 percent of the families children experienced emotional and interactional problems, and behavioral problems in about 20 percent of the families. Imprisonment of the father disrupts family functioning and changes its status to that of a single parent family. (70 references)

477. McGowan, Brenda G., and Karen L. Blumenthal. *Why Punish the Children? A Study of Children of Women Prisoners.* Hackensack, N.J.: National Council on Crime and Delinquency, 1978.

Female arrest rates have increased sharply. 70 percent of these women have children about two-thirds of whom are under the age of ten and nearly one-half of these are black. The authors surveyed 71 institutions and interviewed 65 women at a New York correctional facility. Based on this data plus interviews with children and professionals in child welfare and criminal justice, it was evident that the children of prisoners are neglected. The story of what can happen to a child whose mother is imprisoned has implications for public policy. (Bibliography)

478. Moerk, Ernst L. "Like Father Like Son: Imprisonment of Fathers and the Psychological Adjustment of Sons." *Journal of Youth and Adolescence* 2(4): 303–312 (December 1973).

Twenty-four sons of imprisoned fathers were compared with an equal number of children from divorced families to determine the effects of imprisonment of a parent on the personal and social development of their children. The ages of subjects were between 11.5 and 20 years and father absence had occurred between the ages of six months and fifteen years. Results of several measures used in the study indicated no significant differences between children of imprisoned fathers and children of divorced families. However, profiles of children of imprisoned fathers were more like those of juvenile delinquents and less like those of the norm group than profiles of children from divorced families. (21 references)

479. Pueschel, Jane, and Moglia Ronald. "The Effect of Penal Environment on Familial Relationships." *Family Coordinator* 26: 373–375 (October 1977).

The effects of imprisonment on the prisoner, the family and society are examined through a review of the literature. Prison locations discourage family interaction, and imprisonment itself carries a social stigma that is difficult to erase, especially if there are children. Juvenile delinquency or school dropouts may be a consequence of a lowered socio-economic level that results from father absence. Imprisonment of mothers often results in separation of siblings. Conjugal visits, furloughs, family visiting, and temporary release are viewed as ways to lessen the harmful effects of incarceration. (11 references)

480. Rosenkrantz, Louise, and Virdia Joshua. "Children of Incarcerated Parents: A Hidden Population." *Children Today* (11): 2–6 (January-February 1982).

This article describes a parent-child visitation program, Prison MATCH, that is concerned with the needs of children whose parents are incarcerated in the Federal Correctional Institution at Pleasanton, California. Cases are cited that illustrate how the program works, and its effect on prisoners and their children. A videotape, *Prison*

MATCH: Prison Mothers and Their Children was made by inmate staff members and received a very favorable response. Inmates and prison staff in many states have also made inquiries about the program. (No references)

481. Rubin, Nancy. "Women behind Bars." *McCall's* 114(11): 36–42 (August 1987).

In reviewing the female prison population, the author estimates that 70 percent are mothers, many of whom are single parents. Increasingly their children are placed in foster homes and the parent's custodial rights are placed in jeopardy because of the mother's incarceration. Foster parent-foster child bond may sometimes prevent the foster parent from helping the child reunite with the biological parent following release from prison. Geographic and economic conditions combine to further keep children and mothers separated while the mother is incarcerated. Programs to facilitate mother-child relationships at women's prisons are discussed.

482. Sack, William H. "Children of Imprisoned Fathers." *Psychiatry* 40(2): 163–174 (May 1977).

The effects of their fathers' imprisonment on 24 children from six lower-middle class white families observed over a two-year period are discussed. Clinical observations indicated that for families where imprisonment resulted in divorce, the children in those families were the most disturbed. Children where the marriages remained intact did not exhibit an antisocial element initially, nor did they show worse effects later. Future directions for research are presented. (24 references)

483. Sack, William H., and Jack Seidler. "Should Children Visit Their Parents in Prison?" *Law and Human Behavior* 2(3): 261–266 (1978).

Twenty-two children, five to fifteen years, were interviewed during a visit to see their imprisoned fathers. Findings suggest that children were also found to experience inner conflict over the cause of the imprisonment and separation. Further study of the question of children visiting their incarcerated parents is recommended. (9 references)

484. Sack, William H., et al. "The Children of Imprisoned Parents: A Psychological Exploration." *American Journal of Orthopsychiatry* 46(4): 618–627 (October 1976).

Reactions of 73 children from 31 families with one imprisoned parent were examined in this study. Responses to apprehension and trial of the parent, explanation for the arrest and visitation with the parent are discussed. Temporary behavioral symptoms and antisocial behavior of a few pubertal children are among the effects of stigma and psychological trauma. Suggestions for clinical intervention, short-term counseling and inclusion of the family in rehabilitation are also offered. (18 references)

485. Sametz, Lynn. "Children of Incarcerated Women." *Social Work* 25(4): 298–303 (July 1980).

Prison reforms are proposed that are designed to foster the relationship between incarcerated women and their children. The parental role of the incarcerated mothers, statutory standards of parental unfitness, and protection of the child's best interests are explored. It is concluded that mothers need to be aware of their rights and be provided with parenting techniques. During imprisonment mothers should be allowed to keep infants with them, or the children should be placed in a nurturing environment and frequent and meaningful contact with mothers. Post imprisonment rehabilitation should enable the mothers to function as effective and appropriate parents. (19 references)

486. Savage, James, Jr., et al. *Imprisonment and Child Socialization: A Research Project Executive Summary.* Washington, D.C., Department of Psychology and School of Social Work, 1978. 57pp. (ERIC Microfiche ED200319)

This is the final report and summary of four studies on

the impact of parental absence on the socialization of black children. Five categories of absent-parent families studied included absence due to divorce, death, desertion, separation, and incarceration. Findings showed differences in two major areas: 1) socio-psychological variables affecting parent absent families, and 2) the impact of various social systems and their interaction with families. (12 references)

487. Schiff, Sari S. "The Preschool in Prison Project: OMEP Canada." *Early Child Development and Care* 27(4): 525–532 (1987).

The Preschool in Prison Project focuses on the issue of parental incarceration and its effects on children. The program offers a course in parenting and a child centered space where children can play during visitation. Positive reactions of inmates, wives, and correctional personnel indicate that the project has been successful and it has been replicated in other institutions. (4 references)

488. Schneller, Donald P. "Prison Families: A Study of Some Social and Psychological Effects of Incarceration on the Families of Negro Prisoners." *Criminology* 12(4): 402–412 (1975).

This study examines the effects of imprisonment on 93 families of inmates. A Likert-type scale was constructed to measure the various types of family changes. Findings indicate emotional-sexual change and financial change as problematic for a majority of families. Other negative changes reported included housing, child care, child discipline problems, and various emotional problems experienced by children. (6 references)

489. Showalter, David, and Charlotte Williams Jones. "Marital and Family Counseling in Prisons." *Social Work* 25(3): 224–228 (May 1980).

A marital workshop conducted at the Kansas State Penitentiary for inmates and their wives is described.

Family relationships tend to deteriorate the longer the spouse/father is in prison. Children of inmates may not know where the father is and stories may have been invented to cover up the fact that the father is in prison. The child may experience feelings of rejection, fear and guilt. The authors advocate marital and family counseling within all penitentiaries. (11 references)

490. Stanton, Ann M. *When Mothers Go to Jail*. Lexington, Mass.: Lexington Books, 1980.

The experience of children whose mothers are incarcerated or on probation is the focus of this research. Subjects included seventy-five mothers and their children who were interviewed by the investigators. The mothers' imprisonment did not appear to change their children's school behavior patterns. Mothers' socioeconomic status and prior criminal record had a greater influence on their children's academic preformance than the fact the mother was in jail. Implications for social policies and research are discussed. (Bibliography)

LOSS OF A PARENT THROUGH DIVORCE, SEPARATION, OR DESERTION

BIBLIOGRAPHIES AND LITERATURE REVIEW

491. Ambert, Anne-Marie. "Custodial Parents: Review and a Longitudinal Study." In B. Schlesinger *The One-Parent Family in the 1980's: Perspectives and Annotated Bibliography 1978–1984*. 13–34. Toronto: University of Toronto Press, 1984.

This study explores the long-term effects of divorce on the behavior of parents and children. Twenty custodial mothers and seven custodial fathers were interviewed first from 1978–1980 and again in 1981. Follow-up results showed parents' satisfaction with their children had increased. However, parental satisfaction in these divorced family units occurred strictly in families enjoying a decent standard of living. Custodial mothers experience more difficulties than fathers, although this female disadvantage decreases over time. Both fathers and children view their situation as one that children should be thankful to their fathers. (85 references)

492. Baker, Adrian J. *Divorce and One-Parent Family Counseling.* School of Education, The University of Michigan, Ann Arbor, 1978. 55pp. (ERIC Microfiche ED165083)

These documents represent a computer search of the ERIC database covering the period of November, 1966–1978. It is designed to assist anyone involved in counseling children of divorced parents. Additionally description of exemplary programs and services for persons affected by divorce are provided. (29 references)

493. Bilge, Barbara, and Gladis Kaufman. "Children of Divorce and One-Parent Families: Cross-Cultural Perspectives." *Family Relations* 32(1): 59–71 (January 1983).

Ethnographic and theoretical literature is reviewed to determine the influence of family structure, marital relations, divorce rates, support systems, and social inequity upon the well-being of children in a representative sample of societies of different degrees of socio-cultural complexity. African, Eskimo, Indian, and American societies are compared. The single-parent family occurs in many societies. The conjugal bond can be broken with no adverse effects on children when there are strong personalized support systems. No single family form produces an optimal milieu for a growing child. All who raise children in our society should have adequate material resources and emotional support. (78 references)

494. Bloom, Bernard L., et al. "Marital Disruption as a Stressor: A Review and Analysis." *Psychological Bulletin* 85(4): 867–894 (July 1978).

Research studies linking marital dissolution with various forms of physical and emotional disorders are reviewed. Most of the literature on problems associated with marital disruption focuses on women, who for the most part have physical custody of any children from their marriage, remarry less often than men, and have more problems related to finances. Remedial programs for treating the stresses of marital disruption are reported and evaluated. The need for cross-national research is noted. (174 references)

495. Bloom-Feshbach, Jonathan. "Impact of Marital Dissolution." In *Psychology of Separation and Loss: Perspectives on Development, Life Transitions, and Clinical Practice.* 316–344, San Francisco: Jossey-Bass, 1987.

Presents an overview of current knowledge on the impact of marital separation and divorce on the mental health of children and adults. Differences between the effects of this type of loss from those of other losses are discussed. As divorced parents usually continue to have some contact with each other, the extent to which it is conflict-ridden can determine the degree to which it affects the mental health and adjustment of children and adults. (43 references)

496. Camara, Kathleen A., et al. "Impact of Separation and Divorce on Youths and Families." In *Environmental Variables and the Prevention of Mental Illness,* edited by Paul M. Insel. 69–136, Lexington, Mass.: Lexington Books, 1980.

Research on the impact of divorce and separation on children is reviewed. In general findings show that more minority children than white children are affected by divorce. Factors that influence children's experience with parental divorce are: 1) conflict related to the decision to divorce, 2) loss of a parent or change in relationship with parents and 3) the impact of divorce on the custodial parent and on subsequent parenting behaviors. The age and sex of the children are important in assessing the effects of divorce and in designing appropriate intervention strategies to assist children and youth in coping with separation and divorce. Interventions should aim to improve parenting skills and assist in the resolution of divorce related issues. (184 references)

497. Cantor, Dorothy W. "The Psychologist as Child Advocate with Divorcing Families." *Journal of Divorce* 6(1–2): 77–86 (Fall-Winter 1982).

A state of the art review proposal that the psychologist serve as advocate with divorcing families to reduce stress on children is presented. Indirect and direct ways that the psychologist can work with parents, school personnel and attorneys to help children are suggested. The Family Educational Rights and Privacy Act of 1974 is discussed in context with divorce. Psychologists have a responsibility to educate the legal community about the impact of divorce on children and the impact of custody decisions in particular. It is concluded that children of divorce need an advocate. (13 references)

498. Derdeyn, Andre P. "Child Custody Consultation." *American Journal of Orthopsychiatry* 54(2): 199–209 (October 1984).

The decision-making process in child custody and the limited extent that the needs of the child influences the custody outcome is discussed. A conflicting parent-oriented testimony may not represent the best interests of the child. The author suggests that clinicians can best serve children by acting as consultants for the court rather than the parents. (36 references)

499. Emery, Robert E. "Interparental Conflict and the Children of Discord and Divorce." *Psychological Bulletin* 92(2): 310–330 (September 1982).

Research on the relation between turmoil and behavior

problems in children are reviewed. Type of marital discord, child's behavioral response, sex differences, age effects, parental buffering, and effects of parental psychopathology are outlined. Marital and child problems are interactive. Parents involved in conflict are probably poorer models, more inconsistent in their discipline, and place more stress on their children's involvement in parental conflict. Suggestions are made for future research. (97 references)

500. Fine, Stuart. "Children in Divorce, Custody and Access Situations: An Update." *Journal of Child Psychology and Psychiatry and Allied Discipline* 21(5): 361–364 (1987).

Provided here are annotations of recent papers on divorce related issues that affect children. The literature is grouped according to: 1) prevalence of family disruption, 2) effects of marital breakdown and 3) counteracting detrimental effects. (22 references)

501. Hausslein, Evelyn B. *Children and Divorce: An Annotated Bibliography and Guide.* New York: Garland, 1983.

Articles and books from various disciplines are cited in an effort to provide information on children in relation to divorce for the benefit of lay persons and professionals who must work with them in some capacity. Appropriateness of each book and article for use by teachers, mental health professionals, lawyers, and medical specialists is noted. Lists of organizational resources and audiovisual materials which may be helpful in work with divorcing, and separated families are also included.

502. Hetherington, E. Mavis. "Divorce: A Child's Perspective." *American Psychologist* 34(10): 851–858 (October 1979).

An overview of the divorce process and its potential impact on children is presented. Children vary in their response to divorce according to their individual temperament, sex, developmental status, and past experiences. Changes following divorce, such as economic status, relationship with custodial and noncustodial parents have the potential for cumulating stress. More study of support systems for children is suggested rather than confining the research focus to parent-child relations and the need of divorced parents. Knowledge of support systems that aid the emotional, intellectual and social development of children could help single parent families cope with the changes and stress of divorce. (36 references)

503. Hozman, Thomas L., and Donald J. Froland. "Families in Divorce: A Proposed Model for Counseling the Children." *The Family Coordinator* 25(3): 271–276 (July 1976).

A model designed to facilitate the counseling of preadolescent children whose families are divorcing is presented. Based on the Kubler-Ross concept of loss (1969) the proposed model describes techniques to help the child work through feelings experienced during each step of the divorce process. Although clinical experience shows that not all children respond to divorce in exactly the same way, the model prepares the counselor to deal with those responses that may surface in children. (12 references)

504. Hurley, E. C., et al. "Therapeutic Interventions for Children of Divorce." *Family Therapy* 11(3): 261–268 (1984).

This study presents therapeutic models that have been used with children of divorced parents. The psychodynamic, family therapy and support group models are reviewed in context with findings reported in recent literature. Suggestions are made for future directions in therapy and research. (31 references)

505. Jacobs, John W. "Divorce and Child Custody Resolution: Conflicting Legal and Psychological Paradigms." *American Journal of Psychiatry* 43(2): 192–197 (February 1986).

The competitive theories and models for the resolution of child custody conflict in divorce are reported to be of special concern to legal and mental health professionals. The mediation system that favors joint custody in which both parents continue to play a role in the development of the children and the traditional adversarial system in which child custody and living arrangements favor one parent over the other, are both discussed. It is suggested that a greater synthesis of these systems would provide more options to parents and more stability and security for the developing child. (47 references)

506. Jenkins, Richard L. "Maxims in Child Custody Cases." *Family Coordinator* 26(4): 385–389 (October 1977).

A mental health professional proposes six maxims that have evolved from his experience as an expert witness in child custody cases. Each maxim is related to situations that are encountered frequently in disputed custody and sample cases are presented to illustrate the application. Aspects of custody covered include: dividing or transplanting the child, length of visitation and input from children in custody determination. Advice offered to professionals relates to working on neutral ground, the interests of children in custody recommendations and parental agreements made under pressure. The need for research that evaluates the outcome of cases in which custody decisions were made is suggested. (7 references)

507. Kanoy, Korrel W., and Jo Lynn Cunningham. "Consensus or Confusion in Research on Children and Divorce: Conceptual and Methodological Issues." *Journal of Divorce* 7(4):45–71 (Summer 1984).

Findings in the literature on children and divorce present a confusing picture. The conceptual and methodological features of 18 studies were compared. The studies were selected by using a multistage sampling technique. It was found that both conceptual and methodological issues appear to account for discrepancies in the literature. Future researchers are cautioned to be aware of how conceptual and methodological features of their work will affect their outcomes. (28 references)

508. Gladis, and Barbara Bilge. "Children of Divorce and One-Parent Families: Cross-Cultural Perspectives." *Family Relations* 32(1):59–71 (January 1983).

Examines cross-cultural data on one-parent families headed by females in diverse societies. It was found that overall one-parent families are neither pathological nor inferior and the children in such families often do not suffer from economic or psychological deprivation. The well being of the single-parent household depends upon the availability of sufficient material resources, supportive social networks and the attitudes of cultural groups toward it. It is not the family form, but the support system and the method of socialization that have the greatest impact on children. (71 references)

509. Keshet, Harry Finkelstein, and Kristine M. Rosenthal. "Fathering after Marital Separation." *Social Work* 23(1): 11–18 (January 1978).

Fathers who chose to participate in the rearing of their children following separation or divorce were the subjects of this study. A total of 128 men with children seven years or younger were interviewed and completed a questionnaire during the first two years following the breakup of their marriage. Following an initial period of adjustment, the care of their children did not pose a problem for most men. They tended to focus on spending time with their children in structured activities that lessened the direct interaction between them and was more similar to what they did before separation occurred. The demands placed on divorced fathers can be important in their own growth. (3 references)

510. Lamb, Michael E. "The Effects of Divorce on Children's Personality Development." *Journal of Divorce* 1(2): 163–172 (Winter 1977).

This article reviews the research of developmental psychologists in order to identify significant factors that might have value for child custody decisions. The effects of the absence of fathers and mothers on sons and daughters are examined separately. It was found that children of divorced parents are at greater psychological risk than children from intact families. However, there are no specific sequel that can be identified as the inevitable consequences of family dissolution. Implications for counselors are discussed. (58 references)

511. Levitin, Teresa E. "Children of Divorce." *Journal of Social Issues* 35(4): WHOLE ISSUE (Fall 1979).

This special issue of the journal contains ten articles on the impact of divorce on children. Among the topics examined are the outcomes and long-term effects of divorce on children, the relationship between family structure and family processes, and types of services to help children and their families. The implications of current research and areas in which further study is needed are discussed. (Bibliographies)

512. Lowery, Carol R. "Child Custody Evaluations: Criteria and Clinical Implications." *Journal of Clinical Child Psychology* 14(1): 35–41 (Spring 1985).

This study examines the views of 100 clinical and counseling psychologists and 100 social workers in regard to the relative importance of various criteria in determining child custody in divorce. Considerable agreement was found between the two professions in emphasis on the relationships among the family members and the richness of the social environment in the prospective custodial home. Research demonstrating a relationship between specific variables and children's post divorce adjustment is discussed along with clinician's opinions. Additional research is recommended to determine the adequacy of standards endorsed by clinicians and whether those standards are predictive of children's subsequent adjustment when used in custody determination. (40 references)

513. Lowery, Carol R., and Shirley A. Settle. "Effects of Divorce on Children: Differential Impact of Custody and Visitation Patterns." *Family Relations* 34(4): 455–463 (October 1985).

This paper reviews research literature on children's experience of the restructuring of the family following divorce. Recurrent findings are noted and discussed. The effects of divorce are organized according to differences observed as a function of the child's age, gender, parental conflict, post-divorce family stability, and parent-child relationships. Custody arrangements and visitation patterns that mediate the effects of divorce are identified. (62 references)

514. Luepnitz, Deborah A. "Children of Divorce: A Review of Psychological Literature." *Law and Human Behavior* 2(2): 167–179 (1978).

This paper examines popular myths about one-parent children in contrast with the findings of the best research on this topic. Among the myths about children from divorced families is the assumption that they are more prone to be delinquent, sexually maladjusted, underachievers, and emotionally unstable. A review of the literature indicates that many children do have problems at the time of divorce, and that the symptoms manifested are related to the child's developmental stage. Research data suggests that children are not so much distressed by life in a one-parent home as they are by the level of parental conflict. This does not mean that children of divorce should not be considered at risk. It does mean that lawyers, clinicians, and social workers need to impress on their clients the extent to which children react negatively to family discord. (58 references)

515. Magrab, Phyllis R. "For the Sake of the Children: Review of the Psychological Effects of Divorce." *Journal of Divorce* 1(3): 233–244 (Spring 1978).

The psychological effects of divorce and separation on children are studied through a review of the literature.

The traumatic effects of divorce on children are directly related to how they perceive their home life prior to the divorce. A developmental approach to understanding and providing for the needs of children of divorce is viewed as essential and these needs from infancy to adolescence are discussed. With rapidly increasing divorce rates a policy, programing and support system needs to be developed for children so that the effects of divorce need not be lasting. (30 references)

516. Musetto, Andrew P. "Evaluating Families with Custody or Visitation Problems." *Journal of Marriage and Family Counseling* 4(4): 59–65 (October 1978).

It is more common today for the courts to enlist the help of mental health professionals in family custody disputes. The relationship between the family professional and the court is critical in helping parents to resolve conflicts and arrive at a solution to the problem of custody. Children need to be reassured of consistent parenting regardless of which parent gets custody. The goal of the interview is not to resolve mental problems but to arrive at custody and visitation arrangements that are least detrimental to children and parents. The psychological parent is defined as the one who wants the child, can care for its needs, and recognizes the need to continue positive contact with the noncustodial parent. Guidelines for evaluating and intervening in custody/visitation by the mental health professional are offered. (5 references)

517. Nelson, Geoffrey. "Family Adaptation Following Marital Separation/Divorce: A Literature Review." In *One-Parent Family in the 1980's: Perspectives and Annotated Bibliography 1978–1984*, edited by B. Schlesinger, 97–151. Toronto: University of Toronto Press, 1985.

Research on the impact of marital separation/divorce on the family is reviewed. Adults, children and families experience short term adaptation problems following separation and divorce. Advances in preventive intervention to promote growth and to prevent adverse effects of separation/divorce are noted. Major issues and findings are highlighted, and recommendations are made regarding areas in which further research is needed. Much of the research on separation/divorce focuses on the negative aspects of adaptation and ignores crisis theorists who say that successful mastery of life crises can have growth producing effects. Both positive and negative life changes experienced by adults and children need to be examined.

518. Randall, Kay L. "Separation and Divorce: Annotated Bibliography of Selected Literature for Children and Teens, Also Recommended Reading for Parents." June 1981, 41–48. Parents Without Partners, Inc., Washington, D.C. 1977. (ERIC Microfiche ED143901)

Reading about the experiences of others who have experienced divorce and adjustment to stepparents can be helpful to children undergoing similar experiences. This annotated bibliography was prepared by the *Parents Without Partners* (PWP) Information Center and a representative of the American Library Association Committee on Liaison with National Organizations Serving the Child. Books for children, young adults and parents have been included.

519. Rasmussen, Janis Carol. "The Custodial Parent-Child Relationship as a Mediating Factor in the Effects of Divorce on Children." Research paper for Doctor of Psychology degree, Biola University, California, 1987, 53pp. (ERIC Microfiche ED284146)

This paper explores the ways that the psychological structure and family process variables affect post-divorce functioning in the single-parent family. A search of 25 years of literature dealing with the post-divorce custodial parent-child relationship showed that the following factors influence the effects of divorce on children: 1) parent-child demographics, 2) personal characteristics of the parent, 3) relationship of the parent and the child and 4) use of support networks. Implications for single parents are noted.

520. Rohrlich, John A., et al. "The Effects of Divorce: A Research Review with A Developmental Perspective." *Journal of Clinical Child Psychology* 6(2): 155–21 (Summer 1977).

Research on the effects of divorce on children at different ages is reviewed. Studies show that the consequences of parental loss during infancy, preschool, elementary school and adolescence affect children in different ways at each developmental period. Suggestions for ways to help children cope with parental divorce and new family configurations are offered. (23 references)

521. Santrock, John W. "The Effects of Divorce on Adolescents: Needed Research Perspectives." *Family Therapy* 14(2): 147–159 (1987).

Research literature on the effects of divorce on children is reviewed from a historical perspective and several studies that address the effects of divorce on adolescents are included in this review. The author suggests that the areas in greatest need of research are father custody and joint custody. Methodological problems in earlier studies of divorce are noted. (36 references)

522. Santrock, John W., and Terry D. Madison. "Three Research Traditions in the Study of Adolescents in Divorced Families: Quasi-Experimental, Developmental, Clinical and Family Sociological." *Journal of Early Adolescence* 5(1): 115–128 (Spring 1985).

A selective and critical review of research on adolescents in divorced families from the sociological perspective, from the clinical research of mental health professionals, and research housed in developmental psychology. Information is provided about how each of the research traditions handles sampling, a control group, measures, amount of time spent with subjects, degree of interest in the adolescent's developmental status investigation of demographic variables, and statistical analysis. Discusses ways that sociologists, mental health professional and developmental psychologists might learn and benefit from the other research traditions. Recommends stronger research effort aimed at a better understanding of the effects of divorce on adolescents. (51 references)

523. Sell, Kenneth D. *Divorce in the 70's: A Subject Bibliography.* Phoenix, Arizona: Oryx, 1981.

This bibliography contains 4,760 entries of material published in the United States on divorce or divorce related topics. Some of the areas covered include child custody, child support, children of divorce, father absence, and one-parent families. There is a chapter devoted to nonprint materials on divorce. Author, subject, and geographic indexes are appended.

524. Sorosky, Arthur D. "The Psychological Effects of Divorce on Adolescents." *Adolescence* 12(45): 123–136 (Spring 1977).

The psychological effects of divorce upon adolescents are examined through a review of literature, and observations from private psychiatric practice. Adolescents vary in their ability to cope with divorce and may exhibit a wide range of psychological responses. They are concerned with the effect of their new status on peers, relationship with visiting parent, and dating and remarriage of custodial and noncustodial parents. Divorce may leave the adolescent with a fear of rejection, interrupt resolution of typical adolescent conflicts, and leave a fear of personal marital failure. Knowledge of the typical reactions of adolescents to divorce can help parents identify divorce related issues. Educational programs for parents and adolescents by community agencies and religious organizations can be helpful. (27 references)

525. Wallerstein, Judith, and Joan Berlin Kelly. "Children and Divorce: A Review." *Social Work* 24(6): 468–475 (November 1979).

The emotional impact of divorce on children and adolescents is discussed in context with: 1) the predivorce family, 2) the disruptive process of divorce, 3) the socio-economic post divorce setting and 4) the alterations in the parent-child relationship. Implications of the increase in one-parent families require rethinking of traditional concepts of child development psychopathology, intervention theory and development of theoretical formulas suited to the new family structures. Social Work intervention programs might include: 1) educating parents about children's needs, 2) counseling for parents and children, 3) social support services, 4) training and consultation for schools and 5) new court related services. (56 references)

GENERAL WORKS

526. Abelsohn, David. "An Adolescent adjustment to Parental Divorce: An Investigation from the Theoretial Perspective of Structural Family Therapy." Ph.D. diss., University of Cape Town (South Africa), 1985.

    For a summary see: *Dissertation Abstracts International* 49B(4): 1377.

527. Ahrons, Constance R. "Divorce: A Crisis of Family Transition and Change." *Family Relations* 29(4): 533–540 (October 1980).

    This paper focuses on the relationships between former spouses in postdivorce families in conceptualizing divorce as a process of family change. Stresses related to major role transitions are discussed and common methods of coping used by the family are identified. Clinical guidelines suggested include: maintenance of a good parenting relationship and separation of parental roles from spousal roles. It is suggested that therapists need to clarify their personal perceptions and values about divorce and recognize the divorced family as a continuing family unit. (41 references)

528. ———. "Joint Custody Arrangements in the Postdivorce Family." *Journal of Divorce* 3(3): 189–205 (Spring 1980).

Results of a study of 41 parents, one year postdivorce, who were assigned joint custody by the courts in San Diego California are reported. In-depth interviews in the parents' homes lasted from one and a half to two and a half hours. In San Diego, physical custody is determined separately within the joint custody decision. The parent without physical custody is referred to as the nonresidential parent. Findings support theoretical assumptions and clinical impressions that indicate joint custody is a viable option as most parents were satisfied overall with the arrangements. (25 references)

529. Ahrons, Constance R., and Sandra Arnn. "When Children from Divorced Families are Hospitalized: Issues for Staff." *Health and Social Work* 6(3): 21–28 (1981).

Major issues for social workers and others working with hospitalized children from divorced families are discussed. Understanding of changes in family form is necessary in recognizing that the family's response to the child's hospitalization and illness is significantly related to the child's adjustment. Transitions in divorce, reorganized family forms, custody, and family power plays are factors that need to be taken into consideration by family health professionals who may be able to help all family members cope with the hospitalization of an ill child. (18 references)

530. Ahrons, Constance R., and Roy H. Rodgers. *Divorced Families: A Multidisciplinary Developmental View*. New York: Norton, 1987.

The disorganizing effect of divorce on the family and its reorganization into new structural forms is discussed within a developmental framework. The authors note that behavior problems of children that are frequently attributed to the impact of family dissolution are not unique to this situation, and that similar actions were viewed by society in general in a different light in other areas when divorce was not common. Parental separation, divorce and remarriage, along with the changes in the roles and relationships of individuals in the family and the resulting psychological and sociological effects are discussed. Accomplishments of professionals in research on the binuclear family are reported and suggestions are made regarding the need to continue the development of new intervention strategies and programs. (Bibliography)

531. Alexander, Sharon J. "Influential Factors on Divorced Parents in Determining Visitation Aarrangements." *Journal of Divorce* 3(3): 223–239 (Spring 1980).

A study was made to learn what factors are most important in determining visitation arrangements: visiting parent's best interests, custodial parent's best interests, child's best interests and parental relationship. A questionnaire was completed by 66 divorced parents that included male and female white custodial and noncustodial parents who were members of *Parents Without Partners*. The child's and visiting parent's best interests were found to be more important than the custodial parent's best interests and the parental relationship. Implications for lawyers, judges and marriage counselors are noted. (19 references)

532. ———. "Protecting the Child's Rights in Custody Cases." *Family Coordinator* 26(4): 7–382 (October 1977).

Past and current practices in awarding child custody are reviewed along with related literature. In custody determination, the child's and the adolescent's best interests may differ, and therefore the adolescent is usually allowed to participate in the decision-making process. Sometimes a psychological parent, such as grandparent or other relative, may be preferred over biological parents or an agency. Many states have legislated guidelines to help the judge in arriving at a solution that is best for the child. As the rate of divorce has increased, with more focus being placed on what happens to the child, there have been more voices raised in support of the child's right to his/her own counsel. (20 references)

533. Aller, Robert D. "Differences in Children's Behavior Toward Custodial Mothers and Custodial Fathers." *Journal of Marriage and the Family* 44(1): 73–86 (February 1982).

Children's behavior toward their custodial parents was explored through data collected in-depth interviews with twenty custodial mothers and seven custodial fathers. Custodial fathers reported better child behavior toward them than custodial mothers. Children of custodial fathers verbalized their appreciation for fathers more than they did for mothers. The behavior of children of lower socioeconomic (SES) custodial mothers was much more difficult than that of children of higher-SES custodial mothers. (71 references)

534. Allison, Paul D., and Furstenberg, Frank F., Jr. "How Marital Dissolution Affects Children: Variations by Age and Sex." *Developmental Psychology* 25(4): 540–549 (July 1989).

This assessment of the effect of marital dissolution on children was based on a nationally representative sample of 1,197 subjects who had participated in the 1976 National Survey of Children study. Results of reinterviews conducted in 1981 suggest that marital disolution has significant and long lasting effects in the areas of problem behavior, psychological distress and academic performance. These effects were found to be greater for boys than girls, and are also greater for children who are very young when dissolution occurs. (14 references)

535. Anderson-Khleif, Susan E. "Divorced Mothers, Divorced Fathers and Children: A Study of Interaction, Support, and Visitation in One-Parent Families." Ph.D. diss., Harvard University, 1976.

Not available through UMI.

536. Annunziata, Jane "An Empirical Investigation of the Kinetic Family Drawings of Children of Divorce and

Children from Intact Families." Ph.D. diss., Rutgers University, 1983.

For a summary see: *Dissertation Abstracts International* 45B(1): 342.

537. Aronson, David M., and Steven K. Baum. "Crisp-Psychometric Assessment of Postdivorce Stress/Adjustment in Children." Paper presented at the American Psychological Association, Anaheim, Calif., August 26–30, 1983. 20pp. (ERIC Microfiche ED236235)

A new psychometric instrument for measuring the impact of divorce on elementary school age children was developed: the Child's Report of the Impact of Separation by Parents (CRISP). This structured projective test was specifically designed to assess children's postdivorce stress/adjustment. (31 references)

538. Baden, Clifford, ed. *Children and Divorce: An Overview of Recent Research.* Wheelock College Center for Parenting Studies. Boston, 1980. 164pp. (ERIC Microfiche ED202578)

The Wheelock College for Parenting Studies sponsored a two-day symposium on "Children of Divorce." The effects of divorce on children are the subject of this collection of eight papers by authors from several disciplines (Bibliographies)

539. Bahr, Stephen J. "An Evaluation of Court Mediation: A Comparison in Divorce Cases with Children." *Journal of Family Issues* 2(1): 39–60 March 1981)

This study compares the effectiveness of courts with and without mediation services in divorce cases involving child custody disputes. Data examined came from information provided by family professionals, lawyers, court reports and informal observations. Mediation services were found to reduce the cost of court operations and private legal expenses as well. Data also suggest that mediation increases the rate of compliance with court orders and facilitates post-divorce adjustment. Further research on private mediation is suggested. (56 references)

540. Barenbaum, Nichole B., and Krisanne Bursik. "Parental Acromony and Children's Post-Separation Adjustment." Paper Presented at the Annual Meeting of the American Psychological Association. Toronto, Canada. August 24–28, 1984. 16pp. (ERIC Microfiche ED256476)

Results of a variety of measures administered to 128 recently separated mothers and their children are reported. Both the length of time since the parents' separation and the amount of contact with the father were found to moderate the relationship between parental conflict and children's adjustment. Results show clearly that the level of interparent hostility is an important predictor of children's adjustment in parental separation. (16 references)

541. Barnard, Charles P., and Gust Jenson III. "Child Custody Evaluation: A Rational Process for an Emotion-Laden Event." *American Journal of Family Therapy* 12(2): 61–67 (Summer 1984).

A consultation model for use in child custody determination as an alternative to the adversarial legal process is discussed. The process and procedures used are reported to be in line with what most state laws suggest as criteria to be considered in child custody decisions. The consultation model proposed is viewed as diminishing the destructive impact of the adversarial process. It is suggested that the best interests of the child are served by assessing and considering the overall family operation rather than individuals who comprise the family. (22 references)

542. Barnum, Richard. "Understanding Controversies in Visitation." *Journal of the American Academy of Child and Adolescent Psychiatry* 26(5): 788–792 (September 1987).

Problems in visitation include: understanding the value of visitation, and understanding the meanings of the problems associated with it. It is therefore necessary to be clear about what the visitation is supposed to accomplish and to examine what is at the root of problems that may surface. Several cases are used to illustrate visitation situations. Recommendations for further research are offered. (30 references)

543. Bartz, Karen W., and Wayne C. Witcher. "When Father Gets Custody." *Children Today* 7(5): 2–6, 35 (September-October 1978).

Of 446,000 male-headed single-parent families in the United States, about three-fourths were the result of divorce or separation. Between 1965 and 1976 there was an 80 percent increase in father-headed families. Thirty-four divorced fathers with minor children were interviewed to determine how they adjust to their roles and how their children react to them. Father-headed families were found to have high educational and occupational status, contain male and female children, and averaged two children to a household. Only three of the fathers had been involved in contested custody. Fathers reported adjustments in housekeeping priorities, finding good care for children not in school was a problem. Custody benefitted the parent-child relationship, feelings of security, self-concept, school performance and responsibility improved following divorce. Few fathers had a live in arrangement, although most had an active sexual life. Although this investigation deals with fathers who have succeeded, there are implications for social workers, lawyers and other professionals.

544. Batts, Rachel. "Contested Child Custody and Visitation: A Plight of Children." *Educational Horizons* 58(2): 91–96 (Winter 1979–1980).

The effects that legal and adjustment issues have on the plight of some children whose parents have parted or divorced are investigated. The child's interests are often balanced and made subordinated to adult interests and rights. Various visitation and custody arrangements are discussed along with possible implications in regard to children's adjustments and interests. To resolve responsibly and expediently conflicts of past divorce dispositions, it is suggested that: 1) educational programs be initiated to acquaint legal experts with child development and encourage them to exchange information with mental health professionals and 2) a court-appointed child adversary represents the child regardless of the parents' wishes. (18 references)

545. Beal, Edward W. "Children of Divorce: A Family Systems Perspective." *Journal of Social Issues* 35(4): 140–154 (Fall 1979).

The concepts of family systems theory and clinical interviews were used to examine the emotional attachments that are formed and resolved in the marriage and divorce processes. Participants in the study were 40 families and 100 children 14–18 years of age. The management of emotional attachment in families with a mild and severe degree of child focus is compared and the role of the therapist in helping families decrease the intensity of emotional focus on the child is detailed. It is suggested that the family's emotional stability is important to the healthy functioning of children and parents during and after divorce. The need for further study in this area is noted. (5 references)

546. Beeson, Betty Spillers. "Yours, Mine or Ours: Child Custody Decisions." Paper presented at the Annual Meeting of the Association for Childhood Education International, Cleveland, April 14–17, 1983. 19pp. (ERIC Microfiche ED233818)

Divorcing parents are now being given joint custody. Research results presently available indicate positive aspects of joint custody: parents awarded joint custody are generally satisfied with the arrangement, a continuing relationship with both parents is important for children, and children in joint custody generally adjust well. Evidence further suggests that parents can cooperate in raising their children and that litigation after divorce decreases in joint custody cases.

547. Benedek, Richard S., and Elissa P. Benedek. "Children of Divorce: Can We Meet Their Needs?" *Journal of Social Issues* 35(4): 155–169 (Fall 1979).

The psychological needs of children experiencing divorce, the extent that these needs are being met, and what else needs to be done to better meet these needs is the focus of this paper. Among the services offered to children that are discussed: a grant funded project, court-connected services, community and school education programs and self-help groups. The short-comings of these services are discussed, and a model program of direct and indirect services for children is proposed. Further research to develop and evaluate new services and programs is recommended. (17 references)

548. Benedek, Richard S., et al. "Michigan's Friends of the Court: Creative Programs for Children of Divorce." *Family Coordinator* 26(4): 447–450 (October 1977).

Michigan's Friends of the Court system advises judges of problems, especially those affecting children which are not likely to be brought to the attention of the court by divorcing parents or attorneys. Operations of the system within the scope of its legislated powers and duties are described. The Friends of the Court are primarily oriented toward enforcement, collection, and processing of child support payments. However, social workers are also made available for pre- and post-divorce counseling, for crisis intervention, and to help with visitation arrangements. Replication of the system is encouraged to protect the rights and interests of children. (6 references)

549. Berg, Berthold, and Robert Kelly. "The Measured Self-Esteem of Children from Broken, Rejected and Accepted

Families." *Journal of Divorce* 2(4): 363–369 (Summer 1979).

A random sample of 57 students nine to fifteen years old from rural and urban school systems were subjects of a research study to determine the effect of divorce on the self-esteem of children from divorced families and children from intact and accepted families. The Piers-Harris Children's Self-concept Scale along with items adapted from Coppersmith's Self-Concept Scale and the Minnesota Multiphasic Personality Inventory were used as measures. Self-esteem of children from divorced families was not lower than those from intact accepted families, but was lower in children from intact rejected families. (13 references)

550. Bernard, Janine M. "Divorce and Young Children: Relationships in Transition." *Elementary School Guidance and Counseling* 12(3): 188–197 (February 1978).

Divorce is expected to continue to be one of the major problems facing elementary school counselors, especially since many research studies indicate that younger children have a harder time dealing with the problems of family dissolution than older children. Suggestions are offered for ways that counselors can help children deal with their feelings associated with divorce. Additional research on aspects of divorce and children is encouraged. (11 references)

551. Bernard, Janine M., and Sally Nesbitt. "Divorce: An Unreliable Predictor of Children's Emotional Predispositions." *Journal of Divorce* 4(4): 31–42 (Summer 1981).

Results of two pilot studies which attempted to observe children of divorce without the methodological biases reported in previous research. Subjects were taken from a group of elementary school children in agricultural and urban communities. The Children's Emotion Projection Instrument was developed specifically for use in the investigations to measure the predispositions of children from divorced, disrupted and intact families. Researchers are cautioned to scrutinize their instrument design to prevent their biases from introducing therapeutically dysfunctional interventions into their therapy. Just as adults report positive growth resulting from divorce, children may also experience positive results. (27 references)

552. Bernstein, Barton E. "Lawyer and Counselor as a Interdisciplinary Team: Points for a Woman to Ponder in Considering the Basic Finances of Divorce." *Family Coordinator* 26(4): 421–427 (October 1977).

This article is based on the premise that many women contemplating divorce are not aware of the financial costs involved in establishing a new lifestyle as a single parent. Guidelines for figuring projected income and expenses are presented to aid lawyers and counselors in advising their clients. A schedule of child support payments based on salary can be used to give the client a realistic picture of what she can expect. The chart of expenses to be considered allows for expenses for both mother and children. The husband's expenses are more controllable and predictable than that of the divorced wife with children. Factors that further complicate the financial picture for the single parent family are discussed. (4 references)

553. Bishop, Sue Marquis, and Gary M. Ingersoll. "Effects of Marital Conflict and Family Structure on the Self-Concepts of Pre- and Early Adolescents." *Journal of Youth and Adolescence* 18(1):25–38 (1989).

Sixteen youths from intact families and seventeen youths from separated families and their mothers participated in this study. Results showed that youths from families with low marital hostility and high marital affection had better self-concept scores in both single-parent and intact-parent families. Further study of the effects of parental conflict on children is suggested. (44 references)

554. Black, Melvin, and Wendy Joffe. "A Lawyer/Therapist Team Approach to Divorce." Paper presented at the Annual Conference of the National Council on Family Relations, San Diego, October 12–17, 1977. 18pp. (ERIC Microfiche ED151717)

Mental health clinicians recognize the severe emotional trauma which divorcing families experience. A continuing relationship is often required with the involvement of children; therefore, therapists and lawyers can work as a team to help make the divorce transition less expensive emotionally and financially. The counselor helps the family communicate effectively by differentiating the emotional from the legal issues, while the lawyer acts as an arbitrator in the negotiation of the divorce settlement. A model is presented. (3 references)

555. Blotcky, Mark J., et al. "Treatment of Adolescents in Family Therapy After Divorce." *Journal of the American Academy of Child Psychiatry* 23(2): 222–225 (March 1984).

As the divorce rate has continued to rise, the proportion of children seen by therapists has also risen. This paper presents a therapeutic approach for helping adolescents deal with changes in the relationship between members of a divorcing family, and with feelings toward the excluded parent in particular. A case history is used to illustrate the various stages of a treatment plan suggested for use when other approaches meet with the adolescent's resistance. (7 references)

556. Bolton, F. G., Jr., and Ann MacEachron. "Assessing Child Maltreatment Risk in the Recently Divorced Parent-Child Relationship." *Journal of Family Violence* 1(3): 259–275 (September 1976).

This paper presents a model of Belsky's child maltreatment/parenting model. Three environments of risk are described that relate to: 1) parents' personal psychological resources, 2) the child's individual characteristics and behaviors and 3) contextual sources of stress and support. The critical period is reported to be the first two years following divorce, when the resources of the consistently absent parent are more likely to remain inadequate and insufficient to create the momentum for positive change. Implications for divorce counseling are noted. (56 references)

557. Bonkowski, Sara E., et al. "A Group Design to Help Children Adjust to Parental Divorce." *Social Casework: The Journal of Contemporary Social Work* 65(3): 131–137 (March 1984).

An eight-week, semi-structured group intervention program was designed for latency-age children in divorcing families. A primary objective of the design was to provide an environment that the children could express themselves without fear of parental reaction or retaliation in order to expand their thinking and coping abilities. Confidentiality should be maintained except where the child's safety or emotional well-being is in jeopardy. It is suggested that the group process, in most cases, is the treatment of choice for children of divorcing families and it is thereapeutic for them to be with others who are experiencing similar loss. (13 references)

558. ———. "What You Don't Know Can Hurt You: Unexpressed Fears and Feelings of Children from Divorcing Families." *Journal of Divorce* 9(1): 33–45 (Fall 1985).

Children's concerns, feelings, and questions about their parents' divorces were explored in a group of 46 children ages six to twelve, who participated in an eight-week divorce group. Data was taken from letters the children wrote to their parents during the fourth week of the program asking any questions they wanted answered and expressing their feelings about the divorce. Some of the feelings identified included: longing for the custodial parent, desire for reconciliation, and miscellaneous comments. Boys most often expressed anger about the divorce, while girls expressed a combination of feelings. Implications for mental health professionals and parents

Implications for mental health professionals and parents are noted. (9 references)

559. Booth, Alan, et al. "The Impact of Parental Divorce on Courtship." *Journal of Marriage and the Family* 46(1): 85–94 (February 1984).

This study focuses on the differences in courtship behavior and attitudes between young people from intact and disrupted families. The sample of 2,538 college students included those whose parents' marriage was broken by divorce, death or permanent separation. Findings based on responses to questionnaires show that parental divorce increases courtship activity among offspring. This activity is increased even more if the divorce is accompanied by acrimony during and after divorce, parent-child relationship deteriorates, and the custodial parent remains single. The age that parental divorce occurred seemed not to influence the quality or quantity of courtship activity. Implications for future research are discussed. (14 references)

560. Bornstein, Marcy Tepper, et al. "Children of Divorce: Empirical Evaluation of a Group Treatment Program." *Journal of Clinical Child Psychology* 17(3): 248–254 (September 1988).

A group psychotherapy program that included thirty-one seven-to-fourteen-year-old children of divorce is described. Six sessions of the treatment program focused on identification of feelings, communication skills, and anger management training. The sixth session included both parents and children. Results showed significant group improvement on a teacher measure of child problem behavior. Implications for future research on treatment programs for children of divorce are discussed. (1 Reference)

561. Bowker, Marjorie A. "Children and Divorce: Being in Between." *Elementary School Guide and Counseling* 17(2): 126–130 (December 1982).

The number of elementary school children whose parents are separating, divorcing, or remarrying continues to increase. In-school support groups for children from these families provide participants with the opportunity to share feelings and develop coping skills. This article describes a group counseling approach using audiovisual material, discussion, and bibliotherapy that helped to open lines of communication between parents and children, and improved school behaviors as well. (3 references)

562. Boyd, Donald A., and Thomas Parish. "An Investigation of Father Loss and College Students' Androgyny Scores." *Journal of Genetic Psychology* 145(2): 279–280 (December 1984).

One hundred and thirty college students were administered the Bem Sex-Role Inventory to measure the association between father loss and androgynous self-descriptions. Responses indicated that males who had lost fathers through divorce identified themselves as being more masculine and less feminine than females from divorced families as well as males and females from intact families who had experienced father loss through death. (4 references)

563. Bradford, Arlonial Y., et al. *Parting: A Counselor's Guide for Children of Separated Parents.* South Carolina State Dept. of Education. Columbia Office of General Education. 1982. 38pp. (ERIC Microfiche ED227391)

This group counseling guide, developed in response to counselors' requests for a group counseling booklet for children in grades Kindergarten to eighth grade, whose parents are divorced or separated. It contains materials that were produced, field-tested and evaluated by experienced elementary and middle school guidance counselors. The major components of the guide are outlined in an initial section including specific goals, suggested session formats, activities (group discussions, role playing, films, audiovisual materials and books).

Guidelines for confidentiality and scheduling are given. Five eight-weekly group sessions of 30–60 minutes, suggested group size of ten students and selection procedures. (12 references)

564. Brady, C. Patrick, et al. "Behavior Problems of Clinic Children: Relation to Parental Marital Status, Age and Sex of Child." *American Journal of Orthopsychiatry* 56(3): 399–412 (July 1986).

Seven hundred and three children from a clinic population were examined to determine the significance between family type, age and sex of child. Parents of the subjects in the sample were asked to complete the Conners Parent Questionnaire. Compared with children from intact and step-families, children from separated and divorced families were reported to present more behavioral problems. Children at different ages were found to have different problems and different ways of coping with stress. Differences between the responses of boys and girls were reported. Areas needing further research are identified. (56 references)

565. Braun, Samuel J., and Dorothy M. Sang. "When Parents Split." *Day Care and Early Education* 4(2): 26–29 (November/December 1976).

With each series of legal events in the divorce process, children may repeat the same sequence of behaviors in response to each part. Family dissolution as viewed by children reflects their own developmental needs. Teachers are advised of ways to help children who are acting out feelings of distress. Since all children do not respond to family break-up in the same way, and consequently behavioral responses may not be the same for every child, a variety of remedies for addressing their needs are presented. (4 references)

566. Brumberger, Larry Sheldon. "Identity Constancy: A Cognitive Developmental Analysis of Children's

Understanding of Family Identity and Divorce." Ph.D. diss., Syracuse University, 1986.

For a summary see: *Dissertation Abstracts International* 40B(): 3433.

567. Buehler, Cheryl A., and Janice M. Hogan. "Managerial Behavior and Stress in Families Headed by Divorced Women: A Proposed Framework." *Family Relations* 29(4): 525–532 (October 1980).

An ecosystem approach is proposed to study the relationship between stress and single-parent family management behavior. Change in the composition of the family motivates the female-headed family to reduce stress through better family management. The level of stress is related to the environment and can be created or reduced by systems external to the family and by the family's internal managerial behavior. Professionals who work with single- parent families should be aware of the rules and regulations used by external support systems to aid families in stress reduction and in improving management abilities. (27 references)

568. Burgoyne, Jacqueline, et al. *Divorce Matters*. New York: Penguin, 1987.

The author's focus is on the impact of divorce on British families. Nearly two-thirds of divorces in Britain involve children and about one-third of these are under the age of five. Their picture of divorce is often distorted and there is not much opportunity to discuss it with their parents. Regressive behavior, feelings of guilt, aggression, and academic problems are among reactions exhibited by children when families dissolve. Distress is often short-lived especially in cases where the children's relationships with parents were good. Long-term effects of divorce on children were reported to be slight. Suggestions are offered for helping children cope with the problems they experience. (Bibliographic notes)

569. Camara, Kathleen A. "Children's Construction of Social Knowledge: Concepts of Family and the Experience of Parental Divorce." Ph.D. diss., Stanford University, 1979.

   For a summary see: *Dissertation Abstracts International* 40B(7): 3433.

570. Cantor, Dorothy W. "Divorce: A View from the Children." *Journal of Divorce* 2(4): 357–361 (Summer 1979).

   A play written by a third grade boy is presented and indicates that children are aware of marital discord prior to the formal announcement by parents that a divorce is going to occur. In the "Divorce Play" the discord leading to the divorce is viewed as trivial and they do not understand why parents would leave them. Although many children make a reasonable adjustment following divorce, many develop a chronic maladjustment. It is suggested that professional intervention should occur early during separation to mediate the effects on children. (6 references)

571. Cantor, Dorothy W., and Ellen A. Drake. *Divorced Parents and Their Children: A Guide for Mental Health Professionals.* New York: Springer, 1983.

   Information is presented that will help mental health professionals assist their clients in dealing with some of the common problems divorced parents and children experience. Divorce increases the risk of the development of psychopathology. Although the distress following parental separation may not be lasting it is much like mourning the death of a loved one. Both custodial and noncustodial parents need to develop good parenting skills to avoid negative results in their children. Strategies are suggested for dealing with the problems that emerge while children are trying to cope with family change. Among the issues discussed are visitation, parental dating and remarriage. The appendix includes a special bibliography for professionals, parents and their children. (Bibliography)

572. Cantrell, Roslyn Garden. "Adjustment to Divorce: Three Components to Assist Children." *Elementary School Guidance and Counseling* 20(3): 163–173 (February 1986).

The developmental stage of the child at the time of separation or divorce is related to the quantity and quality of the child's responses. Characteristic responses of children, ages six to eight and nine to twelve exhibited at home and school following family separation are discussed. A three component model that involves parents, teachers and children includes: 1) group counseling aimed at the development of individual problem solving skills, 2) helping parents through conferences to dispel myths, promote understanding of children's responses and suggest ways to help children and 3) educate teachers about the divorce process and its effects on children. (31 references)

573. Charnas, Jane F. "Joint Child Custody Counseling— Divorce 1980's Style." *Social Casework: The Journal of Contemporary Social Work* 64(9): 546–554 (November 1983).

Joint child custody is proposed as a viable and constructive arrangement following divorce and as a superior choice in most cases. Types of joint custody arrangements are discussed and a model for counseling is presented. The model is not aimed at reconciling marital differences and less attention is given to past marital and affective issues. The counselor is urged to make clear that hostile and resistant behavior will not be tolerated from the parents. Confrontation is viewed as a critical necessity. It is acknowledged, however, that joint custody may not work for every divorcing family. (21 references)

574. Chess, Stella, et al. "Early Parental Attitudes, Divorce and Separation, and Young Adult Outcome: Findings of a Longitudinal Study." *Journal of the American Academy of Child Psychiatry* 22(1): 47–51 (1983).

Effects of early parental attitudes, separation and divorce are reported in a longitudinal study of 132 subjects from early infancy. Child adjustment at home was rated at age three and five, and at school at age five. Early adult adaptation ratings indicated that parental conflict, especially over child management, predicted poor adaptation in young adulthood, but separation and divorce without conflict did not. Implications for parent counseling and therapy are noted. (13 references)

575. Chethik, Morton, and Neil Kalter. "Developmental Arrest Following Divorce: the Role of Therapist as a Developmental Facilitator." *Journal of the American Academy of Child Psychiatry* 19(2): 281–288 (Spring 1980).

This article discusses the role of the therapist as a developmental facilitator and surrogate parent in helping the child negotiate the developmental tasks which may be arrested when the child loses a parent. A case study is used to illustrate the role the therapist can play in facilitating the emotional and social growth of the child. It is suggested that therapy may be more effective if the therapist is of the same sex as the absent parent. Longitudinal in-depth studies of the nonclinical population of children from divorced families is suggested in order to probe the effects of divorce on children who do not appear to need treatment on the surface, but who may suffer silently. (12 references)

576. Christensen-Bliss, Jana. "Children of Divorce: The Effects of the Divorced Parental Relationship on the Self-Esteem of their Children." Ph.D. diss., Brigham Young University, 1987.

For a summary see: *Dissertation Abstracts International* 49B(2): 535.

577. Clapp, Genevieve, ed. "Parental Discord and Divorce." In *Child Study Research Current Perspectives and Applications*, 85–110. Lexington, Mass.: Lexington Books, 1988.

Divorce is more than a single crisis in the life of a family. Its effect on a child cannot be separated from its effect on the mother and father. A number of children suffer long-term consequences. Young children adjust better if their environment is highly structured, organized and predictable and when the rules are clearly defined and enforced. The greater the amount of change in the home environment the more likely is the child to develop maladaptive behavior. Some noncustodial parents are able to create and maintain good relationships with their children. These parents without custody sometimes develop relationships with their children that parents in intact homes never accomplish. (73 references)

578. Cline, D., and Jack Westman. "The Impact of Divorce on the Family." *Child Psychiatry and Human Development* 2(2): 78–83 (Winter 1971).

A review of 105 families that had experienced divorce continued family interaction that may or may not be adaptive for the family members. Fifty-two percent of the families studied had hostile post divorce relationships that required at least one court intervention, while 31 percent required two to ten court interventions over a two-year period. Parent interaction related to parenting role, continued conflict between divorced spouses, alliances between one parent and child against the other parent, interaction of divorced spouses with extended family and interaction between divorced children perpetuated by the extended family. Generally court intervention is sought when quarrels over alimony, visitation rights and place of residence cannot be settled between divorced spouses. (13 references)

579. Clulow, Christopher F., and Christopher Vincent, in collaboration with Barbara Dearney, In *The Child's Best Interest? Divorce Court Welfare and the Search for a Settlement*. London: Tavistock, 1987.

The authors explore the conflicts between the public and private interests in Britain when children from divorced families are involved. The work of divorce court workers is described in its social and historical context. Cases are used to illustrate the nature of disputes related to the welfare of children. Incomplete emotional divorce reflected in applications to the divorce court affects its actions. Children have to contend with unexpected changes over which they have no control. They may respond by exhibiting behavior and academic problems and delinquency. (Bibliography)

580. Cochran, Robert F., and Paul C. Vitz. "Child Protective Divorce Laws: A Response to the Effects of Parental Separation on Children." *Family Law Quarterly* 17(3): 327–363 (Fall 1983).

The psychological literature that shows the effect of parental separation and divorce on children and the means of attempting to protect the interests of the children of divorce is examined. There is significant empirical evidence from the field of psychology to establish that parental separation has substantial long-term negative effects on children. Divorce may be beneficial to children where intense continuing conflict between parents and high conflict is avoided following divorce. The trend in recent years has been toward prompt no-fault divorce. It is suggested that a one year waiting period would give parents time to reconsider and to see the effects of separation on their children. (206 references)

581. Colletta, Nancy Donahue. "The Impact of Divorce: Father Absence or Poverty?" *Journal of Divorce* 3(1): 27–35 (Fall 1979).

This study examines whether reported differences in child rearing practices of divorced and married mothers are related to father absence or to the low-income that often occurs with divorce. The sample consisted of 72 divorced and married white working class families. Results of the child-rearing interview support the idea that the consequences of divorce are more strongly related to depressed income than to father absence. When one and

two-parent families are compared and differ only in father
absence, there are no significant differences in child
rearing practices. (25 references)

582. ————. "Stressful Lives: The Situation of Divorced
Mothers and Their Children." *Journal of Divorce* 6(3):
19–31 (Spring 1983).

This study investigates whether the negative effect on
children is due to the divorce itself or to the low-income
situation that frequently follows divorce. The sample
situation contained 48 divorced and 24 married mothers
with preschool children in Buffalo, New York with incomes
varying from $6,000 to $12,000. An open ended interview
was used to measure stress and child rearing practices.
Findings showed that low income one-parent families
had greater stress associated with finances, community
services, living arrangements, employment, and family
illness. When incomes are moderate, stress for both mother
and child decreases. It was suggested that future research
on divorce focus on the forces in the family situation that
affect family stress and what impacts on the child as a
result of the mother's child-rearing practices. (12
references)

583. ————. "Support Systems After Divorce: Incidence and
Impact." *Journal of Marriage and the Family* 41(4):
837–846 (November 1979).

Seventy-two one-parent families were interviewed to
investigate the impact of support systems on post-divorce
family functioning. Results showed that divorced mothers
received less help with the problems of maintaining a
household and financially supporting their families. Those
who reported highly supportive child care arrangements
lived with another person. Mothers in one-parent families
got help mainly from their own families and received
financial support partly from child support payments,
social services or gifts from families. In general, low
income divorced mothers were not satisfied with the

financial support received and their child rearing practices were related to their satisfaction with support. (18 references)

584. Combrinck-Graham, Lee. "When Parents Separate or Divorce: The Sibling System." In *Siblings in Therapy: Life Span and Clinical Issues,* edited by Michael Kahn and Karen Gail Lewis, 190–208, New York: Norton, 1988.

Growing up in a single-parent home following separation or divorce is not in itself, bad for the children involved. The quality of the parents' relationship with the children, the degree of conflict between the custodial parent and the noncustodial parent, and the relationships between siblings are significantly related to children's adjustment. It is suggested that the separation-divorce transition is easier if there are siblings. It seems that children who had siblings were healthier, had more age-appropriate development and had better social relationships. Therapeutic implications are discussed. (10 references)

585. Cooney, Teresa M., et al. "Parental Divorce in Young Adulthood: Some Preliminary Findings." *American Journal of Orthopsychiatry* 56(3): 470–477 (July 1986).

This research explores the reactions of 39 undergraduate students, 18 to 23 years of age, who had experienced parental divorce within three years prior to the study. Results of questionnaires and interviews indicated that emotional stress was greatest early in the divorce process and was greater for women than for men. Positive changes in parental-child relationships were reported but the father-daughter relationship was found to be particularly vulnerable. Additional research on the relationship of family stability at adjustment in young adulthood is suggested. (20 references)

586. Copeland, Anne P. "An Early Look at Divorce: Mother-Child Interactions in the First Post-Separation Year." *Journal of Divorce* 8(2): 17–30 (Winter 1984).

Videotaped play of 61 children, aged six to twelve, with their mothers was studied for observable effects of divorce on children within 12 months of its occurrence. Two determinants of children's reactions to parental divorce are age and gender. Younger children responded more negatively than older children, while mothers interaction with older boys tended to be more positive. Evidence was found that it is the mother's reaction to the child's age that influences their interactions in the immediate post divorce period. Older and younger children exhibit similar behavior in the immediate separation period, but behave differently later in the year. It is suggested that extension of this study into the second post separation year would be of value in understanding the effects of divorce on children. (15 references)

587. ————. "Individual Differences in Children's Reactions to Divorce." *Journal of Clinical Child Psychology* 14(1): 11–19 (Spring 1985).

Children from divorced families and their mothers were interviewed and questioned about their reactions to divorce. Factors surrounding children who had more behavior problems and more recent physical illnesses were examined. Mothers of children with more behavior problems reported more mood disturbances, while boys in this group were less active in play. Boys with more illness had more interactive play with mothers, whereas girls with more illness were less interactive and had more noncontigent play periods. Study of cognitive styles and abilities and other family-or parent-level variables will be important in describing why children react differently to stress. (19 references)

588. Cox, Martha J., and Roger D. Cox. "Socialization of Young Children in the Divorced Family." *Journal of Research and Development in Education* 13(1): 58–67 (Fall 1979).

Studies on the impact of divorce on the socialization of young children are examined. Critical factors for socialization of the child identified by researchers are: quality of parent-child relationship, types of disciplinary techniques used, and parents as models or identification figures for the child. The first year following divorce was found to be the period of greatest stress, conflict and disruption. Individual functioning and the relationships between family members are affected and parenting is more difficult. More research on this stressful period is suggested. (23 references)

589. Crossman, Sharyn M., and Gerald R. Adams. "Divorce, Single Parenting, and Child Development." *Journal of Psychology* 106(2): 205–217 (November 1980).

Twenty-three children from single-parent and two-parent families participated in a preschool education program to determine the effects of the program on psychological functioning following divorce. Results of pretest scores confirmed the delayed development of preschool children from single-parent families. By the end of a supportive intervention program single-parent children performed at levels very much like those of children from intact families. Findings suggest that au@ogram was to raise the level of the subject's self-esteem and foster positive parent-child relationships. Thammend that the program be started with chidren before the two year mark following divorce, and that evaluations take place again at intervals of six months and eighteen months. Teachers and school social workers are urged to investigate significant changes in the behavior of their students. (38 references)

590. DeFrain, John, et al. *On Our Own: A Single Parent's Survival Guide.* Lexington, Mass.: Lexington Books, 1987.

This book is based on data gathered on over 1000 divorced mothers, fathers and children. It is estimated that 12 million children under age 18 live with divorced parents. Children are just as likely to experience negative consequences of divorce as anyone else. There is no way to predict how they will be treated by the courts. It is suggested that children's adjustment to divorce may be related to their mothers' adjustment. Guidelines for self-examinationn by parents considering custody arrangements are offered. The authors include a list of books for preschoolers, elementary-aged children, adolescents and adults. (Bibliography)

591. Derdeyn, Andre P. "Child Psychiatry and Law: The Family in Divorce: Issues of Parental Anger." *Journal of the American Acadamy of Child Psychiatry* 22(4): 385–391 (July 1983).

This paper focuses on the problems of children resulting from parental anger after divorce and the role of the child psychiatrist in treating the clinical manifestations in a hostile family environment. Several cases are used to illustrate the ways in that children may react to parental anger which is not necessarily directed specifically toward them. Boys in divorcing families are shown to be particularly vulnerable. It is suggested that the child psychiatrist needs to be interested and skilled in working with parents in order to be successful in intervening on the child's behalf. (31 references)

592. Desimone-Luis, Judith, et al. "Children of Separation and Divorce: Factors Influencing Adjustment." *Journal of Divorce* 3(1): 37–41 (Fall 1979).

Demographic factors affecting the adjustment of children to parental separation and divorce is the focus of this study. Subjects from *Parents Without Partners* were used to construct profiles of their children based on the Louisville Behavior Checklist. Of some thirty demographic factors only one, a drop in income of at least 50 percent was found to be significant. In addition, of the five deviant profiles, all the children were between six and nine years old at the time of parental separation. It is suggested that future research examine these two factors more fully to determine their contribution to the adjustment difficulties of children. (11 references)

593. Devall, Esther, et al. "The Impact of Divorce and Maternal Employment on Pre-Adolescent Children." *Family Relations* 35(1): 153–159 (January 1986).

Peer relations, responsibilities, self-esteem and activities of 60 boys and girls, ages nine-twelve, of single/employed, married/employed or married/nonemployed mothers were compared in this study. These middle class mothers and children were administered two self report measures. Children from divorced families did not have more responsibilities or participate in fewer activities. The only activity affected by maternal employment was participation in sports. Girls had more personal care responsibilities, and boys more outside chores. Implications of the study for public policy and family practitioners are presented. (21 references)

594. DeWayne, Moore, and Deborah F. Hotch. "Parent Adolescent Separation: the Role of Parental Divorce." *Journal of Youth and Adolescence* 11(2): 115–119 (April 1982).

The effect of parental divorce on emotional separation and personal control in adolescents is examined in 172 college students. Responses of subjects to a questionnaire indicated that for males, parental divorce was significantly related to emotional separation as an important indicator of having left home, while for first-born girls personal control was the important indicator for having left home. Further study of the impact of divorce on parent-adolescent separation was suggested. (15 references)

595. Diamond, S. A. *Helping Children of Divorce: A Handbook for Parents and Teachers.* New York: Schocken Books, 1985.

This book was written by a school counselor to help divorced parents and teachers understand the problems faced by children. Common divorce related reactions that affect academic performance and classroom behavior are discussed and possible solutions are offered for handling them. Suggestions are also made for ways that the school can respond to the special needs of divorced parents. A bibliography is provided for use in classroom discussion and maybe recommended by the teacher to children and parents. Organizations which may be sources of support for divorced parents are also listed. (Bibliography)

596. Doherty, William J., and Hamilton I. McCubbin, eds. "The Family and Health Care." *Family Relations* 34(1): WHOLE ISSUE (January 1985).

The interface between family health and the health care system is discussed. A model focusing on the family health and illness cycle includes those life events and experiences, such as divorce and death, which may precipitate illnesses. Studies indicate that the health of intact families is better than that in divorced families. Collaboration between physicians and other family professionals is encouraged to facilitate the adjustment of children and their parents. In addition to poorer health ratings, children of divorce may suffer from shorter attention spans, loss of energy, decreased motivation, and lack of confidence. The family health model would integrate the family and health research fields to accommodate the complexity of the biopsychosocial nature of individuals comprising the family unit. (Bibliographies)

597. Dominic, Katherine Tasios, and Benjamin Schlesinger. "Weekend Fathers: Family Shadows." *Journal of Divorce* 3(3): 241–247 (Spring 1980).

Nine part-time fathers with an average of two children were interviewed. The fathers had been part-time parents for an average of 3.5 years and their children's ages averaged 10 years. It was found that fathers who settled custody in court did not accept the decision as final, whereas those who settled custody out of court accepted their part-time parent role as permanent and had more frequent visitation with their children. Fathers who settled out of court also felt their ex-wives were good parents.

The need for more information on the coping patterns and parent-child interaction of the weekend father is suggested. (3 references)

598. Donaldson, Mary Beth Williams. "Children of Divorce: A Model for Group Counseling in the Church." Ph.D. diss., New Orleans Baptist Theological Seminary, 1988.

    For a summary see: *Dissertation Abstracts International* 49B(8): 3499.

599. Druchman, Joan, et al. *Helping Youth and Families of Separation, Divorce and Remarriage: A Program Manual.* United States. Youth Development Bureau. August 1980.

    This manual is designed to help agencies and groups to create and expand services for youth and families undergoing separation, divorce and remarriage. Counseling strategies and self-help models reviewed by a panel of experts are presented. Information on ways to use mass and communication media to publicize services and make outreach services more effective is also discussed. The appendix includes lists of measuring instruments, descriptions of programs visited, books for family change curriculum and support groups. (Bibliography)

600. Edgar, Don, and Margaret Harrison. "Children's Participation in Divorce." Paper presented at the Conference of Marriage Counseling Organization. Canberra, Australia. February 16, 1982. 21pp. (ERIC Microfiche ED233264)

    Counselors should begin to think not only of the needs of children involved in the process of their parents' divorce, but of an approach to marriage counseling as a whole. Children participate in the context of divorce as family members in the social interaction that makes a family work or not work. There are, therefore, various stages or points of intervention for counseling children through divorce. Research on childrens' roles in family interaction and marital satisfaction from birth onward has shown that children are included in their parents' affairs and must be allowed to preserve those blood ties or at least to understand why their parents decided to sever the marriage bond that produced them. (53 references)

601. Eiduson, Bernice T. "Child Development in Emergent Family Styles." *Children Today* 7(2) 24–31 (March-April 1978).

This is an update of a study of 200 children from a variety of family styles, including single mother households, social contract couples, two-parent families and communities or living groups. Findings indicate that these family groups, despite differences in value systems, housing arrangements and family environments, socialize their infants in similar ways and their children seem to be physically and psychologically well. Some family units and lifestyles are taking on a more traditional aspect as some marry, some dropouts return to school, and some work in the community where they contribute service. Concern for their children's welfare may have led some parents to modify their lifestyle. (5 references)

602. Elkin, Meyer. "Joint Custody: Affirming that Parents and Families are Forever." *Social Work* 32(1): 18–24 (January-February 1987).

The benefits of joint custody as an alternative that more realistically defines the postdivorce relationship between the child and the parents are explored in this article. The lack of a standard definition of joint custody among legislatures and legal and mental health professionals is noted. It is suggested that a custody plan should include the goal of shared parenting, and that access to both parents is important for young children. However, the author acknowledges that joint custody is not the answer for every family. (22 references)

603. Emery, Robert E., and Daniel K. O'Leary. "Children's Perceptions of Marital Discord and Behavior Problems of Boys and Girls." *Journal of Abnormal Child Psychology* 10(1): 11–24 (March 1982).

A clinical sample of 50 white children between the ages of eight and seventeen were studied to determine the relationship between marital discord and behavior problems. The Short Marital Adjustment Test and the O'Leary-Porter Scale were used as measures of marital adjustment. The Behavior Problem Checklist, the Children's Perception Questionnaire, and Children's Report of Parental Behavior were also used in the study. It was found that marital discord was significantly related to the behavior problems of boys. Behavior problems of boys and girls were moderately accurate in predicting maternal ratings of marital discord. Implications of the study and its limitations are discussed. (35 references)

604. Emery, Robert E., and Melissa M. Wyer. "Divorce Mediation." *American Psychologist* 42(5): 472–480 (May 1987).

This article discusses the growing trend toward the use of mediation as an alternative to the adversarial position in resolving child custody disputes. Exposure to parental conflict, before, during and after divorce has an effect on the child, and relationships with the parents may be strained further by adversary approaches in custody resolution. Data indicate that divorcing parents are more satisfied with mediation than with adversarial procedure. Practical, legal, and ethical issues related to mediation are discussed. Psychologists are encouraged to become involved in developing and evaluating mediation services. (97 references)

605. Epstein, Yakov M., and Charles M. Borduin. "Could This Happen?: A Game for Children of Divorce." *Psychotherapy* 22(4): 770–773 (Winter 1985).

This article describes a game designed for children in

group therapy from divorced or separated parents. The children are asked to respond to a number of hypothetical divorce related situations. These responses to game items are then used by the therapist to assess cognitive and emotional changes over the duration of the treatment. Illustrations of the use of the game with eight- and nine-year-old children in a 12–week program are presented. (1 Reference)

606. Espenshade, Thomas J. "The Economic Consequences of Divorce." *Journal of Marriage and the Family* 41(3): 615–625 (August 1979).

The financial effect of divorce on husbands, wives and children is the focus of this study. Much of the information is based on the Michigan Panel Study of Income Dynamics that included a representative sample of 5,000 families. Children are often the passive recipients of economic changes following divorce. Those who stay with fathers are shown to fare better than those who stay with mothers. While custody is usually awarded to mothers, there is not much consistency in enforcing child support. Wives are not only economically worse off than their former husbands, they face more barriers in the labor market. Suggestions for public policy measures are made in light of the fact that many children will spend part of their lives in single parent families, and more specifically in a female-headed household. (67 references)

607. Falbo, Toni. "Some Consequences of Growing Up in a Nonintact Family." Paper Presented at the Annual Convention of the American Psychological Association. Montreal, Canada, September 1980. 6pp. (ERIC Microfiche ED250079)

The associations between growing up in a family disrupted by divorce and the interpersonal orientations of young adults were investigated in a survey of white college students (N=1720). The majority of subjects (89 percent) came from intact homes. Subjects from divorced families

(N=106) had a more external locus of control and felt lonelier than those from intact families. An investigation of the interacting influences of siblings and family intactness indicated that the impact of siblings was limited to that associated with sibling status, not family size. Middle-born subjects from divorced families scored lower on perceived popularity and internality than those from intact families. (7 references)

608. Farber, Stephanie S., et al. "Older Adolescents and Parental Divorce: Adjustment Problems and Mediators of Coping." *Journal of Divorce* 7(2): 59–75 (Winter 1983).

This study explores the family-disruption problems of college age adolescents and examines some of the factors that aid them in coping with this life transition. A series of pilot interviews with college mental health professionals, a review of the literature on family disruption and a questionnaire were used to identify factors mediating adaptation of adolescents to parental divorce. The questionnaire was sent to the clinical directors of student mental health counseling centers at colleges and universities in the United States. Potential mediators of family disruption identified included age, sex and distance from home of the adolescent. Adolescents were seen as more likely to use more formal sources of support than peers or family members. Implications for prevention and intervention are discussed. (39 references)

609. Farber, Stephanie, et al. "Parental Separation/Divorce and Adolescents: An Examination of Factors Mediating Adaptation." Paper presented at the Annual Conference of the American Psychological Association, Los Angeles, August 24–26 1981. (ERIC Microfiche ED210606)

A series of measures designed to examine the impact of parental separation/divorce on adolescents and to identify salient individual and situational adjustment mediators were administered to subjects. Multiple regression analyses revealed several factors to be particularly salient mediators of the adolescents' post-divorce adjustment, including distance from home, personal coping style, family cohesion, parental remarriage, and the use of family members for support. (No references)

610.   Felner, Robert D., et al. "Party Status of Children During Marital Dissolution: Child Preference and Legal Preference and Legal Representation in Custody Decisions." *Journal of Clinical Child Psychology* 14(2): 42–48 (Spring 1985).

Results of a survey of both attorneys and judges relevant to the custody litigation process are reported. Four issues addressed were: representation for children in divorce cases, the weight assigned representation, weight assigned the child's wishes and the child's competence to participate. The upsurge in the number of divorces has caused the role of the legal system in shaping the familial context that children live to become more prominent. Child advocates argue that the child should be represented by legal counsel. Results of the study showed lack of support for routine representation of children in the custody process, as well as the fact that a majority of legal professionals failed to endorse the child's best interests as among the criteria they consider most critical in making custody decisions. It is suggested that the generation and effective dissemination of empirical data and effective strategies for addressing these concerns by social scientists would aid the legal profession in custody decisions. (22 references)

611.   ———. Risk and Vulnerability in Childhood: A Reappraisal." *Journal of Clinical Child Psychology* 14(1): 2–4 (Spring 1985).

Over one million children experience the divorce of their parents each year and significant numbers receive their primary care each day from alternative caretakers or are on their own, unsupervised for prolonged periods. Situations that are emotionally hazardous are not rare in childhood. Knowledge of what factors place children at risk helps target effective intervention or preventive strategies. Ten to twenty percent of all children may be in need of intensive mental health services. Factors that contribute to resilience and invulnerability in the face of developmentally hazardous situations, if recognized, could aid understanding of children's adaptation in high risk family situations. (22 references)

612. Fergusson, D. M., et al. "A Survival Analysis of Childhood Family History." *Journal of Marriage and the Family* 47(2): 287–295 (May 1985).

The family history of 1,067 preschool children was examined in this study. Findings seem to indicate that once children experience the break-up of the traditional two-parent family, there was a strong likelihood that they would also experience multiple situations involving marriage formation and disolution. Implications of this finding are discussed. (16 references)

613. Fine, Mark A., et al. "Long Term Effects of Divorce on Parent-Child Relationships." *Developmental Psychology* 19(5): 703–713 (September 1983).

One hundred students from families that had experienced divorce seven or more years previously and 141 students from intact families were studied to determine the long-term effects of divorce. These introductory psychology students were given a series of self-report questionnaires to assess their relationship with their parents. Subjects from divorced families perceived their relationships with their parents, particularly with their fathers, less positively than subjects from intact families. Active involvement of the father and added stresses on the mother after divorce were critical determinants of the perceived quality of the current parent-child relationships. Implications for future research are discussed. (31 references)

614. Fine, Stuart. "Children in Divorce, Custody and Access Situations: The Contribution of the Mental Health Professional." *Journal of Child Psychology and Psychiatry and Allied Disciplines* 21(4): 353–361 (October 1980).

The marital turmoil prior to separation seems to be the pathogenic factor that leads to an increased prevalence of conduct disorders and juvenile delinquency among children and adolescents of divorced and separated parents. The mental health professionals can help with education of high school students, pre-divorce counseling, custody conflicts, post-divorce counseling and changes in social and educational practices. Parents may be alerted to the possibilities of divorce mediation and settling of custody disputes out of the courts. Information on the effect of "blended" families, and the importance of extended families and siblings on children of divorced parents is limited. (41 references)

615. ———. "Divorce: Cultural Factors and Kinship Factors in the Adjustment of Children." *Child Psychiatry and Human Development* 17(2): 121–128 (Winter 1986).

This article discusses the way that primitive cultures deal with marital separation and the role of extended family. Research on the role of grandparents and siblings in divorce is examined. Western cultures may profit from some of the practices of primitive societies. Grandparents may provide the least damaging alternative for children of divorced families, and their natural parents would still have access to them. Suggestions for health professionals are made. (23 references)

616. Fisher, Esther Oshiver. "A Guide to Divorce Counseling." *Family Coordinator* 22(1): 55–61 (January 1973).

Divorce counseling is a therapeutic process by which those who experience grief, depression, loneliness, failure, anxiety and hostility can be helped to work through these feelings toward personal growth and adjustment. Guidelines for pre-divorce counseling, divorce counseling, and post-divorce counseling are presented. Differences in the counseling goals for each of these stages of the divorce process are discussed. The counselor has the ultimate responsibility of helping the client clarify his own values and understand their application in regard to ex-spouse, children, relatives and friends. (7 references)

617. Flosi, James V. "Children of Divorce: Ministry to Tangled Lives." *Momentum* 11(3): 30, 32–33 (October 1980).

The challenge of the decade for educators is to administer to the insecurities, failures and guilt feelings of children from divorced families. The process of divorcing is viewed as involving loss of attachment, litigation, transition from married to single life, and the final adjustment or reorganization stage. These stages in the divorce process are discussed in relation to the effects on children's behavior during each period. It is concluded that children do adapt over a period of one to two years and that during this time educators play a significant role in their lives. The difference between counseling and ministering is emphasized and the ways that educators can be supportive of the divorced and their children are discussed. (12 references)

618. Foster, Henry H. "Child Custody and Divorce: A Lawyer's View." *Journal of the American Academy of Child Psychiatry* 22(4): 392–398 (July 1983).

This article reviews the history of child custody laws up to and including the present day practice of considering the child's developmental needs and relationship with family members. The role of the child psychiatrist in helping the court to arrive at custody decisions and helping the child through therapy during the divorce process is discussed. It is recommended that each custody case be decided on its own merits and suggests that caution be exercised in regard to predicting future human behavior. (7 references)

619. Francke, Linda Bird. *Growing up Divorced.* New York: Linden, 1983.

This book focuses on the impact of divorce on children of all ages and its effect on parent/child relationships. Two emotions predominant in the approximately 100 children interviewed were sadness and anger. Findings indicate that boys of all ages seem to have reactions that are deeper than girls. Schools are central to the lives of children and cannot avoid dealing with the consequences of divorce as they affect the teaching learning process. Step-families and child custody arrangements may further complicate the lives of children from divorcing families. Implications for public policy as it relates to single parents and especially to female-headed families are noted. (Bibliography)

620. Fry, P. S., and Jean Addington. "Perceptions of Parent and Child Adjustment in Divorced Families." *Clinical Psychology Review* 5(2): 141–157 (1985).

Perceptions of parent and child adjustment in divorced families are examined from the perspective of four systems and their interactions: 1) the autogenic system focuses on the effects that the child's age, sex and temperament have on adjustment to parental divorce, 2) the ecosystem on the effects of the post-divorce environment and the available support systems on the divorced families, 3) the macrosystem on more general issues of children's rights and status of the single parent and 4) the microsystem on problems arising from inadequate parental coping styles, interparent coping relationships, child custody and visitations. Some appropriate intervention models exist in some court related programs, however experience has shown that the more the parents arrange their own negotiations, the more likely they will continue with the agreement. (38 references)

621. Fulton, Julie A. "Parental Reports of Children's Post-Divorce Adjustment." *Journal of Social Issues* 35(4): 126–139 (Fall 1979).

A representative sample of 560 divorced parents were interviewed in a study of divorce and child custody arrangements. Father's assessment of the effects of divorce on their children was significantly related to whether or not they were the post-divorce custodians. On the other hand, mothers related their children's adjustment to their own level of physical and emotional well-being following divorce. Most of the participants in the study felt that both they and their children had been negatively affected by the divorce, but viewed it as a less painful choice to continuing in an unhappy marriage. (4 references)

622. Furstenberg, Frank F., Jr., et al. "The Life Course of Children of Divorce: Marital Disruption and Parental Contact." *American Sociological Review* 48(5): 656–668 (October 1983).

A sample of 2,279 children ages seven to eleven from 1,747 households spanning 48 states were interviewed in a study of the well-being of children funded by the Foundation for Child Development. Findings reveal that blacks were more likely than whites to have experienced disruption by early adolescence, and within five years a larger number of white children would be in stepfamilies. Frequent contact with the non-custodial parent occurred in only 17 percent of the disrupted families regardless of race. Findings seem to support that contact with the noncustodial parent following divorce ceases or the relationship becomes the equivalent of a ritual form of parenthood. (10 references)

623. ———. "Paternal Participation and Children's Well-Being After Marital Dissolution." *American Sociology Review* 52(5): 695–701 (October 1987).

Data for this study was taken from the National Survey of Children. It focuses on 227 of a sample of 1,423 children aged 11 to 16. Paternal involvement seemed to have little effect on children's academic performance, problem behavior, or psychological distress. Paternal economic support did tend to reduce to some extent the likelihood of problem behavior. Frequency of contact and closeness to the father showed no consistent influence on the available measures of child well-being. (27 references)

624. Gardner, Richard A. *The Boys and Girls Book About Divorce.* New York: Jason Aronson, 1970.

The purpose of this book is to help children from divorced families to get along better with their parents and to help them cope better with the post-divorce situations in which they often find themselves. Children's feelings following divorce, conflict between separated parents, blended families, relationships with parents and peers are among the areas covered. Divorced parents and children who read this book may find it helpful. (No references)

625. ————. "Children of Divorce: Some Legal and Psychological Considerations." *Journal of Clinical Child Psychology* 6(2): 3–6 (Summer 1977).

This article identifies some issues that counselors of separated parents and their children need to keep in mind. Such issues as counselor neutrality, the vulnerability of children at different stages in their development, reactions of children that can be expected, and problems of custody and visitation. Suggestions for social and legal changes aimed at reducing the psychological trauma of divorce are offered. (52 references)

626. ————. *The Parents' Book about Divorce.* New York: Doubleday, 1977.

Parents are informed about the effects of divorce on children and ways that they can be helped through this stressful period are suggested. All children do not react in exactly the same way, and the age of a child at the time of parental separation in addition to the stress present before, during and after the divorce may place the child at increased psychological risk. When remarriage occurs relationships with stepparents, stepsiblings, and half-siblings can further complicate the child's post divorce adjustment. Good relationships between divorced parents lessen the likelihood that children will develop psychological problems. (No references)

627. ———. *Psychotherapy with Children of Divorce*. New York: Jason Aronson, 1976.

The primary focus of this book is on techniques used by the author in treating children of divorce. The task of the therapist who works alone with a child is much more difficult because children's psychopathology is intimately related to their parents' attitudes toward and involvement with them. Advising separating parents, determining when therapy is needed, special therapeutic techniques, children's post divorce feelings, the therapist's role and divorce litigation are among the areas discussed. Divorce itself does not necessarily cause psychopathological reactions in children however, the stresses and traumas that occur before, during and after the separation are potential sources of trouble. (Bibliotherapy)

628. Garfinkel, Irwin, and Elizabeth Uhr. "A New Approach to Child Support." *Public Interest* 75: 111–122 (Spring 1984).

Nearly half of all children in female-headed families are poor. The authors suggest use of a social child-support program with wage deductions from the absent parent which would be enforced by law. Presently, the amount of support an absent parent pays is usually not based on ability to pay, but on varying attitudes of local judges, welfare officials and the parents. A demonstration program in Wisconsin is discussed. (Bibliograpy footnotes)

629. George Washington University. *Single Parent Families*, Parts 1–4. Institute for Educational Leadership; National Public Radio. George Washington University, 1980. 59pp. (ERIC Microfiche ED196563)

Four National Public Radio interviews with single parents, their children and concerned others are recounted in these transcriptions. The interviews cover a wide range of topics, including methods used by single parents to resolve family problems. Additionally, the reactions of a young girl to her parents' divorce, aspects of the relationship between a father and his daughter, and resources providing support to single parents and their children are described. (No references)

630. Glenn, Norval D., and Kathryn B. Kramer. "The Divorce: Marriages and Divorces of the Children of Divorce." *Journal of Marriage and the Family* 49(4): 811–825 (November 1987).

United State national surveys from 1973–1985 were used to provide estimates of the effect of divorce on the divorce proneness of offspring of divorced white males and females, and divorced black males and females. Findings show that there is a tendency for divorce to run in families, at least among white females. A small part of the divorce transmission effect is said to be due to the tendency of children of divorce to marry at an early age. (27 references)

631. ———. " The Psychological Well-Being of Adult Children of Divorce." *Journal of Marriage and the Family* 47(4): 905–912 (November 1985).

The impact of parental divorce on the psychological well-being of white adults was investigated through multiple regression analysis of data from eight recent national surveys. The estimated effects of parental divorce were judged to be almost consistently negative. The authors caution that inferences of "no important long-term effects" which were made on the basis of earlier survey data analyses should be viewed with skepticism. (7 references)

632. Glick, Paul C. "Children of Divorced Parents in Demographic Perspective." *Journal of Social Issues* 35(4): 170–182 (1979).

The purpose of this paper is to report actual and projected demographic changes regarding children under 18 years old with divorced parents. By 1990 it is estimated that one third of the children 18 years of age will have lived with a divorced parent, although the rate of divorce will increase more slowly in the next decade. Social and economic characteristics of divorced parents and the consequences of these patterns are discussed. The low divorce rate of the 60's was accompanied by low ages at marriage, high birth rates, low school enrollment and employment of women. It is suggested that more married persons should place a premium on the goal of a better marriage or accept the consequences of divorce. (19 references)

633. Gray, Mary McPhail. "Separation through Divorce: Supportive Professional Practices." *Child Care Quarterly* 14(4): 248–261 (Winter 1985).

Child care professionals are in a unique position to aid parents and children during the divorce transition process. Economic, time, and communication stressors, as well as the stress of being involved in two households, are discussed and supportive practices are recommended for professionals, in dealing with each specific type of stress. Suggestions help both parent and children during the adjustment period following separation and divorce. (24 references)

634. Green, Barbara J. "Helping Elementary School Children of Divorce: A Multimodal Approach." *Elementary School Guidance and Counseling* 13(1): 31–45 (October 1978).

A multimodal eight session group counseling program for children of divorce is described. The sessions deal with health care, academic achievement, relationships with people, self-image, information about divorce, behavior, and problem solving. Research that supports a group counseling approach is mentioned. Bibliotherapy, audio- and videotapes are used to facilitate communication. (17 references)

635. ———. "Helping Single-Parent Families." *Elementary School Guidance and Counseling* 15(3): 249–261 (February 1981).

This article focuses on the effects of divorce on parents and children and reports on a community program designed to help them make the transition from the traditional family to the single-parent family. The developmental age and sex of the child accounts to a large extent for differences in the way children respond to the divorce process. Changes in behavior, emotional reactions, academic achievement and interpersonal relationships may be noted. A seven-unit model, HELPING, designed for parents' and children's groups, is outlined. Bibliotherapeutic materials include films and books for children and parents. (40 references)

636. Greif, Judith B. "Fathers, Children and Joint Custody." *American Journal of Orthopsychiatry* 49(2): 311–219 (April 1979).

This study examines the separation and post divorce father-child relationship from the father's viewpoint. Forty middle-class fathers were interviewed for the study. Fathers who had the least contact with their children reported decreased paternal influence in the areas of emotional and moral development, discipline and financial decision-making. The greater the father's contact with his child the more he was involved in a parental role after divorce. It is recommended that the contact between the child and both parents be maximized. Children of the subjects ranging in age from five to twelve years did not participate in the study. (12 references)

637. Greif, Geoffrey L. "Mothers Without Custody and Child Support." *Family Relations* 35(1): 87–93 (January 1986).

A sample of 517 mothers without custody were studied in regard to child support payments. These mothers volunteered to complete a questionnaire with over 80 items that was published in *Parents Without Partners*. It was found that mothers who paid child support payments earned higher incomes, were less likely to be living with any of their children and were more likely to describe themselves as being more involved with their children than those who did not pay support. Some mothers pay because the court ordered it, some pay because it seemed fair and some because they wish more involvement with their children. It is suggested that support payments, however small lets the children know the mother cares. Suggestions for practioners are offered. (24 references)

638. Greif, Geoffrey L., and Mary S. Pabst. *Mothers Without Custody* Lexington, Mass.: D.C. Heath 1988.

Five hundred noncustodial mothers were surveyed regarding their relationships with their children. Responses to questionnaires seemed to indicate that the mothers viewed their position as in role conflict and were not clear about what the expectations are for their behavior. Voluntary surrender of custody was found to be a good predictor of adaptation to being a noncustodial mother. The noncustodial mother is advised to keep in contact with children, be truthful in communication with children, and to not attempt child snatching. The need for a support group is indicated. (Bibliography)

639. Grote, Douglas F., and Jeffrey Weinstein. "Joint Custody: A Viable and Ideal Alternative." *Journal of Divorce* 1(1): 43–52 (Fall 1977).

Joint custody is proposed as a more viable option in addressing the rights and remedies of parents who are divorcing than custodial awards as they exist today. The equal rights movement is regarded as pushing fathers to compete for the same custodial power they once had. Traditionally the father was the final authority in the home, and this authority is seen as having potential benefit for a child's sexual identification. It is suggested that mothers and fathers can be expected to try to act like mature parents if they are given legal coequal power that is their right and responsibility. It is concluded that children's emotional and developmental needs are best served by a family system that operates on a freely interacting evolving basis. (16 references)

640. Guerney, Louise, and Lucy Jordon. "Children of Divorce— A Community Support Group." *Journal of Divorce* 2(3): 283–294 (Spring 1979).

Children of Divorce is a community based education support group designed to assist children in adjusting to separation or divorce. Aimed at prevention the program is open to all child volunteer participants. Children meet with volunteer group leaders for six weekly sessions. The program aims to help children: 1) develop realistic appraisals of their situation, 2) acquire problem solving skills and 3) boost self-esteem. Future plans include the development of program packages to train personnel from agencies and institutions and to educate the community to the magnitude of the problems encountered by children of divorce. (13 references)

641. Guidubaldi, John, and Helen Cleminshaw. "Divorce, Family Health, and Child Adjustment." *Family Relations* 34(1): 35–41 (January 1985).

The findings for this study on a comparison of the physical health rating of divorced families with those of intact families were extracted from a national study on the impact of divorce on children. A random sample of 699 first, third, and fifth grade students from divorced and intact families in 38 states was used. While many measures were used in the total study, only selected instruments were used in the analyses of this aspect of the study. Findings indicated that the health status of parents and children are affected by divorce and it changes the focus of concern from mental health to total health of the post-divorce family. Recommendations for school-based support services are made. (25 references)

642. ———."Impact of Family Support Systems on Children's Academic and Social Functioning After Divorce." Paper presented at the Annual Convention of the American Psychological Association, Anaheim, Calif., August 26–30, 1983) 12pp. (ERIC Microfiche ED235887)

This paper focuses on the role of support systems in mediating the impact of divorce on family stress and child adjustment, and in the academic achievement and social functioning of children in particular. Data from an ongoing nationwide study begun at Kent State University in 1981 by the National Association of School Psychologists was the basis for analyses. Adequate support systems and the custodial parent's activities in occupational and educational endeavors were found to be significantly related to child performance and school adjustment. (8 references)

643. Guidubaldi, John, and Joseph D. Perry. "Divorce and Mental Health Sequelae for Children: A Two-Year Follow-Up of a Nationwide Sample." *Journal of American Academy of Child Psychiatry* 24(5): 531–537 (September 1985).

This article presents initial results of a longitudinal study of the effects of divorce on children conducted by the National Association of School Psychologists—Kent State University. One hundred ten children from the original 699 children were evaluated again at the end of two years. Findings showed that children from divorced families performed more poorly on several measures than children from intact families and boys showed more negative effects than girls. When controls for family income were instituted, fewer differences were found between groups, however controls for child's IQ did not change results. (55 references)

644. ———. "Divorce, Socioeconomic Status, and Children's Cognitive-Social Competence at School Entry." *American Journal of Orthopsychiatry* 54(3): 459–468 (July 1984).

One hundred and fifteen kindergarten students were evaluated with a variety of measures to determine the significance of single-parent status on school-entry competencies. Extensive analytical data on intellectual, social academic and adaptive behavior is presented. Results indicate that children from divorced families enter school with significantly less social and academic competence than children from intact families. Single parent status was a more powerful predictor of competencies than socioeconomic status. A longitudinal investigation of the impact of divorce on the behavior and competence of these children in relation to developmental level is planned. (41 references)

645. Guidubaldi, John, et al. "The Impact of Parental Divorce on Children: Report of the Nationwide NASP Study." *School Psychology Review* 12(3): 300–323 (Fall 1983).

The impact of divorce on 699 children from the first, third and fifth grades as reported by 144 randomly selected members of the National Association of School Psychologists is presented. Measures used included parent-child interviews, and Wechsler-Intelligence Scale for Children (WISC-R) and Wide Range Achievement Test (WRAT) scores in addition to ratings by classroom teachers. Boys from divorced families were found to have lower social and academic adjustment than boys from intact families, independent of socio-economic status. Regular contact with the father resulted in better performance by boys on some measures. Directions for intervention suggested by findings are offered. (62 references)

646. ———. "The Role of Selected Family Environment Factors in Children's Post-Divorce Adjustment." *Family Relations* 35(1): 141–151 (January 1986).

Findings of the NASP-KSU Nationwide study of the impact of divorce are reported. A sample of 341 divorced family children were assessed with a variety of instruments to measure social, academic and health criteria. Home environment factors that contribute to healthy child development in the divorced family include interpersonal relationships, child-rearing styles, and changes in home routines. Factors that enhance a child's adjustment after divorce may be different depending on the child's age and sex. Guidelines for professionals who work with divorced families are offered. (61 references)

647. Hammond, Janice M. "Children of Divorce: Implications for Counselors." *The School Counselor* 27(1): 7–14 (September 1979).

This study compares differences in classroom behavior, self-concept and attitudes of children from divorced families with those of children from intact families. The Walker Problem Behavior Identification Checklist, the Piers and Harris Self-Concept Scale, Attitude Toward Family Questionnaire and the Hammond Children of Divorce Questionnaire were administered to 165 students in grades three to six. Boys from divorced families were rated by teachers as having more behavior problems and in turn rated their families as less happy and their mothers as less attentive. More than half of the subjects felt they could talk to school counselors about problems and that counselors could be helpful when parents were separating. Suggestions for individual and group counseling and a list of books on divorce are offered. (21 references)

648. Handford, H. Allen, et al. "Children of Divorced Parents." *Journal of the American Academy of Child Psychiatry* 25(3): 409–414 (May 1986).

A sample of 105 boys and girls, eight to 16 years of age, were studied for depressive syndrome following the loss of one or both parents due to death, divorce, or separation. Students identified as depressed upon admission to school had more house-parent discipline and academic failure nine months later. It is suggested that the Children's Depression Inventory can be used to identify children in an at-risk population early. Implications for therapeutic intervention are noted. (19 references)

649. Haskins, Ron, et al. "Single Parent Families: Policy Recommendations for Child Support." Paper presented at the Conference on Changing Roles of Women in North Carolina (Raleigh, N.C., May 9–10, 1983. 40pp. (ERIC Microfiche ED259820)

A large number of children experience divorce and many live in poverty or in a family with substantially reduced income. Although there have been federal and state efforts to strengthen child support, the problem of low income for female-headed families continues. Four alternative policies that address this issue are examined with regard to seven criteria: equity, efficiency, stigma, preference satisfaction, family privacy, paternal responsibility, and effects on the post-separation family. Social policy recommendations are offered for the state of North Carolina. (59 references)

650. Hess, Robert D., and Kathleen A. Camara. "Post-Divorce Family Relationships as Mediating Factors in the Consequences of Divorce for Children." *Journal of Social Issues* 35(4): 79–96 (Fall 1979).

The social and school behavior of children nine to eleven year old from divorced families was compared with those of children from intact families and the association between family processes and child outcomes were analyzed. The relationships between family members were found to be more significant than the marital status of parents. Positive relationships with both parents mitigated the negative effects of divorce and facilitated developmental progress. Implications for public policy and counseling are noted. (7 references)

651. Hetherington, E. Mavis. "Divorced Fathers." *Family Coordinator* 25(4): 417–428 (October 1976).

Forty-eight divorced parents and their preschool children were compared with 48 intact families two years following divorce. This longitudinal study involved observations, interviews, self reports, rating scales and standardized test measures at two months, one year and two years post divorce. Fathers were coping better with seeing their children infrequently although they continued to experience a great sense of loss and depression. In addition to parent child relations, post-divorce stress affected life style and attitude toward self. Divorced parents made fewer maturity demands on children, had poorer communication, were less consistent in discipline and were less affectionate. (14 references)

652. ———. "Effects of Divorce on Parents and Children." In *Nontraditional Families: Parenting and Child Development*, edited by Michael Lamb, 233–288. Hillsdale, N.J.: Erlbaum, 1982.

It is generally accepted that the outcomes of divorce vary for individuals in a family as the stresses, support systems, and coping strategies differ. In this study of the effects of divorce, seventy-two white, middle-class children and their divorced parents were compared with the same number of children and parents from intact homes. A variety of measures were administered at one month, one year and two years following divorce. The single-parent children who lived with their custodial mothers, suffered more stresses and coping problems than children from intact families. Although there were no victimless divorces, unless severe stress and adversity were encountered, most parents and children adapted to their new family situation within two years. The need to identify and develop adequate support systems for divorced families was noted. (64 references)

653. ———. "Family Interaction and the Social, Emotional and Cognitive Development of Children Following Divorce." Paper presented at the Symposium on The Family: Setting Priorities. May 17–20, 1978. 28pp. (ERIC Microfiche ED156328)

Forty-eight children (24 boys, 24 girls) and parents from single parent families in which custody had been granted to the mother and 48 children (24 boys, 24 girls and their parents) from intact families were compared. A multimeasure, multimethod approach which included observation of parents and children at home and in school was used to investigate family interaction. Overall results indicate that patterns of family interaction change dramatically in the two years following divorce and that the behavior of the divorced father becomes less important than that of the mother in the child's social and cognitive development. However, fathers who maintained frequent contact with their children had more impact on their children's development. (26 references)

654.   ———. "Play and Social Interaction in Children Following Divorce." *Journal of Social Issues* 35(4): 26–49 (Fall 1979).

Forty-eight middle class white preschool children from divorced families were matched with an equal number of children from two-parent families to study the effects of divorce on play and social interaction in children at two months, one year, and two years after divorce. Measures used involved free play and peer nominations, and sociometric measures. Results show that boys from divorced families spent more time playing with younger children than girls in all time periods. At the end of two years, boys were still showing more anxious behavior, but their social behavior had improved. Even after the behavior of boys from divorced families improved they were viewed more negatively by peers and teachers than girls from divorced families. Suggestions are made for additional research. (57 references)

655.   Hetherington, E. Mavis, and Josephine D. Arasteh. *Impact of Divorce, Single Parenting and Stepparenting on Children*. Hillsdale, N.J.: Lawrence Erlbaum Associates, 1988.

This book contains sixteen papers that were originally presented at a conference sponsored by the National Institute of Child Health and Human Development, May

6–7, 1985. They have been updated and revised for this book. They cover such topics as: single parenting in black families, settlement of divorce disputes, custody of children, long-term effects of divorce on children, antisocial behavior in boys from divorced families and sole custody compared with joint custody. (Bibliographies)

656. Hingst, Ann Godley. "Children and Divorce: The Child's View." *Journal of Clinical Child Psychology* 10(3): 161–164 (Fall 1981).

Eighty-four elementary school children whose mothers had responded to a questionnaire on their children's reactions to divorce were interviewed to determine how they felt about the divorce and its aftermath. Children's responses were compared with those of their mothers. The results point to the importance of fathers in the lives of these children, although 23 percent of the children were seen by their mothers as having little opportunity to build a relationship with their fathers. The children's perceptions of the atmosphere in the home, their feelings before and after divorce, and the wisdom of divorce as an alternative differed from the perceptions of their mothers. Mothers tended to diminish the negative effects of divorce on the children. (6 references)

657. Hodges, William F., and Bernard L. Bloom. "Parent's Report of Children's Adjustment to Marital Separation: A Longitudinal Study." *Journal of Divorce* 8(1): 33–50 (Fall 1984).

One hundred and seven children below the age of 18 whose parents recently separated were described in parental interviews at an average of two months post separation and again at six and eighteen months post separation. A questionnaire on parenting and the Child Behavior Checklist were used as measures. Findings reported suggest that parental separation places children at risk, the pattern of adjustment was affected by age of the child, boys experienced more difficulty than girls, and parenting problems are ranked highest as a problem in second marriages. Implications for intervention programs are discussed. (34 references)

658. Hodges, William F., et al. "Divorce and the Preschool Child: Cumulative Stress." *Journal of Divorce* 3(1): 55–66 (Fall 1979).

Fifty-two preschool children from divorced and intact families were studied to determine the effects of divorce on development. Information on children was obtained from parents, teachers and direct observation at five preschools representing various lifestyles and socio-economic groups. Findings indicated no differences in aggression between children of divorce and children from intact families on any measure. There was evidence that the cumulative effects associated with the divorce, as well as presence of younger parents, less money and greater geographic mobility, did result in greater maladjustment. Further study on the interactive effect of divorce in combination with other life stressors is suggested. (32 references)

659. Hoffman, Jeffrey A. "Psychological Separation of Late Adolescents from Their Parents." *Journal of Counseling Psychology* 31(2): 170–178 (April 1984).

The Parental Separation Inventory was administered to 75 males and 75 females undergraduate students to assess aspects of psychological separation from their parents. Results showed that greater conflictual independence was related to better personal adjustment. It is suggested that the effects of divorce on late adolescents may also be mediated by aspects of psychological separation. Implications for psychologists counseling college age adolescents with personal adjustment problems are discussed. (16 references)

660. Holman, Thomas B. "Marital Instability, Maternal Stress, and Sex-Role Development in Children." *Family Perspective* 17(2): 89–100 (Spring 1983).

Interaction techniques used by parents that help define the type of mother-child relationship in unstable marriages are examined for their effect on child development. An examination of theoretical and empirical studies indicates that the more supportive and inductive the interaction of the mother is with the child, the more masculine is the role development of the son. Although marital instability may affect girls' sex-role development, it may take a longer period of time for the full effects to surface. Suggestions for additional study are made. (30 references)

661. Hoorwitz, Aaron Noah. "Videotherapy in the Context of Group Therapy for Late Latency Children of Divorce." *Psychotherapy* 21(1): 48–53 (Spring 1984).

Discusses videotherapy as it is being used by Unified Services for children and Adolescents in Rensselaer County, New York. The therapy takes the form of videotaped dramas created by a group of children with the intent of making a "movie." They discuss what each character was feeling and how those feelings led to troublesome behaviors and unfortunate outcomes. Then alternative cognitive and behavioral solutions that could have been used are explored. Videotherapy should be appropriately timed and used in context with other therapeutic activities. The role of the therapist in videotherapy is almost the same as in most role playing where the therapist directs and coaches to the degree necessary to elicit relevant action from the client. (12 references)

662. Howell, Robert J., and Kate E. Toepke. "Summary of the Child Custody Laws for the Fifty States." *American Journal of Family Therapy* 12(2): 56–60 (Summer 1984).

Laws relating to child custody determinations for 50 states are summarized in Table form. The special issues of joint and shared custody, best interests of the child, the Uniform Child Custody Act, and the acceptance of psychological investigations of the child and/or the child's family are discussed. The approach used by the authors in providing services to the courts in child custody suits is presented. (2 references)

663. Isaacs, Marla Beth, et al. *The Difficult Divorce: Therapy for Children and Families.* New York: Basic Books, 1986.

This book focuses on the difficult divorce in which the parents are unable to control their disputes and subsequently involve their children in the conflict. Therapy can strengthen sibling relationships and combat inappropriate cross-generational alliances. Acceptance of their parents' new partners may take more time than parents anticipate and visitation with the noncustodial parent can cause additional problems. Cases from the authors' clinical practice are used to illustrate therapeutic approaches used in helping children and parents cope with the consequences of divorce. (Bibliography)

664. Jackson, Anna M., et al. "Beyond the Best Interests of the Child Revisited: An Approach to Custody Evaluations." *Journal of Divorce* 3(3): 207–222 (Spring 1980).

An evaluative procedure developed at the Colorado Children's Diagnostic Center involving a team approach to divorce custody is described. The CDC consults directly with District Judges in making custody recommendations. Philosophy and procedures for custody evaluations are presented. Attempts are made to assess parental attitudes and capabilities, the psychological attachment of parent and child, and the impact of the stress of divorce on individuals in the family. Data indicates that a significant number of recommendations are followed by judges and serve as useful guidelines in making legal custody decisions. (10 references)

665. Jacobson, Doris S. "The Impact of Marital Separation/ Divorce on Children: I. Parent-Child Separation and Child Adjustment." *Journal of Divorce* 1(4): 341–360 (Summer 1978).

The first of a larger study on the impact of divorce on children examines the child's psychosocial adjustment and the effect of parental separation. The sample consisted of 30 families with 51 children who were examined within 12 months after marital separation. Two instruments used in the study were the Time Spent Form developed by the researcher and the Louisville Behavior Checklist. Findings suggest the amount of time lost in the presence of the father is a crucial aspect of adjustment following separation of parents. No significant findings regarding the time lost with mother as associated with psychosocial adjustment of the child were observed. Father-presence for children during the first year after parental separation is supported. (2 references)

666. ———. "The Impact of Marital Separation/Divorce on Children: II. Interparent Hostility and Child Adjustment." *Journal of Divorce* 2(1): 3–19 (Fall 1978).

This is the second of three articles on the impact of marital separation/divorce on children aged three to seventeen during the 12 months following parental separation. This paper deals specifically with the effect of interparent hostility on children in divorcing families. Thirty families with 51 children were interviewed. Measures used were the Hostility Schedule Administration and the Louisville Behavior Checklist. It was found that the greater the amount of interparent hostility, the greater the maladjustment of the child. It is recommended that the long-term effects of parental separation where interparent hostility is expressed be studied. The implications for intervention by professionals are discussed. (16 references)

667. ———. "The Impact of Marital Separation/Divorce on Children: III. Parent-Child Communication and Child Adjustment and Regression Analysis of Findings from Overall Study." *Journal of Divorce* 2(2): 175–194 (Winter 1978).

This is the third part of a study on the effects on children aged three-seventeen during the 12 months following separation/divorce. Thirty families with 51 children were subjects of this study. The measures used included the Parent Child Communication Schedule, the Louisville Behavior Checklist and the rating form for the clinical rater judgment concerning attention given to the child in dealing with the separation. The study examines the psychosocial adjustment of the child and the association between this adjustment and 1) the time and activity with each parent, 2) the expression of hostility between parents and 3) the preparatory socialization the child had for the marital separation. Implications for clinicians are discussed. (26 references)

668. Jansen, Livia S. "Children's Perceptions of Their Parents: Relationship to Child Adjustment Following Divorce." Portions of paper presented at the Biennial Meeting of the Society for Research in Child Development (Toronto, Ontario, Canada), April 25–28, 1985. 41pp. (ERIC Microfiche ED256501)

Eighty children, equally divided between divorced female-headed families and intact families, their mothers and teachers completed measures designed to assess perceptions of parents, and the relationship of perceptions to child adjustment. Findings showed children of divorce had less well integrated perceptions of their parents than children from intact families. The level of interparental hostility seemed to mediate some of the group differences. Positive perceptions of parents on content and structural dimensions were positively associated with the ratings of children's social adjustment. (33 references)

669. Jenkins, Shirley. "Children of Divorce." In *Annual Program in Child Psychiatry and Child Development*, edited by Stella Chess, and Alexander Thomas, 283–292. New York: Brunner/ Mazel, 1979.

Child support, custody, emotional adjustment and step relationships are viewed as areas that require attention in evaluating the needs of children of divorce. Each area is discussed and approaches for dealing with the problems encountered in each are offered. Depending on the children's ages and developmental phases they may need special help in working through the effects of divorce. (Bibliography)

670. Johnson, Colleen Leahy. *Ex Familia: Grandparents, Parents, and Children Adjust to Divorce.* New Brunswick: Rutgers University Press, 1989.

This work focuses on the increasing incidence of divorce and its effect on older persons through the intergenerational relationships in families during the divorce process and after. Case studies and anecdotal reports are provided that cover a variety of situations and patterns of family reorganization following divorce. It is suggested that when parents and their divorced children have the freedom to redefine their family system to meet their own needs and interests, intergenerational relationships do not necessarily deteriorate. (Bibliography)

671. Kalter, Neil. "Children of Divorce in an Outpatient Psychiatric Population." *American Journal of Orthopsychiatry* 47(1):40–51 (January 1977).

Records of four hundred children from a clinical population were examined to evaluate the effects of parental divorce. The narrative case history of each subject was coded to fifteen symptom categories. Age and sex were found to be significantly related to marital status of parent and type of symptomatology. Children of divorced parents appeared in larger numbers in the psychiatric clinic than would ordinarily be expected from their numbers in the general population. Girls whose mothers remarry seem to be particularly at risk. Areas deserving further exploration are noted. (13 references)

672. ———. "Conjoint Mother-Daughter Treatment: A Beginning Phase of Psychotherapy with Adolescent Daughters

of Divorce." *American Journal of Orthopsychiatry* 54(3): 490–497 (July 1984).

Three clinical case studies of adolescent girls are presented, which explore developmental stress consequent to parental divorce. Although adolescents claim they are entitled to greater independence, they exhibit behaviors that results in greater supervision by their mothers. This paper discusses conjoint mother-daughter intervention therapy as a means of addressing the social-emotional issues presented by adolescents who have difficulty coping with father loss. (15 references)

673. ———. "Long-Term Effects of Divorce on Children: A Developmental Vulnerability Model." *American Journal of Orthopsychiatry* 57(4): 587–600 (October 1987).

This paper looks at the potential long-term effects of divorce on children are: handling of anger and aggression, separation - individuation and gender identity. It is suggested that co-parenting relationships characterized by mutual respect, minimal hostility and awareness of feeling loved and valued can provide a postdivorce environment that can help children attain key developmental goals. Implications for prevention and therapy are noted. (46 references)

674. Kanoy, Korrel W., and Brent C. Miller. "Children's Impact on the Parental Decision to Divorce." *Family Relations* 29(3): 309–315 (July 1980).

The effect of children on their parents' decision to divorce is explored. Both theoretical constructions and empirical evidence in research literature are viewed in assessing children's impact on divorce and a model conceptualizing these effects is presented. It is concluded that the mere presence or absence of children does not lead to divorce, but that children's potential for creating stress between parents increases its likelihood. Parental value conflicts and children's handicaps may also produce stress and heighten tensions. Very young dependent children seem to serve as a barrier to divorce unless the parents believe the divorce will benefit the children. (30 references)

675. Keilin, William G., and Larry J. Bloom. "Child Custody Evaluation Practices: A Survey of Experienced Professionals." *Professional Psychology: Research and Practice* 17(4):338–346 (August 1986).

Mental health professionals are enjoying an enlarged role in the evaluation and resolution of custody disputes. A questionnaire was completed by 190 professionals with interviews, and a variety of tests were administered to parents and children as part of the evaluation procedures. Single custody determinations were generally based on wishes of the older child, attitudes of the parents toward each other, psychological stability of parents, and the need to keep siblings together. In awarding joint custody, one parent is given physical custody while both parents share in decision making. This was the most preferred and recommended arrangement when a decision for joint custody was made. In general, participants viewed joint custody as appropriate only in specific and limited situations. (31 references)

676. Kelly, Joan B. "Long-Term Adjustment in Children of Divorce: Converging Findings and Implications for Practice. *Journal of Family Psychology* 2(2): 119–140 (December 1988).

This article summarizes research dealing with the long-term effects of divorce on children. Areas of particular focus includes: 1) impact of parental conflict, 2) psychological adjustment of the custodial parent, 3) relationship with the noncustodial parent, 4) child care and 5) custodial arrangements. The role of mental health professionals in educational and therapeutic interventions with divorcing and postdivorce families is discussed. Critical responses to this article by several professionls and the author's reply complete this special section on divorce and its effects. (69 references)

677. ———. "Myths and Realities for Children of Divorce."
Educational Horizons 59(1): 34–39 (Fall 1980).

Seven myths of divorce are discussed in light of new
child-focused divorce research: 1) divorce is better for
children than an unhappy marriage, 2) children anticipate
divorce, 3) are relieved when parents divorce, 4) turmoil
ends with separation, 5) the divorce is in the best interests
of children, 6) children of divorce live in "single-parent
families" and 7) divorce is damaging to children. The
divorce experience is a prolonged and difficult period of
transition. What occurs in the aftermath of divorce is
likely to determine the children's future psychological
development. Divorce needs to occur in such a way as to
enable the children to successfully integrate the family
changes and continue unimpeded in their developmental
progress. (12 references)

678. Kelly, Joan B., and Judith S. Wallerstein. "Brief
Interventions with Children in Divorce Families."
American Journal of Orthopsychiatry 47(1): 23–36
(January 1977).

Preventive clinical interventions developed for children
of different ages whose parents are divorcing are described.
Guidelines for assessment of the child's development and
response to the divorce situation are discussed. Parent-
child relationships, the extended family, peers and
extracurricular activities and psychotherapy as support
systems are examined. Intervention strategies in the
preschool years, early latency, later latency and
preadolescence periods are suggested as part of a
theoretical proposal for planning and implementing age
appropriate therapeutic interventions. A follow-up report
of the 131 subjects of this study is planned. (9 references)

679. ———. "The Effects of Parental Divorce: Experiences of
the Child in Early Latency." *American Journal of
Orthopsychiatry* 46(1): 20–32 (January 1976).

The impact of divorce on 26 children in early latency, as

observed shortly after parental separation and one year later. This material is part of a larger clinical study, begun in 1970, of 60 divorcing families with 131 children. The seven- to ten-year-old showed differences in their respective capacities to deal with divorce. The younger latency group, seven and eight years old when their parents separated, were more immobilized by their suffering, and their defense organization was more vulnerable to regression. The older latency children showed a greater ability to integrate the more extended consequences of the family disruption. The divorce event is not the central factor in determining the outcome for the child, but rather the chain of events set in motion by the separation. (6 references)

680. Khoe, Lynn. "The Effects of Divorce on Children and Implications for Court Custody Cases." Doctor of Psychology Research Paper, Biola University, California, 1986. 47pp. (ERIC Microfiche ED273901)

Based on a review of research literature, this paper explores the effects of divorce on children's psychosocial development, school achievement, and sex role development. Factors found to influence children's adjustment included: children's age at divorce, parental stress and conflict and the quality of the parent-child relationship. There was not enough consistency in findings to draw rigid conclusions about custody decisions based on the effects of divorce on children. However, it is suggested that the emotional characteristics of the parent-child relationship, involvement of the father and a cooperative parental relationship are important factors in making custody decisions. (37 references)

681. Kittleson, Mark J. *Divorce and Children.* 1979. 15pp. (ERIC Microfiche ED169026)

The traumatic effect of divorce on young children is discussed, noting the typical changes in behavior evidenced by children in such a situation. Suggestions are made on ways parents can cope with the child's emotional reactions and alleviate the stress that is natural when a marriage dissolves. (11 references)

682. Koch, Mary Ann P., and Carol R. Lowery. "Visitation and the Noncustodial Father." *Journal of Divorce* 8(2): 47–65 (Winter 1984).

Thirty noncustodial fathers whose names were taken from court records agreed to be interviewed about the amount and quality of visitation with their children. An open-ended interview instrument was developed and the fathers' verbal response was coded by the interviewer. Subjects were white, middle income parents who had been divorced an average of eight months. Findings of the study indicated that 70 percent of the noncustodial fathers saw their children at least twice a month and at least as many provided regular financial support. Visitation was found to be significantly related to the relationship between the parents, and the quality of the father-child relationship was associated with a positive relationship. It is suggested that bimonthly visitation for a majority of divorced fathers is reasonable. (27 references)

683. Kressel, Kenneth, and Morton Deutsch. "Divorce Therapy: An In-Depth Survey of the Therapists' Views." *Family Process* 16(4): 413–443 (December 1977).

This study reports the results of interviews with 21 expert therapists to answer three major questions: 1) what are the criteria for a constructive divorce, 2) what obstacles in a marriage block a constructive divorce and 3) what strategies and tactics are most useful in intervention. Findings: The primary criterion of a constructive divorce was completion of the process of psychic separation and the protection of the welfare of minor children. Strategies in intervention included the need to win the trust and confidence of the partners, promotion of a climate supportive of decision making and resolving those factors that therapists believe inevitable and necessary. Issues needing further study are noted. (14 references)

684. Krueger, Lisa. "Marital Conflict and Children's Cognitive and Emotional Process." Ph.D. diss., University of Southern California, 1988.

For a summary see: *Dissertation Abstracts International* 49B(8): 347.

685. Kulka, Richard A., and Helen Weingarten. "The Long-Term Effects of Parental Divorce in Childhood on Adult Adjustment." *Journal of Social Issues* 35(4): 50–78 (Fall 1979).

Data from two national surveys of adults, 21 years of age or older, were examined to determine psychological and adult functioning in persons who had experienced parental separation or divorce before the age of 16. It was found that the marriage relationships and psychological well-being of adults who had experienced parental divorce was affected to a greater extent than those who had remained in intact families as children. However, when controls for contemporary life circumstances and social backgrounds were included, there was little evidence of any long term effects on those who had experienced parental divorce. (47 references)

686. Kurdek, Lawrence A. "An Integrative Perspective on Children's Divorce Adjustment." *American Psychologist* 36(8): 856–866 (August 1981).

Children's adjustment to their parents' divorce is examined as an interaction among cultural beliefs, attitudes and values, social supports, pre and post-separation functioning, and the psychological competencies of individual children. Research on these and related problems and issues is summarized and guidelines for future research are offered. As no single study could systematically and simultaneously consider all possible interactions of those elements that affect children's adjustment to divorce, the author suggests an integrative approach using teams of psychologists representing various specialties within the field as well as researchers from allied disciplines. (76 references)

687. Kurdek, Lawrence A., and Berthold Berg. "Children's Beliefs about Parental Divorce Scale: Psychometric Characteristics and Concurrent Validity." *Journal of Consulting and Clinical Psychology* 55(5): 712–718 (October 1987).

This study is probing the beliefs about parental divorce in a sample of 170 children aged from six to seventeen years. Children, their custodial parents and teachers completed measures that were compared with each. Many children were found to be anxious, have poor self-concepts in areas related to parents, and reported little social support. However, problematic beliefs were unrelated to parents' and teachers' ratings of children's behavior problems. It is suggested that parents and teachers may not be reliable judges of children's intrapersonal thoughts and feelings. (36 references)

688. Kurdek, Lawrence A., and Albert E. Siesky, Jr. "Children's Perceptions of Their Parents' Divorce." *Journal of Divorce* 3(4): 339–378 (Summer 1980).

Three hundred and thirty-two children five to nineteen years of age were interviewed to determine their perceptions of their parents' divorce. Five measures used in the study are discussed in detail. It was found that the extent to which a child views events as being internally controlled and understands the complexities of interpersonal relations affects the children's perceptions of various aspects of their parents' divorce. It may suggest that adverse reactions to parental divorce may dissipate as the altered family unit attains more equilibrium. Children in the sample seem to have a realistic perception of divorce. They are aware of the interpersonal conflicts that precipitate divorce and see the divorce decision as necessary and perhaps beneficial. (36 references)

689. ———. "Divorced Single Parents' Perceptions of Child-Related Problems." *Journal of Divorce* 1(4): 361–369 (Summer 1978).

Seventy-three divorced single parents were asked to complete a questionnaire in which rated the severity of child related problems. Severity problems did not show a marked change in the post divorce period. However, the problems of greatest concern centered on discipline and behavior problems and lack of a stable male model. The greatest beneficial effect of the separation or divorce was the absence of tension and fear in the home. (8 references)

690. ———. "Effects of Divorce on Children: the Relationship between Parent and Child Perspectives." *Journal of Divorce* 4(2): 85–99 (Winter 1980).

Open-ended questionnaires were administered to 71 divorced single parents and their 130 children who were between five and nineteen years old to measure the children's reaction and adjustment to divorce. Children who were seen as having had adjustment problems were more likely to feel that their friends pitied and sympathized with them, and indicated they were more likely to marry in order to raise a family than for love or companionship. Favorable reactions and adjustments were seen in children who defined divorce in terms of psychological separation, who discussed it freely with friends, and who made positive evaluations of both parents. (11 references)

691. ———. "An Interview Study of Parents' Perceptions of Their Children's Reactions and Adjustments to Divorce." *Journal of Divorce* 3(1): 5–17 (Fall 1979).

Seventy-four single divorced custodial parents were interviewed regarding their children's reactions and adjustments to divorce. Children in this study ranged in age from five to nineteen years. The questions used in the interview are discussed. Findings show: 1) one or both parents tell their children about the impending divorce and children respond in a variety of ways, 2) children's adjustment affects school performance and younger children have more difficulty, 3) most children do not suffer from self-blame, 4) a moderate degree of conflict precedes divorce, and parents feel that children derive positive benefits as a result of their adjustment to divorce. Suggestions for additional study are given. (6 references)

692. ———. "Sex Role Self-Concepts of Single Divorced Parents and Their Children." *Journal of Divorce* 3(3): 249–261 (Spring 1980).

This study examines the effect of divorce on children's sex role self-concept. Subjects were 74 single divorced parents and their 92 children whose ages spanned 10–19 years of age. The Bem Sex Role Inventory was given to parents and a modified version of the same instrument was given to children. Results suggest that divorced mothers and fathers tend to describe themselves in androgynous terms and that sex role self-concept can reflect demands from life situations. Findings also suggest that children of divorced parents may be faced with a situation which causes developmental changes in the nature of their sex role self-concept, and the process may not be the same for boys and girls. (27 references)

693. Kurdek, Lawrence A., et al. "Correlates of Children's Long-Term Adjustment to Their Parents' Divorce." *Developmental Psychology* 17(5): 565–579 (September 1981).

The correlates of adjustment to divorce were assessed in a sample of 58 white middle class children eight to seventeen years old whose parents had been separated about four years. A variety of measures were completed by the custodial parent and children. Children whose parents had been divorced or separated about four years had no severe problems in regard to divorce adjustment. The most negative score was related to news of the divorce and the most positive was related to peer pressure. Findings two years later indicated that the only significant change was a more positive response with regard to the loss of a parent and to peer relationships. Limitations of the study are discussed and a recommendation made for new studies. (62 references)

694. Long, Barbara H. "Parental Discord vs. Family Structure: Effects of Divorce on the Self-Esteem of Daughters." *Journal of Youth and Adolescence* 15(1): 19–27 (February 1986).

The self-esteem of 199 undergraduate females was studied in relation to family structure and parental discord. Intact, separated and reconstituted families were represented in the sample. Subjects were asked to rate the happiness of parental marriages and complete Rosenberg's Self-Esteem Scale. Happiness of biological parents was found to be significantly related to self-esteem, whereas family structure was not. This finding supports the contention that a stable home where parents are divorced is better for children than an intact home where there is marital discord. (20 references)

695. Long, Nicholas, et al. "Self-Perceived and Independently Observed Competence of Young Adolescents as a Function of Parental Marital Conflict and Recent Divorce." *Journal of Abnormal Child Psychology* 15(1): 15–27 (March 1987).

The self-perceptions and observed cognitive and social competence of 40 young adolescents were studied as a function of parental conflict and divorce. A variety of measures involved assessment by subjects, teachers, parents, and independent observers. Findings indicated that the level of parental conflict rather than parents' marital status was highly significant in adolescents' self-perceptions of cognitive and social competence. (25 references)

696. Longfellow, Cynthia. "Divorce in Context: Its Impact on Children." In *Divorce and Separation*, edited by J. G. Levinger and O. C. Moles, 287–306. New York: Basic Books, 1979.

The author contends that much of the findings in the literature on the direct impact of divorce on children is inconclusive. It is therefore suggested that instead of looking for negative effects of divorce on children research should focus on what it is about divorce that troubles children. A more accurate assessment of the impact of divorce would then place this event in the context of the major changes it causes, the single mother's emotional health, the quality of the family's relationships, and the child's own point of view. The young child is more liable to suffer due to limited reasoning abilities which render the child less able to cope. (Bibliography)

697. ———. "Parents and Divorce: Identifying the Support Network for Decisions about Custody." *American Journal of Family Therapy* 12(3): 26–32 (Fall 1984).

This study examines the use of informal social network resources by 55 divorcing couples in regard to child custody and visitation. Subjects' responses to questionnaires showed a greater degree of consulting on custody issues than was reported in earlier research. Parents also expressed in utilizing custody-related services such as educational workshops and mediation. Implications for clinical practice and research are suggested. (22 references)

698. Love-Clark, Peggy Ann. "A Meta-Analysis of Effects of Divorce on Children's Adjustment." Ph.D diss., Texas A & M University, 1984.

For a summary see: *Dissertation Abstracts International* 45A(9): 2807.

699. Luepnitz, Deborah Anna. "A Comparison of Maternal, Paternal, and Joint Custody: Understanding the Varieties of Post-Divorce Family Life." *Journal of Divorce* 9(3): 1–12 (Spring 1986).

This study compares maternal, paternal and joint custody in post-divorce family life. Forty-three families including niney-one children were interviewed. Findings showed that most children were not maladjusted, and adjustment was independent or judged to be better than single-parent custody. However, the author does not endorse mandatory joint custody. (20 references)

700. ———. "Which Aspects of Divorce Affect Children?" *Family Coordinator* 28(1): 79–85 (January 1979).

The effects of divorce on children were studied in a nonclinical sample of 24 college students whose parents divorced before they were 16 years old. Results of interviews with participants indicated that half of them felt the pre-divorce stage was most stressful while one-fourth found the post-divorce stage most stressful. Most of the subjects did not indicate that the divorce had long-term effects on them. Multiple coping strategies used by subjects included withdrawal, avoiding home, confiding in friends and siblings, cognitive restructuring of events, and counseling. It was found that symptoms previously reported in the literature as reactions to divorce were reactions to parental conflict. Implications for therapists are discussed. (18 references)

701. MacKinnon, Carol E., et al. "Effects of Divorce and Maternal Employment on the Home Environments of Preschool Children." *Child Development* 53(5): 1392–1399 (October 1982).

This study addresses the impact of divorce and maternal employment on the home environment of preschool children. The 60 households in this investigation included single-parent and intact families with children from three to six years of age. Evaluations based on the Home Inventory and the Rheingold and Cook Checklist indicated that children with mothers from intact/working and intact/nonworking homes have more toys and games, language and academic behavior, and less punishment than children of divorced mothers. Maternal employment seemed to result in less sex typing of preschool children. It is suggested that the findings in this study be accepted with caution. (13 references)

702. Magid, Kenneth M. "Children Facing Divorce: A Treatment Program." *Personnel and Guidance Journal* 55(9): 534–536 (May 1977).

A six-week intervention program, Children Facing Divorce, operating in Evergreen, Colorado, is described. Videotaped family scenes which are significant for children experiencing divorce are used to stimulate discussion lead by family professionals. Parents meet separately from the children until the final session. Suggestions for counselors of children, consultants to teachers, and consultants to parents are presented. (3 references)

703. McDermott, John F. "Divorce and its Psychiatric Sequelae in Children." *Archives of General Psychiatry* 23(5): 421–427 (November 1970).

This study examines the relationship between family disruption and psychosocial development in 1,487 children from their psychiatric clinical records. It was found that the duration of the presenting problem was shorter in the divorce group and that they had higher rates of delinquency. Depression in the divorce group was rarely mentioned by the parent in the medical history, but was noted by the clinician in 34 percent of the group. It is concluded that there is a large group of vulnerable children when divorce occurs who need help with immediate problems in order to prevent more serious ones later. (17 references)

704. McGurk, Harry, and M. Glachan. "Children's Conception of the Continuity of Parenthood Following Divorce." *Journal of Child Psychology and Psychiatry and Allied Disciplines* 28(3): 427–435 (May 1987).

Three hundred and fourteen children, between the ages of four to fourteen, were interviewed by means of dual play to determine whether they believed that parental status continued beyond divorce. Children whose parents were known to be divorced tended to show more mature levels of understanding than children from intact families. Experience and instruction may modify understandings of parenthood and divorce. (15 references)

705. McKinnon, Rosemary, and Judith S. Wallerstein. "A Preventive Intervention Program for Parents and Young Children in Joint Custody Arrangements." *American Journal of Orthopsychiatry* 58(2): 168–178 (April 1988).

The intervention model presented is a pilot program developed for voluntary joint counseling of parents with very young children by the Center for the Family in Transition. The 25 white middle class families in the program had voluntarily chosen joint custody and were followed for periods of one to four years. The program include assessment interviews, conferences, and counseling at regular intervals. Two cases cited illustrate how children and parents were assisted in dealing with complex life changes, including facilitating changes in child care arrangements. Additional evaluation of the program's effectiveness and applicability is proposed. (9 references)

706. Mcloughlin, David, and Richard Whitfield. "Adolescents and Their Experience of Parental Divorce." *Journal of Adolescence* 7(2): 155–170 (June 1984).

Sixty-four subjects located through divorce court records were interviewed in a study of the reactions of adolescents to the separation and divorce of their parents. While parental divorce has potential for the disruption of adolescent development, it does have some positive aspects in that it can result in the removal of conflict from the home. Behavior of parents is an important factor in determining whether the adolescent can satisfactorily utilize those coping strengths. Parents need to keep their children informed in pre and post-separation periods and avoid denigrating their partner. Discretion and sensitivity when entering new relationships and the parent's conduct in those relationships are important to adolescent adjustment in divorce. (12 references)

707. McPhee, Jeffrey T. "Ambiguity and Change in the Post-Divorce Family: Towards a Model of Divorce Adjustment." *Journal of Divorce* 8(2): 1–15 (Winter 1984).

A role theory orientation is used to present a theoretical viewpoint that suggests relationships between factors affecting divorce adjustment. An overview of research related to divorce finds the post divorce period is one where family members, individually and collectively, adapt roles to compensate for losses caused by divorce and separation. For children, divorce may result in change of schools, loss of friends and new responsibilities in the home. It is suggested that role strain for the child decreases as parent-child communication about the divorce and its effects on the family increases. A model for Divorce Adjustment is proposed and discussed in terms of its applications of such a theory by family professionals. (42 references)

708. Mednick, Birgitte, et al. "Long-Term Effects of Parental Divorce on Young Adult Male Crime." *Journal of Youth and Adolescence* 16(1): 31–45 (February 1987).

This study examines the impact of parental divorce on young adult male crime in a random sample of 323 subjects from a Danish birth cohort. Results indicated a significant relationship between divorce and young adult crime. However, when further path analysis controlled for socio-economic status and father's criminality, the effect of divorce on criminal behavior disappeared. Directions for future research are discussed. (40 references)

709. Melli, Marygold S. "The Changing Legal Status of the Single Parent." *Family Relations* 35(1): 31–35 (January 1986).

A child's mother, as the traditional custodial parent, was

the decision-maker in determining what was in the best interest of the child when parents separated. The unmarried mother, often regarded as the sole parent enjoyed a similar status. This paper considers the changes that have been taking place that alters the equal relationship between parent and child and the reasons for these changes. Implications for policy related to counseling, dispute resolution, and financial responsibility are discussed. Greater participation and responsibility for fathers in the future is predicted. (41 references)

710. Miller, Thomas W., and Lane J. Veltkamp. "Use of Fables in Clinical Assessment of Contested Child Custody." *Child Psychiatry and Human Development* 16(4): 274–284 (Summer 1986).

Contested custody cases are traumatic for both parents and children. The author reviews research on the use of clinical assessment to measure the impact of separation and divorce on children. A psychological assessment strategy based on children's fables is also presented. Clinical data presented by legal and mental health professionals may aid the court in disputed custody cases. (26 references)

711. Mishne, Judith. "Parental Abandonment: A Unique Form of Loss and Narcissistic Injury." *Clinical Social Work Journal* 7(1): 15–33 (Fall 1979).

Through a review of the research findings in the literature, the effects of parental abandonment on the child are discussed in contrast with the effects of other types of parental absence. The abandoned child is seen as exhibiting more narcissistic pathology and therefore traditional treatment used to facilitate the mourning of a lost parent is not as effective in treating the abandoned child. Two case histories are presented in which newer treatment techniques are used. These newer interventions are viewed as offering more promising results for work with abandoned children. (29 references)

712. Mitchell, Ann K. "Adolescents' Experiences of Parental
      Separation and Divorce." *Journal of Adolescence* 7(2):
      175–187 (1983).

      Seventy-one divorced Edinburgh families with 50
      adolescent children were interviewed five to six years
      after divorce to assess the effects of parental separation
      on the children. Preliminary analysis indicated that
      parents' failure to communicate adequately the reasons
      for the separation and failure of the absent parent to
      maintain contact with the child added to the stress of
      separation. Implications of these findings for family
      professionals are discussed. (18 references)

713. ———. *Children in the Middle: Living Through Divorce.*
      London; New York: Tavistock, 1985.

      British children's feelings and experiences related to the
      separation and divorce of their parents are described in
      their own words and compared with the accounts by their
      parents. The quality of access with the absent parent was
      judged to be more important for the child than the
      frequency of the visits. Half of the children interviewed
      did not remember parental conflict before separation and
      the majority thought their family life had been happy.
      Children were not as happy with relationships in
      reconstituted families as parents' accounts reported. Most
      of the fifty children in this study would have preferred
      that their parents not divorce even if the marriage had
      not been happy. Ways that teachers, lawyers, social
      workers could better serve the needs of children from
      divorcing families are discussed. (Bibliography)

714. Moore, Nancy V., et al. "The Child's Development of the
      Concept of Family." Paper presented at the Biennial
      Meeting of the Society for Research in Child Development,
      New Orleans, La. March 17–20, 1977. 6pp. (ERIC
      Microfiche ED140980)

      Twenty-eight boys and girls at each of the three higher
      Piagetian cognitive levels were each given a newly

constructed interview focusing on their concepts of family. Half of each group was from intact families and half from divorced families. Girls showed some advancement of concept over boys, and more often referred to personal proximity factors. Children from divorced families mentioned emotional factors more, listed more activities for adults and used membership as a criterion for family less than children from intact families. (7 references)

715. Morawetz, Anita. "The Single-Parent Family: An Author's Reflection." *Family Process* 24(1): 571–576 (March 1985).

In this paper, the author explores the proposition that separation and divorce should be viewed positively as normal phases in the family life cycle. It is noted that women whose husbands work extremely long hours and spend the weekend resting have much in common with single-parent mothers. Considering the magnitude of the divorce rate, it is suggested that couples and families may cope better if their expectations of marriage and family include the idea of divorce and separation. More family support services, with the idea of education and prevention, rather than resolving problems after they occur, should be advocated by professionals who work with families. (3 references)

716. Muir, Martha F. "Children and Divorce: Opportunities for Continuing Research and Practical Applications—A Guest Editorial." *Journal of Clinical Child Psychology* 6(2): 2 (Summer 1977).

This special issue of the journal focuses on the ideas, research and intervention techniques of prominent investigators of the effects of parental divorce on children. Articles address the issues of the impact on childrens' development, individual, group and community based programs for children and parents from single and reconstituted families and bibliotherapy programs. Suggestion are offered for future research. (No references)

717. Musetto, Andrew P. "Standards for Deciding Contested Child Custody." *Journal of Clinical Child Psychology* 10(1): 51–55 (Spring 1981).

Today's standard for deciding custody is based on the best interests of the child. This standard along with the "least-detrimental- alternative-available" criteria are examined and a modified version that incorporates the merits of both is presented following a discussion of the Uniform Marriage and Divorce Act and specific criteria for determining the best interests of the child. (11 references)

718. National Association of Elementary School Principals. "NAESP Study: Divorce Ranks Third in the Effect on Kids." *Communicator* 6(1): 1, 6 (September 1982).

Divorce ranks third, behind family income and sex, in its effect on children's school performance according to a study by the National Association of Elementary School Principals. Findings show that girls from high income families with one parent do better in school than boys from high income families with two parents, but not better than girls from high income families with two parents. The study also showed that the behavior and school performance of children from remarriage families differ very little from that of children who live with both biological parents. The findings noted here result from a deeper analysis of the 1980 investigation by NAESP and the Kettering Foundation. (48 references)

719. Nelson, Geoffrey. "Moderators of Women's and Children's Adjustment Following Parental Divorce." *Journal of Divorce* 4(3): 71–83 (Spring 1981).

This study was undertaken to determine the strongest moderators of the relationship between parental divorce and the psychosocial adjustment of women and their children. Subjects included mothers who had been separated from their spouse from five to twenty-five months and who had dependent children between four and fourteen years old. The strongest moderators of the adjustment of divorced mothers and their children were determined by stepwise multiple regression analyses. Relationship with the divorced spouse and positive feelings about the ex-husband were the strongest moderators for women. For children of divorced parents, the greater the mother's overall marital happiness, the better the children's behavioral adjustment at home and school. A sudden decision to divorce may avert long drawn out conflict and reduce stress on children. (48 references)

720. Nichols, John F. "The Marital/Family Therapist as an Expert Witness: Some Thoughts and Suggestions." *Journal of Marital and Family Therapy* 6(3): 293–298 (July 1980).

A step-by-step description of the family therapist's participation as an expert witness in legal proceedings is presented. Caution is urged regarding disclosure of unauthorized information. The adversarial nature of divorce and custody litigation often puts the therapist under pressure. The author's presents details of the therapist's involvement in the pre-trial, trial and post-trial process that insures involvement and protection against malpractice action. (2 references)

721. Nichols, Robert C., and James D. Troester. "Custody Evaluations: An Alternative." *Family Coordinator* 28(3): 399–407 (July 1979).

Traditional custodial evaluation places emotional strain on health professionals and aggravates the conflict between parents that lead to the divorce in the first place. The co-authors devised a plan whereby divorcing couples are helped to arrive at a custody/visitation agreement that enables them to determine custody outcome rather than have it imposed on them by others. The procedure used in helping parents reach agreement on custody is described. Results of a questionnaire completed by 13 couples with whom the new approach was used, two months to one year following custody agreement, indicated a continuance of conflicts and attitudes related to custody which the counselors felt had been resolved. However, the counselors view the parental agreement approach to custody as preferable to court ordered custody. (12 references)

722. Nuta, Virginia Rhodes. "Emotional Aspects of Child Support Enforcement." *Family Relations* 35(1): 177–181 (January 1986).

Observations based on work with custodial and noncustodial parents in regard to the financial relationship in child support are reported. Male parents who do not pay support are: the parent in pain, the over-extended parent, the revengeful parent and the irresponsible parent. Nonpaying, noncustodial mothers who do not pay support often feel that it is the man's place to support the children and that single women are disadvantaged economically. How the custodial parent responds to nonsupport is important for them and their children. Practitioners are advised to pay attention to the implication of nonpayment of child support in counseling single parents who may respond in ways that result in negative outcomes for children. (5 references)

723. Omizo, Michael M., and Sharon A. Omizo. "The Effects of Participation in Group Counseling Sessions on Self-Esteem and Locus of Control among Adolescents from Divorced Families." *School Counselor* 36(1): 54–60 (September 1988).

The effectiveness of group counseling for adolescent school children from divorced families is examined in this study. The sixty participants, divided equally into experimental and control groups, were administered locus of control and self-esteem measures. The ten session treatment sessions for the experimental group are summarized. Pretest dependent measures showed no significant differences between the experimental and control groups.

Posttests indicate that students who participated in the group sessions had higher levels of self-esteem and possessed a more internal locus-of-control orientation on aspects of the locus of control measure. Further research on the long-term efficacy of group counseling is suggested. (16 references)

724. ———. "Group Counseling with Children of Divorce: New Findings." *Elementary School Guidance and Counseling.* 22(1): 46–52 (October 1987).

Sixty elementary school children, ranging in age from nine to twelve years were participants in a group counseling intervention program for children from divorced families. Instruments used in the study were the Dimensions of Self-Concept and the Nowicki-Strickland Locus of Control Scale. Brief summaries of the ten group sessions that children from divorced families attended are presented. Findings suggest that the group counseling program helped enhance some areas of self-concept and internal locus of control. Implications for schools and counselors are noted. (22 references)

725. Oversight Hearing on Child Support Enforcement. Hearing before Subcommittee on Select Education of the Committee on Education and Labor. House of Representative, Ninety-Eighty Congress, First Session (New York, New York). September 12, 1983. 104pp. (ERIC Microfiche ED248414)

This document presents the text of the Congressional hearings on nonpayment of child support, examining the link between nonpayment and child abuse, and focusing on possible remedies. The content of the proposed National Child Support Enforcement Act (H.R. 3354) is discussed. Written statements from 12 individuals are included, dealing with the difficulties in enforcing current child support rulings, welfare spending, and court jurisdictions. Collection methods are proposed, including state clearing house, wage attachment, jail and interception of tax refunds. (No references)

726. Parish, Thomas S. "Impact of Divorce on Families."
     Adolescence 16(63): 577–580 (Fall 1981).

     The impact of divorce on 1,409 college students was
     assessed based on their responses to the Personal
     Attribute Inventory that they completed for themselves
     and their parents. Students from divorced families
     evaluated both parents more negatively than those from
     intact families or families where parental loss resulted
     from death. No difference on self-concepts as a function of
     family type was found for the students who participated
     in the study. It is suggested that a longitudinal study be
     undertaken to see if the long-term effect exists. (13
     references)

727. Parish, Thomas J., and Judy W. Dostal. "Relationship
     Between Evaluations of Self and Parents by Children
     from Intact and Divorced Family." *Journal of Psychology*
     104(1) 35–38 January 1980).

     Six hundred and thirty-nine boy and girls from 14 Kansas
     school districts were asked to rate self, mother, father or
     stepfather. Each subject was asked to complete three or
     four copies of the Personal Attribute Inventory of Children.
     Children from divorced families were found to have self-
     concepts that were strongly related to their rating of
     their mothers and stepfathers, but not with their
     evaluations of their natural fathers. Children from intact
     families were found to have self-concepts that were
     significantly associated with the evaluations of their
     fathers and mothers. The study also indicated that
     childrens' concepts of self and parents change during the
     period following divorce. (5 references)

728. Parker, Denise. *The Impact of Divorce on the Lives of
     Children: Alleviating the Trauma of the Divorce Experience
     through Adult Intervention Strategies.* Research Report
     submitted in partial fulfillment of the requirements for
     Master's Degree, Southern Illinois University. August
     1978. 62pp. (ERIC Microfiche ED180615)

This information is directed to many involved in the divorce experience of children: parents, educators, relatives, and friends. The paper reviews current literature pertaining to the effect of divorce on children and makes suggestions regarding general ways that parents and other adults may assist children in coping with divorce. The population of children at which this study is directed includes preschool through latency age children. (27 references)

729. Parkinson, Lisa, ed. *Separation, Divorce, and Families.* London: Macmillan, 1987. (Practical Social Work Series)

The author seeks to provide guidelines for persons working with families in conflict, separated families, and stepfamilies. New developments in conciliation and systems theories are reviewed. Suggestions are offered for helping children cope and for differentiating between children and adult interests in fractured families. Group work with custody decisions and interagency networking are also discussed. There is a bibliography of books about divorce for children and a list of useful organizations. (Bibliography)

730. Payne, Anne T. "Law and the Problem Patient: Custody and Parental Rights of Homosexual, Mentally Retarded, Mentally Ill and Incarcerated Patients." *Journal of Family Law* 16: 797–818 (1977–1978).

This article discusses custody decisions involving homosexual, mentally ill, retarded and imprisoned parents. These categories of parents may be placed at a significant disadvantage in legal custody cases. In each case laws that do not significantly relate to parent-child relationships may affect custody or terminate parental rights. Legal cases related to each parental group are discussed. Results of this research indicate that there is a greater understanding and tolerance for mentally ill parents, than for the mentally retarded parents when it comes to parenting for their biological children. (Bibliographical footnotes)

731. Peterson, Gary W., et al. "Family Stress Theory and the Impact of Divorce on Children." *Journal of Divorce* 7(3): 1–20 (Spring 1984).

Concepts from family stress theory are applied to the findings of research literature on divorce to present a middle range theory that describes the effect of divorce on children. The divorce of a spouse/parent was viewed as a potential stressor on children's social competence. Variables were identified which either increase the crisis-meeting resources or added to the vulnerability of children and custodial parents. The model provides hypotheses that need to be tested. Guidelines for future research are provided in the model. (56 references)

732. Pett, Marjorie G. "Correlates of Children's Social Adjustment Following Divorce." *Journal of Divorce* 5(4): 25–39 (Summer 1982).

Data from interviews with 411 children and 206 randomly selected custodial parents are examined to determine family correlates of the children's social adjustment. A social adjustment scale completed by parents served as the criterion measure of children's adjustment. The quality of the custodial parent's relationship with the child was the single strongest correlate of the children's social adjustment scores. Other significant variables were number of previous marriages, age, social adjustment of parent, and the children's current reaction to the divorce. (29 references)

733. Pett, Marjorie G., and Beth Vaughan-Cole. "The Impact of Income Issues and Social Status on Post-Divorce Adjustment of Custodial Parents." *Family Relations* 35(1): 103–111 (January 1986).

A sample of 256 divorced single parents were studied for the impact of income and social status on post-divorce adjustment. Measures used were the Social Adjustment Scale of Self Report, the General Well-Being Schedule, and personal interviews. Results show that social status and income have a positive correlation, with post-divorce adjustment, the source of equivalent incomes do have an impact. Parents who depend on public funds score lower in social and emotional adjustment than those with equivalent incomes from private earnings. Implications for public policy include the need for child care systems for financially insecure and depressed single parents. (31 references)

734. Phillips, Shelley. "The Child in the Divorcing Family." Unit for Child Studies, Selected Papers No. 22. New South Wales University Kensington, Australia School of Education 1982. 16pp. (ERIC Microfiche ED250090)

A sequence of stages in children's emotional response to parental separation and divorce is described, some effects of continued parent hostility are pointed out, and aspects of children's adjustment to changed-family circumstances are briefly discussed. Long term effects of divorce are discussed in terms of adjustment, sex of children, parenting and problem solving. An educational program designed to assist divorcing parents and their children to express feelings about divorce and to provide some guidelines for counselors and teachers dealing with children of divorce is also described. (16 references)

735. Porter, Beatrice, and Daniel K. O'Leary. "Marital Discord and Childhood Behavior Problems." *Journal of Abnormal Child Psychology* 8(3): 287–295 (September 1980).

The impact of marital conflict and general marital adjustment on the behavior of 64 children from intact families referred to a psychology clinic is discussed. Measures used were the Behavior Problem Checklist, Short Marital Adjustment Test, and the O'Leary-Porter Scale that was developed for this study. Overt marital hostility was found to be significantly related to many of the behavior problems of boys, but not related to the behavior problems of girls. Suggestions for future research are discussed. (23 references)

736. Porter, Blaine R. "Family Life Education for Single Parent Families." *Family Relations* 30(4): 517–525 (October 1981).

The single-parent family is the fastest growing life style in America today. The emotional, social and financial problems that often affect parents and children need programs developed by family life educators to assist them in coping with these problems. The divorced parent, widow/widower, wed parent and single fathers are discussed. Guidelines for development of a family life education program for single parents are presented. It is recommended that the program needs to be (a) application and problem solving oriented, (b) flexible enough to address unique needs, and (c) allow for the expression of feelings while at the same time providing meaningful educational content. (22 references)

737. Price, Sharon J., and Patrick C. McKenry. "Children and Divorce." In *Divorce,* Chap. 5, 73–90. Newbury Park, California: Sage, 1988.

Children in divorcing families experience a feeling of loss, a sense of failure in interpersonal relationship and in adaptation to a new family lifestyle. Many problems associated with children whose parents divorce are related to problems present prior to separation. The responses of children vary both in quality and intensity. The extended family, logically a source of support for children whose parents divorce, often live at a distance too great to help the child cope. Factors that may help mediate reactions to divorce are sex, age, temperament, quality of pre-divorce relations with parents, parenting skills in single-parent home, and the extent and availability of support systems. (4 References)

738. Price, William A., et al. "Children of Divorce: Counseling Guidelines for the Primary Care Physician." *Postgraduate Medicine* 74(2): 93–94 97–100 (August 1983).

Some children involved in divorce suffer personal losses too great to cope with alone and may have a serious negative impact on their lives later. As the divorce rate continues, primary care physicians will encounter more and more children from divorced families. The physician's role is viewed as one which aims to decrease psychological risk to the child, promote positive ways of coping with stress and teach parents new ways of relating to the child. As the family physician may have the first opportunity to counsel children from divorced families, it is suggested that the physician should use a relaxed, empathic approach with a focus on the health of the whole family unit. (18 references)

739. Proulx, Jocelyn, and David Koulack. "The Effect of Parental Divorce on Parent-Adolescent Separation." *Journal of Youth and Adolescence* 16(5): 473–480 (October 1987).

The effects of parent-adolescent separation were examined in 318 Canadian college students from separated and intact families. Subjects completed the Moving Out questionnaire and the Rotter's Internal-External-Locus of Control related conflict was more openly expressed, feelings of personal control increased and feelings about leaving home were less negative. Subjects from separated families had higher emotional separation scores than those from intact families. In addition, males had higher emotional separation scores than females, and females had higher locus of control scores than males. (21 references)

740. Rankin, Robert P., and Jerry S. Maneker. "The Duration of Marriage in a Divorcing Population: the Impact on Children." *Journal of Marriage and the Family* 47(1):43–52 (February 1985).

Demographic data on 11,559 divorcing families from four California counties for the year 1977 were analyzed to disclose the relationships between duration of marriage and presence or absence of children and also between duration of marriage and presence or absence of children below the age of two. Findings show that the presence of children was significant in extending the duration of marriage. However, the presence of children under the age of two was associated with short duration of marriage. Ideas for further research in this area are mentioned along with suggestions for marriage education and family counseling. (34 references)

741. Rasmussen, Janis Carol. "The Custodial Parent-Child Relationship as a Mediating Factor in the Effects of Divorce on Children." Research paper for Doctor of Psychology degree, Biola University, California, 1987, 53pp. (ERIC Microfiche ED284146)

This paper explores the ways that the psychological structure and family process variables affect post-divorce functioning in the single-parent family. A search of 25 years of literature dealing with the post-divorce custodial parent-child relationship showed that the following factors influence the effects of divorce on children: 1) parent-child demographics, 2) personal characteristics of the parent, 3) relationship of the parent and the child and 4) use of support networks. Implications for single parents are noted.

742. Reinhard, David W. "The Reaction of Adolescent Boys and Girls to the Divorce of Their Parents." *Journal of Clinical Psychology* 6(2): 21–23 (Summer 1977).

This study compares the reaction of 46 white middle class boys and girls to parental divorce. The children, between the ages of 12 and 18, completed a 99 item questionnaire. Results showed no sex differences in the reaction of the subjects to their parents' decision to divorce. Although they were disappointed that their parents were not able to find other alternatives to divorce, they indicated that it was probably a sensible thing to do. Suggestions are offered for further research on the subject. (8 references)

743. Reinhart, Gail Eleanor. "One-Parent Families: A Study of Divorced Mothers and Adolescents Using Social Climate

and Relationship Styles." Ph.D. diss., California School of Professional Psychology at Berkeley, 1977.

For a summary see: *Dissertation Abstracts International* 38B(6): 2881.

744. Richards, Arlene, and Irene Willis. *How to the Get it Together When Your Parents are Falling Apart.* New York: David McKay, 1976.

A child psychiatrist reports on interviews with a nonclinical group of 28 teenagers whose parents were separated by divorce. Although it is often not obvious to parents and friends of teenagers, these interviews reveal the pain young people suffer when their parents' marriage dissolves. The author discusses the issues raised, explains the underlying psychodynamics, and suggests a course of action. (Bibliography)

745. Richmond-Abbott, Marie. "Sex-Role Attitudes of Mothers and Children in Divorced, Single-Parent Families." *Journal of Divorce* 8(1): 61–81 (Fall 1984).

One hundred and thirty-four divorced mothers and their children responded to questionnaires designed to determine whether or not single parents and their children have non-traditional sex role attitudes and report non-sex stereotyped behavior. Measures used were the Traditional Family Ideology Scale (Levinson and Huffman, (169) for parents, a modified version for children, and interviews with 25 participants. Mothers in the sample had liberal sex-role attitudes and children followed the same pattern. The more education that the custodial or absent parent had, the more liberal were the children's sex-role attitudes. However, the liberal sex-role attitudes did not transfer to the kinds of chores mothers assigned their children. The children were also likely to get sex-stereotyped gifts and participate in sex-stereotyped activities. Suggestion for other studies are included. (39 references)

746. Rickard, Kathryn M., et al. "An Examination of the Relationship of Marital Satisfaction and Divorce with Parent-Child Interactions." *Journal of Clinical Child Psychology* 11(1): 61–65 (Spring 1982).

This study examines the relationship of marital satisfaction and divorce with parent-child interactions. Forty-one mother-child pairs served as subjects. The children had been referred to the Psychology Clinic at the University of Georgia for treatment of behavior problems. Three groups of mothers at different levels of marital satisfaction were formed. A fourth group consisted of divorced mothers and their children. Measures consisted of parent and child behaviors collected by independent observers and questionnaires completed by parents. Parents who reported a high satisfaction with their marriages used more positive attention with their child than divorced mothers. Research implications are discussed. (17 references)

747. Roberts, Albert R., and Beverly J. Roberts. "Divorce and the Child: A Pyrrhic Victory." In *Childhood Deprivation*, ed. and comp. by Albert R. Robert, 84–97. Springfield, Ill.: Thomas, 1974.

Divorce is sometimes the best solution to a child's well-being. Pre-divorce conflict and custody hearings are most damaging when the child must be a party to the proceedings in which each parent accuses the other of being unfit. When divorce is not handled in the best interests of the child enuresis, acting out behavior, phobias, depression and even suicide may be among the emotional problems exhibited. Awareness of the child's feelings by the parents is one of the most important factors to be considered in trying to mediate the negative effects of divorce. (22 references)

748. Robey, Kenneth L., et al. "The Child's Response to Affection Given to Someone Else: Effects of Parental Divorce, Sex of Child, and Sibling Position." *Journal of Clinical Child Psychology* 17(1): 2–7 (March 1988).

Thirty-two children including intact families and separated or divorced families were studied to assess the children's response to affection given to someone else. Affection shown to one child in a family is often seen by another as lessening the amount left him or her to receive. An instrument was designed to measure the feelings of the children who were eight to twelve years of age. Findings indicate that the non-recipient unhappiness of children of divorce was significantly higher compared with children from intact families. (25 references)

749. Roseby, Vivienne. "A Custody Evaluation Model for Pre-School Children." A paper presented at the American Psychological Association, Toronto, Canada. August 24–28, 1984 (ERIC Microfiche ED257007)

This paper focuses on the needs of mental health consultants involved in making decisions in custody disputes involving preschool children. A custody evaluation model is outlined and discussed. Critical assessment issues are presented and assessment methods for each of these issues are suggested. Factors considered are attachment versus competence identification of the principal parent, authoritative parenting, parent-child communication, and parent role models. Effects of income loss and maternal employment are examined and networks of support are discussed. A seven page bibliography is appended. (23 references)

750. Roseby, Vivienne, and Robin Deutsch. "Children of Separation and Divorce: Effects of a Social-Role Taking Group Intervention on Fourth and Fifth Graders." *Journal of Clinical Child Psychology* 14(1): 55–60 (Spring 1985).

Fifty-seven nine to eleven-year-old children who had experienced parental separation or divorce participated in one of two divorce intervention groups. The experimental group provided training in cognitive social role taking and assertive communication skills. The placebo control group provided no specific skills training, but focused on the identification and discussion of feelings about divorce. Measures used were the Children's Attitude Toward Parental Separation Inventory, Child Depression Scale, and the Devereux Elementary School Behavior Rating Scale. Children who acquired new cognitive skills, improved their understanding of the divorce as measured by CAPSI. However, results suggest that a period of consolidation may be necessary for changed attitudes and beliefs to produce measurable behavioral and emotional change. (32 references)

751. Rosen, Rhona. "Some Crucial Issues Concerning Children of Divorce." *Journal of Divorce* 3(1): 19–25 (Fall 1979).

This study focuses on two issues of the post-divorce situation: custody and access arrangements. Subjects of the investigation were 92 white, middle-class individuals, ranging in age from nine to twenty-eight years, whose parents had divorced within the ten-year period prior to the study.Interviews were conducted with parents and children. Three divorce variables were examined in relation to the child's level of development: 1) sex of custodial parent, 2) degree of contact with non-custodial parent and inter-parental conflict preceding or following divorce. No significant differences were found between mother custody and father custody. Most of the children indicated that contact with the noncustodial parent was important to them and children perceived the divorce as less traumatic where freedom of access was permitted. (17 references)

752. Rosenthal, Perikan Aral. "Sudden Disappearance of One Parent with Separation and Divorce—the Grief and Treatment of Pre-School Children." *Journal of Divorce* 3(1): 43–54 (Fall 1979).

The pathological effect of the sudden departure of one parent due to separation or divorce on young children is examined. Thirty-seven children from twenty families were treated and 24 of the children who were determined to be most pathological were used in the study. Differences in therapeutic approach for the child who loses a parent through death and the child who loses a parent through separation or divorce are discussed. It was found that the feelings following the loss of a parent affect a child less than the relationship the child develops with the remaining parent and a supportive environment. (11 references)

753. ———. "Triple Jeopardy: Family Stresses and Subsequent Divorce Following the Adoption of Racially and Ethnically Mixed Children." *Journal of Divorce* 4(4): 43–55 (Summer 1981).

The adoption of racially causes stress for both parents and children. This study concentrates on problems with 15 black, black-Vietnamese and American Indian children who were adopted by five white middle class families who had two or three biological children. The problems of the children with ethnicity, identity and rejection were further magnified when their parents later divorced. Therefore the need for families considering transracial adoption to be more carefully screened during the preadoption period. Findings in the cases examined in the study were all negative, for the adopted children, biological children and divorced mothers with whom the children lived. (14 references)

754. Rowling, Louise. *Children and Loss.* Part 1: A Teacher's View: The Child in the Single Parent and Blended Family. Part 2: Helping Children Cope with Loss. 1982. 20pp. (ERIC Microfiche ED250093)

This paper is in two parts. Part one discusses areas in family disruption, describes children's experiences of loss, and suggests strategies for helping children cope with such experiences. Part two discusses stages in children's experiences of loss (such as the closeness of the relationship and the psychological impact of the event), and suggests coping strategies, including communication, support systems, anticipation education,use of a divorce adjustment profile to gather information and bibliotherapy.

755. Rubin, Lisa D., and James H. Price. "Divorce and its Effects on Children." *Journal of School Health* 49(10): 552–556 (December 1979).

Divorce results in major changes for the child: loss of father, loss of mother to work, altered income and support systems, and sometimes loss of siblings. Problems of custody and visitation, and continuation of conflicts between parents prior to and following divorce can be particularly stressful to children. The school is in a unique position to mediate some of the effects of divorce by offering the opportunity for group discussion and sharing by children in similar circumstances. Although the discomfort caused by family dissolution is temporary, informed and understanding school personnel can make life a little easier for children undergoing the transition from intact families to single parent families. (36 references)

756. Rugel, Robert P., and Sally Sieracki. "The Single Parent Workshop: An Approach to the Problems of Children of Divorce." *Journal of Clinical Child Psychology* 10(3): 159–160 (Fall 1981).

A workshop designed to deal with the problems of children of divorce and their parents is described. The first 100 persons responding to newspaper advertisements about the workshop were chosen for participation. The group included 30 mental health professionals. Seventy parents volunteered to fill out research questionnaires. The primary measure used to assess changes in the children's behavior as a result of the workshop was the Burks Child Behavior Rating Scale (1968). Findings indicate that parents' ratings of their children's anxiety levels decreased following the workshop. Possible explanations for this finding are discussed. (5 references)

757. Sack, William H. "Gender Identity Conflict in Young Boys Following Divorce." *Journal of Divorce* 9(1): 47–59 (Fall 1985).

This paper addresses the issue of gender identity in father-absent males. Three boys, aged four to seven, dressed in women's clothes followed a divorce where there were problems with visitation and custody decisions. Psychotherapy findings suggested that gender identity was related to loss and aggression. Following treatment all three boys improved. It was concluded that the boys behavior resulted from regression triggered by parental conflict associated with divorce. (10 references)

758. Santrock, John W. "The Effects of Divorce on Adolescents: Needed Research Perspectives." *Family Therapy* 14(2): 147–159 (1987).

Research literature on the effects of divorce on children is reviewed from a historical perspective and several studies that address the effects of divorce on adolescents are included in this reiview. The author suggests that the areas in greatest need of research are father custody and joint custody. Methodological problems in earlier studies of divorce are noted. (36 references)

759. Santrock, John W., and Terry D. Madison. "Three Research Traditions in the Study of Adolescents in Divorced Families: Quasi-Experimental, Developmental; Clinical; and Family Sociological." *Journal of Early Adolescence* 5(1): 115–128 (Spring 1985).

A selective and critical review of research on adolescents in divorced families from the sociological perspective, from the clinical research of mental health professionals and research housed in developmental psychology. Information is provided about how each of the research traditions handles sampling, a control group, measures, amount of time spent with subjects, degree of interest in the adolescent's developmental status investigation of demographic variables, and statistical analysis. Discusses ways that sociologists, mental health professionals and developmental psychologists might learn and benefit from the other research traditions. Recommends stronger research effort aimed at a better understanding of the effects of divorce on adolescents. (51 references)

760. Santrock, John W., and Richard A. Warshak. "Father Custody and Social Development in Boys and Girls." *Journal of Social Issues* 35(4): 112–125 (Fall 1979).

The social development of children in father-custodial homes, mother-custodial homes and intact families are compared. Subjects of the study were 60 white, largely middle class families with children six to eleven years old. Multimethod measures were used in studying family interaction, including videotaped observations. Findings showed that children living with parents of the opposite sex were less well adjusted than those living with parents of the same sex. However, in both types of families, authoritative parenting was positively related to competent social behavior and this was also true when additional caretakers were involved in both types of families. More research is suggested regarding the role of caretakers and their impact on children's social development. (13 references)

761. Santrock, John W., et al. "Social Development and Parent-Child Interaction in Father-Custody and Step-Mother Families." In *Nontraditional Families: Parenting and Child Development*, edited by Michael E. Lamb. 289–313, Hillsdale, N.J.: Erlbaum, 1982.

Sixty-four white, predominantly middle-class families, with children ranging in age from six to eleven years participated in this study that included father-custody, mother-custody and intact household. The multimethod approach included videotaping of family interactions. Findings indicate that the sex of the child, in combination with the sex of the custodial parent and the stepparent strongly influence the child's social behavior. The disequilibrium created by the father's remarriage seems to produce a positive effect for his children several years after divorce. Boys in father custody appear to have made a good adjustment to living in a single family whereas girls have not. When a second major change in family structure occurs, like divorce, a period of disequilibrium is triggered. (35 references)

762. Saucier, Jean-Francois, and Anne-Marie Ambert. "Adolescents' Perception of Self and of Immediate Environment by Parental Marital Status: A Controlled Study." *Canadian Journal of Psychiatry* 31(6): 505–512 (August 1986).

Adolescents' perceptions of themselves and their environment were studied in 1,519 Quebec high school students from divorced, widowed and intact families. Data from questionnaires indicated that divorce was associated with the greatest disadvantage followed by widowhood. However, boys in widowed families were found to be more disadvantaged than girls. Implications for clinicians are noted. (37 references)

763. ———. "Parental Marital Status and Adolescents' Optimism About Their Future." *Journal of Youth and Adolescence* 11(5): 345–354 (October 1982).

A random sample of 4,539 Montreal adolescents completed a questionnaire designed to measure their optimism about their future. It was found that adolescents from intact families expected more than those from broken homes to be successful in the future. Girls who had lost a parent through death seem less optimistic than those whose parents were separated. Longitudinal studies are recommended. (67 references)

764. Scheiner, Lillian C., et al. "Custody and Visitation: A Report of an Innovative Program." *Family Relations* 31(1): 99–107 (January 1982).

An innovative approach to custody/visitation counseling developed by the Camden County Health Services Center Community Mental Health Program in cooperation with the Juvenile and Domestic Relations Court is presented. The goals are based on the Family Systems Theory and the results of clinical and current research findings. Clinical research suggests it is in the best interests of children not to disrupt their lifestyle. The role of the therapist is to halt destructive interaction, provide a therapeutic milieu for communication and change and make recommendations to the court in the best interests of the child. The program involves a great expenditure of time, resources and energy. The final outcome is in the hands of the courts. (14 references)

765. Scherman, Avraham. "Divorce: Its Impact on the Family and Children." Paper presented at the Annual Meeting of American Educational Research Association, San Francisco, April 8–12, 1979. 23pp. (ERIC Microfiche ED172133)

The single most concerning problem facing the mental health professions is divorce and its effect upon children as well as adults. The implications for divorced people suggest an increase in mental and physical illness concurrent with increase in stress. Divorce is a legal, emotion and financial process calling for many adjustments. It is imperative that both parents continue a positive relationship with their children. Most studies occurred after the divorce, this study follows the legal "event" as it transpires. During the project's final phase, a nine session children's group therapy program was established. (65 references)

766. ———. "An Integrated Treatment Model for Children of Divorce." *American Mental Health Counselors Association Journal* 7(1): 24–31 (January 1985).

An intervention model for treatment of children from divorced families is described. The four components of the model relate to the child, the family, support systems, and community value systems. The ways that these components may contribute to the well-being of the child from divorced families are discussed. It is suggested that the model can also be used as a theoretical framework for research. (27 references)

767. ———. "Training Counselors in Divorce Intervention: A Courses Approach." Paper presented at the Annual Convention of the American Association for Counseling and Development. New Orleans, April 21–25, 1987. 30pp. (ERIC Microfiche ED284123)

This article focuses on the legal and psychiatric aspects of parental child stealing. Several cases are used to illustrate the post-traumatic consequences for the child as reported in psychiatric evaluation following kidnapping. It is only recently that parents have been held accountable under state and federal statutes for kidnapping their children and the Uniform Child Custody Jurisdiction Act and the Parental Kidnapping Prevention Act, have been passed. Legislation does not eliminate the problem entirely and it is suggested that child psychiatrists stay alert to possibly identifying parents who are at high risk for kidnapping. (34 references)

768. Schetky, Diane H., and Lee H. Haller. "Child Psychiatry and Law: Parental Kidnapping." *Journal of the American Academy of Child Psychiatry* 22(3): 279–285 (May 1983).

This article focuses on the legal and psychiatric aspects of parental child stealing. Several cases are used to illustrate the post-traumatic consequences for the child as reported in psychiatric evaluation following kidnapping. It is only recently that parents have been held accountable under state and federal statutes for kidnapping their children and the Uniform Child Custody Jurisdiction Act and the Parental Kidnapping Prevention Act, have been passed. Legislation does not eliminate the problem entirely and it is suggested that child psychiatrists stay alert to possibly identifying parents who are at high risk for kidnapping. (34 references)

769. Schlesinger, Benjamin. "Children's Viewpoints of Living in a One-Parent Family." *Journal of Divorce* 5(4): 1–23 (Summer 1982).

Forty children, aged 12–18 years, living in middle class, urban, separated or divorced one-parent families were interviewed about their lives. Findings indicated that nearly half of the subjects had moved to a new neighborhood, most had contact with the absent parent less than once a month, most of the contact with relatives was with in-person visits and most of the children felt that they had enough contact with the custodial parent. In general, it appeared that the hurt lessens over time and the children appear to have a normal life with the one parent at home. (31 references)

770. Schwebel, Andrew I., et al. "Research-Based Interventions with Divorced Families." *Personnel and Guidance Journal* 60(9): 523–528 (May 1982).

This article reports on interventions that have demonstrated their usefulness with other types of clients and could be used to treat problems in families in transition. In particular the authors suggested: 1) mediation of conflict between ex-spouses to foster their involvement with their children, 2) helping parents develop better relationships with their children in the post divorce period, and 3) the use of training methods that draw on the behavioral principles of skill identification, modeling and behavioral rehearsal. (51 references)

771. Seagull, Arthur A., and A. W. Elizabeth. "The Non-Custodial Father's Relationship to His Child: Conflicts and Solutions." *Journal of Clinical Child Psychology* 6(2): 11–15 (Summer 1977).

The impact of divorce on the relationship between the noncustodial father and his children is discussed.

American cultural attitudes toward the roles of husbands and fathers affect his feelings and responses and expectations as a noncustodial parent. The transition period following divorce is usually long and complicated with problems of visitation and sometimes adjustment to remarriage and a stepparent. (6 references)

772. Shaw, Daniel S., and Robert E. Emery. "Parental Conflict and Other Correlates of the Adjustment of School-Age Children Whose Parents Have Separated." *Journal of Abnormal Child Psychology.* 15(2): 269–281 (June 1987).

The impact of parental separation on the psychological adjustment of 40 school age children from lower class families was examined in this study. Results of measures used in the investigation suggest parental acrimony and low income have a significant effect on behavioral adjustment and perceptions of competence among children of separated families. Also found to affect children's adjustment were parental discord and maternal depression. Methodological limitations of the study are discussed. (37 references)

773. Shiller, Virginia M. "Joint and Maternal Custody: The Outcome for Boys Aged Six to Eleven and Their Parents." Paper presented at the Annual Convention of the Orthopsychiatric Association. New York, April 20–24, 1985. 11pp. (ERIC Microfiche ED261273)

The adjustment of 20 boys in joint custody arrangements was compared with that of 20 boys in maternal custody who visited regularly with their fathers. Results of interviews with the boys, their parents, and teachers reports suggested that boys in joint custody had fewer behavioral problems at home and in the classroom. They also had higher self-esteem and less anxiety than boys in maternal custody. The length of time elapsed since the parents divorced was significant for maternal custody boys, but not for boys in joint custody. A follow-up two years later showed better outcomes for boys in joint custody arrangements. (No references)

774. ———. "Loyalty Conflicts and Family Relationships in Latency Age Boys: A Comparison of Joint and Maternal Custody." *Journal of Divorce* 9(4): 17–38 (Summer 1986).

Divorce-related emotional adjustment in 40 boys was examined to determine the differences between those in maternal and joint custody. Test were administered to measure children's feelings toward parents and children's perceptions of the post-divorce family structure. Findings showed that boys in joint custody were more comfortable expressing negative and positive feelings toward parents, and were less concerned with fantasies about parental reconciliation. Additional investigation of the impact of joint custody on other populations is suggested. (30 references)

775. Shufeit, Lawrence J., and Stanley R. Wurster. *Frequency of Divorce among Parents of Handicapped Children*. July 1975. 52pp. (ERIC Microfiche ED113909)

Seventy-six parents of handicapped children were surveyed to compare the frequency of divorce in the same population to that of the U.S. population. The survey showed that the presence of a child with a handicapping condition causes a certain degree of stress within the family and the marital dissatisfaction is highest in families that have children. Results showed that the frequency of divorce for the sample population was not significantly higher than that of the U.S. population. (28 references)

776. Slater, Elisa J., and Karen S. Calhoun. "Familial Conflict and Marital Dissolution: Effects on the Social Functioning of College Students." *Journal of Social and Clinical Psychology* 6(1): 118–126 (1988).

This study examines the effect of parental divorce and perceived family conflict in childhood on the social functioning of college students. A variety of questionnaires were administered to 253 subjects. Results suggest that family background and conflict are important interacting variables associated with long-term social adjustment.

Males were found to be less well adjusted than females. Subjects from low conflict situations reported more social support. Implications of these findings are noted. (21 references)

777. Slater, Elisa J., and Joel D. Haber. "Adolescent Adjustment Following Divorce as a Function of Familial Conflict." *Journal of Consulting and Clinical Psychology* 52(5): 920–921 (October 1984).

The effect of continuing familial conflict on adolescent adjustment and self-concept was investigated in a group of 217 adolescent high school students. Responses to the Family Environment Scale, the Tennessee Self-Concept Scale, Locus of Control Scale For Children, and the State-Trait Anxiety Inventory showed that children from high conflict families had lower self-concepts, more anxiety and less internal control regardless of whether or not divorce occurred. Low conflict in families did not differentially affect adjustment of adolescents even if a divorce did occur. Implications of these findings are discussed. (7 references)

778. Smollar, Jackeline, and James Youniss. "Parent-Adolescent Relations in Adolescents Whose Parents are Divorced." *Journal of Early Adolescence* 5(1): 129–144 (Spring 1985).

Three groups of adolescents living in single-parent mother custodial homes were defined through assignment of positive and negative adjectives for parent-self relationships. These same subjects also chose mothers or fathers as the persons with whom they would discuss six kinds of topics and with whom they were most likely to communicate five qualitative ways. Subjects in the three groups perceive their relations with custodial mothers differently. Questionnaire responses were examined for disruption of the coordination found in the "division of labor" of typical two-parent families. The mother-negative subjects showed the most disruption of coordination as their mothers seem to have taken on the characteristics other subjects assigned to their fathers. (15 references)

779. Sorosky, Arthur D. "The Psychological Effects of Divorce on Adolescents." *Adolescence* 12(45): 123–136 (Spring 1977).

The psychological effects of divorce upon adolescents are examined through a review of literature, and observations from private psychiatric practice. Adolescents vary in their ability to cope with divorce and may exhibit a wide range of psychological responses. They are concerned with the effect of their new status on peers, relationship with visiting parent, and dating and remarriage of custodial and noncustodial parents. Divorce may leave the adolescent with a fear of rejection, interrupt resolution of typical adolescent conflicts, and leave a fear of personal marital failure. Knowledge of the typical reactions of adolescents to divorce can help parents identify divorce related issues. Educational programs for parents and adolescents by community agencies and religious organizations can be helpful. (27 references)

780. Southworth, Suzanne, and Conrad J. Schwarz. "Post-Divorce Contact, Relationship with Father and Heterosexual Trust in Female College Students." *American Journal of Orthopsychiatry* 57(3): 371–382 (July 1987).

This study probes the expectations in 104 female college students in regard to men, work and marriage in order to explore possible connections between their attitudes and their pre- and post-divorce father/daughter relationships. Based on responses to several questionnaires, it was found that the experience of divorce and its consequences had longterm effects on young women's trust in males and on their plans for the future. However, these effects were not found to be significantly connected to the kind of relationships the subjects had with their father in the period following divorce. (20 references)

781. Stack, Carol B. "Who Owns the Child? Divorce and Child Custody Decisions in Middle-Class Families." *Social Problems* 23(4): 505–515 (April 1976).

This article questions the right of the custodial parent to permit or deny the noncustodial parent access to the child and criticizes the custody guidelines presented in *Beyond the Best Interests of the Child* by Goldstein, Freud and Solnit (1973). Adoption of uniform statutes for child custody is proposed. Joint custody is advocated in divorce cases unless the court finds overriding reasons why this would not be in the best interests of the child. (No references)

782. Stolberg, Arnold L., and James M. Anker. "Cognitive and Behavioral Changes in Children Resulting From Parental Divorce and Consequent Environmental Changes." *Journal of Divorce* 7(2): 23–41 (Winter 1983).

Environmental change due to divorce is viewed to explain the processes leading to psychopathology in some children of divorce. Subjects included 39 children of divorced parents who had been separated from six months to three years and 40 children from intact families. Measures used were: Recent Life Changes Questionnaire, Environmental Changes Questionnaire and Child Behavior Checklist. Processes leading to child psychopathology were identified as types of changes, changes in parent-child relations and increased demands on the custodial parent. Application of the research data to intervention programs is discussed. (25 references)

783. Stolberg, Arnold L., and Joseph P. Bush. "A Path Analysis of Factors Predicting Children's Divorce Adjustment." *Journal of Clinical Child Psychology* 14(1): 49–54 (Spring 1985).

Eighty-two mother-child pairs from divorced homes completed measures assessing life change events, marital hostility, parenting skills, parent and child adjustment, and children's self-concept. Four variables measuring children's postdivorce outcomes were predicted with significant accuracy based on 14 family history, parent adjustment, and child-rearing environment variables. It was found that mothers with more children reported better postdivorce social and emotional adjustment and practiced better parenting techniques. The use of more effective parenting techniques was associated with better skills and less internalized psychopathology in their children. Externalize pathology may be modelled after observed parental behaviors. (21 references)

784. Stuart, Irving R., and Lawrence Edwin Abt. *Children of Separation and Divorce: Management and Treatment.* New York: Van Nostrand Reinhold, 1981.

The first edition of this book (1972) examined problems and issues related to divorce from the point of view of parents and the effects of this action as seen by their children. This edition focuses on matters of management and treatment of problems affecting children as they are seen by specialists in a variety of areas. Among the issues covered are children's legal rights and difficulties, developmental consequences of parent-loss, psychiatric aspects of visitation and custody, foster-care, and children of incarcerated parents. Treating children in gay families and remarried families is also discussed. Suggestions are offered for identifying children at risks, determining needs, and timing interventions. (Bibliography)

785. Sullivan, Kenneth, and Anna Sullivan. "Adolescent-Parent Separation." *Developmental Psychology* 16(2): 93–99 (March 1980).

Results of adolescent-parent separation were probed in a study of 242 white adolescent male students who were to either board at college or live at home and commute. Parents and students were administered pretest and post-test questionnaires. Findings showed that more boarders attended four year colleges, had higher SAT scores, exhibited increases in affection, communication, independence, and satisfaction in relation to parents. Therefore, this study suggests that separation from parents facilitated the adolescent boys' growth toward becoming functionally independent of parents. (15 references)

786. Taylor, Laura. "The Effects of a Non-Related Adult Friend on Children of Divorce." *Journal of Divorce* 5(4): 67–76 (Summer 1982).

The idea of helping a child cope with divorce by having a neutral friend with whom the child could discuss the event is explored. A number of communities have programs to provide a non-related adult friend for the children many professionals consider at risk. Results of a study of Big Brother/Big Sister of Des Moines are reported. Analysis of responses to a questionnaire in a review of the literature was not supported. The data collected gives no clear indications of the factors that help or hinder the development of a mutually enjoyable and helpful relationship. (10 references)

787. Teleki, Jane K., et al. "Factor Analysis of Reports of Parental Behavior by Children Living in Divorced and Married Families." *Journal of Psychology* 112(2): 295–302 (November 1982).

A factor analysis of the responses of children to the Child's Report of Parental Behavior Inventory by 59 children from divorced and intact families was compared in this study. Results showed that children's reports of divorced mothers did not differentiate the factors of acceptance and lax discipline to as high a degree as did children reporting for married mothers, married fathers, or divorced fathers. (20 references)

788. ———. "Parental Child-Rearing Behavior Perceived by Parents and School-Age Children in Divorced and Married Families." *Home Economics Research Journal* 13(1): 41–51 (September 1984).

This study focuses on parental behavior in divorced and married families. Children and parents from 29 divorced and 30 married families responded to the Child's Report of Parental Behavior Inventory. Children from divorced families reported their father as being more lax in discipline than their mother, and their fathers as being more lax in discipline than did children of married fathers. The children in divorced families felt themselves as accepted by their fathers and mother as children from married families. (37 references)

789. Terre, Lisa, et al. "Child Custody: Practices and Perspectives of Legal Professionals." *Journal of Clinical Child Psychology* 14(1): 27–34 (Spring 1985).

Attitudes and practices of judges and attorneys are explored in regard to custody arrangements and the criteria used to formulate custody decisions. Legal professionals do not see joint custody as the most desirable or most appropriate arrangement in most cases and should not be arranged at the cost of maintaining or prolonging the child's involvement in a highly conflictual situation. The emotional stability and maturity of the parents and their relationship to each other were keys in custody arrangement, rather than the importance of the child's relationship to both parents and/or the enhanced well being of the noncustodial parent. (32 references)

790. Tessman, Lora Heims. *Children of Parting Parents.* New York: Jason Aronson, 1978.

This book is based on the authors' experience in working with children, adolescents, and adults who were trying to cope with parental loss through separation, divorce and death. Reactions to separation from parents, that are similar to those of mourning the loss of a loved one are discussed. It is suggested that when remarriage occurs, the young child's security may be threatened unless he can call one or the other parental abodes "home base." Ill-suited custody arrangements, relationships with stepparents, siblings and step-siblings, school problems and the need for a supportive human network are among the topics explored. (Bibliography)

791. Tiktin, Emily A., and Catherine Cobb. "Treating Post-Divorce Adjustment in Latency Age Children: A Focused Group Paradigm." *Social Work with Groups* 6(2): 53–66 (Summer 1983).

When parental divorce occurs during latency, the subsequent disruption in the lives of children may interfere with their development. A model group program for children seven to twelve years of age was developed by the authors to broaden children's understanding of divorce, to teach healthy expression of feelings, and to provide a forum for sharing experiences with peers. Reports from parents and children plus observations of therapists indicate that the group model had a positive effect on children's post-divorce adjustment. (23 references)

792. Tooley, Kay. "Antisocial Behavior and Social Alienation Post Divorce: the Man of the House and His Mother." *American Journal of Orthopsychiatry* 46(1): 33–42 (January 1976).

The structure of the post divorce single family and its impact on the developing personality of male children between four and seven years of age is examined. Emotional responses of the parent to the post divorce situation frequently affect the behavior of their children. Clinical experience reviewed in this report suggests that mothers and sons derive great benefit from family interventions focused on recognizing and utilizing aggression. (9 references)

793. Trunnell, Thomas L. "Johnnie and Suzie, Don't Cry: Mommy and Daddy Aren't That Way." *Bulletin of the American Academy of Psychiatry and the Law* 4(2): 120–126 (1976).

This paper focuses on child custody litigation. The author describes many of the complex problems facing children, parents, attorneys, child psychiatrists, and other family professionals involved in custody disputes and child placement in divorce. Procedures developed for use at the Child Guidance Clinic at San Diego are recommended for use in making custody decisions. It is suggested that those who represent the rights of children need to be experts in child development as well as adult pathology. (No references)

794. United States. Congress. Senate Hearings before the Subcommittee on Juvenile Justice of the Committee on Judiciary. Parental Kidnapping, Washington, D.C.: Govt. Printing Office, 1983. 192pp. (ERIC Microfiche ED245145)

Thirty-five cases involving contested child custody and visitation are reviewed and the techniques used by experienced divorce mediators to help couples resolve their differences are discussed. Mediators were lawyers and mental health professionals. Project clients were identified by clerks, referees and investigators of Denver metro area courts. To generate custody agreements, mediators provided couples with orientation to mediation, and helped them overcome emotional and other obstacles. Variations in the ways mediators deal with expressions of emotions and the amount of control they exercise are presented. (34 references)

795. Vanderskooi, Lois, and Jessica Pearson. "Mediating Divorce Disputes: Mediator Behavior, Style and Roles." *Family Relations* 32(4): 557–566 (October 1983).

Thirty-five cases involving contested child custody and visitation are reviewed and the techniques used by experienced divorce mediators to help couples resolve their differences are discussed. Mediators were lawyers and mental health professionals. Project clients were identified by clerks, referees and investigators of Denver metro area courts. To generate custody agreements, mediators provided couples with orientation to mediation, and helped them overcome emotional and other obstacles.

Variations in the ways mediators deal with expressions of emotions and the amount of control they exercise are presented. (34 references)

796. Wadsworth, M. E., and M. Maclean. "Parents' Divorce and Children's Life Chances." *Children and Youth Services Review* 8(2): 145–159 (1986).

Data from cross-sectional and longitudinal studies in Great Britain were used to investigate long term consequences of divorce for children. Lower educational achievement for males and females, and lower socio-economic status for males in their mid-twenties was found for those who had suffered parental divorce or separation before they were 14 years of age as compared to their peers from intact families. Related research in Great Britain and the United States is discussed. (40 references)

797. Walker, Glynnis. *Solomon's Children: Exploding the Myths of Divorce.* New York: Arbor House 1986).

This book is based on the responses to 368 questionnaires on separation, divorce, remarriage, and later on. The pros and cons of a variety of custody arrangements, mothers who don't want custody, serial marriages, and profiles of parents and children in these various situations are discussed. Most respondents felt blameless for their parents' divorce and did not favor reconciliation, although they frequently cited feelings of rejection, embarrassment, puzzlement, and sadness following separation and divorce. The author suggests that it is a disservice to the children of divorced families to consider them damaged or different from children in traditional families. (Bibliography)

798. Wallerstein, Judith S. "Children of Divorce: Preliminary Report of a Ten-Year Follow-Up of Older Children and Adolescents." *Journal of the American Academy of Child Psychiatry* 24(5): 545–553 (1985).

This article reports preliminary results of a ten-year longitudinal study of 113 children and adolescents from divorced families in Northern California. Initially all children in the study had been reported by parents and teachers as a significant number were considered psychologically troubled. Forty of these subjects between 19 and 29 years old regard their parents' divorce as a major continuing influence on their lives and expressed feelings of sadness and resentment. Females in this group appeared especially troubled. Sibling relationships seem to provide a significant supportive network with the capacity to buffer the family ordeal and nuture family relationships. (6 references)

799. ———. "Children of Divorce: Preliminary Report of a Ten-Year Follow-Up of Young Children." *American Journal of Orthopsychiatry* 54(3): 444–458 (July 1984).

This is a preliminary report from a ten-year longitudinal study of responses of children and parents following separation and divorce. Results of interviews with 30 children and 40 parents indicated that the children who were youngest at the time of family breakup fared better than their older siblings. Memories, perceptions and attitudes regarding parents and divorce were among adjustment issues examined. (14 references)

800. ———. "Children of Divorce: The Psychological Tasks of the Child." *American Journal of Orthopsychiatry* 53(2): 230–243 (April 1983).

Divorce is a special kind of stress for the child who has been raised in a two parent family. The child's experience in divorce is comparable in some ways to the experience of the child who loses a parent in death or the child who loses his or her community in a natural disaster. Six psychological tasks that the child must face are: acknowledging the reality of the marital rupture, disengaging from parental conflict and distress and resuming customary pursuits, resolution of loss, resolving anger and self-blame, accepting the permanence of the divorce, and achieving realistic hope regarding relationships. Even when these tasks are successfully resolved, there will remain some residue of sadness, anger, and anxiety about the potential unreliability of relationships that may surface at critical times during the adult years. (19 references)

801. ———. "Children of Divorce: Report of a Ten-Year Follow-Up of Early Latency-Age Children." *American Journal of Orthopsychiatry* 57(2): 199–211 (April 1987).

This study reports findings from a ten-year follow-up of 38 children from 54 of the original 60 families whose parents divorced during the children's early latency. Responses to interviews and questionnaires suggest that familial separation and transition to adulthood fostered feelings of anxiety in regard to relationships with the opposite sex, a sense of powerlessness and lowered expectations of themselves. Regardless of the family's legal status, young people still turn to the appropriate parent for help at various developmental stages. (13 references)

802. ———. "The Impact of Divorce on Children." *Psychiatric Clinics of North America* 3(3): 455–468 (December 1980).

In the California Children of Divorce Project 106 children and adolescents were studied close to the time of separation and five years after the divorce. Prior to family disruption, all children had reached age appropriate development as rated by parents and teachers. During the divorcing process, few children experienced relief with their parents' decision to divorce and evidence suggested that many were not adequately supported by parents and distant extended family. Preschool children were likely to exhibit regression, five to eight year old children were likely to show symptoms of grief, nine to twelve-year-old children often felt intense anger, while some adolescents exhibited anxiety. In the post divorce period changes in relationship with visiting and custodial parents were noted. Five years following the divorce 37 percent of the children were psychologically distressed. Professional help is suggested for helping families through this difficult period. (27 references)

803. Wallerstein, Judith S., and Sandra Blakeslee. *Second Chances: Men, Women and Children A Decade After Divorce*. New York: Ticknor & Fields (Houghton Mifflin), 1989.

This longitudinal study began in 1971, the impact of divorce on 131 children from 60 middle-class families. Twelve to eighteen months following parental divorce, many families were still in crisis, exhibiting symptoms worse than at the time of the divorce. At the end of five years about 37 percent of the families were found to be depressed. Ten years after the divorce 41 percent were not doing well. Some families were followed for as long as 15 years. Many children emerged competent with help of inner resources and the support of parents and kin or mentors. Almost half of the children entered adulthood worried, underachieving and self-deprecating. Children exposed to post-divorce parental conflict were at greater risk. (Bibliography)

804. Wallerstein, Judith S., and Joan Berlin Kelly. "California's Children of Divorce." *Psychology Today* 13(8): 67–76 (January 1980).

Results of an indepth study of the children in 60 families who had experienced divorce. One hundred thirty-one children, aged two to eighteen from white, black and interracial families participated in the study. This study reports results of interview five years after the breakup. Although individuals among the children had improved or worsened, the percentages within broad categories of good and poor adjustment had remained relatively stable. Joint legal custody is viewed as a positive step. Shared "physical" custody was suggested as an area for future study. It is also noted that the divorced family, in many ways, is less adaptive economically, socially and psychologically to the raising of children than the two parent family. (4 references)

805. ———. "Divorce Counseling: A Community Service for Families in the Midst of Divorce." *American Journal of Orthopsychiatry* 47(1): 4–22 (January 1977).

A conceptual framework for the development of child-centered, preventive clinical services for divorcing families is presented. The structure and components for intervention including treatment strategies, successful interventions, failures, therapist role transference and counter transference responses and professional dilemmas are discussed after five years of work with 60 families whose children were between the ages of three and 18 at the time of divorce. (9 references)

806. ———. "The Effects of Parental Divorce: Experiences of the Child in Later Latency." *American Journal of Orthopsychiatry* 46(2): 256–269 (April 1976).

Discusses the impact of divorce on 31 children in later latency as observed shortly after the initial parental and one year later. The material is part separation of an on-going clinical study begun in 1970 of 131 children from 60 divorcing families. The data for this paper focuses on the experiences of 31 children from 28 families who were between nine and ten years old at the time of the initial study. Efforts to cope include seeking coherence, by denial, by courage, by bravado, and by seeking support from others. Half of the children suffered a decline in school performance and changes in parent-child relationships were also noted. Although the divorce experience had been muted somewhat at the end of a year, few children were able to maintain a good relationship with both parents. (10 references)

807. ———. "The Effects of Parental Divorce: Experiences of the Preschool child." *Journal of the American Academy of Child Psychiatry* 14(4): 600–614 (Autumn 1975).

This paper reports the initial responses of 34 preschool children from a sample of 131 children and adolescents who are part of a larger study of the effects of parental divorce. Regression in children younger than four was found to be temporary when there was continuity of physical and loving care. Self-esteem and self-image in children under five may be threatened by the lack of dependability and seemed to survive family turmoil without adverse effects or appeared clinically worse at follow-up. There seemed to be a significant relationship between postdivorce that was not related to the mothers' employment outside the home. (8 references)

808. ———. *Surviving the Breakup: How Children Actually Cope with Divorce*. New York: Basic Books, 1980.

This book is addressed to family professionals who come in contact with divorcing parents and are concerned about the children in these families. The experiences of sixty California families and 136 of their children are analyzed. Although it was found that the children respond to family dissolution in a variety of ways, the immediate post-separation period was especially critical. At the end of the five-year study the authors concluded that the successful post-divorce family can experience an improved quality of life, whereas the failed divorce families may experience low self-esteem, depression, and feelings of anger and deprivation that can last for years. It is suggested that divorced parents need to maintain separate social and sexual roles while continuing to cooperate as parents on behalf of their children. (Bibliography)

809. ———. "The Effects of Parental Divorce: The Adolescent Experience." In *The Child in his Family: Children at Psychiatric Risk*, edited by E. Jones Anthony and Cyrille Koupernik, 479–505. New York: Wiley, 1974.

This paper is the first report from a three year study of the effects of divorce on children at the time of divorce and one year following divorce. Sixty families with 131 children between the ages of three and nineteen availed themselves of counseling directed toward easing the effects of divorce on children. The subjects were interviewed again 12 to 18 months following the six week counseling period. Findings indicate that parental divorce is an extremely painful experience for young people who are undergoing the changes that occur during adolescence. However, most of the young people studied were able, one year following divorce to take up their individual agendas as they moved toward adulthood. Except in cases where the response to divorce caused delays in development, these young people continue at a level equal to their previous achievement. (28 references)

810. Warner, Nancy S., and Carla J. Elliot. "Problems of the Interpretive Phase of Divorce-Custody Evaluations." *Journal of Divorce* 2(4): 371–382 (Summer 1979).

Problems encountered by clinicians in child custody evaluations in divorce are the focus of this article. The evaluation processes used in the Children's Diagnostic Center in the Child Psychiatry Division of the University of Colorado Medical Center are those where there have been lengthy allegations by each parent regarding the fitness of the other. Evaluations consist of pediatric, psychiatric, psychological and psychoeducationl exams of the children as well as the parents. A problem with divorce-custody evaluations is the lack of long-term follow-up studies to determine the effectiveness of methods used. (9 references)

811. Warren, Nancy J., and Ingrid A. Amara. "Educational Groups for Single Parents: The Parenting after Divorce Programs." *Journal of Divorce* 3(2): 79–96 (Winter 1984). (Also ERIC Microfiche ED244217)

The Parenting After Divorce project was designed to help parents facilitate their children's adjustment by providing educational prevention programs. The impact of intervention on family, children and parents was measured by a variety of instruments. The divorce group that this paper focuses on is described in detail sufficient to permit replication or close adaptation of the model project. Group response indicates that parents with the greatest post-divorce stress benefit the most. Data collected from the 35 parents in the group studied show that parents especially valued the skills learned which enabled them to understand their children better and to communicate more effectively with them. (30 references)

812. Warshak, Richard A., and John W. Santrock. "Children of Divorce: Impact of Custody Disposition on Social Development." In *Life-Span Developmental Psychology: Non-Normative Life Events*, edited by Edward J. Callahan and Kathleen A. McCluskey, 241–263. New York: Academic Press, 1983.

Not until the twentieth century was a tradition of awarding mothers custody of their children established. Sixty-four white middle-class families with children six to eleven years of age, were subjects of the Texas Custody Research Project. A multimethod approach was used in assessing the social development of children in father custody. Results of the investigation do not support reliance on generalizations that give prior claims to either the father or the mother. Instead, it suggests that a variety of factors that include the sex of the child, aspects of the custodial parent-child relationship, and the availability and use of extrafamilial support systems. Limitations of study are discussed and implications for future research noted. (Bibliography)

813. Weiss, David Charles. "Margaret S. Mahler's Separation-Individuation Phase of Early Childhood Development and Responses to Marital Separation." PhD. diss., Boston University, 1980.

For a summary see: *Dissertation Abstracts International* 40B(12): 13219.

814. Weiss, Robert S. "The Impact of Marital Dissolution on Income and Consumption in Single-Parent Households." *Journal of Marriage and the Family* 46(1): 115–127 (February 1984).

Data on 5,000 households with separating and divorcing mothers were taken from the Michigan Panel Study of Income Dynamics in a study of the effect of marital dissolution on income and consumption in single-parent households. Separation and divorce was found to result in reduced income at all income levels. Approximately 50 percent of the income in single parent households went for food and housing, the remainder goes largely for clothing, child care and transportation. As income does not increase substantially over the years, single parent families are trapped in reduced living standards and studies have shown that many of the problems of single parent children are related to reduced income. (12 references)

815. Weiss, Warren W., and Henry B. Collada. "Conciliation Counseling: the Court's Effective Mechanism for Resolving Visitation and Custody Disputes." *Family Coordinator* 26(4): 444–446 (October 1977).

Counseling services offered for mitigation of custody/ visitation disputes by a California court are discussed. The conciliation service, an adjunct of the court, employs professional marriage and family counselors whose primary business is to assist parents in reaching a custody/ visitation agreement that best serves the interest and needs of their children. The negotiation process involves parents, children and attorneys with the judge rendering the final decision. A sample case is presented which illustrates the conciliation process. Benefits of custody visitation counseling a reduction in cases returned to the court and a reduction in cost not possible with the old system. (No references)

816. Wesley, Valerie Wilson. "Children of Divorce: What the Law Says." *Essence* 14(2): 74+ (July 1983).

Courts dealing with child custody and support will only consider what is relevant to the child's physical and emotional well being. Support allowances will depend on a child's needs and be regularly adjusted with the cost of living. If visitation is denied, a parent can file a contempt of court motion. Parents should seek the advice of attorneys specializing in family law. Parents must document their claims in court. Fathers are liable to pay their wives legal fees. Legislation allows unsupportive parents to be traced and payment enforced. Under the Uniform Reciprocal Enforcement Act, parents in another state can be made to give support. Unwed mothers must prove paternity before support will be provided. Unwed fathers rights are improving. (No references)

817. Westman, J. D., et al. "The Role of Child Psychiatry in Divorce." *Archives of General Psychiatry* 23(5): 416–420 (November 1970).

The divorce process is very stressful for children. Custody and visitation adjustment, interference from relatives, and child support may add to the turbulence of the postdivorce period and children may become the pawns in the continued parental conflict. Finding in this clinic study suggests that most divorces involving children are not followed by legal conflicts over financial and child rearing arrangements. However, one-third of the divorces involving children were followed by continuing conflict between parents. Implications of the study for child psychiatry and divorce courts are discussed. (12 references)

818. Whitehead, Linette. "Sex Differences in Children's Responses to Family Stress: A Re-Evaluation." *Journal of Child Psychology and Psychiatry and Allied Disciplines* 20(3): 247–254 (July 1979).

This study investigates the relationship of marital discord to antisocial and neurotic behavior in children as assessed by parental questionnaire. Data on 1775 first-born children aged seven years old were taken from the first follow-up of the National Child Development Study. Results of the investigation show that divorce, separation or desertion have some relationship to maladjustment in young children and that marital discord may be associated with antisocial and neurotic disturbances in children of both sexes. Divorce may be more closely associated with disturbance in boys, although there is some question as to whether social factors or greater psychological vulnerability are responsible. (8 references)

819. Williams, Bonnie Myhre, et al. "A Model for Intervention with Latency-Aged Children of Divorce." *Family Therapy* 10(2): 111–124 (1983).

A model for intervention with latency-aged children from divorced families is described. Examples from clinical work and a review of literature are discussed. The latency-aged model for children of divorce involves parents, children, and peers. It is suggested that this model reduces anxiety in children and parents during a stressful period in their lives. (32 references)

820. Wolchik, Sharlene A., and Paul K. Karoly. *Children of Divorce: Empirical Perspectives on Adjustment.* New York: Gardner Press, 1988.

The ten chapters of this book were written by persons whose names are well known to professionals who work with children and parents from divorced families. Topics discussed include: children's reactions to divorce, the postdivorce environment, child custody arrangements, the impact of divorce on children's school behavior and academic performance, mediation of post divorce arrangements and current issues in family law. (Bibliographies)

821. Wolchik, Sharlene A., et al. "Events of Parental Divorce: Stressfulness Ratings by Children, Parents, and Clinicians." *Journal of Community Psychology* 14(1): 59–74 (February 1986).

This research focuses on 62 events that children experience during parental divorce and the stressfulness they caused as rated by children, parents and clinicians. Of 125 children who participated in the study, 90 percent were Caucasian, three percent were black, and five percent were Hispanics. The Divorce Events Schedule for Children and the Stressfulness Rating Form were used to measure stressfulness. Results seem to indicate that there are similarities in the way that children, parents and clinicians view the impact of divorce in relation to stress. When significant differences occurred, both parents and clinicians rated the events more stressful than the children rated them. There was also an absence of age and sex effects on the item stressfulness ratings. It is suggested that study can aid in design of intervention programs to help children cope with impact of divorce. (24 references)

822. ———. "Maternal Versus Joint Custody: Children's Postseparation Experiences and Adjustment." *Journal of Clinical Child Psychology* 14(1): 5–10 (Spring 1985).

This study compares the experiences and adjustment of children in joint and maternal custody arrangements. Subjects included 133 children, ages eight to fifteen who had experienced parental separation. Interviews and questionnaires were used to assess anxiety, depression, self-esteem and hostility. Children in joint custody had a greater number of positive experiences than children in maternal custody. Knowledge of parents' motivation for selecting joint custody may help in understanding why joint custody is beneficial in some cases and not in others. It is suggested that a data base be developed to allow custody decisions based on empirical findings rather than theoretical fancy. (33 references)

823. Woody, Robert Henley. "Fathers with Child Custody." *Counseling Psychologist* 7(4): 60–63 (1978).

The Uniform Child Custody Jurisdiction Act has resulted in the questioning of existing child custody practices and an increase in the number of fathers who get custody. Research on custody and father absence is reviewed along with developmental implication for children who suffer father loss. An attempt is made to define the role of the counseling psychologist in custody cases through ten recommendations that lean toward father custody while advocating objectivity. (22 references)

824. ———. "Sexism in Child Custody Decisions." *Personnel and Guidance Journal* 56(3): 168–170 (November 1977).

Recent sex equity legislation pretends changes in custody award practices. This study examines sexism in custody determination based on responses to a questionnaire by lawyers, psychiatrists, psychologists, and social workers. Findings indicated that, with all conditions equal, psychiatrists and older professionals favored mother-custody, while most of those opposed to mother-custody had never been married. The majority of the respondents did not believe that placement of the child with a parent of the same sex was of any special significance. It is suggested that counselors need to recognize their own attitudes, beliefs and values about custody in order to arrive at a position of objectivity in their role as counselor. (5 references)

825. Wyman, Peter A., et al. "Perceived Competence, Self-Esteem, and Anxiety in Latency-Aged Children of Divorce." *Journal of Clinical Child Psychology* 14(1): 20–26 (Spring 1985).

Ninety-eight children, nine to twelve years old, from divorced families were compared to demographically similar children from intact families on measures of perceived competence, self-worth, anxiety and sources of support. Latency aged children of divorce had lower perceived cognitive competence, higher anxiety and fewer potential sources of social support. Results show the need for developing effective preventive intervention incorporating support principles for children of divorce aimed at pinpointing problem areas and mediators of good postdivorce adjustment. (43 references)

826. Young, David M. "A Court-Mandated Workshop for the Younger Children of Divorcing Parents: A Description and Program Evaluation." *Early Child Development and Care* 13(3–4): 292–307 (January 1984).

A description and empirical evaluation of a pre-divorce workshop established by the Family Court of Allen County, Indiana, for younger children (seven to eleven) of divorcing parents. The concerns of the children and the approaches taken by the staff are highlighted. Post workshop evaluations were collected and a content analysis of children's perception of problems are also discussed as well as the preventive nature of the program. (15 references)

827. Young, David M., and Gordon L. Bodie. "The Accuracy of Parents' Perceptions of Children of Divorce." *Early Child Development and Care* 13(3–4): 309–320 (January 1984).

The relationship between self-reported attitudes and adjustment of 48 young children of divorce and their parents was studied. Compared to the traditional family control group, the divorced parents were able to accurately assess their children's current attitudes about the family situation with the following exceptions: child's self-rating of feeling upset, sad or worried, current behavior problems at school and estimates of father's emotional state. Although the differences in perception are not great, it is recommended that the impact needs to be explored. (6 references)

LOSS OF A PARENT THROUGH DEATH

BIBLIOGRAPHIES AND LITERATURE REVIEW

828. Aradine, Carolyn R. "Books for Children about Death." *Pediatrics* 57(3): 372–378 (March 1976).

This article reviews books about death for preschool and school aged children that will aid them in their understanding of death. It is suggested that awareness of this literature can be helpful to pediatricians and nurses in advising parents who are concerned about their childrens' reactions to death. These books are recommended for children from a preventive mental health perspective rather than for use with children who are terminally ill. (21 references)

829. Berlinsky, Ellen B., and Henry B. Biller. *Parental Death and Psychological Development*. Lexington, Mass.: Lexington Books, 1982.

A critical review of the literature on the child's adjustment and development following parental death is presented. Following parental death the child and surviving parent need immediate assistance in reducing the tendency to become overwhelmed and unable to function. Surrogate support systems can be helpful in the period immediately following the crisis. Cognitive and projective personality test responses may not remain constant over a long period of time. Reasons for initiating psychotherapy are discussed along with preventative techniques designed to help the child. (Bibliography)

830. Bernstein, Joanne E. *Books to Help Children Cope with Separation and Loss*. 2nd ed. New York: Bowker, 1989.

Children's reactions to separation and loss are discussed and bibliotherapy is recommended as a means of helping children cope with the effects of the trauma they experience in these situations. An annotated list of 633 books, graded for reading levels, is presented in context with a variety of losses such as divorce, death, desertion, hospitalization, single-parent family, war and displacement, reconstituted families, adoption, and facing foster care.

831. Cook, Sarah Sheets. *Children and Dying: An Exploration and a Selective Professional Bibliography.* New York: Health Science Publishing, 1973.

An understanding of children's perceptions of death and their reactions to it is essential for those in the helping professions. Four essays one by a nurse, one by a physician, and two by clergymen, address the responses of children and adolescents to death. A list of 22 books and 36 articles, primarily from medical journals, is presented. (Bibliography)

832. Crook, Thomas, and John Eliot. "Parental Death During Childhood and Adult Depression: A Critical Review of the Literature." *Psychological Bulletin* 87(2): 252–259 (March 1980).

The relationship between parental death in childhood and depression in adult life is examined through a review of literature on the subject. Results of this study lead to the conclusion that parental death in childhood is not significantly related to adult depression or any subtype of adult depression. It is also suggested that studies that have found a higher incidence of childhood bereavement in depressed patients evidenced flawed methodology. (31 references)

833. Critelli, Tecla. "Parental Death in Childhood: A Review of the Psychiatric Literature." In *The Child and Death,* edited by John E. Schowalter, et al., 89–103. New York: Columbia University Press, 1983. (Foundation of Thanatology)

Literature on long-term effects of parental death in childhood is reviewed, with flaws in research design noted.

Serious depressive illness associated with early bereavement was reported in many studies, and additionally age at loss, family composition, and circumstances were also found to affect outcomes. Further study of the extent to which normal childhood bereavement overlaps with that of childhood depressive states is suggested. (90 references).

834. Griggs, Shirley A. "Annotated Bibliography of Books on Death, Dying, and Bereavement." *School Counselor* 24(5): 362–371 (May 1977).

An annotated list of over 50 books on death, dying, and bereavement is presented which can be useful for children, parents, family, professionals, and others. Cultural differences in viewing death, differences in philosophy among religious groups, explaining death and counseling the child, and the psychological aspects of death and dying are among some of the areas covered.

835. Epstein, Gerald, et al. "Research on Bereavement: A Selective and Critical Review." *Comprehensive Psychiatry* 16(6): 537–546 (November/December 1975).

This article presents a critical review of research on investigations of parental loss, conjugal loss and predictors of unfavorable bereavement outcomes. Problems with research design are noted and more sophisticated methodology in the study of the relationship between childhood bereavement and later behavioral pathology is suggested. Some studies find that the death of one or both parents in childhood is common among attempted and actual suicide victims. (54 references)

836. Finkelstein, Harris. "The Long-Term Effects of Early Parent Death: A Review." *Journal of Clinical Psychology* 44(1): 3–9 (January 1988).

Because a child is not mature enough to function independently, early death of the mother can be expected to have some impact on the behavior and attitudes of children. A review of research on early parental death suggest that it may be associated with depression, alcoholism and possibly a number of other negative outcomes in adulthood. Age, emotional stability of the individual child, sex of the deceased and the bereaved, quality of the relationship between the child and the deceased, and the nature of social supports following parental loss were viewed as variables that may mitigate the long-term effects of loss. (58 references)

837. Hare, Jan, et al. "The Child in Grief: Implications for Teaching." *Early Child Development Care* 25(1): 43–56 (1986).

This paper is based on a review of the literature on child bereavement. Child educators are in a position to provide a safe environment in which children can explore the concepts of death and dying. The classroom is a place where the bereaved child can find support and the opportunity to express feelings. Parents may also learn from teachers what behaviors children display in expressing grief. Together with parents, teachers may help children to respond and recover from loss. (14 references)

838. Kastenbaum, Robert, and Paul T. Costa. "Psychological Perspectives on Death." *Annual Review of Psychology* 28: 225–249 (1977).

This article is a critical survey of the psychology of death from a historical perspective. Research indicates that children often perceive death-related phenomena and try to understand them much earlier than many theorists assume. It is suggested that the two forms of bereavement that have the most powerful effects on the survivor are: the parent who loses a child and the child who loses a parent. Research on anticipatory grief is encouraged for its implications for the mental health of those who will survive, and for the adjustment to death when it occurs. (169 references)

839. Lamers, Elizabeth. "Books for Adolescents." In *Adolescence and Death*, edited by Charles A. Corr and Joan N. McNeil, 97–118. New York: Springer, 1986.

A bibliography of books for use with adolescents in opening up channels of communication for discussing loss through death is the focus of this chapter. In consideration of the variance in reading abilities of adolescents, the annotated list of books is divided by primary level, middle grades, and age twelve and up. The author tells how the 44 books might be used with readers and mentions other sources of books as well. (Bibliography)

840. Mace, Gillian S., et al. *The Bereaved Child: Analysis, Education, and Treatment: An Abstracted Bibliography.* New York: IFI/Plenum, 1981.

This comprehensive abstracted bibliography contains over 550 items that focus on the reactions and coping responses of children and adolescents to the death of parents, siblings, friends, teachers, pets and presidents.The supporting roles that adults can play in facilitating the mourning process and the developmental effects of the death experience on children are also covered. Titles of journals that are devoted exclusively to the subject of death, dying, and bereavement are listed in a separate section.

841. Nelson, Richard C. "Counselors, Teachers, and Death Education." *School Counselor* 24(5): 322–329 (May 1977).

Teachers and counselors need to be able to deal effectively with death in their own lives and in their work with children before they can provide leadership in death education. Classroom learning experiences that may help develop a healthy awareness related to death are discussed. Newspaper accounts of accidents, motion pictures, television dramas, and books are useful in launching a discussion of death and the feelings related to it. Guidelines for forming a group of counselors and teachers to explore the impact of death and to discuss related concerns and attitudes are offered. Teachers may then be in a better position to understand the problems grieving students face and help them work through the grief process. (5 references)

842. "Outstanding Children's Books About Death." In *Children and Death: Perspectives from Birth Through Adolescence.* 195–215, edited by John E. Schowalter, et al., with editorial assistance of Jeanne D. Cole. New York: Praeger, 1987.

This is an annotated list of recent children's books about death for young readers. The titles are part of a bibliography, *Books to Help Children Cope with Separation and Loss.* 2nd ed., New York: Bowker, 1983. The 12 books included here are graded for reading level and may be used to promote discussion and open lines of communication related to children's feelings about loss through death.

843. Pacholski, Richard A. "Audiovisual Resources." In *Adolescence and Death,* edited by Charles A. Corr and Joan N. McNeil, 251–274. New York: Springer, 1986.

One hundred and fifty-five audiovisual titles that might be used in discussing death with adolescents are described. The annotated list of films and videotapes that address death resulting from a variety of causes may be used at all academic levels. A list of addresses for audiovisual distributors is also provided.

844. Palombo, Joseph. "Parent Loss and Childhood Bereavement: Some Theoretical Consideration." *Clinical Social Work Journal* 9(1): 3–33 (Spring 1981).

The effects of parental loss in childhood are examined through a critical review of major research findings. It was concluded that children do not necessarily respond to the loss of a parent in the same way and therefore no single psychoanalytic position can provide an answer to the complexity of the effects of parental death on a child. Suggestions for further study are offered. (48 references)

845. Speece, Mark W., and Sandor B. Brent. "Children's Understanding of Death: A Review of Three Components of a Death Concept." *Child Development* 55(5): 1671–1686 (October 1984).

This article examines three components of children's understanding of the concept of death: irreversibility, nonfunctionality and universality. Findings in a review of the literature suggests that most children in modern urban-industrial societies achieve an understanding of all three components by the age of seven. Suggestions for future research related to these specific components are offered. (68 references)

846. Stambrook, Michael, and Kevin C. Parker. "The Development of the Concept of Death in Childhood: A Review of the Literature." *Merrill-Palmer Quarterly* 33(2): 133–159 (April 1987).

Although research findings vary, a pattern is present that suggests that children tend to move from viewing death as temporary and reversible to seeing it as an internal and universal biological process. Factors that have been mentioned as contributing to the development of the concept of death are: death experiences, religious training, life circumstances, cognitive development, emotional development, education, mass media and sociocultural influences. The adequacy of measuring instruments and the exclusive use of cross-sectional data collection for research are discussed. (57 references)

847. Tennant, Christopher, et al. "Parental Death in Childhood and Risk of Adult Depressive Disorders: A Review." *Psychological Medicine* 10(2): 289–299 (May 1980).

The authors review results of studies that conclude that parental death in childhood predisposes parent-loss children to depressive disorders in adulthood. The composition of experimental samples and control groups and lack of control of variables were judged to be factors that contributed to methodological limitations that resulted in a lack of consistency in findings. Where the experimental and control groups were carefully matched there was no association found between parental bereavement in childhood and later depressive disorders. (58 references)

848. Wass, Hannelore, and Charles A. Corr, eds. *Helping Children Cope with Death: Guidelines and Resources.* 2nd ed. Washington: Hemisphere, 1984. (Series in death education, aging and health care).

This book was written to help those who are most commonly involved in helping children cope with the death of parents. Basic requirements for helping children who have suffered loss, common problems that follow a child's experience with death, and guidelines for those who help the child are among the topics covered by the authors. An extensive annotated bibliography of books and audiovisual resources for use with children at all age levels may be useful to those who work with individuals and groups. (Bibliography)

GENERAL WORKS

849. Adam, Kenneth S. "Childhood Parental Loss, Suicidal Ideation, and Suicidal Behavior." In *The Child in His Family: The Impact of Disease and Death,* edited by E. James Anthony and Cyrille Koupernik, 275–298. New York: Wiley, 1973. (Yearbook of the International Association for Child Psychiatry and Allied Professions, v.2)

Following a critical examination of literature on the subject, this paper discusses the relationship of early parental loss to suicidal ideas and behavior. It is suggested that loss or separation from a parent that occurs during a critical period in childhood may result in pathological suicidal ideas that remain in an unconscious form throughout life and may be triggered later by certain events. A research problem designed to test this hypothesis is described. Preliminary findings seem to indicate that early parental loss is a significant factor in the development of suicidal tendencies later in life. (37 references)

850. Albert, Robert S. "Cognitive Development and Parental Loss Among the Gifted, the Exceptionally Gifted and the Creative." *Psychological Reports* 29(1): 19–26 (August 1971).

The focus of this study is on descriptions of children in research studies who have IQ's of at least 155, and who are labeled as exceptionally gifted. Compared to groups with IQ's between 110 and 150, the exceptionally gifted persons started their careers at a much earlier age, were physically larger, had unusual memory, and preferred the company of older persons. Sudden transitions from no reading to reading and from one word statements to simple sentences characterize the gifted and exceptionally gifted child. Subjects designated as 'eminent' or 'historical geniuses' had a greater parental loss rate than the average college population, and greater father loss to mother loss. (21 references)

851. Anthony, James E. "Mourning and Psychic Loss of the Parent." In *The Child in His Family: The Impact of Disease and Death*, edited by James E. Anthony and Cyrille Koupernik, 255–264. New York: Wiley, 1973. (Yearbook of the International Association for Child Psychiatry and Allied Professions, v.2)

The psychic loss of a parent may manifest itself in a sense of alienation or abandonment. Factors that may affect a child's response are the child's age, phase of development, sex as related to the psychotic parent, and support given by the non-psychotic parent. There is the wish that the parent will return to the prepsychotic state. Earlier reactions to loss, such as sibling birth, weaning, and going off to school may give some indication as to how children will react to psychic loss through psychosis. Like divorce or desertion, psychic loss is incomplete. (3 references)

852. Barnes, Gordon E., and Harry Prosen. "Parental Death and Depression." *Journal of Abnormal Psychology* 94(1): 64–69 (January 1985).

The Center for Epidemiological Studies Depression Scale (CES-D) was administered to 1,250 patients in general practitioners' offices to examine the association between depression and parental loss by death. Subjects were asked whether they had lost a parent by death and their age at the time of loss. A significant association between father loss and depression was found. No significant effect for mother loss occurred. The father loss effect remained the same when demographic factors, such as city of testing, sex, marital and occupational status, age, and education were controlled. (23 references)

853. Barnes, Marion J. "The Reactions of Children and Adolescents to the Death of a Parent or Siblings." In *The Child and Death*, edited by Olle Jane Z. Sahler, 185–201. St. Louis: Mosby, 1978.

An expression of grief after an important loss often does not occur until the finality of death is accepted. Children under the age of five need special attention. Psychologically, a period of time is required before a child confronts the reality of loss and the surviving parent can help abolish misconceptions related to death. Several cases illustrate the reactions of children to parental death. Although young children may not ask painful questions directly, their feelings may be expressed in symbolic play and stories. Older children who are coping with the stresses of adolescence need a great deal of emotional support and the opportunity to verbalize their feelings. (10 references)

854. Bascue, Loy O., and George W. Kreiger. "Death as a

Counseling Concern." *Personnel and Guidance Journal* 52(9): 587–592 (May 1974).

This article focuses on the need for counselors to be informed and prepared to address the topic of death in order to deal with its impact on those individuals they serve. It is suggested that these professionals should be aware of related research and clarify their own feelings and beliefs, prior to development of a counseling program including young children who exhibit problems that are death related. (25 references)

855. Bedell, John Wesley. "The Maternal Orphan: Paternal Perceptions of Mother Loss." In *Bereavement: Its Psychosocial Aspects*, edited by Bernard Schoenberg, et al., with Editorial Assistance of Lillian G. Kutscher, 191–207. New York: Columbia University Press, 1975.

Forty-one widowers were interviewed in an effort to assess the fathers' perception of the impact of mother loss on children. Based on the responses of participants in the study, there was little change in the socio-emotional adjustments of children following the death of their mothers. However, fathers became more aware of their children's problems after they became the primary caretakers. In general the children were judged to be healthy both physically and mentally and not more than 20 percent had any of the problems studied. Limitations of the study are noted. (19 references)

856. ———. "The One-Parent Family: Mother Absent Due to Death." Ph.D. diss., Case Western Reserve University, 1971.

For a summary see: *Dissertation Abstracts International* 32A(8): 4734.

857. ———. "Role Organization in the One-Parent Family: Mother Absent Due to Death." *Sociological Focus* 5(2): 84–100 (Winter 1971).

Role reorganization in 41 Cleveland, Ohio, families headed by widowers was examined in this study. Responses to questionnaires indicate that the role of children in decision-making is smaller than before the mothers' deaths and many take on chores formerly performed by their fathers. Household tasks are prioritized and some omitted. Extended family, as well as hired help, play a role in many families. Group and individual needs are met through family role diversity after the death of the wife and mother. (9 references)

858. Bendiksen, Robert, and Robert Fulton. "Death and the Child: An Anterospective Test of the Childhood Bereavement and Later Behavior Disorder Hypothesis." *Omega: Journal of Death and Dying* 6(1): 45–59 (1975).

This conference paper explores the long-term effect of parental death in childhood on later behavior disorders. The retrospective approach in previous studies is reviewed and shortcomings in methodology noted. A sub-sample of 401 persons from the original Minnesota Multiphasic Inventory study of 1954 by Hathaway and Monachesi were asked to complete a questionnaire for the study. Data showed that subjects from homes broken by death or divorce reported more major illnesses and more extreme emotionally distressful experiences than subjects from intact families. Siblings of those subjects who had suffered parental loss were reported as having similar experiences. (35 references)

859. Berg, Constance DeMuth. "Cognizance of the Death Taboo in Counseling Children." *School Counselor* 21(1): 28–32 (September 1973).

Cultural taboos may hamper a child's ability to express emotions related to death in the same way that all persons are affected by attitudes toward the discussion of death. When adults, as role models, act as if death does not occur and act as controlled as possible when it does occur, it is difficult for a child to understand the emotional impact of death, or not to feel that his or her feelings about death are something that must be kept inside. Adults and children need to communicate their feelings about death, and adults need to encourage children to discuss their memories and anxieties. (19 references)

860. Birtchnell, John. "Depression in Relation to Early and Recent Parent Death." *British Journal of Psychiatry* 116(532): 299–306 (March 1970).

This study uses data from case records of 500 psychiatric patients whose reactions to parental death were reported in earlier studies by the author. Depressed and nondepressed patients, and severely and moderately depressed patients were examined in regard to early and recent parent death. Findings indicate that the death of a parent in childhood or during the years prior to admission of patients was equally common in depressed patients as in other types of patients. The early death of one parent combined with the recent death of the other is significantly more common in the severely depressed. (19 references)

861. ———. "Early Parent Death and Mental Illness." *British Journal of Psychiatry* 116(532): 281–288 (March 1970).

The relationship between early parental death and mental illness was explored in a sample of 482 psychiatric patients who were compared with a control group of 476 persons from the local population. Results of the study suggest that death of a parent before the age of ten is an etiological factor in mental illness. The findings of this study are compared with those of other studies on the effect of early parent loss. It is concluded that it is not so much the trauma of separation from the parent, as the continued absence of the parent throughout childhood, which is the important effect of early parent death. (13 references)

862. ———. "Early Parent Death and the Clinical Scales of the MMPI." *British Journal of Psychiatry* 132(5): 574–579 (May 1978).

This article explores the relationship between early parent death and the severity of adult depressive illness. Subjects in this study were taken from a sample of 524 referrals for psychiatric services at North East Scottard who had completed the Minnesota Multiphasic Inventory. Findings indicate that early bereavement affects the severity of depression rather than a disposition to develop a more psychotic form of depression. (16 references)

863. ———. "The Effect of Early Parent Loss upon the Direction and Degree of Sexual Identity." *British Journal of Medical Psychology* 47(2): 129–137 (June 1974).

This study, conducted in Great Britain, examines the effect of parental loss in childhood on sexual identity. Masculinity and femininity scores, as measured by the Krout Personal Preference Scale that administered to a clinical sample of 696 persons, showed no significant differences between bereaved and nonbereaved, for both men and women. The author anticipates questioning of results due to the low incidence of early bereavement and early parental loss in the groups studied and explores hypothetically how the results in a larger number of subjects might be affected. (16 references)

864. ———. "Recent Parent Death and Mental Illness." *British Journal of Psychiatry* 116(532): 289–297 (March 1970).

Case records of 500 psychiatric patients were examined to determine the relationship between parental bereavement and patients' illness or need for admission. These subjects were compared to a control group of 473 subjects from the register of a general practitioner. It was found that the patient group had experienced almost twice as many parental deaths in the most recent five-year period than in the less recent period. A definite relationship was found between parent death and first admission. The period following parent death was one of adjustment and relative instability. (9 references)

865. ———. "Relationship Between Attempted Suicide, Depression, and Parent Death." *British Journal of Psychiatry* 116(532): 307–313 (March 1970).

This is one of a series of studies that explores the relationship between parent death and mental illness.Data for the report was obtained from selected records of a group of 500 psychiatric patients and examines the relationship between attempted suicide, depression, and parental death. Findings showed that there were twice as many attempted suicide patients in the more severely depressed group than in less depressed patients or in non-depressed group. It is suggested that severely depressed patients with a history of early parental loss may be at high risk for attempted suicide. (12 references)

866. Black, Dora. "The Bereaved Child." *Journal of Child Psychology and Psychiatry and Allied Discipline* 19(3): 287–292 (July 1978).

An attempt is made to summarize what is presently known about childhood bereavement and to identify variables that might affect the outcome. Research seems to indicate that children and adults are more likely to develop depression when parental death occurs during childhood. However, frequently the time lag between the experience with death and the onset of psychiatric disorder is such as to raise questions about causation. Children at greatest risk are those bereaved at three to five years and during early adolescence. Further study of therapeutic interventions with children and the surviving parent is suggested. (29 references)

867. Black, Dora, and Tony Kaplan. "Father Kills Mother: Issues and Problems Encountered by a Child Psychiatric Team." *British Journal of Psychiatry* 153: 624–630 (November 1988).

When one parent kills another, their children lose both parents at the same time. The impact of this type of tragedy on 28 children from 14 families is examined.

Psychiatry in association with social work is recommended for all children who lose a parent because one parent killed the other. Wardship or full care orders should be carried out until permanent arrangements can be made. Establishment of a central, regional, or national information source to provide assistance in handling this kind of parental loss is suggested. (17 references)

868. Black, Dora, and M. A. Urbanowicz. "Family Intervention With Bereaved Children." *Journal of Child Psychology and Psychiatry and Allied Discipline* 28(3): 467–476 (May 1987).

This paper describes an intervention study with 45 families in which 83 children had experienced parental loss before the age of 16. Following the six-session treatment plan, the subjects were seen again at the end of one year, and two years in the post-loss period. Findings indicate that the group benefited from the brief intervention program and this should be a consideration in treatment of childhood bereavement. (31 references)

869. Brown, George W., and Tirril Harris. "Social Origins of Depression: A Reply." *Psychological Medicine* 8(4): 577–588 (November 1978).

This article responds to criticism of the authors' work by Tennant & Bebbington (1980). The authors address the issues of bias in sampling, case identification procedure, and vulnerability factors. The authors state that their book on ORIGINS OF DEPRESSION discusses many of the issues raised in the criticism of their work. (20 references)

870. Brown, George W., et al. "Depression and Loss." *British Journal of Psychiatry* 130(1): 1–18 (January 1977).

A random sample of 458 women in Britain was studied for onset of depression related to recent loss as distinguished from losses occurring more than two years earlier. Of past losses, it was found that loss of mother before the age of 11 is associated with greater risk of depression. However, past loss of a father before 17, or a mother between 11 and 17, is not associated with a greater chance of developing depression. It is suggested that there be more investigation of the relationship between loss and depression in association with social processes and cognitive and emotional states. (50 references)

871. Bunch, J., et al. "Suicide Following Bereavement of Parents." *Social Psychiatry* 6(4): 193–199 (December 1971).

In this investigation of suicide following parents' death, 75 consecutive suicides were compared with 150 living cases comparable in age, sex, marital status, and area of residence. Findings suggest that suicide was significantly associated with a loss by death of either parent and of a mother in the previous years. Unmarried men who have lost mothers seemed to be at higher risk for suicide in the period following their mothers' death. Predisposition to mental illness of the suicides, plus lack of a close supportive alternative relationship were suggested as possible reasons they were unable to cope with grief in a normal way. (12 references)

872. Burgess, Ann Wolbert. "Family Reaction to Homicide." *American Journal of Orthopsychiatry* 45(3): 391–396 (April 1975).

This pilot study focuses on the experience of families of homicide victims. The crisis phase consists of an acute grief process, including the period immediately following the homicide, the funeral, and police investigations. The long-term reorganization phase includes psychological issues of mourning and the socio-legal issues of the criminal justice process. Reactions to the death by homicide of parent and siblings are reported and special intervention situations discussed. (11 references)

873. Cain, Albert C. "The Impact of Parent Suicide on

Children." In *The Child and Death*, edited by Olle Jane Z. Sahler, 202–210. St. Louis: Mosby, 1978.

A number of clinical studies of children whose parents committed suicide suggest family vulnerabilities. Children are frequently directly involved in, or immediately confronted with, some aspect of the parent's suicidal act. The parent's suicide is superimposed on the preexisting personality structure and stage of development in the child. The child's reactions caused by guilt feelings, denial, and identification are discussed. Obstacles to mourning are the post-suicide effects of stigma, gossip, social embarrassment, and the tendency of family members not to talk about the event. Professionals need to be alert to concealed parent suicides in patients' backgrounds. (25 references)

874. Cain, Albert C., and Irene Fast. "Children's Disturbed Reaction to Parent Suicide: Distortions of Guilt, Communication, and Identification." In *Survivors of Suicide*, edited by Albert C. Cain, 93–111. Springfield, Ill.: Thomas, 1972.

This study is based on case records of 45 disturbed children who had lost one parent through suicide. The subjects were seen from a few days to more than ten years after the parent's death. Symptoms included psychosomatic disorders, academic problems, obesity, running away, tics, delinquency, sleep walking, fire setting, fetishism, and encopresis. Specific incidents prior to the suicide, involving some form of misbehavior, were seen by the children as related to the suicidal act. Family avoidance of communication with the children about the suicide did not help relieve feelings of guilt. Children whose parents committed suicide may experience fears that they may commit suicide themselves. (22 references)

875. Cantalupo, Paul. "Psychological Problems and Parental Loss." *Science News* 113(2): 21 (January 14, 1978).

This article summarizes clinical findings on psychological problems resulting from parental loss reported at a meeting of the American Psychoanalytic Association in New York. A survey of patients over a 2 1/2 year period showed that each of the 36 persons had suffered parental loss of some kind by age 15, or that one parent had suffered a similar loss by early adolescence. Through therapy many of these patients have been able to understand that death-related voids in their development caused major pathology. It is suggested that while parental loss may not be the major cause of emotional problems, where pre-loss psychic conflict is present for other reasons, parental loss may result in a neurotic outcome.

876. Cardarelle, James A. "A Group for Children of Deceased Parents." *Social Work* 20(4): 328–329 (July 1975).

A Minnesota public welfare agency formed an outreach group to aid the grieving process of teenage children who had lost a parent through death. It is suggested that this specialized group is just as beneficial for well-adjusted children as it is for those who exhibit acting-out behaviors that may be attributed to parental loss. The success of the program encouraged the agency to establish similar groups in other schools. (5 references)

877. Carroll, Marguerite R., and Shirley A. Griggs, Editors. *School Counselor* 24(5): WHOLE ISSUE (May 1977).

This special issue of the journal focuses on death. Articles report on three ways that counselors may have to respond to death related needs: 1) by counseling individual students 2) serving as consultants to teachers and 3) by providing a program of death education. A wide ranging list of books on various aspects of death, dying and bereavement is also featured, along with reviews of audiovisual materials. (Bibliographies)

878. Crase, Dixie R., and Darrell Crase. "Death and the Young Child: Some Practical Suggestions on Support and Counseling." *Clinical Pediatrics* 14(8): 747–750 (August 1975).

Many parents try to shield children and adolescents from a knowledge of, or experience with, death. By age nine, children are capable of understanding the finality of death, but their conceptions are to some extent dependent upon their family's providing honest answers to questions, acknowledging their reactions to death, giving simple explanations, and presenting them with a concept of death. (9 references)

879. ———. "Single-Child Families and Death." *Childhood Education* 65: 153–156 (Spring 1989).

The death of a parent is especially traumatic for a young child. The child's age, cognitive level, and the availability of other sources of love and support are significant factors in mediating loss. Death by accident, homicide, or suicide may be more difficult for the child to cope with than death by natural causes. Family environment can help the child overcome loss through death. (16 references)

880. Crook, Thomas, and Allen Raskin. "Association of Childhood Parental Loss with Attempted Suicide and Depression." *Journal of Consulting and Clinical Psychology* 43(2): 277 (April 1975).

This article examines the relationship between suicide, depression and parental loss in childhood. Comparison of depressed and suicidal patient groups and nonclinic subjects indicated that significantly more parental loss from divorce, desertion, or separation had been experienced by the suicidal group. This finding suggests that marital discord and intentional separation of parent and child is a significant factor in causing suicidal behavior in adult life. (2 references)

881. Cvinar, Stephen E. "Children and Loss." *The National Montessori Reporter* 5(2): 1–2 (April 181).

Although this article focuses on the death of a parent in childhood, the difference between father loss due to death and father loss due to divorce is discussed also. Death results in a permanent absence and grief does not represent disloyalty to the surviving parent and therefore can be expressed more openly. Understanding the variety of behaviors that may be exhibited following the death of a parent enables the surviving parent to help the child through the period of grief. Possible behavioral responses are outlined and ways to help the child are offered.

882. Darlington, Susan. *Young Women's Phenomenological Sense of Father and Parental Marital Relationships and Their Relation to Parental Loss.* 1979. 7pp. (ERIC Microfiche ED183984)

This study attempts to examine the meaning father has for women as they are growing up by measuring women's perceptions of their father on a number of factors to determine how this sense varies as a functions of father loss, cause and time of loss, perception of parental marital relationships and presence of an older brother. The use of women's perceptions instead of direct observations follows the frequently expressed theory that a person's perception or phenomenological sense of a situation has more influence on the person's behavior and/or emotion than its objective reality. (6 references)

883. Dietrich, David Robert. "Psychopathology and Death Fear: A Quasi-experimental Investigation of the Relationships between Psychopathology and Death Fear and Fantasies as Psychological Sequelae in Young Adults Who Experienced the Death of a Parent During Childhood or Adolescence." Ph.D. Washington University, 1979.

For a summary see: *Dissertation Abstracts International* 40B(2): 910.

884. Dorpat, T. L. "Psychological Effects of Parental Suicide on Surviving Children." In *Survivors of Suicide,* edited by Albert C. Cain, 121–142. Springfield, Ill.: Thomas, 1972.

This study examines the long term psychological effects of parent suicide on 17 patients who were treated in adulthood. Psychological symptoms evident in the group were guilt, depression, preoccupation with suicide, and self-destructive behavior. Loss of a parent by suicide has a different and more disturbing meaning to a child than does any other kind of parental death. Survivor suicides and anniversary suicides are not uncommon. (28 references)

885. Eisenstadt, J. Marvin. "Parental Loss and Genius." *American Psychologist* 33(3): 211–223 (March 1978).

This study attempts to explain the development of the eminent individual or genius by showing a relationship between achievement and parental loss by death. Six hundred ninety-nine subjects were selected from the Americana and Britannica encyclopedias. The orphanhood rates for these eminent persons were found to be higher than for the general population. Factors associated with parental loss that may be responsible for producing a creatively gifted individual are discussed. It is suggested that the creative mourning process operated in such a way that the loss triggered a crisis requiring mastery on the part of the bereaved person. (74 references)

886. Elizur, Esther, and Mordecai Kaffman. "Factors Influencing the Severity of Childhood Bereavement Reactions." *American Journal of Orthopsychiatry* 53(4): 668–676 (October 1983).

This report is part of a longitudinal study of 25 preadolescent kibbutz children who lost fathers in the October War of 1973. Results of interviews with mothers and teachers indicated that the combination of several factors determined the intensity of the bereavement response. The pre-traumatic family and environmental situations are significant determinants of the length and severity of bereavement. (9 references)

887. Felner, Robert David. "An Investigation of Crisis in Childhood: Effects and Outcomes in Children Experiencing

Parental Death or Divorce." Ph.D. diss., University of Rochester, 1977.

For a summary see: *Dissertation Abstracts International* 39B(3): 1475.

888. Felner, Robert David, et al. "Family Stress and Organization following Parental Divorce or Death." *Journal of Divorce* 4(2): 67–76 (Winter 1980).

This study examines whether children of separation and divorce experience more disorganization and stress than those in homes broken by death or from intact families. The 468 subjects were drawn from the Primary Mental Health Project, a school-based program for the early identification and prevention of emotional problems in primary grade children. Findings indicated that children from separated and divorced families were subject to more family stressors, received less educational stimulation from parents, and experienced greater parental rejection, economic stress, and general family problems than those from homes broken by parental death or from intact families. Planning of preventive interventions is discussed. (34 references)

889. ———. "Parental Death or Divorce and the School Adjustment of Young Children." *American Journal of Community Psychology* 9(2): 181–191 (April 1981).

The effect of parental divorce or death on the school adjustment of young children is the subject of this study. Subjects were all children who had been referred to the Primary Mental Health Project for behavioral or educational problems and 145 children who were not in the project. Measures used in the study were the Teacher Evaluation Form and the Ridgeway Health Resources Inventory. Findings indicated that children who had suffered parental loss through death or divorce had greater overall school maladaptation than children who did not have similar histories. Limitations of the study are noted. (41 references)

890. Fulmer, Richard H. "A Structural Approach to Unresolved
      Mourning in Single Parent Family Systems." *Journal of
      Marital and Family Therapy* 9(3): 259–269 (July 1983).

      The special problems of the single-parent family in dealing
      with unresolved mourning is discussed. When a loss occurs
      in a single-parent family, the pressures on the surviving
      spouse in taking over additional responsibilities often
      prevents that person from completing the mourning
      process. This delays the making of new attachments to
      peers and to work that would enrich the family's life and
      lessen chances of over involvement with children.
      Unresolved mourning may be masked by behavioral
      symptoms of children. Techniques of Structural Family
      Therapy used to facilitate the mourning process are
      presented. (22 references)

891. Furman, Erna. *A Child's Parent Dies: Studies in
      Childhood Bereavement*. New Haven: Yale University
      Press, 1974.

      This book on parental loss is based on research undertaken
      at the Cleveland Center for Research in Child
      Development. The process of grief and mourning in
      children is illustrated through case studies.
      Understanding death, accepting its finality, trust in the
      surviving loved person, and the latter's love for the child
      and familiarity with the ways in that the child was cared
      for, can help the child in adjusting to parental loss.
      Therapeutic approaches used in clinical cases are
      described along with the results obtained. (Bibliography)

892. ———. "Helping Children Cope with Death." *Young
      Children* 33(4): 25–32 (May 1978).

      In this article the author shares information based on her
      experience in working with children who experienced
      parental loss. The first step in helping children cope with
      the death of a parent is to make certain that they
      understand death. Observations suggest that some
      children as young as two mastered this tragic loss while

some older children were not able to cope with parental loss alone. Ways that children can be prepared to face loss and ways to facilitate the mourning process are discussed. (4 references)

893. ———. "On Trauma: When is the Death of a Parent Traumatic?" *Psychoanalytic Study of the Child* 41: 191–208 (1986).

Not all parentally bereaved children experience the death of a parent as a trauma. Four cases of children who lost a parent are described along with their responses to the loss. It is suggested that the initial experience of trauma and the recuperative process may be mediated by the quality of mothering the child receives. Implications for psychoanalysis are discussed. (19 references)

894. ———. "Studies in Childhood Bereavement." *Canadian Journal of Psychiatry* 28(4): 241–247 (June 1983).

A group of 23 children enrolled in psychoanalytic therapy and who had lost a parent were studied. Behavioral manifestations included academic and social problems, delinquency and neurosis. Factors found to be helpful in mastering bereavement are: good adjustment prior to loss, understanding what death means, deriving satisfaction from being alive, and mourning the one who has died. Suggestions are made for ways that the surviving parent can aid the bereaved child. (25 references)

895. Furman, Robert A. "A Child's Capacity for Mourning." In *The Child in His Family: The Impact of Disease and Death*, edited by E. James Anthony, and Cyrille Kouprenik, 225–231. New York: Wiley, 1973. (Yearbook of the International Association for Child Psychiatry and Allied Professions, v. 2)

This paper discusses the child's capacity for mourning, factors that interfere with mourning, and the consequences for the child who fails to complete this task. From age four and older the child is said to have the capacity for completing the mourning process, but may not display grief in the externally visible way that adults do. Death is best explained when a child encounters it in insects and animals. With loss of a parent, the child needs to understand that his/her needs will continue to be provided for. An unmourned loss prevents the making of lasting object relationships. (12 references)

896. Garber, Benjamin. "Some Thoughts on Normal Adolescents Who Lost a Parent by Death." *Journal of Youth and Adolescence* 12(3): 175–183 (June 1983).

Teenagers who were not part of a clinic population were studied to determine the effects of the death of a parent. Seven teenagers, selected from 350 normal adolescents used in a longitudinal study, had lost a parent between the ages of seven and ten and a half. Interviews with the seven subjects were reviewed at ages 12 and 13. All individuals were traumatized by their loss and reactions to the event persisted one to six years after the loss. Most of the subjects were functioning and progressing developmentally, but half had some type of therapeutic contact. Children's ability to extract from the environment the necessary help and support (from therapy, peers, or siblings) may determine how successfully they can cope with loss. (14 references)

897. Gardner, Richard A. "Children's Reactions to Parental Death." In *The Child and Death*, edited by John E. Schowalter, et al., 104–124. New York: Columbia University Press, 1983. (Foundation of Thanatology series)

Some psychological reactions of children to parental death could be prevented if they were better prepared to deal with death. It is generally agreed that the child must be old enough to differentiate himself from the dead parent in order to mourn the loss. Normative responses to loss are discussed along with pathological reactions that can occur beyond the mourning period. Most therapists agree that many disorders can be prevented by the meaningful concern and involvement of the surviving parent. (32 references)

898. Giacalone, Gail M., and Eileen McGrath. "The Child's Concept of Death." In *Bereavement Counseling: A Multidisciplinary Handbook*, edited by B. Mark Schoenberg, 195–212. Westport, Conn.: Greenwood Press, 1980.

This chapter focuses on the psychosocial and religious aspects of preparing children to deal with the area of thanatology and the role of supportive others in the child's life. Researchers do not all agree about the young child's ability to grieve and mourn. Through education children can be taught to cope with loss in their daily lives. They will then be better prepared to face separation and death. Loss of a toy, failing an exam, losing a pet, can help children learn to deal with loss and bereavement. Suggestions are made for clergy and religious counselors who must help those who are overcome with grief. A natural explanation of the cause of death for young children is recommended. (25 references)

899. Glicken, Morley D. "The Child's View of Death." *Journal of Marriage and Family Counseling* 4(2): 75–81 (April 1978).

This paper reviews current theory on the way that children cope with death and their continuing adaptation to the concept of death. Loss of a parent in early life may be associated with psychiatric disorders, and delinquency. Their fears of separation and abandonment may be revealed in play, stories, songs, dreams, or art. Children must have intellectual understanding of death before they can deal with it emotionally. There is disagreement about the age at that a child should be able to attend a funeral. If the child attends, he/she should be told what to expect. Sudden death is harder to cope with. In the case of a dying mother the child's care should be transferred gradually to her successor so that the child knows his/her needs will be fulfilled. (18 references)

900. Gray, Ross E. "Adolescent Response to the Death of A Parent." *Journal of Youth and Adolescence* 16(6): 511–525 (December 1987).

This study examines the effect of parental loss based on responses to a variety of measures by 50 adolescents whose parents had died within five years prior to the testing and interviews. Factors found to be significant in facilitating a healthy adjustment included good post-death social support, good relations with the surviving parent, balanced personality in the bereaved, and the presence of religious beliefs. Suggestions are offered for future research. (36 references)

901. Greenberg, Lois I. "Therapeutic Grief Work with Children." *Social Casework* 56(7): 396–403 (July 1975).

Intrafamilial communication where feelings are shared helps the bereaved disassociate from the deceased. In the absence of family participation, the therapist becomes the surrogate. Case illustrations are used in describing therapeutic techniques used to help three children. The funeral ritual can help the child to begin to deal with death and accept its reality. Books, play, and fantasy may be used to explore grief at various levels. Positive outcomes of grief are characterized by future-oriented children with enhanced self esteem who have developed the will to survive. (6 references)

902. Hagin, Rosa A., and Carol G. Corwin. "Bereaved Children." *Journal of Clinical Child Psychology* 3(2): 39–41 (Summer 1974).

Although the effect of parental death on children is great there seem to be some hesitation on the part of adults to discuss death with them. Research studies show that 1) there is a considerable incidence of parental loss in large samples of psychiatric patients, 2) maternal death at age eight years appears to place the child at risk for psychotic disorders and 3) girls who experience parental loss between the ages of ten and fourteen seem to be especially at risk for suicide in later life. Children who have suffered parental loss may be less able to handle separation and loss later in life than those persons who have not experienced parent loss. Principles of grief management in children are discussed. (24 references)

903. Hajal, Fady. "Post-suicide Grief Work in Family Therapy." *Journal of Marriage and Family Counseling* 3(2): 35–42 (April 1977).

This article reports the case history of the treatment of a family following the death by suicide of the husband and father. The attempt of the child patient to keep the memory of the dead father alive prevented the natural resolution of the mother's mourning. The ways that the family members were helped to deal with the unresolved grief reaction are described. The intervention was designed to reduce the risk of repeating the suicide experience, actively or passively, by the survivors. (9 references)

904. Hammond, Janice M. "A Parent's Suicide: Counseling the Children." *School Counselor* 27(5): 385–388 (May 1980).

A school counselor discusses parental suicide and the effect of parental loss on children and their family relationships based on a case history that features many of the elements commonly encountered during this crisis. Several books that may be helpful to children, parents, teachers and counselors are noted. The child's family is advised to: 1) tell the child about the death of a parent as soon as possible, 2) encourage the child to express his or her feelings, 3) take the child to the funeral, 4) talk with the child about the missing parent in the weeks following, and 5) let the child feel free to discuss the death with others. (11 references)

905. Hart, Edward J. "Death Education and Mental Health." *Journal of School Health* 46(7) 407–412 (September 1976).

This article focuses on the need for school health programs to reflect society's concern with death and dying. Four mental health issues said to be associated with death are: guilt, interpersonal relationships, fear, anxiety, and aggression. Suggestions are made for helping children understand these death related reactions. (8 references)

906. Hawener, Rebecca, and Phillips Wallace. "The Grieving Child." *School Counselor* 22(5): 347–352 (May 1975).

Although divorce, separation, and desertion leave children with a deep feeling of loss, the death of a parent, perhaps because of its finality, is a more traumatic loss. Death means little to children before the age of four, and it is only by about the age of nine that they accept it as a biological event. Children's ability to cope with the death of a parent is related to the quality of their relationships with adults. Feelings of guilt and hostility are viewed as they affect the child and result in negative behavior in school. Children need help in resolving grief and counselors may help by being accessible to parents, teachers, and children. Three factors cited as being highly important in helping the grieving child are listening, communicating and understanding. A bibliography of books to help counselors understand their own attitudes and beliefs relating to death is presented. (12 references)

907. Hayes, Richard L. "Coping with Loss: A Developmental Approach to Helping Children and Youth." *Counseling and Human Development* 17(3): 1–12 (November 1984).

This article discusses the losses in life, loss as a cumulative experience, and how to help mediate the loss of others. It is suggested that the ability of individuals to understand the smaller losses in childhood influences their ability to handle the greater disappointments of adulthood. Children's responses to death at various stages in their lives are discussed in terms of their development and understanding at each stage. Both children and youths need adult guides who will encourage them to express their feelings and help them understand their reactions to loss. Guidelines for helping youngsters mediate loss at their developmental level are offered. (35 references)

908. Hetherington, E. Mavis. "Effects of father absence on Personality Development in Adolescent Daughters." *Developmental Psychology* 7(3) 313–326 (November 1972)

Twenty-four white adolescent girls were studied for the effects of father loss due to death or divorce. A variety of measures were used to assess the personality development of the subjects. Findings suggest that the effects of father absence on girls surface during adolescence and primarily affect their ability during adolescence to interact appropriately with males. Daughters of divorced mothers were involved earlier in dating and sexual activities than daughters of widows. Suggestions are offered for future investigations. (27 references)

909. Huston, Kathleen Anne. "Personality Characteristics of Adults Who Have Experienced Parental Death in Childhood" Ph.D. diss., University of Denver, 1986.

For a summary see: *Dissertation Abstracts International* 47A(10): 3705.

910. Huttunen, Matti O., and Pekka Niskanen. "Parental Loss of Father and Psychiatric Disorders." *Archives of General Psychiatry* 35(4): 429–431 (April 1978).

The relationship between maternal stress in pregnancy and psychiatric behavior disorders in children is explored in this study. One hundred sixty-seven persons whose fathers died before their births and 168 persons whose fathers died during the first year of their life were subjects of this investigation in Finland. It was found that maternal stress during the third to fifth, and ninth to tenth months of pregnancy may increase the risk of the child for psychiatric disorders. (20 references)

911. Ilan, Eliezer. "The Impact of a Father's Suicide on His Latency Son." In *The Child in his Family: The Impact of Disease and Death*, edited by E. Anthony, and C. Koupernik. 299–306. New York: Wiley, 1973. (Yearbook of the International Association for Child Psychiatry and Allied Professions, v.2)

Children are encouraged to mourn the death of a parent in the belief that this will prevent the development of psychopathology in later life. A case history of a boy who lost his father through suicide when he was ten years old and who developed problems five years later is described. The youth was denied the opportunity to mourn and shielded from information about the cause of death at the same time that he benefited from the absence of marital discord. His psychological adjustment problems appear to have been triggered by the possibility of his mother's remarriage. It is suggested that even a short period of psychotherapy can be helpful in redirecting the child along a healthier course. (4 references)

912. Jackson, Edgar N. "Helping Children Cope with Death." In *Children and Dying*, edited by Sara S. Cook, 24–27. New York: Health Sciences, 1973.

A former pastor discusses how adults can help children cope with death. He cautions that adults must face their own feelings and curb their tendency to provide more information than a child wants or needs to answer his or her questions. An honest discussion that helps the child see that natural death is not tragic is recommended. Suggestions are offered for dealing with unnatural and untimely death. (Bibliography)

913. ———. *The Many Faces of Grief*. Nashville, Tennessee: Abingdon Press, 1977.

Children and adolescents may respond to death with anger, guilt, self-deception, acting-out and/or depression. Their reactions may vary according to age, quality of emotional support, and the individual's capacity for coping with stress. The need to give accurate and simple answers to questions, and to give permission for children to participate in family ceremonies is stressed. (No references)

914. Jenkins, Richard A., and John C. Cavanaugh. "Examining the Relationship between the Development of the Concept

of Death and Overall Cognitive Development." *Omega: Journal of Death and Dying* 16(3): 193–199 (1985–86).

This study replicates and extends previous research findings relating to the development of the concept of death in children. Several measures were given to 32 elementary school white children, including four from non-intact families were administered to assess their understanding of death. Findings indicate that children's concept of death is related to chronological age and developmental age. Directions for future research are suggested. (22 references)

915. Johnson, Patricia A. "After a Child's Parent has Died." *Child Psychiatry and Human Development* 12(3): 160–170 (Spring 1982).

This study explores surviving parents' and childrens' perceptions of family relationships following the child's loss of a parent. Responses to interviews and the Kvebaek Family Sculpture test indicate that parents and children differ in their expectations for and experience of communications about the parent's death as well as in their levels of perceived closeness in the family. These findings have significance for the child's future emotional development. (14 references)

916. Johnson, Patricia A., and Paul C. Rosenblatt. "Grief Following Childhood Loss of a Parent." *American Journal of Psychotherapy* 35(3): 419–425 (July 1981).

Grief that continues following the childhood loss of a parent, and that which develops later as a result of maturation and new experience, is examined in relation to implications for psychotherapeutic treatment. Mechanisms of incomplete mourning specific to a child's grief are discussed and differentiated from grief triggered by new situations that arise as an individual matures. It is important for therapists to recognize the difference and not evaluate the grief of children with models derived from studies involving adult-level understandings. (25 references)

917. Jones, W. "Death-Related Grief Counseling: The School
     Counselor's Responsibility." *School Counselor* 24(5):
     315–320 (May 1977).

     Although the death of a mother is often more traumatic
     to a child, counselors are most often faced with counseling
     children who have lost fathers. Grief reactions of children
     and adults are similar, but in children may vary with the
     stage of the child's psychological development. Mourning
     and grief may last for months or years. On the child's
     return to school, informal support systems may disappear.
     Some of the ways that the school counselor can intervene
     to help the grieving child are discussed. Books that may
     be used with young children for reading and discussion
     are suggested. School counselors have the skills to help
     grieving students in nonpathological grief situations. (9
     references)

918. Kaffman, Mordecai, and Esther Elizur. "Bereavement
     Responses of Kibbutz and Non-Kibbutz Children
     Following the Death of the Father." *Journal of Child
     Psychology and Psychiatry and Allied Disciplines* 24(3):
     435–442 (July 1983).

     This report is part of a larger study of the early effects
     and long-term consequences of parental loss on pre-
     adolescent children in Israel. Mothers of both Kibbutz
     and city school children reported symptoms of grief in
     their children 18 months after the father's death. In
     every case where the father played a significant role in
     the child's life, his death resulted in severe and prolonged
     bereavement responses. The supportive environment of
     the Kibbutz that protects children against many stressful
     situations was found lacking in providing a protective
     shield in the case of death of a father. (1 reference)

919. Kaltreider, Nancy B., et al. "Relationship Testing after
     the Loss of a Parent." *American Journal of Psychiatry*
     141(2): 243–246 (February 1984).

     Thirty-five adults with symptoms of pathological grief
     following parental death were compared with 37 subjects

without symptoms in order to assess the impact of the death of a parent on current love relationships. Of the 35 patients, nearly half had experienced ruptures in relationships, and three-fourths had problems with negative self-images triggered by parental loss. Psychotherapy focused on repairing the negative images, thus allowing the patients to rework current relationships. (10 references)

920. Kane, Barbara. "Children's Concepts of Death." *Journal of Genetic Psychology* 134 (Pt. 1): 141–153 (March 1979).

Children's concepts of death were investigated in a sample of 122 white middle-class children between the ages of three to twelve. Subjects were interviewed informally in school or at home. A three-stage development of death concept was noted: Realization, Separation, and Immobility. The sequential development of concepts of death was the same for each subject and was found to be related to age. Children who had experience with death had accelerated rates of death concept development. Children at three years old had developed a realization of death, at eight to twelve years old they were found to have ideas about death similar to adults. (35 references)

921. Katz, Sheri, and Virginia Flynn. "A Young Child's Response to Death." *Day Care and Early Education* 10(1): 22–25 (Fall 1982).

This article probes the impact of the death of her father on a young girl in a day care center. In a discussion of the day care center's role in helping the child to cope with parental loss are guidelines which may prove helpful to other teachers with children who have experienced death. Five books are listed that may be used with children to help them understand their loss. (11 references)

922. Ketchel, Judy Ansell. "Helping the Young Child Cope with Death." *Day Care and Early Education* 14(2): 24–27 (Winter 1986).

Children may react differently to loss by death. The child that does not show emotion outwardly may grieve inwardly. School-age children need caring adults who talk openly about death, lessen fears, and correct misconceptions. Four books for use with children are discussed by the author. Information about death that is presented to children needs to be developmentally appropriate. Following the death of a loved one (such as a parent) every effort should be made to keep the child in the same environment. (16 references)

923. Kilman, Gilbert. "Facilitation of Mourning During Childhood." In *Perspectives on Bereavement*, edited by I. Wiener, et al., 76–100. New York: Arno Press, 1979.

This paper describes several forms of treatment of bereaved children, most of whom were orphans. Same sex and opposite sex parental loss and reactions associated with this type of loss are among the cases presented to illustrate intervention strategies used at the Center for Preventive Psychiatry in White Plains, New York. The author concludes that mourning is more difficult and often more incomplete for young children than for adolescents and adults. It is suggested that bereaved or one-parent children entering nursery, headstart, or day care centers are prime targets for the development of services for prevention of mental illnesses. (Bibliography)

924. Koocher, Gerald P. "Talking with Children about Death." *American Journal of Orthopsychiatry* 44(3): 404–411 (April 1974).

Seventy-five children between the ages of six and fifteen were questioned about their perceptions of the meaning of death and about their expectations in regard to their own death. The children experienced little anxiety in discussing death, and their ideas about it varied according to their age levels. Suggestions are offered for discussing death with a child who has suffered a loss. (7 references)

925. Krupnick, Janice L. "Bereavement During Childhood and Adolescence" In *Bereavement: Reactions, Consequences and Care.* edited by Marian Osterwers et al., 99–141. Washington, D.C.: National Academy Press, 1984.

The author suggests that the imposition of adult models on children has resulted in confusion and misunderstanding about children's grieving. Children's reactions to loss by death are significantly related to age and developmental stage at the time of loss. Developmental strategies used by children may include idealizing the lost parent as the good parent while transferring hostility to the surviving parent. Adolescence appears to be an especially vulnerable time for coping with loss. The mother's assertiveness in coping with loss and the availability of a surrogate father figure can influence the outcome for a child. (143 references)

926. Lebovici, Serge. "Observations on Children Who Have Witnessed the Violent Death of One of Their Parents: A Contribution to the Study of Traumatization." *International Review of Psycho-Analysis* 1(1–2): 117–123 (1974).

This study focuses on clinical observations in several cases of children who had been present when one parent met a violent death. It was noted that society in general gives little thought to the effect of violent parental death on children. In a case cited, the court supported the request by a wife-killer to be reunited with his children. Even though there may be evidence that witnessing the violent death to a parent has traumatized a child, psychiatric services may not be utilized. (2 references)

927. Lester, David, and Aaron T. Beck. "Early Loss as a Possible 'Sensitizer' to Later Loss in Attempted Suicides." *Psychological Reports* 39(1): 121–122 (August 1976).

Two hundred forty-six subjects who had attempted suicide were studied to see whether an earlier loss was related to a suicide attempt following a recent loss. Female subjects showed a significant relationship between permanent loss of parents and experience with recent loss. For males this association was not found. The relationship between suicide attempts following recent loss by females was also significantly related to loss of parents before the age of ten. Permanent loss of both parents was found to be a critical factor triggering a suicide attempt following later loss. (1 Reference)

928. Lifshitz, Michaela. "Long Range Effects of Father's Loss: the Cognitive Complexity of Bereaved Children and Their School Adjustment." *British Journal of Medical Psychology* 49(2): 189–197 (June 1976).

This investigation probes the relationship between family structure, cognitive development, and social behavior in a sample of 136 Israeli children, 34 of whom had experienced father loss through death. Responses to the Bieri Test of Cognitive Complexity, classroom observations, and teacher interviews suggest that the cognitive level of children and their dealings with situations outside the home were more constricted for father-loss children than for children from intact families. A controlled intervention program that teachers focus on fatherless children had been started. (34 references)

929. Linzer, Norman, ed. *Understanding Bereavement and Grief: Proceedings of Two Interdisciplinary Educational Conferences in 1974 and 1975.* New York: Ktav, 1977.

This volume contains the proceedings of two interdisciplinary educational conferences, held in 1974 and 1975, that were intended to open lines of communications between helping professionals, including funeral directors, who work with bereaved and grieving persons. The section on children cites the death of a parent as perhaps the most traumatic loss a child can experience. A grieving surviving parent may not be able to provide the support a child needs to cope with parental death. Suggestions are offered about ways that members of the various professions may help the child accept parental loss from divorce and death. (Includes Bibliographies)

930. Lopez, Thomas, and Gilbert W. Kilman. "Memory, Reconstruction, and Mourning in the Analysis of a 4–Year-Old Child: Maternal Bereavement in the Second Year of Life." *Psychoanalytic Study of the Child* 34: 235–271 (1979).

The case of a child whose mother committed suicide when she was 19 months old, and who began analysis at the age of four, is described. In therapy, the child was drawn into profound mourning by presenting specific details about her mother's death, including burial under the ground. Sessions with the therapist were conducted five times a week during the first year and three times a week during the second year. Psychoanalysis is credited with aiding the mourning process and overcoming the symptoms that resulted from the mother's suicide. (34 references)

931. Mallan, Lucy B. "Young Widows and Their Children: A Comparative Report." *Social Security Bulletin* 38: 3–21 (May 1975).

This study of the economic situation of young widows, in contrast with divorced and separated women, was based on the Current Population Survey by the Bureau of Census that contained a sample of 50,000 households. Even with Social Security Benefits one-third of the widows were poor. Poverty was more likely if there were three or more children. Over one-half of divorced or separated mothers who did not have these benefits relied on public assistance, savings, veteran benefits, and living with relatives. (No references)

932. Miller, Jill Menes. "The Effects of Aggressive Stimulation upon Young Adults Who have Experienced the Death of a Parent During Childhood and Adolescence." Ph.D. diss., New York University, 1973.

For a summary see: *Dissertation Abstracts International* 35B(2): 1055.

933. Morris, Barbara. "Young Children and Books on Death." *Elementary English* 51(3): 395–398 (March 1974).

Research studies on the degree of children's understanding of death at various age levels are reviewed. Death occurs with increasing frequency in books for young children and this may be a means of helping them understand its reality. Eight children's books with death related themes are discussed. However, the question is raised as to what extent it is necessary to intervene in the process of children's understanding of the reality of death. (17 references)

934. Moss, Sidney, and Miriam S. Moss. "Separation as a Death Experience." *Child Psychiatry and Human Development* 3(3): 187–194 (Spring 1973).

This article is based on a paper presented at the Fourth Annual Conference, Family Institute of Philadelphia, October 12, 1972. The similarities in responses to separation and death, and the dynamics of long-term and permanent separations are explored. Family separation is particularly traumatic for the young child who is limited in his understanding of the meaning of death. Early losses may influence relationships with others later in life. Implications for therapeutic intervention are discussed. (15 references)

935. Murphy, Patricia Ann. "Parental Death in Childhood and Loneliness in Young Adults." *Omega: Journal of Death and Dying* 17(3): 219–223 (1986–87).

This study examines the relationship between self-esteem and response to parental loss in childhood as reported by 184 young adults. Four questionnaires, including a modified UCLA Loneliness Scale, the Coopersmith Self-Esteem Inventory and the Mourning Behavior Checklist were used to gather data. It was found that self-esteem was the most significant single predictor of loneliness. It is suggested that children who experience mourning behaviors may resolve their grief and be spared loneliness as adults. (28 references)

936. Nelson, Christine Whiteley. "Childhood Loss and Later Consequences." Ph.D. diss., University of Massachusetts, 1981.

   For a summary see: *Dissertation Abstracts International* 42B(8): 3433.

937. Oshman, Harvey, and Martin Manosevitz. "Death Fantasies of Father-Absent and Father-Present Late Adolescents." *Journal of Youth and Adolescence* 7(1): 41–48 (March 1978).

   Parental perceptions of 256 father-absent and father-present college students were examined. The Thematic Apperception Test and Michigan Pictures Test were used as measures in the study. Father-present females produced more themes of death than did females who had actually lost fathers. Father-absent males produced more themes that indicated feelings of guilt. Further study using this model for adolescent males is suggested in order to enlarge present information on how adolescents experience and cope with death and loss. (14 references)

938. Owen, Greg. "Death at a Distance: A Study of Family Survivors." *Omega: Journal of Death and Dying* 13(3): 191–225 (1982–1983).

   This study reports findings of questionnaires and interviews with 558 bereaved persons, including spouses, parents, and adult children. The type of relationship the subject enjoyed with the deceased person was deemed to be especially significant in determining the nature of the grief of the survivors. The adult child group seemed to have less illness during bereavement than surviving parent and surviving spouse groups. Cultural and sociological factors that affect responses to death are discussed. (15 references)

939. Perman, Joshua. "The Search for Mother: Narcissistic Regression as a Pathway of Mourning in Childhood." *Psychoanalytic Quarterly* 48(3): 448–464 (July 1979).

In this paper the author discusses his findings that children do mourn loss of a parent, but their mourning differs from that of adults. The mourning of children often takes the form of identification with the lost object. Narcissistic regression and associated autoerotic activities may result. Case material is presented in the analysis of a latency child and an adult, both of whom had suffered mother loss in childhood. (28 references)

940. Raphael, Beverley. "The Anatomy of Bereavement." In *The Bereaved Child*, edited by Gillian S. Mace et al., 74–138. New York: Basic Books, 1983.

The death of a parent is especially stressful for the young child. If the surviving parent or surrogate figure takes over the tasks that meet the physical and emotional needs that ensure the child's survival, he/she may feel secure enough to mourn and grief may be short lived. When support for the expression of grief is lacking, the child is at greater risk of psychiatric disorder that may not surface until additional stresses place too great a burden on the child. The child who is overt and aggressive may gain the care he needs, while the child who withdraws may be viewed as coping and may be denied the understanding he needs.

941. Rosenman, Linda, et al. "Widowed Families with Children: Personal Need and Societal Response." Working Paper No. 7. Institute of Family Study, Melbourne, Australia. May 1984. 26pp. (ERIC Microfiche ED255810)

This paper examines data on the needs of children who had experienced parental death as reported by 126 parents in a larger survey of widowed men and women in Australia. Children's responses to a parent's terminal illness differed according to the extent of change it produced in their routines. Reactions to the actual death of a parent also varied and were largely age related. Many children showed signs of insecurity years later and a few showed signs of emotional disturbance, especially in cases of parental suicide. In addition to coping with grief, children faced economic and social changes related to reduced family income. Re-evaluation of policy and services for children was suggested. (21 references)

942. Roy, Alec. "Parental Loss in Childhood and Onset of Manic-Depressive Illness." *British Journal of Psychiatry* 136(1): 86–88 (January 1980).

Two hundred and thirty-one manic-depressive patients were studied to determine whether there was any significant connection between early onset of mental illness and parental loss in childhood. Findings in this study indicate that parental loss in childhood, maternal death or separation before the age of 11, had no significant relationship to early onset of manic-depressive illness. (6 references)

943. Rozendal, Frederick G. "Halos Versus Stigmas: Long-Term Effects of Parent's Death or Divorce on College-Students' Concepts of the Family." *Adolescence* 18(72): 947–955 (Winter 1983).

This study investigates the impact of parental death or divorce on concepts of the family in a sample of 72 college students as compared with 53 students from intact families. Children from divorced families think less favorably of fathers and evaluate family concepts more negatively than children from death families or intact families. Thus it was concluded that a stigma applies to fathers of children from divorced families although there was no substantiation of an halo effect for dead fathers. It is suggested that additional investigation needs to be made in regard to the functioning of these subjects in their own families. (19 references)

944. Sahler, Olle Jane Z., ed. "Survivorship." Section III. In *The Child and Death*, 179–225, St. Louis: Mosby, 1978.

This section of the book contains chapters on the reactions of children and adolescents to the death of a parent, and the effects of parental suicide on children. Adolescents need much emotional support and the opportunity to discuss feelings and concerns in order to clarify misconceptions about death. Parental death resulting from suicide places the child at greater risk of developmental disturbances. Stigma, gossip, denial, and conspiracies of silence place additional burdens on surviving family members. The need for early intervention to prevent later personality disorders is stressed. (Bibliographies)

945. Samaniego, Lupe-Rebeka. "Parent-Loss in Childhood: Ego Functions, Death and Mourning." Ph.D. diss., Oklahoma State University, 1977.

For a summary see: *Dissertation Abstracts International* 38B(11): 5593.

946. Schiff, Harriet Sarnoff. *Living Through Mourning: Finding Comfort and Hope When a Loved One Has Died.* New York: Viking, 1986.

The author discusses bereavement in relation to the deaths of parents, spouses, children, siblings, and friends. Cases are used to illustrate responses to death and outline the mourning process. Coping with the death of a parent is said to be the most difficult task a child can face. Suggestions are offered for ways that children can be aided during the mourning process. (No references)

947. Schowalter, John E. "Parent Death and Child Bereavement." In *Bereavement: Its Psychosocial Aspects,* edited by B. Schoenberg et al., 172–179. New York: Columbia University Press, 1975.

The author reviews research on children's bereavement responses to the loss of a parent. A child reacts to parental death in a variety of ways depending on age and developmental stage at the time of death. It is the author's contention that the latency or preadolescent child's dependency and immature cognitive functioning is such that we see only the defenses against the pain of mourning and that the mourning task is not completed until later in life. However, he concludes that childhood bereavement can have delayed as well as immediate effects and suggests that family professionals give bereaved children priority attention. (34 references)

948. Sekaer, Christina. "Toward a Definition of Childhood Mourning." *American Journal of Psychotherapy* 41(2): 201–219 (April 1987).

Although a child does not mourn like an adult, optimal responses to loss may be distinguished from pathological ones. Aspects of mourning such as identification and decathexis must be related to the child's developmental level. Children like adults need to be able to express and work through feelings related to the loss and need adult help to understand the "facts" of death. (33 references)

949. Sekaer, Christina, and Sheri Katz. "On the Concept of Mourning in Childhood: Reactions of a Two and a Half-Year-Old Girl to the Death of Her Father." *The Psychoanalytic Study of the Child* 41: 287–314 (1986).

This paper focuses on the reactions of a young female child to her father's death when she was 28 months old. A general review of published research related to the understanding of death and mourning precedes the case report of the child's response to father loss. The subject of this study exhibited no serious fixations or conflicts affecting her development in the period immediately following her father's death. However, with a sympathetic teacher who had a special interest in childhood bereavement she was encouraged to discuss her father's death in order to help her understand and mourn her loss. (29 references)

950. Seligman, Roslyn, et al. "The Effect of Earlier Parental

Loss in Adolescence." *Archives of General Psychiatry* 31(4): 475–479 (October 1974).

This study examines the impact of earlier parental loss in 85 adolescents referred for psychiatric evaluation, as compared with 179 adolescents from a school population and 185 from a medical clinic. Two case histories are reported to illustrate the types of cases in the referral and clinic samples. A high frequency of earlier parental loss was found in the inpatient and the outpatient groups. The outpatient group was generally referred because of neurotic conflict, the inpatient group had usually been referred because of self-destructive behavior or drug overdose. It is suggested that factors at work in latency may prevent the mourning of parent loss, which may later resurface due to the biological and psychological stresses present in adolescence. (20 references)

951. Shepherd, D. M., and B. M. Barraclough. "The Aftermath of Parental Suicide for Children." *British Journal of Psychiatry* 129(9): 267–276 (September 1976).

Thirty-six children, two to seventeen years old, whose parents had committed suicide were studied five to seven years later. Of the 18 with dead parents, 17 out of 18 suffered from some form of psychiatric disorder. An incidence of psychological morbidity greater than that of a comparison group was noted. Some children could cope with parental suicide without serious effects. For some it was a relief from an abnormal home environment created by pre-suicide stresses. (10 references)

952. Silverman, Phyllis, and Sue Englander. "The Widow's View of Her Dependent Children." *Omega: Journal of Death and Dying* 6(1): 3–20 (1975).

The widow's view of her children's reaction to death and her ability to maintain her own maternal role following father-husband death is explored in the Widow-to-Widow program for preventive intervention. Mothers do not always understand that children's reactions to death may differ from adult mourning and do not connect their children's behavior with feelings about the father's death. Mothers' preoccupation with loss may affect their maternal role. In the 64 cases examined, most mothers felt that relatives offered them little help during the first year of bereavement. (18 references)

953. Silverman, S. M., and P. R. Silverman. "Parent-Child Communication in Widowed Families." *American Journal of Psychotherapy* 33(3): 428–441 (July 1979).

This article attempts to examine communication between children and surviving parents as it is influenced by their inability to accept death as final. The adolescent and the parent are alike in their difficulty in accepting the finality of death and may not be able to talk about it. The young child who is less self-conscious does not have problems discussing the death of a parent although he may not be able to differentiate between reality and his wishes. Inability to accept the finality of death blocks communication between surviving spouse and child. Memorials and rituals aid acceptance of death and children should be included in these events. (27 references)

954. Simos, Bertha G. "Grief Therapy to Facilitate Healthy Restitution." *Social Casework* 58(6): 337–342 (June 1977).

The fears of loss and separation are responsible to some extent for much of the pathology seen in clinical work. Cultural emphasis on competence, adequacy, and strength may prevent the family from experiencing the emotions that are necessary for the resolution of grief. Early losses and reactions to loss set the pattern for later reactions to separation and loss. A healthy resolution of grief can lead to growth and creativity. (No references)

955. Wakerman, Elyce. *Father Loss: Daughters Discuss the Man That Got Away.* Garden City, New York: Doubleday, 1984.

Six hundred and eight women volunteered to complete

questionnaires for a father loss study. Subjects included single women who had lost fathers through death or divorce, women who had lost fathers through death or divorce and whose mothers remarried, and women from intact families. It was noted that fathers are important to sex role development, the fostering of a positive feminine identity, and achievement orientation that enables daughters to acknowledge and develop the many aspects of themselves. An unrealistic picture of the father may negatively affect childhood, adolescence, attitude toward self, relationships, careers, and family. (Bibliography)

956. Warren, Max. "Some Psychological Sequelae of Parental Suicide in Surviving Children." In *Survivors of Suicide*, edited by Albert C. Cain, 112–120. Springfield, Ill.: Thomas, 1972.

A parent's suicide may be viewed by the child as a personal rejection. Arrest of emotional development, attempts by the family to conceal the suicide and suppress discussion, fear of suicide, and regression are factors that need to be considered in psychotherapy. Suggestions to aid the therapist in working with children who have experienced parental suicide are presented. (5 references)

957. Watt, Norman F., and Armand Nicholi, Jr. "Early Death of a Parent as an Etiological Factor in Schizophrenia." *American Journal of Orthopsychiatry* 49(3): 465–473 (July 1979).

The role of early parental death in the etiology of schizophrenia is examined in three separate studies— "Mayberry" (MASS), Harvard (College), and Gottingen (University). It was found that early bereavement appears not to be a critical etiological factor for disorders other than schizophrenia. The average age of subjects at parental loss was five through seven years. It is noted that parental death is a single event, and the implications for a child's psychological development are complex and contingent upon many other factors. (27 references)

958. Weber, Joseph A., and David G. Fournier. "Family Support and a Child's Adjustment to Death." *Family Relations* 34(1): 43–49 (January 1985).

A sample of 91 children from 50 families who had experienced death were interviewed along with parents who completed a questionnaire to determine the factors related to family influence on a child's understanding and adjustment to death. The Family Adaptability and Cohesion Evaluation Scale (FACES) was used to measure adjustment. Variables studied included family cohesion and adaptability, decision making about a child's understanding of death, and the ability to conceptualize death and adjust to loss. (28 references)

959. Wessel, Morris A. "Children, When Parents Die." in *The Child and Death*, edited by John E. Schowalter, et al., 125–133. New York: Columbia University Press, 1983. (Foundation of Thanatology Series)

The child's ability to cope with the death of a parent is significantly related to the way that the adults who take care of his needs support him as he copes with this stressful event. Giving the child honest answers to questions, allowing participation in burial ceremonies, or later visits to the grave site may help the child adapt to the reality of the loss. Ways that the physician may provide support for the child or adolescent are suggested. (No references)

960. Wolfelt, Alan. *Helping Children Cope with Grief*. Muncie, Ind.: Accelerated Development, 1983.

This book was written for caregivers, parents, teachers, and counselors who are in a position to help children cope with loss through death. Since children may suffer more from the loss of parental support than from the death experience, it is important to have a loving and caring environment. Children's grief may be seen more in their actions than in their words. The child's response to death, skills needed by helping adults in responding to expressions of grief, preparing others to help children, and guidelines for developing a community education program related to children and grief, are among topics discussed. (Bibliography)

961. Wolfenstein, Martha. "The Image of the Lost Parent." *Psychoanalytical Study of the Child* 28: 433–456 (1973).

Loss of a parent by death while the child is still growing is extremely stressful. This article explores the effects of the child's inability to separate himself from the lost object, as well as the ability of some children, under favorable circumstances, to achieve some detachment from a lost parent in ways that differ from adult mourning. Effects of parental loss in early boyhood is illustrated in the cases of A. E. Housman and Rene Magritte. In the images of the poet and the painter, the lost parent is both dead and alive. Children who lose a parent at an early age tend to retain their intense cathexis of the image of the parent at the same time they superficially acknowledge the parent's death. (25 references)

962. Wulf, Virginia Clare. "Parent Death in Childhood and Later Psychological Adjustment." Ph.D. diss., Michigan State University, 1976.

For a summary see: *Dissertation Abstracts International* 37B(12): 6357.

963. Zeligs, Rose. "When a Parent Dies." In *Children's Experience with Death*, 192–210. Springfield, Ill.: Thomas, 1974.

Parental death destroys balance in the family and creates the need for change and adjustment. When death results from unexpected disasters, it is important not to fragment surviving family groups. It is easier for a child to cope with parental death from illness, when the child has been prepared for this event. The sex of the dead parent affects the child and his role in the family in different ways. The young child who loses a parent has no background for coping with this experience. Some children are more vulnerable than others and require more care than those who are stronger. (Bibliography)

IV

SINGLE-PARENT CHILDREN AND THE SCHOOLS

BIBLIOGRAPHIES AND LITERATURE REVIEW

964. Bently, Eloise. *Children and Broken Homes: Sources for the Teacher.* 1975. 10pp. ERIC Microfiche ED128735)

It is not unusual to find large numbers of children in the schools who live in one-parent families. A young child may believe that his/her situation is abnormal and that he/she is inferior to his classmates. This may create an emotional attitude that works against the learning process. A teacher who is prepared can counter this tendency. An annotated bibliography lists materials that offer an introduction to the problem, and provide insight into ways the young child may be helped to cope with his/her situation. (23 references)

965. Drake, Ellen A., and Sylvia Shellenberger. "Children of Separation and Divorce: A Review of School Programs and Implications for the Psychologist." *School Psychology Review* 10(1): 54–61 (Winter 1981).

Increasingly schools are being forced to deal with behavior and learning problems of children affected by separation and divorce. Programs that have been developed to deal with the difficulties children experience in these crisis situations are reviewed. Direct, indirect and preventive approaches that the psychologist can use with children, parents and school professionals are described. Implications for changes and modifications in school policies and procedures that facilitate the adjustment of children and enhance the functioning of single-parent families are noted. (28 references)

966. Gay, Velva Bere. "How the Schools Can Meet the Needs of the Children of Divorce." (April 1981). 23pp. (ERIC Microfiche ED201623)

One hundred years of fiction books for children with one-parent families are discussed. Two hundred and fifteen titles are analyzed.

967. Hopkins, Lee Bennett. "Book Bonanza: Mama (or Daddy) Doesn't Live Here Anymore." *Teacher* 98(7): 24–26 (March 1981).

This article cites 16 books that deal with separation/ divorce and results of this experience as it impacts the lives of children. The list includes picture books for very young children, reference books for mature readers, novels for middle grade readers, and a research book by a divorced father of eight children. Teachers will find these books helpful in getting children to realize that others have similar experiences and that they are not alone. The books may also serve as a basis for classroom discussion and a means of getting children to discuss their feelings openly and share experiences with each other. (Bibliography)

968. Lopez, Frederick G. "The Impact of Parental Divorce on College Student Development." *Journal of Counseling and Development* 65(9): 484–486 (May 1987).

The effect of parental divorce on college student development and adjustment is explored through a review of the literature published during the past twenty years. Results of studies suggest that parental divorce may hasten parent-young adult psychological separation, ego maturity, and courtship activity. Methodological shortcomings of many studies are said to be responsible for failure to find clear and conclusive group differences. Researchers are urged to address these limitations. (34 references)

969. Mallett, Jerry J. "Classroom Reading." *Learning* 5(6): 24–25 (February 1977).

There are many good books on one-parent families that may be beneficial to all children especially as many more children will find themselves in one-parent families before they reach maturity. A list of 15 titles that may be used with children in one-parent families are discussed. Recommendations for ages four to thirteen and summaries for each book are included. (Bibliography)

970. Olsen, Henry D. "Bibliotherapy to Help Children Solve Problems." *Elementary School Journal* 75(7): 422–429 (April 1976).

Bibliotherapy is a program of activity involving reading that is planned, conducted and controlled by a professionally trained librarian. It is a resource to help children deal with problems that influence their education and socialization. Literature on the therapeutic effects of reading is reviewed and a list of books is presented which the teacher can use to begin developing a collection to be used with children who have minor social, emotional or psychological problems. Results will be more successful if readings are suggested rather than assigned and appropriate follow-up activities are necessary if personality change is to take place. (6 references)

971. Randall, Kay L. *The Single-Parent Child in the Classroom*, June 1981. 52pp. (ERIC Microfiche ED204027)

This annotated bibliography focuses on the needs of single-parent children in the schools. The four major areas covered are: problems encountered by single parents, the impact of divorce on children's behaviors in the classroom, implications of increasing numbers of single-parent children for teachers and schools and types of counseling available to single-parent children. Research studies are summarized and recommendations are offered.

972. Voza, Judith. "A Comparison of Reading Scores of Children from One-Parent and Two-Parent Families." 1984. M.A. Thesis, Kean College of New Jersey. 24pp.

Reading achievement scores of 12 children in grades two through four who lived in one-parent families were compared with scores of 12 children from two parent families. Findings showed that the mean score of students in one-parent families was higher than those of students in two-parent children. A review of literature on the academic achievement and behavior of single-parent children is appended. (Bibliography)

GENERAL WORKS

973. Adams, Gerald R. "The Effects of Divorce:Outcome of a Preschool Intervention Program." Paper presented at the Annual Meeting of the American Education Research Association, New York, March 19–23, 1982. 10pp. (ERIC Microfiche ED214667)

The two studies described in this article investigated the effectiveness of educationally-based programs as crisis intervention strategies for limiting the negative effects of divorce on preschool-age children. Two experimental groups including seven children from divorced homes and eight children from intact families were given an 18–week preschool program experience. A further eight children from intact homes served as controls for maturation effects. It is concluded overall for the two studies that some but not all behaviors might be assisted by placing young children of recently divorced parents in preschool programs. (27 references)

974. Allen, Henriette L., and James A. Tadlock. "Pupil Achievement as Related to Social Class, Gender, and Number of Parents in the Household." Paper presented at the Annual Meeting of the Mid-South Educational Research Association, Memphis, November 19–21, 1986. 27p (ERIC Microfiche ED277134).

A sample of 6,000 fourth, sixth, and eighth grade pupils in a Tennessee school district was examined to determine the relationship of gender, class, and family structure to school achievement. Investigators administered the California Achievement Test (CAT) that was disaggregated over a three-year period. Findings showed that upper social class students did better than lower social class students, although the difference narrowed over the three year period. Lower social class students from two-parent homes did better than one-parent children in the same class. Females, two-parent children, and upper-class children performed better on the CAT. Policy implications are noted. (8 references)

975. Allers, Robert D. "Children from Single-Parent Homes." *Today's Education* 71(3): 68–70 (1982).

When a child loses a parent through divorce or death, the child's behavior in school will often be affected. Many of the problems may result from pre-divorce conditions in the family. The child who is living with one parent may find more or different challenges in life than the child living with two. Teachers may help by noticing signs of stress, offering friendship, planning programs around the child's needs, being aware of comments, assignments and events that affect the child negatively and encouraging the noncustodial parent to attend conferences. (No references)

976.   ———. *Divorce, Children, and the School*. Princeton, N.J.:
       Princeton Book Company, 1982.

The number of school children from divorced families has
increased. As these children make an effort to cope with
the change in family structure and the turmoil that
frequently accompanies it, poor academic performance
and problem behaviors may surface. The authors describe
typical reactions of children experiencing divorce in their
families, and offer suggestions and guidelines for teachers
who must work with parents and chldren. The majority
of these children do not need individual counseling but
need to be reassured that they are not alone and that
there are persons who care about what is happening to
them. The bibliography contains books for children,
adolescents, and adults. (Bibliography)

977.   ———. "Helping Children Understand Divorce." *Today's
       Education* 69(4): 26–29 (November-December 1980).

Children of divorce face major changes that are frequently
stressful. Almost 25 percent of the children in the U.S.
live with a single parent who is divorced, separated, or
remarried. They must learn to cope with parents who
date, double holiday celebrations, baby sitters, less money
to live on, and new relatives when one or both parents
remarry. Feelings of anger, guilt and loneliness affect
behavior and achievement in school. Since therapy and
counseling are not available to every child, teachers may
need to help children deal with their feelings about divorce.
Suggestions for teachers that may help them to provide
support for children experiencing this crisis in their lives
are outlined. (No references)

978.   Annunziata, Albert Leonard. "The Relationship of Family
       Intactness and Achievement of Children in Suburban
       Private Elementary Schools." Ph.D. diss., Boston College,
       1981.

For a summary see: *Dissertation Abstracts International*
42B(9): 3803.

979. Appel, Karen W. "America's Changing Families: A Guide for Educators." *Fastback 219* Bloomington, Ind.: Phi Delta Kappa Educational Foundation, 1985. Also (ERIC Microfiche ED256768).

The changing structure of American families, due to divorce, out of wedlock births, and new options for adoption, are viewed as they relate to the school's role in helping children adjust. Emotional, mental, and financial stresses of parents and children related to the process of family change are discussed along with ways that the school may help children cope with problems.

980. Armstrong-Dillard, Peggy. "Developing Services for Single Parents and Their Children in the School." *Social Work in Education* 3(1): 44–57 (1980).

Problems related to the impact of the increasing divorce rate on children and schools are discussed. Crying, disruptive behavior and decrease in academic performance are common reactions of children to family dissolution. School social workers can help by providing individual and group counseling for students and parents, leading student discussion groups, and providing in-service programs for educating teachers about the effects of divorce. An alliance with the school librarian is suggested as a means of ensuring that appropriate reading material is available for students and that books on divorce are also accessible to parents. (17 references)

981. Baldwin, Eugene Millard. "Middle School and Junior High School Teachers" Expectations of Adolescents from Single-Parent Families." Ed.D. diss., University of Pennsylvania, 1983.

For a summary see: *Dissertation Abstracts International* 44A(4): 0920.

982. Barton, Wayne Arthur. "The Effects of One-Parentness on Student Achievement." Ph.D. diss., Pennsylvania State University, 1981.

For a summary see: *Dissertation Abstracts International* 42A(7): 2944.

983. Bergman, Mary Andrews. "The Effectiveness of an In-Service Training Program on Teachers' Perceptions of the Problems of Single-Parent Children." Ed.D. diss., Northern Arizona University, 1985.

For a summary see: *Dissertation Abstracts International* 46A(6): 1493.

984. Bernstein, Barbara Elaine. "How Father Absence in the Home Affects the Mathematics Skills of Fifth-Graders." *Family Therapy* 3(1): 47–49 (1976).

Past research studies have suggested that early father-absence has a negative effect on the math skills of children. One hundred and seventeen middle-class fifth grade students were administered the Iowa Test of Basic Skills for this study. It was found that boys' math skills were not depressed significantly below their verbal skills as a result of father absence. However, this was not the case with girls. (54 references)

985. Berry, Kenneth K., and Michael Poncini. "Father Absence and School Achievement in Australian Boys." Paper presented at the Annual Meeting of the American Psychological Association, Washington, D.C., August 23–27 1982. 13pp. (ERIC Michofiche ED222277)

The effects of early and late father-absence on school achievement, cognitive development, and emotional development were examined in 27 Australian males between nine and twelve years of age. Three groups of boys who were evaluated included children who had experienced father absence before the age of five. Responses on all achievement measures for boys with fathers present were superior to those of boys whose fathers were absent. However, no significant differences were found between the early and late father absent groups, nor were any differences found between these groups on self concept measures. Findings are discussed and compared with similar studies in other countries. (10 references)

986. Bianchi, Suzanne M. "Children's Progress through School: A Research Note." *Sociology of Education* 57(3): 184–192 (July 1984).

This research focuses on ethnic differences associated with family structure and variation in age-appropriate school progress. Data for the study came from the October school enrollment supplement to the 1979 Current Population Survey. It was found that living in poverty and having a parent with low educational attainment increases the likelihood that a child will be enrolled below the grade that is modal for his or her age. Children in single-parent families were more likely to be enrolled below mode than children living with both parents. (31 references)

987. Black, Kathryn Norecross. "What About the Child From a One Parent Home?" *Teacher* 96(5): 24–26, 28 (January 1979).

A College Entrance Examination Board panel has cited one-parent families as one of the societal factors possibly responsible for the decline in Scholastic Aptitude Test Scores over the past 14 years. Research on the school achievement of one-parent children do not always produce the same findings. The loss of one parent, even in part, is a psychological loss that is painful to children. If schools cannot offer direct assistance to the single parent in child management, they should be able to offer information about possible resources. Educators can learn skills to help children from one-parent homes regardless of their feelings about divorce. (No references)

988. Blanchard, Robert W., and Henry B. Biller. "Father Availability and Academic Performance Among Third-Grade Boys." *Developmental Psychology* 4(3): 301–305 (May 1971).

Class grades and academic performance were used to measure the effects of father availability on the school achievement of 44 white third-grade boys. The academic performance of boys who saw their fathers more than two hours per day was found to be higher than boys who saw their fathers less. Boys who experienced father absence before the age of five were generally underachievers. This study suggests that early father absence has negative effects on the academic performance of their children. (28 references)

989. Bledsoe, Eugene. "Divorce and Values Teaching." *Journal of Divorce* 1(4): 371–379 (Summer 1978).

An educator discusses the impact of divorce on children in relation to teaching human values in the curriculum. Although the school is not the only available support system, many of the problems children manifest in the post separation/divorce period are observed in the school. As the divorce rate is increasing, school professionals need to exchange information, have access to an up-to-date professional library, and workshops need to be held to help develop new methods for teaching human values along with facts and concepts in each course content area. (No references)

990. Blum, Heather Munroe, et al. "Single-Parent Families: Child Psychiatric Disorder and School Performance." *Journal of the American Academy of Child and Adolescent Psychiatry.* 27: 214–219 (March 1980)

The Ontario Child Health Study included 1,869 families with 3,294 children. The incidence of emotional and somatic disorders, hyperactivity, and school performance were investigated. Compared with two-parent children, single-parent children were found to be at a small but statistically significant increased risk for a negative outcome. When income, welfare status and family dysfunction are controlled, childhood psychiatric disorders and poor school performance, as factors in single-parent family status are reduced to nonsignificance. The implications of these findings are discussed. (16 references)

991. Bolgiani, Sally Ann. "A Comparison of Fourth and Fifth Grade Children of One-Parent Families with Those of Two-Parent Families on Measures of Academic Achievement and Self-Esteem." Ed.D. diss., Wayne State University, 1984.

For a summary see: *Dissertation Abstracts International* 45A(3): 735.

992. Brenes, Margarita E., et al. "Sex-Role Development of Preschoolers from Two-Parent and One-Parent Families." *Merrill-Palmer Quarterly* 31(1): 33–46 (January 1985).

The sex role development in 41 preschool children from divorced, separated, and two-parent families was examined in this study. Cognitive aspects of sex roles, sex-role stereotypes, and toy preferences were assessed. Single-parent families had more knowledge of stereotyped concepts of sex roles and were less sex-typed in use of toys than two-parent children. They did not differ in their concept of gender identify. It is concluded that the pattern of sex role adoption of single-parent children is not indicative of gender confusion. (21 references)

993. Brown, B. Frank. "A Study of the School Needs of Children from One-Parent Families." *Phi Delta Kappan* 61(8): 537–540 (April 1980).

It is not known to what extent lower pupil performance results from parental separation but it is known that serious behavioral problems often characterize children of one-parent families. A study by the Kettering Foundation and the National Association of Elementary School Principals was designed to measure school performance and compare the functioning of one-parent children with two-parent children in 26 schools. Finding showed that children from one-parent homes were more mobile, had lower achievement, a higher incidence of tardiness, and a higher rate of absenteeism. It is suggested that schools should recognize the problems of one-parent families, review and update school records, revise school services and curricula, and provide programs in the field of parenting.

994. Burbank, J., and Kris Kissman. "Single-Parent Students: Obstacles and Opportunities." *Early Child Development and Care* 29(3): 261–272 (1987)

Implications of the growth of single-parent families for higher education are explored. Twenty-five mothers who were attending college and using the services of daycare centers completed questionnaires through interviews. The most frequently cited problem for mothers was too little time and too little money. Parents, relatives, or boyfriends were mentioned as sources of encouragement. All women with preschool children felt that colleges could offer more daycare service. The author suggests that colleges need to identify and address the problems of single parents. (15 references)

995. Burns, Christine W., and Marla R. Brassard. "A Look at the Single-Parent Family: Implications for the School Psychologist." *Psychology in the Schools* 19(4): 487–494 (October 1982).

The effects on parents and children of living in a single-parent family are reviewed through a survey of literature. The age of the child at the time of loss and the cause of the separation may affect the ways that a child responds to the loss. An adaptation of the Divorce Specific Assessment Measure is recommended for use by school psychologists to assess the needs of single-parent children. Discussion groups for children, bibliotherapy, parent education programs, in-service programs for teachers, and referrals to community agencies, are among ways the school psychologist may help. The need for school policies that address the special needs of single-parent families is also discussed. (35 references)

996. Butler, Annie L. "Tender Topics: Children and Crises." Paper presented at the Annual Study Conferences of the Association for Childhood Education International, Minneapolis, April 10–13, 1977. 16pp. (ERIC Microfiche ED147019)

This paper describes children's feelings and reaction to divorce, death, hospitalization and parent imprisonment. It is suggested that adults can help children cope with crisis situations by providing accurate information, by encouraging the expression of feelings, and by managing their own feelings and attitudes toward the situation. The paper also describes ways that outside supportive services, teachers' initial relationships and responses to a crisis situation can help children cope with crisis. (11 references)

997. Calabrese, Raymond L., et al. "The Identification of Alienated Parents and Children: Implications for School Psychologists." *Psychology in the Schools* 24(2): 145–152 (April 1987).

This study investigated predictors of parental alienation in a sample of 49 urban fourth grade students. As measured by the Dean Alienation Scale, high levels of alienation were associated with single, unemployed female parents, whose child had few perceived friends. Implications for school personnel are discussed. (18 references)

998. Camiletti, Y., and V. Quant. "Children of Divorced Parents: Anticipatory Counseling for Adolescents of Divorced Parents." *School Guidance Worker* 39(1): 20–23 (September 1983).

Adolescents from divorced families may have feelings of guilt, insecurity and abandonment. Counseling prior to parental separation may mitigate some of the negative effects. A school program illustrating anticipatory counselling is described. Recommendations for replication of similar programs are offered.

999. Cantor, Dorothy W. "School-Based Groups for Children of Divorce." *Journal of Divorce* 1(2): 183–187 (Winter 1977).

This paper proposes the establishment of situation/transition groups within the school to help children cope with the crises of divorce. Suggestions are made for establishing a program that school psychologists, social workers, and guidance counselors would serve as group leaders. One such program is discussed in detail and results of evaluations by teachers, parents and children are reported. It is concluded that a situation/transition program established in a school can provide ongoing support and avert serious personality disorders later. (13 references)

1000. Cantrell, Roslyn Garden. "Adjustment to Divorce: Three Components to Assist Children." *Elementary School Guidance and Counseling* 20(3): 163–173 (February 1986).

The developmental stage of the child at the time of separation or divorce as it relates to the quantity and quality of the child's reactions is discussed. Characteristic responses of children, exhibited at home and school, following family separation were identified. The author offers a three component intervention model, that involves parents, teachers and children and includes: 1) group counseling aimed at the development of individual problem solving skills, 2) helping parents through conferences to dispel myths and promote understanding of children's responses, and suggest ways to help children and 3) programs to educate teachers about the divorce process and its effects on children. (31 references)

1001. Chapman, Michael. "Father Absence, Stepfathers, and Cognitive Performance of College Students." *Child Development* 48(3): 1155–1158, (September 1977).

Ninety-six white college students from father-absent, step-father, and father-present families were administered the Embedded Figures Test and these scores along with quantitative and verbal scores from the SAT were used to assess the effects of father-absence and stepfathers on cognitive performance. Findings suggest that a stepfather can be an effective substitute in the child's cognitive development. Absence of a father figure was associated with field dependence and lower SAT scores for males. Consistent father absence effects on the cognitive development of females was not found. However, field independence for females from stepfather families was greater than for those from father-absent families. (12 references)

1002. Cherian, Varghese I. "Academic Achievement of Children of Divorced Parents." *Psychological Reports* 64(2): 355–358 (April 1989).

The academic achievement of 242 students from divorced families and 713 students from intact families were compared. These pupils of Transkei, South Africa, were administered a questionnaire to identify family structure. The academic achievement of children from divorced or separated families was found to be significantly lower than that of those children from intact families. (14 references)

1003. Clarke-Stewart, K. Alison. "Single-Parent Families: How Bad for the Children." *NEA Today* 7(6): 60–64 (January 1989).

Children from divorced families frequently have more responsibilities thrust upon them at a younger age than their peers. Other changes in their lives include less regular routines less consistent discipline, and a lowered standard of living. Each year teachers will encounter children in the classroom who are experiencing some phase of parental divorce or remarriage. These children, boys in particular, are likely to exhibit acting-out-behavior, shortened attention span, withdrawal, and decrease in academic achievement. During this troubled time both the children and their parents need support rather than criticism. Teachers can prepare themselves to deal with single-parent children by workshops, reading, and discussing problems and solutions with colleagues. (6 references)

1004. Clay, Phyllis L. "School Policy in Observing Rights of Noncustody Parents." *Education Digest* 46(5): 20–22 (January 1981).

The national Committee for Citizens in Education surveyed 1200 noncustodial single parents nationwide to determine what access they had to school records and the level of communication with school personnel. The family Educational Rights and Privacy Act of 1974 provides noncustodial parents the right to their children's school records. However, schools vary in their compliance with this law and in the extent to which they communicate with the noncustodial parents. Parents who know about their children's school performance and who participate in school activities can offer more support to their children. This article is condensed from *Network*.

1005. Coffman, Shirley Gwinn. "Conflict-Resolution Strategy for Adolescents with Divorced Parents." *School Counselor* 36(1): 61–66 (September 1988).

Single parent children are more often engaged in conflict in their schools than children from intact families. This article provides a conflict-resolution model suitable for the adolescent with divorced parents. It is a simple strategy which adolescents can be trained to use as needed. The model encourages communication and exchange of information as a basis for establishing more cooperative relationships. (24 references)

1006. Coffman, Shirley Gwinn, and Albert E. Roark. "Likely Candidates for Group Counseling: Adolescents with Divorced Parents." *The School Counselor* 35(4): 246–252 (March 1988).

The impact of parental divorce may interfere with the completion of the development tasks necessary for the transition from adolescence to adulthood. Group counseling may be the best method of providing support for adolescents whose parents are separated or divorced. A conceptual model for group counseling is discussed. Students can cope more successfully with the psychological issues of divorce in an environment where they have the opportunity to express their feelings, obtain information, and still have access to individual counseling if warranted. (10 references)

1007. Colarusso, Calvin. "Johnny, Did Your Mother Die?" *Teacher* 92(6): 57 (February 1975).

Most teachers have encountered a situation in the classroom where the student was having a difficult time adjusting to parental death. Frequent hospitalization of a terminally ill parent may intensify the child's difficulty in accepting the permanent absence of the parent who has died. Most experts agree that the six-year-old child is not capable of understanding death. This article suggests ways that the teacher may help the child cope with the stages of grief as they may be exhibited in classroom behavior and help his or her classmates arrive at an understanding of appropriate responses in these circumstances. (No references)

1008. Collins, Betty G. "Self-Concept: A Study of Junior High Students from One-Parent Families and Two-Parent Families." Ed.D. diss., University of Toledo, 1979.

For a summary see: *Dissertation Abstracts International* 41A(4): 1400.

1009. Conley, Louise M. "The Effect of Divorce on Children." *Independent School* 41(2): 43–50 (December 1981).

Between 15 and 20 million children have experienced the departure of one parent from their daily lives because of divorce. School personnel might help children of divorce more if they understood better what these children are going through. Divorce can affect the formation of ego ideals as children develop their identity. Negative behavior exhibited by children may include hyperactivity, restlessness, loss of concentration, forgetfulness, test-taking anxiety, mocking other children, lying, aggressiveness, cutting classes, and bodily pains. The key to helping these children is to provide alternative ego ideals. A human support network that can be made up of older relatives, brothers and sisters, substitute families, teachers, counselors, administrators, church people, coaches, scout leaders and others may provide a sense of continuity and caring. (No references)

1010. ———. "Loss through Death." *Independent School* 41(1): 35–38 (October 1981).

Behavioral changes, usually temporary, are not uncommon in young persons who have experienced the loss of a parent, brother, or sister. School professionals need to know what constitutes healthy mourning. Assessing the strength of the surviving parent from conversation can give some measure of the parent's ability to provide emotional strength and support to children at home. Sharing positive memories and anecdotes may be helpful. Time is the ultimate comforter for the healthy mourner. (No references)

1011. Conyers, Mary G. "Comparing School Success of Students from Conventional and Broken Homes." *Phi Delta Kappan* 58(8): 647–648 (April 1977).

A three year study of the effect of family dissolution on school children supports the contention that children from single-parent families perform more poorly academically and have more problems at school. Absences, truancies, suspensions, expulsions, and dropouts were significantly higher for children who lived with one parent and their grade-point averages were lower than for children who lived with both natural parents.

1012. Cook, Alicia S., and Jean McBride. "Divorce: Helping Children Cope." *The School Counselor* 30(2): 89–94 (November 1982).

Children's reactions to the divorce process and the ways that adults can promote growth and adjustment are explored. Not all children react to divorce in the same way. However, they often respond with unfamiliar behaviors such as frequent crying, regression, bodily disturbances, fear, and guilt. School counselors can help parents who are unsure of their children's needs during the divorce process. The school counselor can assist teachers by helping them understand what behavior to expect from a child at this time. In addition counselors may provide individual and group counseling. (23 references)

1013. Courtney, Dan, and Leo M. Schell. "The Effect of Male Teachers on the Reading Achievement of Father-Absent Sixth Grade Boys." *Reading Improvement* 15(4): 253–256 (Winter 1978).

The effect of male teachers on the reading achievement of father-absent sixth grade boys was the focus of this investigation. Ninety boys assigned to male teachers, and one hundred and three boys assigned to female teachers were administered the Reading Comprehension subtest. The assignment of male teachers was found to have no significant effect on the reading scores of father-absent boys. The chief implication of this study is that educators must search for other strategies to help improve the reading achievement of father-absent boys and begin intervention as soon as the problem has been identified. (14 references)

1014. Covell, Katherine, and William Turbull. "The Long-Term Effect of Father Absence in Childhood on Male University Students' Sex-Role Identify and Personal Adjustment." *Journal of Genetic Psychology* 141 (pt.2): 271–276 (December 1982).

The long-term effects of father absence in childhood were studied in a sample of 173 male college students. Subsections of the California Personality Inventory and

Bem's Sex Role Inventory were completed by father-absent and father-present subjects. Males who had experienced father absence prior to age five scored significantly lower on self-esteem, self-confidence, and social interaction. No differences were found in performances on sex-role measures. Single-parent subjects were no more masculine or feminine than those in two-parent families. Whereas sex-role disruption may be overcome, father absence prior to age five may have lasting effects on the self-esteem and self-confidence of males. (18 references)

1015. Damon, Parker. "When the Family Comes Apart: What Schools Can do." *National Elementary Principal* 59(1): 66–75 (October 1979).

The impact of divorce on the school is complex because children and their families will be, at different times, at various stages in the divorce process and its consequences. Although individual attention is warranted, the number of divorce situations faced by the schools dictate a group or program approach. Real-life examples are used to illustrate some of the emotional, social and financial impact of divorce on children. Parents are one source of information on what schools can do to help single-parent families. Suggestions for taking a poll of the community as another means of getting information to facilitate school planning are also offered. Ten recommendations for teachers who deal with single-parent children are outlined. (5 references)

1016. Davidson, Charles W., et al. "The Prediction of Drug use through Discriminate Analysis from Variables Common to Potential Secondary School Dropouts." *Journal of Educational Research* 76(6): 313–316 (July-August 1979).

Seventy-eight secondary school students from male-present and male-absent families were studied in regard to self-image, ability to communicate with parents, sex of student and drug use, and employment status of parents. Findings indicated that the best predictor of drug use was the presence or absence of an adult male. Self-image and perceived ability to communicate with parents were the next best predictors. It is recommended that drug education programs focus on enhancement of student self-concept and improvement of communication with parents. (21 references)

1017. Delaney, Eline, et al. "A Study of the Single Parent Child in Catholic School." *Momentum* 15(4): 41–43 (December 1984).

Several instruments were used to measure the school behavior of 483 parochial school children from single-parent and two-parent families. It was found that students from divorced families differed most from those in intact families in the areas of interpersonal skills and relationships. Teachers rated the school behaviors of children from intact families more positively, than they did those of single-parent children. However, teachers' perceptions of the single-parent children were more positive than the children's perception of themselves. It is suggested that schools and teachers need to be more alert to signals indicating that a child is under stress and that modifications in curriculum and instruction may be needed. (4 references)

1018. Deutsch, Francine. "Classroom Social-Participation of Preschoolers in Single-Parent Families." *Journal of Social Psychology* 119(1): 77–84 (February 1983).

Social interactions, peer contacts and play activity of thirty-five white, first-born and only child preschoolers from one and two-parent lower class families were compared. Single parent children in the study exhibited more advanced types of play and had more contacts with their peers than children from intact families. Gender and birth order were found to have little effect on interactions. The need for caution in interpreting research findings is discussed. (33 references)

1019. Drake, Ellen A. "Children of Separation and Divorce: School Policies, Procedures, Problems." *Phi Delta Kappan* 63(1): 27–28 (September 1981).

School policy tends to ignore issues involving children of separation and divorce although single parent children comprise approximately 20 percent of school enrollments. The school administrator needs to determine that children are legally enrolled in the school they are entitled to attend, although decisions about residency should be made on an individual basis. Access to school records should not be affected by custody. However, release of children from school, absent parent's school visits and medical emergencies may be affected by custody. Activities for father/son or mother/daughter may need to be altered. Administrators may also help staff become more aware of the special needs of children of separation and divorce by providing inservice training. (8 references)

1020. ———. "Helping the School Cope with Children of Divorce." *Journal of Divorce* 3(1): 69–75 (Fall 1979).

The educational and social effects of divorce on children as reflected in their academic achievement, peer relationships, relationships with teachers and other school personnel are examined. The school is a source of stability in the child's life. An examination of research studies showed no definition of the characteristics of children exhibiting change in school adjustment from those children showing no change. Steps for divorce-specific assessment are outlined and suggestions are offered for direct and indirect intervention techniques by school professionals. The importance of the school's role is viewed in light of the fact that it is not the divorce itself but the length of the divorce process that can have developmental implications for the child. (8 references)

1021. Edgar, Don, and Freya Headlam. *One-Parent Families and Educational Disadvantage.* Institute of Family Studies. Melbourne, Australia. 1982. 15pp. (ERIC Microfiche ED229693)

Data from two Australian studies of the effects of single parenting on the educational achievement of children was examined. Teachers' assessment of one parent children's educational performance, aspirations and emotional stability showed that most teachers viewed one-parent children the same as two-parent children, but a significant minority saw one-parent children as worse. Data on the one-parent family and single-parent views on child-school relationship, parent-child relationship, and labeling are reported. Implications of the studies are noted. (48 references)

1022. Effron, Anne Kurtzman. "Children and Divorce: Help from an Elementary School." *Social Casework* 61(5): 305–312 (May 1980).

A twelve week intervention program for elementary pre-adolescent children who were experiencing the stress of parental divorce is described. A combination of role playing, discussion, games, films and creative writing projects were used with a group of eight children referred by teachers because of declining academic performance and problems in relationships with peers. Behavior traits noted were aggressiveness, depression and immaturity. The program received a positive appraisal from parents, teachers and participants. Although the short term program was not enough for some children, it did identify problem areas about which parents could be informed. (16 references)

1023. Ellison, Edythe. "Classroom Behavior and Psychosocial Adjustment of Single-and-Two-Parent Children." Paper presented at the Biennial Meeting of the Society for Research in Child Development, San Francisco, March 15–18, 1979. 14pp. (ERIC Microfiche ED168710).

This study compared the psychosocial adjustment and social behavior of children from divorced or separated single-parent families with that of children from two-parent homes. Observations and ratings of 38 children by teachers were used in the investigation. Teachers' ratings of children from single-parent homes based on observations of gaze-directed behavior suggest that two-parent children may adapt better to the shifting demands of the classroom than single-parent children. During social periods, single-parent children of both sexes spent more time in dyadic conversation with male peers than older two-parent children. These findings are discussed in relation to attachment theory, peer relations and the academic performance of single-parent children. (12 references)

1024. Evans, Al, and John Neel. "School Behaviors of Children from One-Parent and Two-Parent Homes." *Principal* 60(1): 38–39 (September 1980).

This study examines the school behaviors of children from single-parent and intact families based on data from the National Association of Elementary School Principals-/I/D/E/A/ Consortium for the Study of School Needs of Children from One-Parent Families. The SPSS Statistical package was used to perform a multivariate analysis of variance. It was found that there is less difference in the school behavior of one and two-parent children in low-income families. However, in general, the behavior of two-parent children is significantly different from that of one-parent children and more closely meets school expectations. (No references)

1025. Faber, Stephanie S., et al. "Older Adolescents And Parental Divorce: Adjustment Problems and Mediators of Coping." *Journal of Divorce* 7(2): 59–75 (Winter 1983).

This study explores the family disruption problems of college age adolescents and examines some of the factors that aid them in coping with this life transition. A series of pilot interviews with college mental health professionals, a review of the literature on family disruption, and a questionnaire were used to identify factors mediating adaptation of adolescents experiencing parental divorce. The questionnaire was sent to the clinical directors of student mental health counseling centers at colleges and universities in the United States. Potential mediators of family disruption identified included age, sex, and distance from home of the adolescent. Adolescents seemed more likely to use more formal sources of support than peers or family members. (39 references)

1026. Farquhar, Carolyn Lewellen. "A Study to Determine the Needs of East Lansing, Michigan, Middle School Youngsters from Single-Parent Families in Relation to Their Adjustment in Assuming Their New Roles." Ph.D. diss., Michigan State University, 1973.

For a summary see: *Dissertation Abstracts International* 34A(9): 5581.

1027. Felner, Robert D., et al. "Parental Death or Divorce and the School Adjustment of Young Children." *American Journal of Community Psychology* 9(2): 181–190 (April 1981).

Two potentially crisis-producing experiences, parental divorce or death, are examined for their effects on the school adjustment of young children. Subjects in this study were primary school children identified in a program for early detection and prevention of school maladaptation. The program uses trained nonprofessional child-aides, working under professional supervision, as direct help-agents for the children. Children with family histories of death and divorce were found to show greater overall school maladaptation than children without such histories. It is suggested that effective preventive and interventive strategies be developed for these children. (41 references)

1028. Fowler, Patrick C., and Herbert C. Richards. "Father Absence, Educational Preparedness, and Academic Achievement: A Test of the Confluence Model." *Journal of Educational Psychology* 70(4): 595–601 (August 1978).

The impact of early and continuing father absence on

school achievement was the focus of this investigation. One hundred amd twenty, lower-class black kindergarten boys and girls were assessed on twelve educational preparedness measures and tested again two years later to measure achievement in math, reading and language arts. Findings indicated no difference in educational preparedness between father-present and father-absent children. Analysis of achievement criteria favored father-present subjects, with the math performance of girls aided more than boys by the presence of fathers. The need for additional research is discussed. (24 references)

1029. Friedlander, Brian Scott. "Teachers' Expectation of Children from One-Parent Families: An Analogue and Observational Study." Ph.D. diss., University of Pennsylvania, 1988.

For a summary see: *Dissertation Abstracts International* 49A(6): 1408.

1030. Fuller, Mary Lou. "Teachers' Perceptions of Children from Intact and Single-Parent Families." *School Counselor* 33(5): 365–374 (May 1986).

This study examines 91 elementary school teachers' perceptions of children from intact and single-parent families. Findings based on responses to a questionnaire indicated that teachers over 35 years old were more apt to attribute negative behaviors to children from single-parent families, whereas teachers 35 and under were apt to attribute positive behaviors to single-parent children. It is therefore concluded that students from intact families and single-parent homes are receiving messages that have the potential for influencing their self-perceptions and behaviors. Implications of these findings for school counselors are discussed. (28 references)

1031. Garvin, James P. "Children of Divorce—A Challenge for Middle School Teacher." *Middle School Journal* 16(1): 6–7 (November 1984).

Frustrations and concerns of children whose parents have separated affect their school behavior and teachers need to take time to understand the unique needs of school age children as they relate to behavior and achievement in school. Teachers need to show understanding and concern, keep contact with divorced parents, abandon stereotyped vocabulary, select literature to help adolescents cope, adjust the curriculum to recognize children from single-parent families, and encourage out-of-class programs that aid socialization. The child's self-concept should be reinforced to give the student the strength to cope with problems of divorce at home and at school. (No references)

1032. Gatlin, Beverly G., and Robert M. Brown. *Effects of Father Absence on Educational Achievement of Rural Black Children*. North Carolina (Halifax County) 1975. 9pp. (ERIC Microfiche ED216072)

Data was collected on 116 black rural school children, 52 percent of whom came from two-parent families, 32 percent from single-parent families, and 16 percent who lived with grandparents. Data on academic achievement seemed to be significantly related to parental status in the language arts areas. Findings suggest that living with the mother only has a negative effect on the children's academic performance, while father absences seemed to have little effect. Children who lived with their grandparents did as well as those who lived with both parents. (7 references)

1033. Gross, Dorothy W. "Shopping the Issues II: Improving the Quality of Family Life." *Childhood Education* 54(2): 50–54 (November/December 1977).

The rising divorce rate, increased incidence of teenage pregnancies, more mothers joining the workforce and the disappearance of the home based extended family have changed the traditional image of the family in America. It is suggested that schools, like day care centers, Head Start programs, and nursery schools, need to expand their role to adoption of a family model. Schools would then provide day care for infants and children, adult education, parent support groups, tutoring, and other support programs that meet the special needs of today's families. Along with the expanded role suggested for schools is a call for new teachers trained to meet the needs of today's families. (3 references)

1034. Guidubaldi, John, and Joseph D. Perry. "Divorce, Socioeconomic Status, and Children's Cognitive-Social Competence at School Entry." *American Journal of Orthopsychiatry* 54(3): 459–468 (July 1984).

One hundred and fifteen kindergarten students were studied to determine significant predictors of school-entry competencies for children of single parents. A variety of predictor and criterion variables were used in the investigation. Socio-economic status and single-parent status consistently predicted school entry competencies. Academic, visual-motor and social development of the child were significantly related to single-parent families. Since single parenthood resulted from divorce, findings suggest that children from divorced family homes begin school with less academic and social competence than those from intact families. There are implications for professional interventions for children at risk. (41 references)

1035. Guidubaldi, John, et al. "The Impact of Parental Divorce on Children: Report of the Nationwide NASP Study." *School Psychology Review* 12(3): 300–323 (Summer 1983).

The impact of divorce on 699 children from the first, third and fifth grades as reported by 144 randomly selected members of the National Association of School Psychologists is presented. Measures used included parent-child interviews, WISC-R and WRAT scores in addition to ratings by classroom teachers. Boys from divorced families were found to have lower social and academic adjustment than boys from intact families, independent of socio-economic status. Regular contact with the father resulted in better performance by boys on some measures. Directions for intervention suggested by findings are offered. (62 references)

1036. Hainline, Louise, and Ellen Feig. "The Correlates of Childhood Father Absence in College-Aged Women." *Child Development* 49(1): 37–42 (March 1978).

A sample of college women between 17 and 23 years of age from father-absent and intact families were studied to determine correlates of father absence. This investigation attempts to replicate Hetherington's (1972) study of father-absent adolescent girls. Results of several measures used with the college women showed few deviations between father-absent and father-present groups for nonverbal behavior response to a male interviewer, locus of control, self-image, attitude toward sex and degree of sex-role typing. Differences between the findings and the Hetherington study are discussed. (20 references)

1037. Hammond, Janice M. "Children, Divorce and You." *Learning* 9(7): 83–84, 88–89 (February 1981).

Although the stigma of divorce has lessened because of the growing numbers of families involved, divorce may be one of the most traumatic events a child has to face. Teachers can create a more positive environment for children from divorced families by not expecting failure, being sensitive to language used and avoiding familial stereotypes, being a good listener, using social studies units to discuss divorce and single parent families, making books about divorce available, communicating with parents, being aware of custodial arrangements and by not shutting out the non-custodial parent. (No references)

1038. ———. "Children of Divorce: Implications for Counselors." *The School Counselor* 27(1): 7–14 (September 1979).

This study compares differences in classroom behavior, self-concept and attitudes of children from divorced families with those of children from intact families. A variety of measures were administered to 165 students in grades three to six. Boys from divorced families were rated by teachers as having more behavior problems and in turn rated their families less happy and their mothers less attentive. More than half the subjects felt they could talk to school counselors about problems, and that counselors could be helpful when parents were separating. Suggestions for individual and group counseling are offered. (21 references)

1039. ———. "Children of Divorce: A Study of Self-Concept, Academic Achievement and Attitudes." *Elementary School Journal* 80(2): 55–62 (November 1979).

The effects of divorce on self-concept, academic achievement and attitudes were studied in a sample of 165 elementary school children. Information was furnished by students and teachers and a variety of measures were also used. Findings indicated no significant differences in self-concept or reading achievement between children from divorced families and children from intact families. Boys from divorced families were rated lower in mathematics and also rated their family less happy than boys from intact families. Implications for teachers and school administrators are discussed. (19 references)

1040. Harlamert, Elizabeth Kay. "A Study of the Relationship of a Parenting Program to Reading Achievement Scores of Single-Parent Children." Ed.D. diss., Ball State University, 1986.

For a summary see: *Dissertation Abstracts International* 47A(9): 3259.

1041. Hempe, A. Henri, and William Decker. "Prudent Policy Can Keep Your Schools Out of the Child-Custody Cross Fire." *The American School Board Journal* 27(6): 174–176 (June 1987).

Many school boards do not have systemwide policies for dealing with problems related to child custody rights of divorced parents. A policy developed for the Beloit, Wisconsin, School District in 1982 allows the noncustodial parent the same access to school reports and notices about the student that the custodial parent receives, unless specifically forbidden by court order. Other issues related to child custody are also discussed. (No references)

1042. Henderson, Anne J. "Designing School Guidance Programs for Single-Parent Families." *School Counselor* 29(2): 124–132 (November 1981).

A school program to aid in the development of guidance programs for single-parent families is presented. The step-by-step evolution of the support groups for parents and children is described in sufficient detail that the program could be easily replicated in other school systems. Suggestions for changes in the program based on individual responses from children and parents are reported. Sixty-five percent of 131 children gave a positive rating to the program. Child Care, Visitation, and New Family Roles received high ratings. Implications for guidance are noted. (33 references)

1043. Herzog, J. D. "Father-Absence and Boy's School Performance in Barbados." *Human Organization* 33(1): 71–83 (Spring 1974)

This paper examines the relationship between father-absence and school achievement in a sample of boys in Barbados. The study controls for socioeconomic status, race, cultural attitudes toward birth status test and school data. Findings showed that father-absence during the earliest years was benefical to have their fathers return after age two or three. It is suggested that the effect of father-absence on white middle-class Americans is not necessarly the same for boys in other social or cultural groups. (43 references)

1044. Hetherington, E. Mavis, et al. *Cognitive Performance, School Behavior, and Achievement of Children from One-Parent Households.* National Institute of Education. 1981, 264pp. (ERIC Microfiche ED221780)

The impact of divorce and single-parenting on the school achievement and intellectual functioning of children was examined through a review of research. Factors that were found to be related to academic achievement included reason for single-parent status, gender, race, and socioeconomic status. Quality of parent-child relationship, effective family functioning, and use of support services are among those factors that may mediate the negative effects of post-divorce stress. (Bibliography)

1045. Hodges, William F., et al. "Parent-Child Relationships and Adjustment in Preschool Children in Divorced and Intact Families." *Journal of Divorce* 7(2): 43–58 (Winter 1983).

Quantitative and qualitative aspects of child rearing and their effect on child adjustment were examined in relation to the marital status of parents. Mothers of 30 children of divorced families and 60 children from intact families in Denver, Colorado were subjects of the study. Few differences were found that were associated with marital status, the quality of parenting, and predicted adjustment. Boys were more likely to have behavioral problems than girls. It is concluded that differences between divorced and intact families are not as clear as some studies have implied. (22 references)

1046. Hoffman, Carol Elaine. "Family Dissolution: An Issue for the Schools-Group Sessions in a Middle School." *Children Today* 13(4): 25–27 (July-August 1984).

Early adolescence is a period of great change in a child's life and coping with parental separation and divorce adds additional stress. A group discussion program used in a Virginia school system is described. In the middle school, children have a more realistic understanding of custody and financial arrangement and may participate in the custody decision. The need to advise teachers as well as parents about the impact of parental dissolution on children is noted.

1047. Holzman, Terry. "Schools Can Provide Help for the Children of Divorce." *American School Board Journal* 171(5): 46–47 (May 1984).

Support groups and a curriculum that reflect the needs of children in changing families have been offered in Newton, Massachusetts, since the 1970's. Programs aimed at children from divorced and separated families are described. An address for obtaining more information about curriculum materials is provided. (No references)

1048. Horns, Virginia, and Gypsy Abbott. "A Comparison of Concepts of Self and Parents Among Elementary School Children in Intact, Single Parent, and Blended Families." Paper presented at the Annual Meeting of the Mid-South Education Research's Association, Biloxi, Miss., November 1985. 31pp. (ERIC Microfiche ED265481)

This study examines the differences in children's self-concepts and their concepts of the adults with whom they live in a variety of family structures. Participants included girls and boys in grades two to five from middle to high socioeconomic status families. The Personal Attribute Inventory was used to assess interpersonal and intrapersonal evaluations. Few differences on self-concept and concepts of parents were found. Differences in specific feelings were reported, with single-parent children evaluating themselves as less calm, less complaining, but more afraid and nicer than other children. Areas for further research are suggested. (29 references)

1049. Houtz, Paul L., ed. "The American Family Minus One." *National Elementary Principal* 59(1): WHOLE ISSUE (October 1979).

With the increasing divorce rate schools may be the chief

source of stability in the lives of children who must cope with the loss of a parent. This issue of the journal is devoted to children and their single parents. The National Association of Elementary School Principals, I.D.E.A., and the Ditchley Foundation of England sponsored the meeting on which this issue is based and excerpts from the discussion are included. (Bibliographies)

1050. Hulbert, Jackeline Luce. "Social Adjustment and Reading Achievement of Children from Single-Parent and from Two-Parent Military Service Family Enrolled in the DoDDS—Germany." Ed.D. diss., University of Southern California, 1987.

For a summary see: *Dissertation Abstracts International* 48A(12): 3048.

1051. Isaacs, Marla Beth, and Irene Raskow Levin. "Who's in my Family? A Longitudinal Study of Drawings of Children of Divorce." *Journal of Divorce* 7(4): 1–21 (1984).

Self-Concept Scale, Attitude Toward Family Questionnaire and the Hammond Children in grades three to six. Boys from divorced families were rated by teachers as having more behavior problems and in turn rated their families less happy and their mothers less attentive. More than half of the subjects felt they could talk to school counselors about problems and that counselors could be helpful when parents were separating. Suggestions for individual and group counseling are given. (21 references)

1052. Jenkins, Jeanne E., et al. "Parental Separation Effects on Children's Divergent Thinking Abilities and Creativity Potential." *Child Study Journal* 18(3): 149–158 (1988).

The effect of parental separation was studied in a sample of 116 elementary school children from one-parent and two-parent families in New York City. The Revised Art Scale and Divergent Thinking Exercise were used as measures. No significant effect on children's divergent thinking processes was found. Single-parent children scored higher on measures of creativity -related measures. It is suggested that this may mean that single-parent children may respond favorably to instructional arrangements that allow for more individualized interpretation and expression. (26 references)

1053. Kalter, Neil, et al. "School-Based Development Facilitation Groups for Children of Divorce: A Preventive Intervention." *American Journal of Orthopsychiatry* 54(4): 613–623 (October 1984).

A model school-based intervention program designed to help children successfully meet developmental tasks related to divorce and the post-divorce experience is described. Telling a child about divorce, identifying divorce issues that are upsetting to children, and the development of coping strategies are discussed. Multiple brief interventions related to developmental tasks created by change in custody, parental loss, parental dating, stepfathers, and live-in boyfriends are discussed. Children may continue to face divorce related problems years after family dissolution occurs. (24 references)

1054. Kealey, Robert J. "The Image of the Family in Second-Grade Readers." *Momentum* 11(3): 16–19 (October 1980).

This study examines the image of the family as it is presented in second grade readers in six basic textbook reading series. About 76 percent of the readers include children and adults in some type of family relationship. However adoptive and foster parents are not included. About 38 percent of the children in the basic reader stories live in single-parent families, reflecting the current situation and future trends. The high number of references to father and child mirrors recent attention to fathers in a parenting role and as a custodial parent. No mention was found of deceased or divorced parents. Stories of single parents may be used as a form of bibliotherapy. (12 references)

1055. Kelley, Charles Edward. "A Study of Students from Single-Parent and Two-Parent Families in Terms of Progress Toward High School Graduation." Ph.D. diss., Auburn University, 1984.

For a summary see: *Dissertation Abstracts International* 45A(9): 2713.

1056. Kelly, Joan B., and Judith S. Wallerstein. "Children of Divorce." *National Elementary Principal* 59(1): 51–58. October 1979.

This discussion of single-parent children is based on a five year longitudinal study of 60 divorcing families and their 131 children. Children in the study found the divorce highly stressful, were concerned about the continuity of the parent-child relationship and hoped for a reconciliation. Children below the age of five to eight seemed more directly affected by father-absence. Teachers reported changes in classroom behavior for about two-thirds of the children following the separation of their parents. At the end of five years findings suggested that the quality of support received from both parents was linked significantly with the child's adjustment to divorce. Recommendations for teachers and school policies to better meet the needs of single-parent children are offered. (11 references)

1057. King, Jodie, and Ron Moreland. "Rx for Children of Broken Homes." *Thrust* 12(5): 30–31 (February-March 1983).

Children from one-parent homes present more problems in school when they fail to learn coping skills. The project called STAGES is described. It is designed to increase coping skills through the experientially based curriculum based on the process of adjustment. The program was developed for use at the primary and intermediate grade levels. Results indicate positive responses in academic achievement and school behaviors. (No references)

1058. Kohn, Sherwood Davidson. "Coping with Family Change." *National Elementary Principal* 19(1): 40–50 (October 1979).

Despite the growing incidence and acceptance of divorce, the term "broken home" still carries negative connotations and society as a whole is predisposed to react in certain predictable ways that are not supportive of the single parents and their children. The issues related to one-parent families and the school are viewed as societal rather then simply a matter of scheduling, training, counseling and administrative adjustment. The most sensitivity to single-parent families shown by schools occurs where these families are most numerous. Public policy implications for single-parent families discussed with the secretary of HEW further underline the disadvantages faced by single females and their children. (No references)

1059. Kopf, Kathryn E. "Family Variables and School Adjustment of Eighth-Grade Father-Absent Boys." *Family Coordinator* 19(2): 145–150 (April 1970).

Fifty-two mother-son pairs were studied to assess the relationship between school adjustment and with father-absence. A school adjustment measure was developed for the eighth grade boys, and an interview schedule was constructed for use with mothers. Results showed that the degree of father and extended family support were not significantly related to adjustment. Participation in household tasks, positive attitudes toward the father and son, and some joint mother-son social activities were found to be related to good adjustment in school. The attitudes and behavior of the mothers of father-absent boys can therefore enhance or impede their sons' school adjustment. (10 references)

1060. Krantz, Susan E., et al. "Cognition and Adjustment among Children of Separated or Divorced Parents." *Cognitive Therapy and Research* 9(1): 61–77 (February 1985).

This study tested the hypothesis that coping with stress is associated with the individual's cognitive appraisals of the stressor (events) and of their resources for coping with the stressor. Fifty-two children between 8.5–12 years of age whose parents were separating or divorcing were given a measure of appraisals of coping options. The Louisville Behavior Checklist and A-M-L Behavior Rating Scale were used to determine whether the primary appraisals of separation and the secondary appraisals of coping options are related to post divorce functioning in children. Boys' evaluation and appraisals of events involved in parental divorce were associated with behavior in the home but not in school. (62 references)

1061. Krein, Shelia Fitzgerald. "Growing Up in a Single-Parent Family: The Effect on Education and Earnings of Young Men." *Family Relations* 35(1): 161–168 (January 1986).

The educational and economic attainment of young men from single-parent families is examined. Data sets in the matched mother/son sample used were taken from the National Longitudinal Survey of Labor Market Experience. Living in a single-parent home has a negative effect on educational attainment but only a marginal effect on earnings when education is taken into account. The effect is most pronounced for those who lived in single families during the preschool years. Implications for public policy and practioners are discussed. Further research on the impact of variables such as child care, educational activities, schools, teachers, peer and social support among others that may have an impact on educational attainment of those living in a single-parent family is discussed. (25 references)

1062. Krot, Sandra. "Adolescent in the Transitional Family: How the Schools Can Help." *Educational Horizons* 61(4): 205–208 (Summer 1983).

The Families in Transition Project works with local schools in Eugene, Oregon, to provide services to youth whose families are divorcing by providing family counseling, parent education classes, and self-help support groups for parents and youth. The program for youth focuses on helping them to cope with their feelings and to understand the feelings of their parents. The program demonstrated the effectiveness of a private agency and a public school working together to help students with the insecurity related to family transition. (2 references)

1063. Levine, Elinor Reah. "Teachers' Academic and Psycho-Social Expectations for Children from Single-Parent Families." Ed.D. diss., 1981.

For a summary see: *Dissertation Abstracts International* 41A(12): 5033.

1064. ———. "What Teachers Expect of Children from Single-Parent Families." Paper presented at the Annual Convention of the American Personnel and Guidance Association, Detroit, March 17–20, 1982. 26pp. (ERIC Microfiche ED219692)

Single-parent children may experience discrimination through school policies and teachers' attitudes. Responses to questionnaires completed by 100 teachers suggest teachers had lower expectations for children from single-parent families. One hundred and two parents were asked to respond to the same questionnaire in the way they believed a teacher would respond. They indicated they believed that teachers would have lower expectations for children from single-parent families. These findings suggest that teachers' negative expectations for single-parent children may have an impact on their students' performance. (30 references)

1065. Lewis, Wade. "Strategic Interventions with Children of Single-Parent Families." *School-Counselor* 33(5): 375–378 (May 1986).

This article focuses on school related problems of single-parent children and the use of the family systems perspective. The parent should be asked to help the school solve the child's problem. Teacher, therapist, and parent should agree on a plan to solve the presenting problem and age appropriate activities for the child should be encouraged. The parent should be encouraged to participate in social and physical activities in order to increase the support network. These and other intervention techniques may be used alone or in various combinations with elementary and junior high school students. (7 references)

1066. Louwes, Wiepke, and Rie Bosman. "School Careers of Children from One-parent and Two-parent Families: A One-Parent Family on the Educational Attainment of Children." *Netherlands Journal of Sociology—Sociologia Neerlandica* 7(24) 117–131 (October 1988).

A nationally representative sample of students from one-parent and two-parent families were matched and compared on variables known to influence educational achievement. Results suggest that father absence does not necessarily, by itself, contribute to the poorer academic performance of their children. Despite equal achievement test scores, teachers advised children from divorced mothers to aim lower in their secondary schooling than children from two-parent families. Socioeconomic factors may also be responsible for placing single-parent children at additional risk. (45 references)

1067. Manfredi, Lynn A. "Divorce and the Preschool Child." *Day Care and Early Education* 4(5): 18–20+ (May/June 1977).

The feelings and fears of a preschool child as they related to the various changed situations in his/her life following the separation of parents are discussed from the child's viewpoint. Although divorce does not cause serious problems for all children, all children do feel guilt, fear, and worry when the family disintegrates. Changes in a child's behavior that indicate stress or anxiety in response to divorce should be reported to the parents by the day care teacher. In the classroom, the teacher can provide the extra love and attention that the child needs at this time. Other ways in which the teacher can also help reduce the trauma of divorce for the preschool child are also offered. (No references)

1068. McAdoo, Harriette Pipes. "Youth, School, and the Family in Transition." *Urban Education* 16(3): 261–277 (October 1981).

This article discusses the implications of changes in family structure, changing roles of women, and decreases in family income for schools and communities. Single mothers must spend so much time trying to meet the economic needs of their families, they have little time left to handle school related problems of their children. Unemployment rates are higher for blacks and Hispanics. Children of minorities therefore suffer more detrimental effects. They are not only economically deprived, but lack role models of regularly employed adults. Unlike in the past, higher education is not always associated with upward mobility for minorities. The author predicts deterioration of urban schools in the coming decade due to an aging population and geographic shifts of young families. (39 references)

1069. McDaniel, Susan H. "Treating School Problems in Family Therapy." *Elementary School Guidance Counseling* 15(3): 214–222 (February 1981).

This article considers how family therapists and elementary school counselors can work together in helping children and their families with problems. School psychologists are often the first to notice behaviors in children which are related to a crisis in the home. The most frequent problems occur because of parental divorce or remarriage. The assessment process and the need for school professionals to work with mental health clinicians in the community are discussed. (11 references)

1070. Michaels, Carol S. "Summary of a Study of Father Fantasies of Preschool Children with Nonresident Fathers." Paper presented at the Annual Meeting of American Psychological Association Los Angeles, August 24–28, 1981. 11pp. (ERIC Microfiche ED208987)

Preschool children's fantasies of their nonresident fathers were investigated in 96 pairs of black, white, and Hispanic mothers and children. Of 18,846 fantasies produced by the children, 46 percent included the absent father. "Good" father fantasies accounted for 21 percent of the father fantasies and were significantly associated with the maternal attitude variable. Eight to six percent of the "Bad" fantasies were related to several variables of which gender was most important. "Silhouette" fantasies, relatively free of strong emotion and personal conflict, accounted for 15.1 percent of the responses in the children's play. The purpose and role of idealization of the nonresident fathers in the child's future growth and developments is not determined. (19 references)

1071. Miller, David R. "Sensitizing New Teachers about Father-Absent Boys." *Action in Teacher Education* 8(3): 73–78 (Fall 1986).

As the divorce rate continues to rise, teachers of elementary and middle school children may become the first line of defense for troubled children and may need to serve as surrogate parents as well. A brief summary of research findings from studies on the impact of parental absence identifies common responses of children to this crisis in their lives. (19 references)

1072. Miller, Helen L. "Helping Kindergarteners Deal With Death: A Teacher's Response." *Childhood Education* 64(1): 31–32 (October 1987).

A former kindergarten teacher describes her experience in helping children deal with the death of a father, grandfather and sister. Listening and providing children with the opportunity to express their feelings and share their experience with others are important in resolving grief. It is also important for children to know that whatever happens, there are people who care. (No references)

1073. Milne, Ann M., et al. "Single Parents, Working Mothers, and the Educational Achievement of School Children." *Sociology of Education* 59(3): 125–139 (July 1986).

The relationship of the mother's employment and the school achievement of children who live in one-parent families is explored in new research studies. Data used for this investigation was based on a national survey of 12,429 elementary school students and 2,720 high school students. Results show that the effects of the mother's employment on the school achievement of children living in a one-parent family can have negative effects but that these effects differ by age, race, and family structure. (39 references)

1074. Moffitt, Terrie E. "Vocabulary and Arithmetic Performance of Father-Absent Boys." *Child-Study Journal* 10(4): 233–241 (1981).

The impact of father absence on the verbal and mathematics aptitude of 60 Danish boys ranging in age from ten to twenty is examined. Subtests of the Weschsler Intelligence Scale for Children (WISC) for Arithmetic and Vocabulary were used as measures. Results indicated a slight decrease in verbal and mathematical abilities for father-absent boys of low socio-economic status. Ability scores were nearly identical for boys from father present families of low and high socio-economic status. The amount of separation from the father was not significantly related to the subjects' performance on the Arithmetic or Vocabulary subtests. Suggestions for future studies of the effects of father separation are offered. (21 references)

1075. Monteith, Mary K. "The Reading Teacher vs. Children of Divorce." *The Reading Teacher* 35(1): 100–103 (October 1981).

The reading teacher may provide students of divorced or divorcing parents with a collection of books to help sustain them during this stressful period. Since children's classroom behavior is often negatively affected by stress, the reading teacher and the child are frequently in an adversarial relationship during the divorce process. The teacher is encouraged to recognize the signals of stress that indicate a child needs help. Problems that arise due to movement between custodial and noncustodial homes may affect the image the child presents at school. Five bibliographies of books for children and teens are cited, along with a discussion of the historical role of bibliotherapy in the treatment of stress. (7 references)

1076. Morgan, John D. "Death and Loss: How Can You Help the Kids? *Guidance and Counseling* 2: 37–41 (November 1986).

This article discusses the effect of loss through death on the child and the need to provide support for the bereaved. Unresolved grief may place children at risk for problems in later life. Although a child may not show signs of continuous grief, the need for support extends beyound just the first few weeks after death loss. The teacher and the school counselor are important sources of intervention during the bereavement process. (10 references)

1077. Morris, Douglas Thomas. "Is Student Success Dependent on the Number of Parents in One Family?" Ed.D. diss., Saint Louis University, 1982.

For a summary see: *Dissertation Abstracts International* 43A(5): 1375.

1078. Myers, David E., et al. *Single Parents, Working Mothers and the Educational Achievement of Secondary School Age Children.* Department of Education, Washington, D.C., June 1983. 55p. (ERIC Microfiche ED234093)

This study examined the effects of maternal work on secondary school age children in single-parent families and two parent families. Data used for the investigation came from a national longitudinal survey of 58,270 high school students and their parents. The effect of mothers working in two-parent families was found to have negative total effects on students' achievement and positive total effects in one-parent black families. However, the total effect of number of parents on students' achievement for secondary school age students tended to be negligible. (33 references)

1079. Nassib, Bridget. "Case Studies of Three Kindergarten Children from Single-Parent Families in an Urban School District." Ed.D. diss., University of Pennsylvania, 1985.

For a summary see: *Dissertation Abstracts International* 47A(7): 2447.

1080. National Association of Elementary School Principals. *The Most Significant Minority: One-Parent Children in the Schools*. Institute for Development of Educational Activities, Dayton, Ohio, July 28, 1980. 28pp. (ERIC Microfiche ED192438)

First-year report of a longitudinal study of the needs of school children from one-parent families conducted by a consortium of twenty-six elementary and secondary schools in fourteen states. The study was co-sponsored by the National Association of Elementary School Principals and the Institute for Development of Educational Activities. Participating schools reported on every student enrolled within the first five days of each semester. Findings confirmed that students living with only one parent show lower scholastic achievement, more absence, tardiness and discipline and health problems than their two parent peers. They therefore need more help from school than they receive. (12 references)

1081. National Association of Elementary School Principals Staff Report. "One-Parent Families and Their Children: The School's Most Significant Minority." *Principal* 60(1): 31–37 (September 1980).

The study of the needs of single-parent children undertaken by NAESP and the Institute for Development of Educational Activities (/I/D/E/A/) involved a consortium of 26 schools. The 1979–80 study netted 36,115 responses. Findings indicated that children from one parent families have lower academic achievement, more discipline problems, more absence and tardiness, and perhaps more health problems. Directions for future studies are noted and implications of the present study for schools are discussed. Education consultant Mitchell Lazarus assisted with the preparation of this report by the NAESP staff. (9 references)

1082. National School Boards Association. "School Systems and the Growing Minority." *Updating School Board Policies* 14(7): 1–3 (August 1983). (ERIC Microfiche ED236772)

Studies about the effects of growing up in a single-parent family present a variety of conclusions. School policies should recognize the change in family structure and keep both parents informed about their children. State and federal laws provide guidelines regarding the rights of parents. Many school systems provide extended day care programs that ensure that the children are safe during the parents' workday. Teaching homemaker and survivor skills to young latchkey children is another way schools may assist single-parent families.

1083. Noe, Ine Nijhuis. "An Exploratory Study of Single-Parents' Perceptions of Issues Related to the Schooling of Their Children." Ed.D. diss., George Washington University, 1986.

For a summary see: *Dissertation Abstracts International* 47A(2): 493.

1084. Ourth, John. "Children in One-Parent Homes: The School Factor." *Principal* 60(1): 40 (September 1980).

This article examines the role of the school in meeting the needs of all children. The school cannot fulfill its function of instruction until children from families in crisis have been helped to the extent that they can cope with the demands of the classroom. The school can help children and their families without invading their privacy. It is suggested that the most important thing educators can do is to reexamine their attitudes toward children from single-parent homes and learn to recognize signs of confusion and stress. (No references)

1085. Palker, Patricia. "How to Deal with the Single-Parent Child in the Classroom." *Teacher* 98(2): 50–54 (September 1980).

With the increasing numbers of single-parent homes, research on the effects of parental separation, divorce and death has accelerated, as have programs to help single parents deal with their lives and families. Schools sometimes show insensitivity to the needs of single parent families, not intentionally, but by oversight. Patience, understanding and listening are the keys to dealing with children who show trouble signs. Special counseling programs help children who can not deal with divorce on their own. Another option is "advance education" that would provide some general information to parents and children relative to problems they could face if a divorce should occur. (7 references)

1086. Parish, Thomas S., and Mary K. Philip. "The Self-Concept of Children from Intact and Divorced Families: Can They be Affected in School Settings?" *Education* 103(1): 60–64 (Fall 1982).

A group of teachers who attended an in-service workshop on the use of Maslow's Hierarchy to assess the needs of students, were asked to assess their students' needs and attempt to fulfill them. Based on pre and post-test measures the entire group of 376 grade-school students manifested significantly higher self-concepts after the teachers had been trained and encouraged to implement what they had learned. However, children from intact families, not those from divorced, remarried, or divorced non-married families, were the ones who were found to adopt significantly more positive self-concepts. Parents and teachers should be provided the knowledge they need to better understand children's needs and how to fulfill them. (12 references)

1087. Parrow, Alan A. *Race, Father Absence and the Educational Ambition of Adolescent Males.* Revised version of a paper presented at the Annual Meeting of the Southern Sociological Society, Atlanta, March-April 1977. 48pp. (ERIC Microfiche ED148984)

This paper reports on an investigation of the effect of father absence on educational ambition of adolescent public school males. Data for the study was obtained from surveys completed by the boys and interviews with their mothers. Evidence was found that father absence depressed ambition to a greater extent among blacks than whites, at least for boys in the 12th grade. Neither academic performance nor the boys' views of the opportunity structure mediated much of the father absence effect on ambition. However, a substantial portion of that effect was passed through the mothers' expectations for their sons' ultimate level of attainment. Areas for further study are suggested. (48 references)

1088. Patten-Seward, Patricia. "Assessing Student Emotional Behavior after Parental Separation or Divorce." *Journal of School Health* 54(4): 152–153 (April 1984).

Divorce affects 12.5 million children in the United States. The child's age at the time of divorce influences directly the feelings presented by the child. Preschoolers' feelings include: fear, regression, self-blame, grief, yearning for the departed parent, or feelings of conflict in loyalty to parents. Children nine to twelve years old may wish to be active, feel anger, have a shaken sense of identity, and may align themselves with one parent. School nurses need to understand how divorce affects children and have the skills to assess children of divorce for possible emotional problems. (1 Reference)

1089. Pedro, Carroll, et al. "Preventive Intervention with Latency-Aged Children of Divorce: A Replication Study." *American Journal of Community Psychology* 14(3): 277–290 (June 1986).

The assessment of the effectiveness of a school program of preventive intervention for children from divorced families is reported. One hundred and thirty-two, fourth-to-sixth-grade students from divorced and intact families were participants in the intervention group. Five school health professionals were trained to increase their understanding of divorce related problems of latency-aged children. Adjustment changes in subjects were evaluated by teachers, parents and children. Children from divorced families who were less well adjusted than their peers improved significantly and by the end of the intervention period approached the adjustment level of children from intact families. Follow-up studies of short-term findings are suggested. (30 references)

1090. ———. "The Children of Divorce Intervention Program: An Investigation of the Efficacy of a School-Based Prevention Program." *Journal of Consulting and Clinical Psychology* 53(5): 603–611 (October 1985).

This paper examines results of a school-based intervention program offered to 72 fourth through sixth-grade students. The ten-week group program was designed to enable students to share divorce-related feelings, clarify misconceptions, teach problem-solving, and to teach other coping skills. Teacher and parent ratings of children following the program indicated improvement in problem behaviors and adjustment. (37 references)

1091. Ramey, Craig T., et al. "Predicting School Failure from Information Available at Birth." *American Journal of Mental Deficiency* 82(6): 525–534 (May 1978).

This study investigates the value of using information on birth certificates to identify children entering school for the first time who may need special education services. One thousand randomly selected first grade students constituted the sample. A variety of measures were used in the study. Race and education of the mother were found to be significant predictors of intelligence, academic achievement, visual-motor integration performance, and teachers' ratings. Birth order, prenatal care, survival of older siblings, child's legitimacy, plus mother's race and education were predictors of children likely to be at severe risk. (13 references)

1092. Reyes, Tito Fidel. "Father Absence and the Social Behavior of Pre-School Children." Michigan State University, 1977.

For a summary see: *Dissertation Abstracts International* 39A(1): 185–186.

1093. Ricci, Isolina. "Divorce, Remarriage, and the Schools." *Phi Delta Kappan* 60(7): 509–511 (March 1979).

The traditional American family is being replaced with new family forms. Terms such as "parent with custody," "parent without custody," and "stepparent" are replacing the words "mother" and "father." Schools resist probing new family structures. Complex legal arrangements, the need to respect families' right to privacy and budget restraints prevent them from meeting the changing needs of families. Educators can change outdated "one home" policies, develop effective procedures for access to school records by all the child's parents, provide inservice training for teachers and create a family/school dialogue that involves the family, school and child working together. Finding more positive ways to encourage divorced and remarried parents to maintain responsible and continuous relationships with their children strengthens family life. (7 references)

1094. Riley, Barb. *Education and the Children of One-parent*

Families: A Background Paper. (ERIC Microfiche ED222838)

Current literature about single-parent children can provide educators with information on the effects of single-parenting on the child's personality, behavior, and academic performance. Findings of research studies suggest that at the elementary school age level children often fear abandonment, act agressively, and exhibit attention-getting behaviors when their parents have separated. Secondary school age children are likely to blame themselves, show anger or withdrawal, and have difficulty with heterosexual relationships. Sometimes the experience can lead to greater independence and personal strength. Discussion groups and peer counseling can often be helpful for children in single- parent families. (48 references)

1095. Roddy, Patricia Palker. "A Closer Look at Children in Single-Parent Families." ERIC/CUE Digest Number 23 (June 1984). (ERIC Microfiche ED254587)

Although schools must accommodate students' differences in background and experiences, including those related to an increasing number of one-parent families, educators are cautioned against expecting trouble from the child from a one-parent family. Research findings suggest that single-parent children tend to have more behavioral problems in school, and are at greater risk in terms of truancy and dropout rate. The likelihood of a child having cognitive or behavioral problems depends upon such factors as quality of child care arrangements, number of siblings, structure of home and school environment, amount of nurturing received, age, sex and race of child, socioeconomic level and the circumstances related to parental separation. (14 references)

1096. Roosa, Mark W. "Adolescent Mothers, School Drop-Outs and School Based Intervention Programs." *Family Relations* 35(2): 313–317 (April 1986).

Recent studies of school based intervention programs for
teenage mothers are examined. School programs for teen
mothers may have positive effects, but miss those
adolescents who drop out early in the pregnancy/parenting
process. It is suggested that drop-outs could be reduced
by providing 1) parenting programs in neighborhood
schools, 2) infant care at the site of the program and 3)
flexible attendance school attendance policies. (26
references)

1097. Rosenberg, Judith Kate. "Early Childhood Separation:
Effects During Latency on Personal Behavior, School
Behavior and Attitude." Ph.D. diss., United States
International University, 1980.

For a summary see: *Dissertation Abstracts International*
41B(4): 1524.

1098. Rothschild, Marie Stupp. *Public School Center VS. Family
Home Day Care: Single Parents' Reasons for Selection.*
99p. (ERIC Microfiche ED162759)

A sample of 30 single parents who selected day care
centers for their children, and 23 parents who placed
their children in school centers were asked to rank the
reasons for their decisions. Responses indicated that
parents chose their child care because the facility offered
a structured program, had trained and competent staff,
focused on the needs of the child offered flexible hours
and was easily assessible. (23 references)

1099. Roy, Crystal M., and Dale R. Fuqua. "Social Support
Systems and Academic Performance of Single Parent
Student." *The School Counselor* 30(3): 183–192 (January
1983).

This study was designed to test the hypothesis that single-
parent families of high-achieving children would have
greater social support than single-parent families of low-
achieving children. Subjects of the study were the parent
and the oldest school age child of single-parent families

who responded to the questionnaires. Results suggest that an adequate social support system may mediate the negative effects of single-parent families' status on children's academic performance. Helping single-parent families develop adequate support systems through education and training may be more effective than treating only symptoms of the maladjustment. (11 references)

1100. Salant, Edna G. "Johnny: A One-Parent Preschooler." *Art Education* 33(4): 22–24 (April 1980).

Preschool children are particularly vulnerable to disruption in family life. Although they are too young to adequately express their feelings in words, art therapy presented early may provide the child with a means of expressing painful feelings that could otherwise lead into greater psychopathology. An art therapy program that was designed for use in a preschool, especially for children of separated or divorced parents, is discussed. A case study is also presented to illustrate the value of art therapy in helping a four-year-old adopted child through his feelings about the loss of his father. (8 references)

1101. Samans, Elaine Mae. "Investigations of Differences Among Children from One and Two-Parent Families Through four Case Studies in a Suburban School District." Ed.D. diss., University of Pennsylvania, 1983.

For a summary see: *Dissertation Abstracts International* 44A(4): 0985.

1102. Santrock, John W., and Russell L. Tracy. "Effects of Children's Family Structure Status on the Development of Stereotypes by Teachers." *Journal of Educational Psychology* 70(5): 754–757 (October 1978).

This study examines the possibility that teachers' ratings of children may be influenced by the bias of the rater and his or her mistaken perception of the child's behavior. Thirty teachers were asked to view a videotape of an eight-year-old boy, rate him on personality traits and predict what his behavior would be like in five specified school situations. Half the subjects who were told the boy was from a divorced home rated him less favorably on happiness, emotional adjustment and ability to cope with stress than the other half of the subjects who were told that the boy was from an intact family. The finding suggests that the child from a father-absent home is likely to be seen more negatively by his teachers than a similar child from an intact family. (9 references)

1103. Schell, Leo M., and Dan Courtney. "The Effect of Male Teachers on the Academic Achievement of Father-Absent Sixth Grade Boys." *Journal of Educational Research* 72(4): 194–196 (March-April 1979).

This study probes the effect on academic achievement of the assignment of male teachers to father-absent sixth-grade boys as compared with that of similar boys assigned to female teachers. Subjects comprised 193 boys identified through school records. The Iowa Test of Basic Skills was used as a measure and IQ scores from the previous year were consulted. Results showed no significant evidence of improved academic achievement for boys assigned to male teachers. It is suggested that intervention should be instituted in earlier grades if father-absent boys are to benefit academically. (14 references)

1104. "The School and the Single-Parent Student: What Schools Can Do to Help." *Principal* 62(1): 24–26, 31–33, 38 (September 1982).

Divorce is a traumatic experience for children. Schools can help without adding costly programs or singling out a particular group of students and parents for special treatment. A child's school record should be made available to the noncustodial parent, attitudes and curriculum materials should be examined for possible negative impact on one-parent families, school events should be scheduled during nonworking hours, a homework hotline could be staffed by teachers on a rotating basis, business and community groups could help with the extra costs associated with special activities. (7 references)

1105. Schoyer, Nancy L. "Divorce and the Preschool Child." *Childhood Education* 57(1): 2–7 (September-October 1980).

Young children need help as they struggle with the changes that take place when their parents divorce. They may use defensive techniques to cope with difficult situations that include regression, premature detachment from parents, trouble with toilet use and fantasying about the things they would like in reality. School behavior may indicate inability to play creatively, problems sitting still, noisiness, kicking, hitting and biting peers. Among implications for teachers are the need to work closely with parents, help the child express feelings verbally, or for the young child, through some other medium. A list of five books are recommended for readers who want more information on separation/divorce and children. (7 references)

1106. Sciara, Frank J. "Effects of Father Absence on the Educational Achievement of Urban Black Children." *Child Study Journal* 5(1): 45–55 (1975).

Achievement test scores in reading and arithmetic were collected over a two-year period for 1003 black fourth-grade children from eight Model Cities Midwestern schools. Variables of years, sex, family status and intelligence were considered in analyzing data. Findings showed significant differences which suggested that children from father-present homes achieved more academically than children from father-absent homes. The impact of father absence on achievement was much greater for those students who had IQ's above 100. (16 References)

1107. ——. *Father Absence, an Overlooked Factor in the Lack of Achievement of Black Children in Title I Schools.*

Institute for the Preparation of the Disadvantaged, Teachers College, Ball State University. 13pp. (ERIC Microfiche ED137493)

The effects of father absence upon the academic achievement of black children are examined in this investigation. Students in the study were enrolled in remedial reading and remedial math programs at 20 Title I schools in a midwestern metropolitan school district. Children placed in the Title I remedial programs were those judged to be of normal intelligence, but whose achievement test scores were below average. Findings indicated that black children from father-absent homes were over-represented in the Title I remedial programs. The author cautions against any attempt to generalize this effect beyond the sample studied since the information was based on children in remedial programs only. (17 references)

1108. Shackelford, James Noble. "A Comparison of the School Adjustment of Ninth Grade Students from Conventional Parent Families and from Single Parent Families in the Parkway School District. Ph.D. diss., Saint Louis University, 1978.

For a summary see: *Dissertation Abstracts International* 39A(10): 6053.

1109. Shaw, Lois B. "High-School Completion for Young Women; Effects of Low Income and Living with a Single Parent." *Journal of Family Issues* 3(2): 147–163 (June 1982).

This study investigates the effects of living in a single-parent home on the educational chances of young women in addition to possible effects of low income. The discrepancy between the income of female-headed families and intact families contributes to a higher high school dropout rate for single-parent families. However, in black families, even when incomes were comparable with white families, black daughters were more likely to fail to complete high school if they lived with a single parent.

Data from the National Labor Survey indicated that black girls were more likely to drop out of school because they were pregnant, while white girls were more likely to drop out because of early marriage. (27 references)

1110. ———. *Does Living in a Single-Parent Family Affect High School Completion for Young Women?* Center for Human Resource, Columbus, Ohio State University. March 1979. 24pp. (ERIC Microfiche ED174700)

A sample of mothers and daughters from the National Longitudinal Surveys of Labor Market Experience is examined to determine the relationship between living in a one-parent family and a daughter's completion of high school. Multiple regression analysis shows failure to complete high school varies according to the length of time spent in a one-parent family, level of family income during high school, educational level of mother, and knowledge of the world of work. Findings indicated that low income is the single most significant factor accounting for the probability of a daughter dropping out of high school, for both white and black women. (22 references)

1111. Shea, Catherine A. *Schools and Non-Nuclear Families: Recasting Relationships.* 1982. 28p. (ERIC Microfiche ED234333).

The traditional home-school relationship is being challenged by the need to adjust to increasing numbers of single-parent families and stepfamilies. Society and educators need to examine attitudes and perceptions that tend to compare non-nuclear families unfavorably with traditional families. It is suggested that institutions provide training to help teachers gain the skills needed to work with children and parents from these new family forms. Additional areas where change is recommended include curriculum, record keeping, instruction, awareness of legal issues, and intervention techniques. (30 references)

1112. Sheridan, John T., et al. "Structured Group Counseling and Explicit Bibliotherapy as In-School Strategies for

Preventing Problems in Youth of Changing Families."
The School Counselor 33(2): 134–141 (November 1984).

Prevention methods used in a structured group counseling
program involving children from changing families are
outlined. A Group of 48 students from grades seven
through nine were selected because they were judged to
have problems so severe that extensive personality change
seemed necessary. Results indicated that group member
attitudes of youths in the prevention programs were more
positive at the end of the program. Short-term and long-
term studies are recommended. (22 references)

1113. Shilling, Frederick, and Patrick D. Lynch. "Father Versus
Mother Custody and Academic Achievement of Eight-
Grade Children." *Journal of Research and Development
in Education* 18(2): 7–11 (Winter 1985).

The effects of parent custody on the academic performance
of 3,160 eighth grade single-parent children was
investigated in this study. The Educational Quality
Assessment inventory was used to measure cognitive
skills, attitudes and interests of students. Findings
showed: 1) while mother-headed families were of lower
socioeconomic status, a higher level of perceived interest
in school was indicated, 2) children living with single-
parent mothers also scored higher in reading and
mathematics than children in single father headed
families. These results support the courts' practice of
giving mothers custody of children at least while the
children are in the eighth grade. Directions for future
studies are offered. (14 references)

1114. "Single-Parent Families Change Elementary Education."
Report On Education Research 21(8): 3–4 (April 19, 1989).

This article reports results of a study by the National
Association of Elementary School Principals (NAESP),
"Meeting the Needs of Children in Single-Parent
Families." Most of the principals agreed that children
from single parent families are educationally

disadvantaged, but could not say whether family structure, poverty, or some other factor was responsible. More than 90 percent of the 500 principals participating in the study reported making some changes to accommodate the needs of single-parent children and their parents. (No references)

1115. Skeen, Patsy, and Patrick C. McKenery. "The Teacher's Role in Facilitating a Child's Adjustment to Divorce." *Young Children* 35(5): 3–14 (July 1980).

Information is presented to help teachers provide positive support for children and families during divorce. Parent child relationships are altered and parenting becomes difficult as the family structure breaks down and parents must cope with interpersonal adjustments. Teachers can look for behavioral cues that reveal how a child is feeling, make a plan to aid intervention, help the child understand cognitively, be consistent in expectations of the child, and examine personal attitudes. Finally, teacher-parent communication should be supportive and positive. (23 references)

1116. Smith, Trudy Hensley. "An Exploratory Study of the Relationship of Amount of Time Spent with Children and Home Educational Environment in One-Parent and Two-Parent Families to Academic Achievement of Second Grade Students." Ed.D. diss., University of Georgia, 1982.

For a summary see: *Dissertation Abstracts International* 43A(11): 3505.

1117. Snyder, Alicia Allman, et al. "Children from Broken Homes: Visits to the School Nurse." *Journal of School Health* 50(4): 189–194. (April 1980).

The incidence of visits to the school nurse was based on 610 elementary school students from intact and single-parent families. It was found that students from broken homes visited the school nurse more frequently and in greater numbers than those from intact families. The nature of their complaints suggests the possibility that they were psychomatic. Implications of the study for school nurses are noted. (19 references)

1118. Solari, Robert Lee. "Correlation of One-Parent Family and Achievement Scores of Children in Selected Urban Central City Elementary School." Ph.D. diss., University of Michigan, 1976.

For a summary see: *Dissertation Abstracts International* 37A(3): 1391.

1119. Sonnenshein-Schneider, Mary, and Kay L. Baird. "Group Counseling Children of Divorce in the Elementary Schools: Understanding Process and Technique." *Personnel and Guidance Journal* 59(2): 88–91 (October 1980).

Children of divorce exhibit shock, depression, anger, shame, fear, and insecurity that are manifested in poor concentration, outbursts, fighting, withdrawal, and inferior schoolwork. Guidelines and techniques for elementary school counselors to set up peer-group counseling sessions are discussed. Children in the middle years seek self-discovery and self-affirmation through peer-group interactions. The only requirement for group membership is that the child's parents are separated or divorced. Piaget's theory on the development of understanding in the child forms the theoretical foundation for the techniques used in the children's groups. Elementary school counselors are presented with a reality-based perspective on divorce groups. (4 references)

1120. Southworth, Nicki. *A Comparative Study of Single-Parent Children and Two-Parent Children in Behavior, Achievement, and Emotional Status.* M.A. Thesis, Kean College, New Jersey, May 1984. 43pp. (ERIC Microfiche ED245200)

The academic achievement, classroom behavior, and emotional stability of 42 elementary school students from single-parent families and intact families are compared in this study. Behavior checklists were used to determine classroom behavior, and academic achievement was assessed through analysis of test scores on the Educational Records Bureau Comprehensive Test. In addition, human figure drawings were used to interpret the children's emotional status. Findings showed that children from single-parent homes had lower math and reading achievement, poorer school deportment in some areas, and less emotional stability than students from nuclear families. Recommendations for further investigation are offered.

1121. Spohn, Donald Eugene. "The Relationship between Perseverance in School and Childhood Loss of Parents in One MidWestern School District." Ph.D. diss., Michigan State University, 1978.

For a summary see: *Dissertation Abstracts International* 39B(10): 5050.

1122. Stanley, Barbara K., et al. "The Effects of Father Absence on Interpersonal Problem-Solving Skills of Nursery School Children." *Journal of Counseling and Development* 64(6): 383–385 (February 1986).

Fifty rural Kentucky nursery school children ages four to five from father-absent and intact families were given the Preschool Interpersonal Problem Solving Test to determine the effects of father absence on children. Father-absent children scored lower in their ability to solve problems relating to interpersonal real-life situations. It is suggested that intervention in the form of discussion and problem-solving groups in kindergarten-primary grades could help minimize effects of father absence. (14 references)

1123. Stansbury, Glenda Wells. "The Hurting Doesn't Stop at 8:45—Divorced Kids in the Classroom." *Contemporary Education* 56(4): 236–238 (Summer 1985).

A teacher's observation of the effects of divorce on children in the classroom is reported. The divorce process has

negative effects on children and educators need to note
the impact and provide support during the period of
readjustment. The teacher also needs to be familiar with
the stages of grief that children may exhibit. The impact
of post-divorce arrangements such as new home situations,
and visitation and custody, affects who is notified of
emergencies, conferences and special events. It is
suggested that both parents be contacted for conferences,
provided with copies of report cards, testing information,
and school bulletins. (6 references)

1124. Stickles, Patricia Adele. "The Influence of Single-Parent
Living Conditions on the Social Development of Six and
Seven Year Old Children Enrolled in a Regular First
Grade Program." Ph.D. diss., University of South Carolina,
1981.

For a summary see: *Dissertation Abstracts International*
41A(10): 4355.

1125. Stone, Judith P. "Problems of the Single Parent of the
Preschool Child." *Day Care and Early Education* 5(3):
16–17 (Spring 1978).

Single parents may be unwed, divorced, adoptive, widow,
widower, foster parent, or older sibling. Money is a critical
factor in the lives of the working single parent because of
the cost of child care. Age of parent, emotional stability,
and racial and ethnic considerations are significant in
their relationship to the parent and child support system.
Parents and child care staff must share a partnership
where the parents share what happens at home with the
staff, and the information is taken into consideration by
the school in its child care plans. This partnership, that is
based on goals that are mutually agreeable, is important
for the child's development and adjustment.

1126. Taylor, Velma Williams. "An Investigation of the Effect
of Bibliotherapy on the Self-Concepts of Kindergarten
Children from One-Parent Families." Ph.D. diss., Jackson
State University, 1982.

For a summary see: *Dissertation Abstracts International* 43A(11): 3505.

1127. Teleki, Jane K. "Parental Child-Rearing Behavior Perceived by Parents and School-Age Children in Divorced and Married Families." *Home Economics Research Journal* 13(1): 41–51 (September 1984).

This study focuses on parents' perceptions of acceptance, psychological control, and lax discipline as a function of belonging to a divorced or married family. A revised Child's Report of Parental Behavior Inventory was used in the investigation. Responses from 59 families, including divorced and intact parents, and 59 children, indicated no significant difference for the dimension of acceptance based on family type. Children from divorced families reported their fathers more lax in discipline than their mothers, while divorced mothers saw themselves as less firm disciplinarians than married mothers. Further research is suggested. (37 references)

1128. Theus, Robert. "The Effects of Divorce upon School Children." *Clearing House* 50(8): 364–365 (1977).

Some of the potential effects of divorce on school children are examined through a review of the literature. Predivorce parental relationships, child placement and custody, relations with noncustodial parent, and remarriage of parents are examined in association with possible effects on children. Implications for public policy and future research on the effects of parental absence are discussed. (5 references)

1129. Touliatos, John, and Byron W. Lindholm. "Teachers Perceptions of Behavior Problems in Children from Intact, Single-Parent, and Stepparent Families." *Psychology in the Schools* 17(2): 264–269 (April 1980).

The behavior problems of 3,644 Caucasian children, kindergarten through eighth grade, from intact, single-parent, and stepfamilies were the focus of this study.

Quay's Behavior Problem Checklist and teacher input
was used to provide data on the children. Results indicated
that children from broken families evidenced a greater
degree of maladjustment than those from intact families.
The effect of sex, social class, and grade in school was
greater for the children from broken homes.
Recommendations for future research are offered. (25
references)

1130. True, Judy, and Duane Googins. "Extended Learning
      Opportunities for the Single Parent Family." Paper
      presented at the National Reading and Language Arts
      Educator's Conference, Kansas City, September 26–28,
      1984. 11pp. (ERIC Microfiche ED252321)

When designing school support systems educators need
to consider the problems faced by single parents in terms
of time, earnings, and energy. Two programs in
Minneapolis, Minnesota designed with the needs of single-
parent families as well as families of more traditional life
styles are described. One program provides facilities and
direction for parents to help their children become better
readers. In the second program college of education
students from local colleges and universities work with
students in public libraries and elementary schools.

1131. Turner, Pauline H., and Beverly Gallegos. "A Comparison
      of the Day-Care Needs, Attitudes, and Practices of Intact
      and Single-Parent Families." *Journal of Employment
      Counseling* 21(1): 19–30 (March 1984).

Day-care needs, attitudes, and practices of both married
and single parents are compared. A questionnaire
assessing demographic factors revealed that both groups
were similar in age, ethnic background and religion.
Differences in education were not significant. However,
married parents reported a mean income nearly three
times that of single parents. Single parents were also
found to have a more positive relationship with their
children. Although single and married parents ranked

daycare needs differently, all parents seemed to need centers which were conveniently located, clean, and reasonably priced. Implications for employers are discussed. (9 references)

1132. Turner, Pauline H., and Richard M. Smith. "Single Parents and Day Care." *Family Relations* 32(2): 215–226 (April 1983).

The day care needs, attitudes, and practices of 252 single parents with dependent children are assessed. The sample used in the study was diverse in terms of age, income, educational level, and number and ages of dependent children. It is suggested that parents need: 1) adequate day care services that are convenient to either home or work 2) that are affordable 3) information about the criteria for selecting quality day care care, and 4) a greater variety of day care options. The projected increase in the number of children being reared by single-parents places high priority on the need for more day care options. Improving day care services now will be more cost effective overall. (21 references)

1133. Uslander, Arlene S. "Divorce: You Too Must Pay Child Support." *Learning* 5(6): 23–32 (February 1977).

Although all children do not respond in the same way to parental divorce, for many it is a difficult experience requiring many adjustments. Factors that affect the way children react are: age, level of maturity, custody arrangements, coping mechanisms or support systems, and relationship with parents. Some of the various ways children may respond to divorce are illustrated from classroom examples. Teachers may provide emotional support but should not adopt the role of psychologist by asking personal questions or attempting to solve family problems. They may create an atmosphere of understanding and acceptance by helping the child toward a positive self-image, avoiding embarrassing the child by inappropriate assignments, helping the child understand he or she is not alone and providing suitable books on divorce for reading and classroom discussion. (No references)

1134. Wasserman, Herbert L. "A Comparative Study of School Performance Among Boys from Broken and Intact Black Families." *The Journal of Negro Education* 41(2): 137–141 (Spring 1972).

This study explores the relationship between the school performance of black boys and family structure. The sample of 117 boys was limited to families living in low-income housing projects. Only minor variations were found between the school performance of one-parent boys and two-parent boys. It was found that boys under the age of 12 generally performed at higher levels in age-appropriate classes than boys 12 or over. Implications of these findings are discussed. (4 references)

1135. Waters, Faith H. "The Effect of Family Structure on Behavior and Attendance of Central Bucks High School Students." Ph.D. Ed.D. diss., University of Pennsylvania, 1983.

For a summary see: *Dissertation Abstracts International* 44A(4): 0952.

1136. Werner, Marion S. "Alienation or Alliance?" *The Pointer* 15(1): 46–50 (Fall 1980).

For the single parent, a school crisis is an added burden in what is frequently an already overwhelming life situation. Time pressures and job commitments can limit the single parent's involvement with the school. A serious crisis in school often brings the parent and school personnel together as adversaries at a time when the student may be needing help. Examples are given to demonstrate efforts of different schools to involve single parents during times of crisis. Principals and school professionals can support single parents by offering to work as a team. Guidelines for intervening with single parents in crisis situations are recommended. (No references)

1137. Williams, Mary Beth, and Carol Elaine Hoffman. "Family Dissolution: and Issue for the Schools; An Elementary School Program." *Children Today* 13(4): 24–25 (1984).

Group discussion programs for elementary and middle school children experiencing difficulty in dealing with family dissolution are discussed. The group process is viewed as facilitating the opportunity for children to share questions and experiences with peers and to realize the universality of their experiences. Books used to stimulate discussion are limited to child-centered issues. It is suggested that schools are in a unique position to help divorced families cope with stress by recognizing their problems and providing group support, counseling and mediation programs for both children and parents. (8 references)

1138. Willis, Irene Jolley. "The Relationship of Teachers' and Principals' Attitudes Toward Single-Parent Families to Their Expectations for the School Performance of Single-Parent Children." Ph.D. diss., New York University, 1984.

For a summary see: *Dissertation Abstracts International* 47A(7): 2027.

1139. Winfield, Evelyn T. "Relevant Reading for Adolescents: Literature on Divorce." *Journal of Reading* 26(5): 408–411 (February 1983).

The dramatic increase in the divorce rate has caused many adolescents to find themselves in one-parent families. Characters in current fiction often encounter issues that reflect those in real life situations. Relevant to adolescent development, and found in junior novels about divorce, are four social roles: family member, friend, group member, and self. Representative titles that teachers may use to help adolescents recognize the value of nurturing positive social roles while adjusting to divorce are discussed. Other resources that may motivate students to investigate issues includes brief book talks, film clips, media displays, guest authors, and sharing sessions. (13 references)

1140. Womack, Mark Allen. "Children with Learning Disabilities from Divorced and Intact Family Systems: A Comparison of Personality Characteristics with Regard to Family Structure, Gender, and Age." Ed.D. diss., George Peabody College for Teachers of Vanderbilt University, 1987.

For a summary see: *Dissertation Abstracts International* 48A(10): 2545.

1141. Yehl, Suzy. "The Hurting Child: Only an Open, Caring Teacher Can Reach-and Teach-the Child from a Fragmented Family." *Momentum* 17(4): 20–21 (December 1986).

Death, separation or divorce was the cause of over 14 million children living in single parent homes in 1984. Parents who want to spare their children the painful details of such events often do not communicate adequately with their children and the children may not understand what is happening. Age level reactions of children to divorce and death are cited to help teachers identify associated behaviors. Suggestions for ways to help children through family disruption are offered.

1142. Zakariya, Sally Banks. "Another Look at Children of Divorce: Summary Report of the Study of School Needs of One-Parent Children." *Principal* 62(1): 34–37 (September 1982).

Data on one-parent children was obtained from a study co-sponsored by National Association for Elementary School Principals and the Institute for Development of Educational Activities. Results of the study reported in 1980 showed that single-parent children had lower academic achievement than children from two-parent families. They were also more likely to be in low income families, more likely to move during the school year, and be referred more often for disciplinary problems. A special analysis indicated that girls from higher income two-parent families ranked highest in achievement. More black families were headed by a single parent and more single-parent children disliked their school. Implications for school policy and areas for further study are suggested. (5 references)

GEOGRAPHIC INDEX

PROGRAMS, PROJECTS, ASSOCIATIONS, AND INSTITUTIONS INDEX

AUTHOR INDEX

SUBJECT INDEX

ACHIEVEMENT
Achievement 195, 206, 209,
212, 220, 281
Academic achievement 25, 50,
72, 135, 165 171
death of parent 874, 885,
1022
and divorce 206, 543, 579,
642, 644, 645, 648,
718, 796, 803, 806,
820
fatherless families 86, 187,
190, 219, 220, 281,
874, 885
ill and hospitalized parents
439
military families 451, 461,
463
school 972, 974, 976, 977,
984, 985, 986, 987,
988, 990, 1002, 1013,
1028, 1032, 1039,
1040, 1043, 1050,
1066, 1073, 1074,
1076, 1077, 1078,
1080, 1081, 1087,
1095, 1099, 1103,
1107, 1110, 1113,
1116, 1118, 1121,
1134, 1143 (*See also:*
EDUCATION;

COGNITIVE
DEVELOPMENT;
TESTS AND
TESTING)

ADJUSTMENT, BEHAVIOR,
MENTAL HEALTH,
MENTAL ILLNESS,
EMOTION, STRESS,
etc.
Acting-out 10, 747, 834, 876,
913, 470, 473, 1003
Adjustment
death of parent 829, 835,
839, 843, 855, 875,
880, 940, 958, 961,
962, 963, 1024, 1089
divorce 492, 495, 502, 526,
527, 530, 537, 544,
563, 572, 574, 590,
592, 608, 615, 616,
617, 626, 647, 657,
667, 698, 747, 752,
779, 804
incarcerated parents 470,
476
military families 447, 448,
451, 456
motherless families 300,
285
reconstituted families 320

477